MW00830062

"Libraries are replete with books
theologians, and analyses of past
apply historical developments to ~~~~~~~~~~~~~~~~~~ of contemporary challenges and their implications on the future. *Southern Baptist Identity* is a
valuable compilation confronting this formidable task. With contributions
from notable denominational leaders, this volume acknowledges the phe-
nomenal growth of Southern Baptists but recognizes the impact a changing
world and postmodern society will have on the future of its churches and
collectively on the Southern Baptist Convention. While readers will not
necessarily agree with the insights and conclusions of each writer, they will
find the diverse perspectives valid as they grapple with the contemporary
realities of denominational life and trends."

—JERRY RANKIN, President, International Mission Board,
    Southern Baptist Convention

"The Southern Baptist Convention is preparing for a new generation of
global witnesses. To understand the purpose and passion of the world's
largest cooperative network of evangelical churches, read this book. I am
grateful for this scholarly insight and spiritual challenge as we seek to fulfill
the Great Commission in the twenty-first century."

—JACK GRAHAM, Former President, Southern Baptist Convention;
    Pastor, Prestonwood Baptist Church

"All Baptists should draw water from these wells of provocative essays
and lectures in order to avoid historical amnesia or political euphoria. We
are reminded that we dare not be content with kicking the convention can
further down the road; instead, we must be forward-leaning, asking the
hard questions about present and future. This work calls us to a rigorous
and serious mapping of the contours of our convention road."

—HAYES WICKER, Senior Pastor, First Baptist Church, Naples, FL

SOUTHERN BAPTIST IDENTITY

An Evangelical Denomination Faces the Future

Edited by

DAVID S. DOCKERY

CROSSWAY BOOKS
WHEATON, ILLINOIS

Trade paperback ISBN: 978-1-4335-0679-6

PDF ISBN: 978-1-4335-0680-2

Mobipocket ISBN: 978-1-4335-0681-9

Library of Congress Cataloging-in-Publication Data
    Southern Baptist identity : an Evangelical denomination faces the
future / edited by David S. Dockery.
      p. cm.
    Includes bibliographical references and index.
    ISBN-13: 978-1-4335-0679-6 (tpb)
    1. Southern Baptist Convention. I. Dockery, David S. II. Title.
BX6462.7.S66   2009
286'.132—dc22   2008046623

VP		19	18	17	16	15	14	13	12	11	10	09
15	14	13	12	11	10	9	8	7	6	5	4	3	2	1

To

HARRY and BETH SMITH,

special friends and
coworkers together
for the sake of the gospel.

CONTENTS

PART ONE
THEOLOGICAL AND HISTORICAL PERSPECTIVES

PART TWO
MINISTRY AND CONVENTION PERSPECTIVES

CONTRIBUTORS

Daniel L. Akin, President, Southeastern Baptist Theological Seminary

Morris H. Chapman, President, Executive Committee of the Southern Baptist Convention

Michael Day, Executive Director of Missions, Mid-South Baptist Association

David S. Dockery, President, Union University

Nathan A. Finn, Assistant Professor of Church History, Southeastern Baptist Theological Seminary

James Leo Garrett Jr., Distinguished Professor of Theology, Southwestern Baptist Theological Seminary

Timothy George, Dean, Beeson Divinity School

Richard Land, President, Ethics and Religious Liberty Commission of the Southern Baptist Convention

R. Albert Mohler Jr., President, The Southern Baptist Theological Seminary

Russell D. Moore, Dean, School of Theology, and Vice President for Academic Administration, The Southern Baptist Theological Seminary

R. Stanton Norman, Provost, Oklahoma Baptist University

Paige Patterson, President, Southwestern Baptist Theological Seminary

Thom S. Rainer, President, LifeWay Christian Resources

Jim Shaddix, Pastor, Riverside Baptist Church, Denver, Colorado

Ed Stetzer, President, LifeWay Research Center

Gregory A. Wills, Professor of Church History and Director, Southern Baptist History Center, The Southern Baptist Theological Seminary

PREFACE

THE SOUTHERN BAPTIST CONVENTION is now more than 160 years old. During that time these unique people of God have changed in several obvious ways. What was once a small, Southern, predominantly white denomination has become large, multi-regional, and multi-ethnic. Southern Baptists now worship and serve in dozens of languages all across North America. Southern Baptist missionaries serve in every continent across the world. During these 160 years, the history of Southern Baptists has been dotted with tension, concerns, and at times outright heresy. Southern Baptists have indeed experienced the need for renewal, and as we move forward in the early years of the twenty-first century, we need a fresh work of God's Spirit once again to bring renewal to Southern Baptist identity.

At the turn of the twentieth century, there were questions raised as to what it means to be a Southern Baptist. An important work titled *Baptist, Why and Why Not*[1] expressed the consensus positions of the day. The key chapters were written by Baptist Sunday School Board leader J. M. Frost, Union University graduate T. T. Eaton, and Southern Seminary professor F. H. Kerfoot. It was in this volume that Frost so powerfully contended for the all-sufficient and infallible nature of Holy Scripture, insisting on its sole authority for Southern Baptists.

From time to time there has been a need for Baptists to once again reflect on who they are and what they believe, particularly in light of what can be called the historic orthodox consensus throughout the history of the church. *Baptist, Why and Why Not* was produced at a time when American Christianity at-large was coming to grips with the influence of Charles Darwin and the rise of historical criticism. Eminent historian E. Brooks Holifield has recently claimed in his *Theology in America*[2] that a survey of theological opinion from the late nineteenth and early twentieth centuries leads one to recognize that the consensus of the age of orthodoxy had ended. Certainly the challenges that Southern Baptists faced at the

---

[1] *Baptist, Why and Why Not* (Nashville: Sunday School Board, Southern Baptist Convention, 1900).
[2] E. Brooks Holifield, *Theology in America* (Yale University Press, 2003).

beginning of the twentieth century are now as great or greater in the first decade of the twenty-first century. The contributors to this book seek to offer ways to help Southern Baptists think about ways to address some of these most significant challenges.

We offer this volume with the hope that churches across the Southern Baptist Convention (SBC) can be strengthened. It is our prayer that the gospel and its entailments can be proclaimed. Challenges facing Southern Baptists are addressed by seasoned Baptist leaders as well as by fresh voices in our convention. Important matters are explored from both theological and historical perspectives, as well as from ministerial and convention-oriented vantage points.

Some of the chapters in this book were originally presented at Baptist Identity conferences at Union University in recent years. Gregory A. Thornbury and Charles A. Fowler helped coordinate these important conferences. To each of them I offer my deep appreciation. I also want to say a big thank you to Melanie Rickman, Cindy Meredith, and Taylor Worley for their significant contributions to the preparation of this volume. I am grateful for the encouragement of Lanese, Jon, Sarah, Ben, Julie, Tim, and Andrea as this book was completed. I am extremely thankful to friends at Crossway for their wonderful support of this project.

I am preparing this preface at the 2008 Southern Baptist Convention in Indianapolis. This year's convention powerfully addressed the issue of regenerate church membership, an issue at the very heart of the identity of Southern Baptists.[3] This year's convention also called over and over for a renewed commitment to global missions, to convictional confessionalism, and to collaborative cooperation. Hopefully, this book will carry forward these important themes, as well as others, that will illuminate a way forward for Southern Baptists in the twenty-first century. We offer this volume with the prayer that God will renew our life together for the good of Southern Baptist churches, agencies, entities, and academic institutions, and for the glory of God.

Soli Deo gloria.

David S. Dockery
June 2008

---

[3]See Mark Kelly, "Dockery: Spiritual Issues at the Heart of Debate Over 'Total Membership' Statistic," *Baptist Press* (June 5, 2008).

SOUTHERN BAPTISTS IN THE TWENTY-FIRST CENTURY

David S. Dockery

THE SBC IS THE LARGEST evangelical denomination in the country, with over 44,000 churches in all fifty states. Southern Baptists have often functioned separately from the rest of American Christianity because of their sectionalism, their inability to separate from Southern culture, their parochialism, and their self-sufficiency, though there are some indicators that these things are beginning to change. For almost three decades the Convention has been embroiled in controversy regarding theological issues and denominational polity. We now find ourselves asking important questions about the future and identity of the SBC.[1]

The SBC world in which many of us were nurtured—Bible drills, GAs, RAs, Training Union, WMU, Brotherhood, and so on (not to mention uniform Sunday school lessons, the Baptist hymnal, and similar worship patterns)—no longer exists in every SBC church. For almost five decades, during the middle of the twentieth century, Southern Baptists followed the same organizational patterns, the same programs, and the same Sunday school lessons. These practices were to Southern Baptists what the Latin Mass was to Roman Catholics. It provided all within the SBC a sense of continuity and security. This programmatic uniformity all hung together around a ubiquitous commitment to missions and evangelism, expressed in giving through the Cooperative Program and support for Lottie Moon and Annie Armstrong. It was absolutely ingenious. Throughout most of the twentieth century, being a Southern Baptist had a cultural and program-

---

[1]See David S. Dockery, *Southern Baptist Consensus and Renewal: A Biblical, Historical, and Theological Proposal* (Nashville: B&H, 2008).

matic identity to it unlike anything else. This kind of intactness provided Southern Baptists with a denominational stability unmatched by any other denomination in the country. Martin Marty, the influential American church historian, was not exaggerating when he said that Southern Baptists were the Roman Catholic Church of the South, because their identity was so intact and their influence so pervasive, providing an umbrella over the entire culture in almost every dimension of life. We were a very practical people, with heart religion—carried out in rather uniformly pragmatic and programmatic expressions.

But for a variety of reasons, this intactness has been challenged by the growing fragmentation of recent years. Even without the "Controversy," the intactness had started to unravel over the past thirty years due to the growth of multiple Bible translations, the impact of parachurch groups, the expanding diversity of music, varied worship patterns, and the unexpected reality that church models and heroes for many Southern Baptists now come from outside the SBC. Today Southern Baptists seem to be a gathering of loosely connected, if not balkanized, groups. By and large, we don't know our heritage, our history, or our theological identity. We don't know Furman, Manly, Broadus, Johnson, Frost, Mullins, Carroll, Conner, Moon, or Armstrong, all heroes of yesteryear. We hardly know more recent leaders like Lee, Rogers, Hobbs, and Criswell. If you can't identify a Southern Baptist now as you could in the 1950s—by a King James Bible, a uniform Sunday School lesson, a six-point envelope system, fall and spring revivals, and a preaching service that concludes by singing all the verses of "Just As I Am"—then what does it mean to be a Southern Baptist in the twenty-first century? That is the question that must be answered in the next few years, and it lies behind the various chapters in this book.

TOWARD CONSENSUS AND RENEWAL

We now find ourselves at a different moment in American Christianity, and in world Christianity in general. Contemporary culture is being overtaken and submerged by a new spirit, often referred to as postmodernism and sometimes described by the growing trends toward secularism. It is in this changing context that we are made aware that Southern Baptists are at once beneficiaries and victims of tradition. We are beneficiaries who receive nurturing truth and wisdom from God's faithfulness from past generations, and we are victims who now take for granted things that possibly need to be questioned or reexamined. Southern Baptists are both beneficiaries of good, wise, and sound traditions, as well as victims of poor, unwise, and unsound traditions.

The Bible must be the "last word" in sifting through and evaluating both our traditions and our challenges. Paul's word in 1 Thessalonians 5:21 is a helpful reminder for us at this important moment in the SBC: "Test everything. Hold on to the good" (NIV). In our "testing," we must avoid the extremes of those who stress human moral experience as the primary basis for our message and theological understanding. At the same time we must avoid those who have equated cultural norms and forms of philosophical rationalism with the truth of Scripture. It would be naïve for us to think that the answers to the current challenges we now face in the SBC are simple or that we are the only ones facing such challenges, as if we lived in a vacuum. We must explore issues of identity, while seeking to establish a new consensus, lest we drift apart. This is imperative. Such a consensus must be centered around the gospel and must be connected to the churches. We will need to distinguish between markers of Southern Baptist identity and markers of Southern Baptist consistency. In doing so, we can emphasize primary and core convictions. We cannot, however, ignore necessary boundary markers. The ultimate danger to the gospel lies not in the nuances of our differences, but in the rising tides of liberalism, neo-paganism, and postmodernism that threaten to swamp Southern Baptist identity in cultural accommodation. We must remember that current frustrations and disappointments could reignite a battle—one in which those who are engaged are prone to concentrate on the frustrations or disappointments, while never thinking of the ultimate issues or implications for which the battle is being fought.

CONVICTIONAL AND CONFESSIONAL BELIEFS

We celebrate and give thanks that this generation of Southern Baptists has received the truth of the gospel and recognizes the need to pass on this body of truth to the next generation. Our responsibility is to faithfully pass on what we have received from wells we did not dig and from gardens we did not plant.

We now find ourselves in a culture which often fails to recognize that there is an identifiable body of truth, and that truth is the Christian faith. One of the reasons that Southern Baptists now need to ask the hard questions about a regenerate church membership, a historic and foundational Baptist tenet, is that people have confused the Christian faith for substitutes. The Christian faith is not mere moralism; it is not faith in faith, some subjective amorphous feeling, or a self-help theory. The Christian faith is the manifestation of God's truth revealed in his Son and made known to us today in his Word. What is needed today is a renewed commitment to confess and teach the truth in congregations, academic institutions, and agencies across the SBC and literally around the world.

There remains a sector of Southern Baptist life that is quite hesitant to acknowledge the place of normative, doctrinal confessions for fear of its resulting in creedalism. Behind much of this fear is a misplaced emphasis on individualism and soul competency that has produced a false dichotomy between "a living faith" and "a confessional faith." While we would never want to put any confession on the same level as Scripture itself, or confuse a doctrinal statement *about* Jesus with a dynamic trust *in* Jesus, it is certainly a misunderstanding of our Baptist heritage to deny the importance of a confessional faith.

In response to this false dichotomy, James Leo Garrett Jr. has keenly observed that the opposite of a confessional faith is not a living faith, but an undefined faith that lacks content and depth. Thus, there is no need to construct a false choice between "a living faith" or "a confessional faith." Instead we need a living faith that we confess and a confessional faith that we live and proclaim. We can no more work safely in a frameless building or eat beef from a boneless cow than we can practice and communicate the Christian faith without basic affirmations of doctrinal truth.[2]

Today, we see the growing impact of secularization and pluralization expanding all around us in seemingly exponential ways—as has been so well documented in R. Albert Mohler Jr.'s insightful analysis of the New Atheism.[3] This changing world in which we live has been masterfully described in Charles Taylor's 874-page volume, *A Secular Age*. Taylor claims that once people assumed faith as the norm for making sense of life, and thus had to have a reason *not* to believe, but today the paradigm has shifted so that people now have to be given a reason *to* believe, because he says at best faith in our day is seen as only one option among many in our pluralistic society.[4]

While Taylor's insights about the world in which we live are absolutely brilliant, we recognize, however, that challenges to the Christian faith are not new to the twenty-first century, for false teachers have existed since

---

[2]See James Leo Garrett Jr., *Systematic Theology: Biblical, Historical, Evangelical* (Grand Rapids, MI: Eerdmans, 1990), 1:5.
[3]See R. Albert Mohler Jr., *Atheism Remix* (Wheaton, IL: Crossway Books, 2008).
[4]See Charles Taylor, *A Secular Age* (Cambridge, MA: Belknap, 2007).

the apostolic period. And while today believers face challenges from both inside the church and out, we need to understand that many of these challengers are merely the contemporary heirs of Marcion, Arius, Pelagis, Abelard, and others. What seems new today is often a repackaging of older errors and heresies. In response we need an authentically confessional faith, grounded in Scripture and the best of our Baptist heritage, a convictional faith that will not give in to this secular age with a spirit of defeat.

COLLABORATIVE AND COOPERATIVE SERVICE

We need an SBC characterized not only by a confessional and convictional faith, but by a collaborative and compassionate sense of cooperation. The recovery of a convictional confessionalism has kept us from going the way of so many mainline denominations who have become untethered to Scripture and have lost their way. Yet the need of the hour also includes the need to regain a spirit of collaborative cooperation. I know that some wonder if we can find a way to cooperate together—after all, we are so different. No longer can a programmatic pragmatism or a cultural homogeneity alone be the foundation for our cooperation. The call to cooperate in 2008 differs greatly from the world of M. E. Dodd in 1925, but we need to reclaim the spirit of M. E. Dodd for our day.[5]

Southern Baptists in the twenty-first century are rapidly changing. A quick look reveals that we are Asian, Hispanic, black, brown, and white. We have dark skin and light, we are young and old, our churches are small and large, and we worship in rural communities and in sprawling metropolitan areas. We are educated and uneducated, well known and anonymous, bloggers and non-bloggers, rich and poor, theologians and practitioners, and while we remain predominately Southerners, SBC congregations are found across this land in the West, East, and North as well. One of the things, however, that gets the attention of the world and authenticates our confession is the way Christians love each other, celebrate our diversity, and serve together in harmony. I believe the absence of such love and cooperation breaks our Savior's heart.

Some think that neither conviction nor cooperation really matters. On the contrary, the reality is this: much is at stake, including the health of the SBC and the eternal life or the eternal condemnation of individuals. We need both collaborative cooperation and convictional confessionalism. Those who emphasize cooperation are prone to compromise. Those who

---

[5]M. E. Dodd was known as the father of the Cooperative Program in the SBC, which was adopted at the annual convention in Memphis in 1925.

emphasize conviction are prone to be cantankerous. So, choosing between compromised beliefs or a cantankerous spirit is not an inviting option.

I think we would do well to hear again the words of Carl F. H. Henry. About 60 years ago he maintained that our witness to the world will be stronger when the church is united. Cantankerousness, he claimed, often leads to additional and unnecessary fragmentation, thus diminishing opportunities for cooperation and collaboration, for reform and renewal.[6] As we look toward the future, let us suggest some important steps that might help us focus on our identity, build consensus, and work toward renewal.

INITIAL STEPS TOWARD RENEWAL

1. We must begin afresh to appreciate the best of Baptist history/ heritage.

2. We must balance a commitment to the material principle of the gospel and the formal principle of inspired Scripture. As Mohler has recognized, "the material and formal principles constitute not only a center, but rightly understood they also establish boundaries."[7] We cannot focus on the center alone and ignore the circumference, for one influences the other. Millard Erickson has suggested that there surely comes some point where the line has been crossed (from either direction) and at least a hybrid orthodoxy can develop.[8] D. A. Carson similarly notes that there comes a time to "draw lines" even when "drawing lines is rude." He offers four reasons why this must be done:

    a) because truth demands it;
    b) because distinctions between orthodoxy and heresy must be maintained;
    c) because a plurality of errors calls for it; and
    d) because the implications of the gospel confront our culture and must be lived out in a consistent way.[9]

3. The new consensus must be built upon a full-orbed doctrine of Scripture, which affirms that only those beliefs and practices that rest firmly on scriptural foundations can be regarded as binding on Southern Baptists, because as "people of the Book," we are first and foremost Biblicists. Southern Baptist theology and spirituality rests on Scripture as the central

---

[6]Carl F. H. Henry, *The Uneasy Conscience of American Fundamentalism* (Grand Rapids, MI: Eerdmans, 1947).
[7]See R. Albert Mohler Jr., "Reformist Evangelicalism: A Center without a Circumference," in *A Confessing Theology for Postmodern Times*, ed. Michael S. Horton (Wheaton, IL: Crossway Books, 2000).
[8]See Millard J. Erickson, *The Evangelical Left* (Grand Rapids, MI: Baker, 1997).
[9]See D. A. Carson, *The Gagging of God* (Grand Rapids, MI: Zondervan, 1999).

legitimating source of Christian faith and theology, the clearest window through which the face of Christ may be seen. We must recognize that to allow one's ideas and values to become controlled by anything or anyone other than the self-revelation of God in Holy Scripture is to adopt an ideology rather than a theology.[10]

4. Defining the circumference is necessary, but we should not expect or demand uniformity, lest we impose a straightjacket on our fellow Southern Baptists. Similarly, this new consensus must be grounded in the gospel that is not enslaved to rationalism nor denatured by an alien individualism, experientialism, or postmodernism.

5. We must recognize that a confession of the Bible's truthfulness is an important safeguard, a necessary, albeit an insufficient, statement for the SBC to maintain consistent evangelical instruction and theological method, which is needed for an orthodox statement on matters of Christology, the doctrine of God, and salvation. Certainly there are differences among us. The pressures from a rapidly changing culture will only continue to create significant challenges in our efforts to rediscover a Southern Baptist consensus. We must also clearly affirm the importance of worship, regenerate church membership, and local church autonomy and cooperation, as well as believer's baptism and the Lord's Supper.

6. A model of dynamic orthodoxy must be reclaimed. The orthodox tradition must be recovered in conversation with Nicea, Chalcedon, Augustine, Bernard, Luther, Calvin, Wesley, the Pietists, and the revivalists. In sum, our Southern Baptist identity must be rooted in the *consensus fidei* of the Christian church.

7. We must recognize that Southern Baptists have historically reflected considerable diversity. While we do not hold out doctrinal uniformity as a goal, we do call for renewed commitments to the inspiration, truthfulness, and authority of Scripture, with an accompanying commitment to a hermeneutic of acceptance over against a hermeneutic of suspicion, as well as a reestablishment and reaffirmation of the gospel center.[11]

8. We must take seriously the biblical call to unity (John 17; Ephesians 4) in accord with the Nicene affirmation of the oneness and universality of the church, as reflected in the Orthodox Confession (1678): a oneness that calls for humility, gentleness, patience, forbearance with one another in love, and a diligence to preserve the unity of the Spirit in the bond of peace (Eph. 4:2–3), and a universality with a renewed dedication to racial

---

[10]See David S. Dockery, *Christian Scripture* (Nashville: B&H, 1995).
[11]Ibid.

reconciliation, looking forward to a day in which a great multitude from every nation and all tribes, people groups, and tongues shall stand before the Lamb (Rev. 7:9).

9. We need to be reminded of where Southern Baptists might be were it not for the conservative resurgence—as well as a recognition of where we could be if we ever become untethered to Holy Scripture. We are reminded that there are first-order gospel issues that define both our core and needed parameters. Simultaneously, we cannot forget that some secondary and tertiary matters belong, as the great W. A. Criswell was so fond of saying, to the "imponderables of God."

10. We need a new spirit of mutual respect and humility to serve together with those with whom we have differences of conviction and opinion. It is possible to hold hands with brothers and sisters who disagree on secondary and tertiary matters of theology and work together toward a common good to extend the work of Southern Baptists around the world and advance the kingdom of God. We need a like-mindedness on first-order issues—particularly on the exclusivity and uniqueness of the gospel that is found only in Jesus Christ and in him alone (John 14:6).

11. We want to begin to build a new and much-needed consensus around the gospel of the Lord Jesus Christ—a consensus that was present at the first Triennial Convention in 1814 and again at the inaugural convention of Southern Baptists in 1845.[12] This consensus carried forward into the 1950s, but it moved from being a theologically informed consensus to a programmatic and pragmatic one. When that cultural and programmatic consensus dissipated, we found ourselves looking for a new direction. It is time to move from controversy and confusion to a new consensus and renewed commitment to cooperation. We need to take a step back, not just to commit ourselves afresh to missions and evangelism, as important as that is. We need to commit ourselves foremost to the gospel, the message of missions and evangelism, the message that is found only in Jesus Christ and his atoning death for sinners.

12. Twenty-first-century Southern Baptists need not only to affirm the Bible's truthfulness and the saving power of the gospel, but we need to evidence our concern for these matters by careful biblical interpretation and theological reflection, faithful churchmanship, proclamation, worship, repentance, and prayer. We can thus trust God to bring a fresh wind of renewal to Southern Baptist theology, evangelism, missions, worship, education, and service. We can relate to one another in love

---

[12]See David S. Dockery, *Southern Baptist Consensus and Renewal*, 38–45.

and humility, bringing about true fellowship and community not only in orthodoxy, but orthopraxy before a watching world. May God grant to us a renewed commitment to the gospel, to the church, and to the truthfulness of Holy Scripture that will help forge and shape a new consensus among us, bringing about genuine transformation and a renewed spirit of cooperation.[13]

---

[13]Ibid., 201–20.

PART ONE

THEOLOGICAL AND HISTORICAL PERSPECTIVES

CHAPTER ONE

SOUTHERN BAPTIST IDENTITY: IS THERE A FUTURE?

R. Albert Mohler Jr.

ADDRESSING THE FUTURE OF any movement is an inherently dangerous affair. Winston Churchill once remarked to one of his classmates that he was certain that history would treat him well. His schoolmate, a bit incredulous, asked how he could be so certain. Churchill raised an eyebrow and said, "Because I intend to write the history." That is certainly one way to make sure history looks favorably upon you—provided you have the luxury of writing it yourself. The rest of us, however, are left simply wondering whether the historians of some future age will look back and say we got it even approximately correct. That is a risky business, of course, but it is even more dangerous not to envision the future. The greatest risk is assuming the future will somehow "just happen" in a way that brings glory to God.

As we consider the Baptist movement in the twenty-first century, we can look back on four centuries of Baptist history, Baptist work, and Baptist witness. By no accident, that history also includes four centuries of debate over Baptist identity and the Baptist future.

I have to begin with some word of autobiography. I can remember as a small child explaining to my neighbors that I belonged to the Baptists. That was the terminology—I never knew a time when I did not consider myself a Baptist. Of course, now I know better theologically, but I was a part of the tribe before I ever understood the theology. I was a Baptist by custom before I came to be a Baptist by conviction. That Baptist heritage leads me to feel at home in this discussion. I understand something of the grandeur, something of the vibrant texture of faith that has produced not only the Baptist movement as a whole but the SBC as we know it now.

I was raised by parents who were convictionally Baptists. They were so Baptist, in fact, that when I wanted to become a Boy Scout, my parents would not let me until I was also a Royal Ambassador. This was an extreme position in my view. The Boy Scout troop was sponsored by the same Southern Baptist church as the Royal Ambassadors, so it was essentially the same boys dressing up in different uniforms on different nights. It was a very small world. To me, the external world was a panoply of different faiths—people called "Methodists" and "Presbyterians." There was a sectarianism there, to be sure, but one that is not to be despised; it was a deeply held sense of belonging. We Baptists knew who we were, and thus we would know whom we should be looking to in the future.

Understanding the present and preparing for the future requires us to consider not only our own autobiographies, but also the biography of a great denomination, the SBC. One of the key issues for our understanding the current situation is to recognize that Baptists have always debated our identity. From the very beginning, there has been a both/and character to the Baptist understanding of what it means to be a Christian. First, Baptists did not intend to start a new faith. The seventeenth-century Baptists were never about the task of creating a new Christian religion. In fact, they went to great lengths to point out that they stood in continuity with the faith "once for all delivered to the saints." Yet at the same time, Baptists were defined by certain unique theological convictions that framed our understanding. Those convictions were of such passionate strength and theological intensity that the early Baptists had to set themselves apart even from other English separatists and nonconformists. Essentially, our Baptist forebears were nonconformists even within the world of nonconformity. So they joined themselves together in congregations of like-minded believers who were uniquely committed to three principles.

The first of those principles was regenerate church membership. If there is any one defining mark of the Baptist, it is the understanding that membership in the church comes by personal profession of faith in the Lord Jesus Christ. The church is not merely a voluntary association of those who have been born to Christian parents—even to Baptist parents—or of those who might have been moistened as infants. Rather, the church is an assembly of those who make a public profession of faith in the Lord Jesus Christ and gather together in congregations under the covenant of Christ.

The second principle, a derivative of the first, was believer's baptism—

the conviction that baptism is to be administered only upon an individual's profession of faith. Baptism is not only a symbol, but an act of obedience and entry into the covenant community of the church. To reject believer's baptism is therefore to paint a picture of the church that is much distorted.

The third principle was congregational church government. Baptists have made several and various attempts to define exactly what congregational church government should look like. At its root, however, congregationalism affirms that it is the covenanted community that must take responsibility for the ordering of the church, for the preaching of the gospel, and for everything else that God has assigned to the church in this age. There is no sacerdotalism; there is no priestly class, no one who can be hired to do the ministry of the gospel, and no franchise to be granted. The church itself, the covenanted community of baptized believers, must take responsibility for the fulfillment of all Christ has commanded his people.

Much more could be added to Baptist ecclesiology, but these three principles are an irreducible minimum of Baptist identity. When any one of them is compromised—much less denied—then whatever is left may call itself Baptist only by asserting a lie. It is something less than Baptist when any one of these principles is absent.

THEOLOGICAL ISSUES

With these historic principles in mind, we turn to consider some theological issues that now face the SBC and should therefore have our very careful attention. The first of these is the conservative resurgence in the SBC, a movement that emerged most publicly in 1979, even though its roots go back to at least 1963.

The public controversy of 1979 did not emerge out of a vacuum; there was a history behind it. By the 1960s, the Enlightenment had come to Dixie. A region that had long believed itself immune to history suddenly found itself grappling with the very questions that Northern evangelicals had confronted decades earlier and that European Christians had faced in the previous century. Now, Kant, Hume, Locke, and Hobbes arrived at the very threshold of the SBC.

The controversy that erupted in the SBC centered first and foremost on issues of truth and authority. With modernity having already reached our ranks, higher criticism and other ideological denials of the truthfulness of Scripture now presented themselves as challenges. Southern Baptists were thus forced to make a decision whether to assert, affirm, and cherish the

Bible as the written Word of God, or merely to receive it as a human testimony of human religious experience.

Yale University professor Gabriel Josipovici once said that we should see the Bible as an arbitrarily collected group of scrolls, writings of tremendous spiritual interest and substance, but which say more about the persons who wrote them than about the God by whom they claim to be inspired. At such a fork in the road, there are only two options: either we will affirm the total truthfulness and verbal inspiration of Scripture, or we will decide that Scripture is to some extent simply a fallible witness to human religious experience. Southern Baptists first faced that choice in the 1960s, but they denied it for a number of years and papered over it for another decade. They tried to find some bureaucratic means of denying the elephant in the middle of the denominational room, but eventually the elephant grew so large it could be contained no longer.

By the 1970s, Southern Baptists had coiled into two separate parties: a truth party and a liberty party. Some tried to join both, but ultimately the controversy forced a choice. The issues became so narrowly focused and so intense in application that individuals eventually had to understand that the candidates running for the office of president of the SBC represented one of these sets of consuming interests.

The truth party understood doctrine to be the most basic issue confronting the convention. They were suspicious that heterodoxy had entered the ranks of Southern Baptists, and they had documentation to back up their claims—reports from students at colleges, universities, and seminaries. Soon, what had begun as a grassroots concern became an organized movement convinced that if the truth was compromised, all would eventually be lost.

The liberty party might best be described with what became a bumper-sticker slogan of the movement: "Baptist means Freedom!" To this party, liberty itself was the *leitmotif* of the Baptist movement. Now, it is certainly true that members of the liberty party also cherished truth, and members of the truth party had an understanding of Baptist freedom. But for the truth party, freedom had to fit within the truthfulness of God's Word and the parameters established by divine revelation. For the liberty party, on the other hand, it was truth that had to be accommodated to the more important issue of freedom. Any parameters thus became not only awkward, but eventually impossible. This issue of freedom raises a host of questions, most obviously: "Freedom from what?" and "Freedom for what?" Eventually, the majority of Southern Baptists came to understand that if freedom were the only motif—or even the driving motif—of the denomination, it would finally mean freedom from accountability and freedom from doctrinal responsibility.

From 1963 to 1990, these two parties—truth and liberty—struggled to define the SBC and chart its course into the future. The issues over which they clashed were serious and substantial theological matters. They were not small, they were not minor, and they were not negotiable. Now, it is willful ignorance to suggest that Southern Baptists were not separated by theological differences of tremendous depth and great intensity. Those who say otherwise should simply read the evidence. The inerrancy and infallibility of the Bible were the primary issues of debate, though of course there was always more than that. Questions of epistemology, truth, and authority were only the entryway into an entire complex of debate that included virtually every major doctrinal issue and would ultimately affect the entire shape of the theological task.

At the end of the nineteenth century, Charles Spurgeon understood the Baptist Union in Britain to have slipped into what he called a "downgrade," antiquarian language that nevertheless accurately communicated the reality of his day. Spurgeon saw the downgrade and gave the warning, but he was not successful in calling the Union to theological accountability. Today, the Baptist Union is a shell of its former self, hardly holding on to its declining membership. Southern Baptist conservative leaders in the 1960s, and especially in the 1970s and 1980s, put their lives, their careers, and their ministries on the line to prevent Southern Baptists from following a similar trajectory.

John Shelton Reed of the University of North Carolina (who once held the Margaret Thatcher chair of American studies at the London School of Economics) is one of the greatest historians of the American South. He recently characterized the Southern Baptist controversy as a "pitchfork rebellion." Southern Baptists heard the issues, became alarmed, and were motivated to action. The true heroes of the conservative resurgence in the SBC were men and women who slept in their cars because they could not afford a hotel room. So motivated were they by the cause of truth and concern for the gospel, they would go wherever they had to go and sleep wherever they had to sleep in order to elect a president who represented their hope for the future of the SBC.

Where does the SBC stand now? Can we look back at the conservative resurgence and say the theological issues were settled forever? Absolutely not. Southern Baptists are now exceptional in the broader theological world. On same-sex marriage and a host of other cultural issues, the SBC is consistently recognized by the news media as being the one exception to a trend of churches acquiescing to liberal agendas. We cannot take confidence in that exceptionalism, for that would be a false confidence established on a very flimsy hope. In the conservative resurgence, the SBC was given a second chance, not a guaranteed future. It was not given a pass from history, or from the theological debates of the future.

That being the case, Southern Baptists have to grow out of a posture of inherent defensiveness and move to a positive agenda that points to the glory of God in the comprehensive embrace of biblical truth and takes delight in confessing the faith. We live in a day that is averse to theology and irritated by doctrine. If Southern Baptists find themselves being irritated by doctrinal questions, we will soon find ourselves sharing the fate of the mainline denominations—just slightly delayed. The tectonic plates of the contemporary theological landscape are shifting. Southern Baptists must accept the challenge of confronting these issues, not merely by defending against them, but by actually using contemporary debates to proclaim a theological reality that is firmly grounded in Scripture.

Of first importance in this challenge is a full embrace of classical orthodoxy. For one thing, we must be unapologetic in speaking about tradition. G. K. Chesterton was not the first to invoke the "democracy of the dead." Even the author of Hebrews refers to one who, "though he died . . . still speaks" (Heb. 11:4, ESV). Tradition—that backward glance at what Christians throughout the centuries have confessed and how they have understood the great doctrines of the faith—allows the dead to have a vote. We are not the first persons to read the Bible, nor are we the first to confess the Christian faith. We must therefore distinguish between tradition and traditionalism. As Jaroslav Pelikan has noted, traditionalism is the dead faith of the living; tradition is the living faith of the dead. Moreover, fully embracing classical orthodoxy will require us to move beyond the issues of urgent and immediate debate to an embrace of the whole. The alternative is to be constantly dealing with peripheral matters and never with the center of the faith.

Second, we need to return to a robust confessionalism. Just as Michael Walzer argues that there are "thin ethics" and "thick ethics," we might speak of thin confessionalism and thick confessionalism. A *thin* confessionalism is one that is merely a matter of requirement—a signature and a statement of allegiance and subscription. Doctrine is a contract rather than a covenant. *Thick* confessionalism, on the other hand, understands that

it is a privilege for a person to say, "I stand on these truths with this covenanted community. And as a matter of mutual accountability before God,
and under the authority of Scripture, we join together to hold ourselves
accountable to contend faithfully for the faith once for all delivered to the
saints, even as we address the urgent issues of the contemporary hour." This
is the kind of confessionalism our Baptist forebears espoused, and it is the
kind we must recover in the twenty-first century.

Third, we need to seek a recovery of Baptist principles. On regenerate
church membership, for instance, there has been too much compromise.
Baptist ecclesiology is not merely a matter of church organization. It stands
at the very center of the Baptist vision and goes to the very heart of our theology. When Baptist principles are compromised, everything is affected—
including our understanding of the gospel, the work of regeneration, and
the role of a covenant community as the congregation of faith.

Fourth, we must recover the discipline of theological "triage," a word
normally associated with the emergency room. Patients are brought in
with a great variety of injuries—sprained wrists, gunshot wounds, slight
stomachaches, and spider bites. In that situation, someone has to make an
evaluation of what is most urgent and what can wait. Otherwise, confusion
will reign. That triage nurse in the emergency room provides a good model
for our theological debates.

In the vast world of theological controversy, there are first-order issues,
second-order issues, and third-order issues. Unfortunately, most of our time
is usually spent dealing with secondary and tertiary issues, when we should
be focusing our attention on the primary issues. Primary issues are those
that distinguish Christians from non-Christians. I remember a student once
asking Dr. Lewis Drummond how one should relate to Christians who do
not believe in the bodily resurrection of Christ. Dr. Drummond replied,
"You relate to them as lost people." He was exactly right. Those who deny
the bodily resurrection are not believers in the Lord Jesus Christ. That is a
first-order issue.

Second-order issues are those that would prevent two Christians from
joining the same covenant community, even though they would still call one
another "Christians." A church, for instance, will either baptize babies, or
it will not. A church will either ordain women as pastors, or it will not.
This does not mean we would necessarily say that those who ordain women
as pastors are non-Christians. Nor would we say that those who baptize
babies are non-Christians. Nevertheless, we must affirm without apology
that a theological seminary, a denomination, and even individual churches

will have to stand with one confession, not a multiplicity of diverse choices. These second-order issues are the right place to focus much of our debate, so long as we remember where they rank.

Third-order issues are those that would not prevent two Christians from joining together in a covenant community. These are not unimportant issues; all truth is important. Yet they are not of such importance that disagreement on them means we cannot cooperate with each other. Many current debates within our churches—including everything from questions about the timing of the millennium to issues of cultural engagement—stand on this third level. As such, they are ripe for discussion, but they should not become cause for division.

Without the discipline of theological triage, we are constantly at risk of confusing third-order issues for first-order issues—the original besetting sin of fundamentalism. At the same time, we are also at risk of mistaking first-order issues for third-order ones—the besetting sin of liberalism. Keeping our equilibrium requires that our triage be clear and self-conscious, articulated and accountable.

ORGANIZATIONAL ISSUES

Having considered some of the theological issues that the SBC will face in coming years, we turn now to a second category—organizational issues. The SBC, like the Baptist movement as a whole, has experienced transformation over time. When Southern Baptists established themselves in Augusta, Georgia, in 1845, it was something new under the Baptist sun. The SBC was not merely a Southern version of the Triennial Convention; it was an entirely new model of the convention itself. The Southern Baptists organized their convention with a centralized purpose and sense of identity that drove it forward in a way the Triennial Convention was never intended to be driven.

Southern Baptists adjourned their convention in 1845 with just two boards, but over the next fifty years they negotiated their way into several others. They did not found a seminary in 1845; that would happen in 1859, when the Convention founded what would become The Southern Baptist Theological Seminary. By 1925, the SBC had grown, innovated, and been remarkably transformed. Still largely regionalized in the South after the Civil War and Reconstruction, it began the twentieth century by founding a second seminary—Southwestern Seminary in Fort Worth, Texas—even as the mission boards were continuing to test the limits of Southern Baptist vision. The Memphis convention in 1925 was perhaps the most critical turning point in the denomination's history. At that one convention and at that specific time, more crucial decisions were made than at any SBC held before or since. Messengers adopted the Cooperative Program, organized the Executive Committee, and accepted the *Baptist Faith and Message* in the first convention-wide, self-conscious adoption of a confession of faith.

The question is sometimes raised as to why the issue of religious liberty became so central at that particular moment. About that same time, Al Smith had run with the Democratic nomination for president in the 1920 election, and Southern Baptists were concerned. What would a Roman Catholic President mean? Even more urgently, World War I had been a disastrous experience for Southern Baptists. In fact, they had pulled all their chaplains out of the war effort because the War Department declared that chaplains had to function as nondenominational religious workers. More than anything else, that rankled the Baptist conscience, and religious liberty became a driving concern—one of the concerns, in fact, that led George W. Truett to preach his famous sermon, "Baptists and Religious Liberty," on the steps of the United States Capitol.

Not only were religious liberty issues a matter of concern, but so was the fundamentalist and modernist controversy being fought most hotly in the Northern denominations. Southern Baptists managed to reach an accommodated settlement, a solution possible only because they thought heterodoxy to be confined to the periphery of the denomination's experience, nowhere near the center. E. Y. Mullins, a statesman of unparalleled and unprecedented power, was able to articulate for Southern Baptists a way to the future that appeared to give them another pass through history. And it appeared to work for some time.

The adoption of the Cooperative Program and the organization of the Executive Committee showed that the SBC realized it could no longer operate as an ad-hoc meeting on an annual basis. There were fifty-two weeks in the year, all of which brought serious business to be done on the denomination's behalf, and in which the interests and gifts of the churches had to be channeled into some structure of support and accountability.

Fast forward to 1945 and the end of World War II, and not only did America enter a time of unprecedented prosperity and international influence, but the SBC also began a remarkable institutional, organizational, and denominational advance. The SBC became a national denomination by awkward default in the years from 1945 to 1965. Because no one needed any sort of denominational permission to start a Baptist church, Baptists were doing just that all across the country. Some of these churches operated without even acknowledging they were Southern Baptist, until they came out of the closet and sent messengers to an annual meeting. All of a sudden, Southern Baptists found themselves to be a national denomination with churches in all fifty states.

More subterranean developments pointed to the future as well. The SBC's Executive Committee hired Booz Allen Hamilton, the organizational and efficiency experts that had recently reorganized General Motors, to help them rethink their own denominational structure. In this way, the SBC took on the safeguards of a modern multinational corporation, with various branches like those of General Motors—Chevrolet, Oldsmobile, Buick, and Cadillac lines. The SBC now had various branches and institutions, all orchestrated in a very tight logic of efficiency.

That sort of organizational structure worked well because it fit the American mind. Moreover, so long as Southern Baptists assumed themselves to be together theologically, they could energize themselves around their institutions and pursue their goals of greater reach, expansion, and efficiency through the streamlined logic of the corporation. The slippage from that ideal began even in the mid-1960s, because if the SBC was a corporation, it had become very confused about its mission. Its own constituency was divided, and its senior executives were not even certain of the direction it should go. The SBC's corporate identity began to fall apart in the 1960s and 1970s, until the conservative resurgence brought a new energy and a new rallying point.

Along with the theological matters at stake in the conservative resurgence, there was also a renewed sense that the structure of the denomination no longer fit the needs of the time. In 1995, the Program and Structure Study Committee presented to the convention a covenant for a new century. The proposal was a partial reversal of the corporate logic that had prevailed for so long. It was a significant step, reducing the total number of entities from nineteen to twelve—something which, to my knowledge, no denomination had ever done, except in response to a financial crisis. Southern Baptists did it because they wanted a new structure that was leaner, more mission-oriented, easier to understand, and more accountable to the denomination and its churches.

Not only have changes taken place at the national level, but associational principles are also being rewritten in our day. An understanding of general Baptist bodies is being recovered, even by people who do not know the term "association." There is a renewed understanding that Baptists can rethink the way we relate to each other, and it is the churches that are driving that change—again, without asking for permission. The large infra-structure of modern Southern Baptist life may not survive in the postmod-ern age, but that decision will not be made by the executives of Southern Baptist agencies, or by the executives of state conventions. It will be made, eventually, by the churches.

In the 1900s, the primary issue was efficiency. In the twenty-first cen-tury, the primary issues are credibility and accountability. For the younger generation, the issue is this: "Is the SBC the answer to a question anyone is asking?" I would suggest the response to that is both "yes" and "no." There is a new congregationalism now being established. It is real, and it is evolv-ing. We can see it in churches such as Second Baptist Church in Houston, Texas, which now has a *third* location—in other words, one church in multiple locations. Such a thing was unheard of among Baptists in the past, but it is becoming more and more common because churches are beginning to understand that being a covenanted community may no longer mean we all have to be in one room at one time. Any church that holds multiple services in one location has already made the great theological jump, so going from two services to two locations is not too complicated or radical. Churches are also experimenting with a redefinition of the role of a deacon and a renegotiation of the role of an elder. There are real questions here about how we as Baptists should appropriate our tradition and maintain our understanding of congregational church government, especially when it is so easy to look at other alternatives and different denominations that may be more efficient, but that are also less Baptist.

PARACHURCH, TECHNOLOGICAL, AND DEMOGRAPHIC ISSUES

Three other issues deserve mention here. First, the parachurch will be a very significant part of the Southern Baptist future. By necessity market-driven, parachurch organizations offer expertise in customization and relevance. They emerge because they are generally able to meet a particular need faster than a denominational structure, and they can adjust themselves faster and get closer to the local church more quickly than a denominational entity accountable to 40,000 churches. The rise of parachurch organizations will spell a very different future for the SBC.

The second issue is the rise of a technological society. Churches are no longer dependent upon the SBC as they were just a few decades ago. The

SBC essentially has lost its monopoly, and that monopoly will never be recovered. In the same way, local newspapers have also lost their monopoly because people can go to the Internet and find newspapers from virtually anywhere in the world. Cable television was once the wave of the future. Now it is largely a thing of the past, because people can look on the Internet and even beat the reporters to a news story. The SBC is being affected by the information age in much the same way, and the only way it will be able to recover a sense of affection, accountability, and relevance with the churches is by understanding the real needs of real churches and reshaping itself to meet those needs.

The third great issue is demographic realities. In the first volume of his new history of the United States of America, William McDougal does what historians do not normally like to do—he makes judgments. McDougal says that over the last 400 years, the most important event in world history was the emergence of the United States of America. As much as others in the world may hate that assertion, he argued, "Try to discuss anything in contemporary history without making essential reference to the United States of America." Since 1845, the SBC has grown, and its expansion has taken place in the midst of this American reality. In just over 160 years, we have seen it grow from being a denomination embedded in an essentially agrarian social context to being a denomination that is now engaging a highly mobile, highly professional, and largely metropolitan society. Today's society is radically different from the one that gave birth to the SBC; in fact, it is almost impossible to imagine a citizen of the United States of America in 1845 recognizing much of the shape that America has taken today.

All this has led to changes in the SBC, and to a variety of new church types. We have seen the rise of megachurches and micro-churches—megachurches that understand growth and size to be an essential component in responding to an expanding metropolitan reality, and micro-churches that fit a niche for particular communities within those metropolitan areas. These megachurches and micro-churches have become models for others—especially the megachurches, which have been our denomination's great innovators of ministry for the last twenty years. With this phenomenon, however, has come an understandably low level of denominational commitment. Not only did the SBC lose its monopoly, but now many members of these large churches are not even aware that they are Southern Baptist. Megachurches are communities that are largely self-defined, and they do not need the SBC in order to conduct their seven-day-a-week ministry. They may connect with the SBC for missions, theological education, and other causes, but many of the members of these churches have only a vague awareness of what their denomination is, or should be, or could be.

Southern Baptists are still clustered in the South, but we are now in the New South—or maybe the *New* New South. In this highly mobile society, made up of the driving energy of young professionals in metropolitan areas, we face a missiological challenge that is different from anything we have seen before. Ponder this: if current statistical trends hold, by the year 2010 the majority of the people who attend our churches on any given Sunday morning will do so in just 19 metropolitan areas in the United States of America. In other words, most of the people who attend Southern Baptist churches now live in the cities and suburbs. This situation leads to statistical confusion, for often we hear that only about half of Southern Baptist pastors have a seminary degree. That may be true, but 90 percent of the people who hear a sermon on Sunday morning are hearing a seminary-educated pastor. The statistic mentioned above tells only half the story, and indeed a misleading part of the story. The SBC's energy has moved from its rural roots, where it began, to the metropolitan areas that have become the future of the nation. This was not done by any strategy, but simply by the shape of economic, political, and social dynamics—from transportation and the interstate highway system to the shape of the modern economy. That presents a tremendous challenge to Southern Baptists, one we ignore to our great detriment.

Another demographic challenge is the rise of ethnic and minority groups. The 1950 American census did not even record Hispanics as a category. Now Hispanics comprise the largest minority group in America. Just recently I was listening on CSPAN as a Republican strategist said, "You have to realize there are more Hispanic voters in Los Angeles than there are *voters* in Chicago." Once that fact is taken into consideration, it becomes obvious that the shape of the United States of America is not well represented by the annual meeting of the SBC. In terms of the ethnic diversity of this country, we are more than just a few years behind; we are in a different world altogether, and it will take the most concerted denominational leadership to address this challenge well.

There is also a generational challenge. Thanks to advances in medical technology, people are living longer. Not only so, but their vitality and energy have also been extended. Demographers are now being forced to talk about not only the old, but also the "old old," which might lead us to speak also of the "young old." These "young old" are the most underutilized generational cohort in our churches today. These are persons who are recently retired, who have great gifts and sound leadership experience, but who are being largely ignored because the church has bought into a pagan understanding of retirement. In pagan terms, retirement means "You're done." As Christians, however, we should understand retirement years not as "vacation time" in which we are to be left alone, but rather as an opportunity to work full-time for the glory of the Lord Jesus Christ and the good of his church. This "young old" cohort represents a great—but so far largely overlooked—opportunity for the church.

If the "young old" are the underutilized generation, there is also a generation that is almost entirely missing from the SBC—pastors and leaders between the ages of thirty-five and fifty-five. There is a tremendous younger generation coming, and there are many pastors fifty-five and older who are demonstrative leaders, servants of the Word, and preachers of power; but the most difficult pastoral search to conduct right now is for someone between age thirty-five and fifty-five. That is not to say, of course, that there is no one between the ages of thirty-five and fifty-five, but statistically speaking, this is an area of urgent vulnerability.

The worst news, however, is this: we are not even baptizing our own teenagers. Statistics can be interpreted in many different ways to make many different arguments, but one can only grieve over the figures on adolescent baptisms. According to some estimates, we are now baptizing only slightly more than 14 percent of our own teenagers. It is often noted that the years between twelve and twenty-five are the prime ages for making major decisions in life, including a public profession of faith in Christ. Ninety percent of persons who are baptized in our churches are baptized before age twenty-one. If we are reaching 14 percent of the twelve to twenty-five cohort, we are therefore missing 86 percent of them. The SBC's organizational issues must take a backseat here. If Southern Baptists do not address this problem quickly, an entire generation of young people who have grown up in our churches will not be defining the future of the SBC—they will instead be absorbed into a pagan America.

Despite all this, there is hope to be seen in the students on many university campuses and on the campuses of the SBC seminaries. There you will find hundreds of very serious young Christians ready for leadership. They are more conservative than their forebears, and they are more committed because they were not raised in a context of cultural Christianity. They have fought their way to every decision, and they made their public profession of faith in Christ when it was not popular. They are not interested in *laissez-faire*, lighthearted Christianity. They want the real thing, the red meat, a serious challenge, and they want to be taken seriously. It is not too much to say that this generation is our denomination's hope for the future.

CULTURAL AND MORAL ISSUES

We are also being confronted by a host of cultural and moral issues. One author has said that in the 1960s, Southern Baptists were at ease in Zion. The South was largely intact and basically unaffected by many of the social problems that had torn apart the North, not to mention post-Christendom in Europe. By the1970s, the culture wars had arrived at the doorstep of the SBC. In 1973, when *Roe v. Wade* was handed down by the United States Supreme Court, the SBC went on the record about abortion—and on the wrong side, to our denominational shame. It was not until 1979 that the SBC adopted a resolution that reversed that pro-choice affirmation. Incidentally, the issue of abortion was far more important in the conservative resurgence than most people have recognized. While most sociologists would describe the inerrancy issue as an opaque issue—one that is hard for laypeople to understand—there is nothing opaque about killing a baby in the womb. The evil of such a thing is obvious.

In the 1980s, the culture wars broke open with intensity, and we now face a panoply of issues, each of which seems more insistent than the one before. Genetic engineering, biotechnology, germ line therapy, embryo research, stem cell experimentation, in vitro fertilization, human cloning, euthanasia, assisted suicide—each of these issues presents the church with a formidable challenge. Already, over a dozen SBC churches have had trans-gendered persons present themselves for membership, and those congregations have had to decide right then and there what they believe. The church in this age cannot avoid giving an answer to these questions. The rising cultural confusion around us will eventually demand it.

Pastors are already facing questions about euthanasia and assisted suicide. People in our churches are also making decisions about reproductive technologies, and the day is not far off when they will be confronted with the issue of cloning. These are not distant issues. We cannot avoid giving an answer much longer. The culture wars are no longer "out there" or "up there" in the North. They are right here, in our churches and in our denomination. We as Southern Baptists will either muster the courage to address these issues in the comprehensive truthfulness of God's Word, or we will join the other mainline Protestants in their utter confusion. The sexual revolution, the clash of worldviews, the issue of homosexuality, the personal autonomy theme, the rise of moral relativism, the theological culture, the psychologies of the self, and the pervasiveness of postmodern worldviews all present inescapable challenges to our denomination, our seminaries, and our churches, and to Christian fathers and mothers.

Our denomination will be involved in controversy from now on. Our children will face these questions in their schools. Our families will face them in the workplace. What will your church members do on "Gay Day" at the local corporation, when someone comes by passing out gay-pride flags and the executive warns that it will not go well on evaluation day for anyone who refuses to celebrate? Philosophers such as Robert Audi are now arguing that the only assertions that should be allowed in the public square are those with a secular rationale, a secular purpose, and a secular effect. According to this logic, arguments about homosexuality that rely on scriptural teaching would be ruled out of bounds—if not silenced altogether. How will Southern Baptists react to the legal sanction, social ostracism, and prejudice that will soon be heaped upon us?

FINANCIAL ISSUES

The final issue to consider is our denomination's financial challenges. Other matters we have discussed are far more important, but the questions surrounding our denomination's finances also demand some attention. From 1987 to 2002, church receipts in the SBC grew 120 percent to a high of $9.5 billion. During that same period, the missions budget grew only 55 percent—about half the growth of total receipts. Similarly, giving to the Cooperative Program grew only 49 percent—less than half the total budget. The percentage of undesignated receipts given from local churches over the last fifteen years fell one-third from 7.85 percent to 5.3 percent. On a straight-line projection, that means the Cooperative Program would die in thirty years. Of course, such a scenario is unlikely, but it is clear that we are renegotiating the way we finance the work of this denomination and its entities, and once again, the churches are driving that change.

Two considerations are especially important in this matter. First, the rise of an American investor class means that patterns of giving are remarkably different at the local church level than they have been in the past. People are no longer looking forward to pensions established on a guaranteed benefit plan. Instead, they have to invest, and their future is dependent upon the protection of that money. Therefore, people are no longer giving out of accumulated wealth, but are increasingly waiting to give a portion of their estates after they die. If a 55-year-old man makes a major estate gift to Southern Seminary right now, we would thank him heartily for the gift. But actually speaking, that gift probably will not come to Southern Seminary for another thirty years. Thus, a great deal of the wealth transference upon which Christian churches and Christian organizations have always depended is now being delayed for years and even decades—a reality that will make the next twenty or thirty years a significant financial challenge for churches and Christian institutions.

Another sobering statistic is that in the metropolitan sectors of America, the average couple in their thirties is living on 115 percent of their annual income, which means they simply do not have much money to give. These economic realities immediately impact the bottom line. Is this a spiritual issue? Of course it is. Is it a stewardship issue? Of course it is. But the problem will not be reversed quickly. As Christians in the twenty-first century, we must entirely rethink the way we look at wealth, retirement, income, and materialism.

CONCLUSION

For all the challenges we will face in the future, this is a great time to be a Baptist. We now have the opportunity to recover our nonconformist roots. That is where we began. We were outsiders, not insiders. In fact, Baptists are always better when we are outsiders. When Baptists are forced to be nonconformists, we are forced to go back home. We have an opportunity now to think more clearly about what it means to be a Baptist, to be a covenanted community, and to be a Christian in communion with like-minded, Christ-professing, mutually accountable believers.

We have an opportunity to rekindle the Baptist vision of the church. Baptists have always understood Christianity in the context of the congregation. There can be no lone rangers, no theme of personal autonomy. Baptists understand that we are mutually accountable to each other. For it is in the context of the covenanted community—where Word and Spirit come together by the preaching of the Word and the nurture of Christian fellowship—that the Holy Spirit conforms us to the image of Christ.

We have an opportunity to reestablish our commitment to the *consensus fide*. Baptists are different from every other Christian denomination—and yet the same. We must remember that sameness as we stand together with others in the faith, even if they are not members of our own covenanted communities.

We have an opportunity to recommit ourselves to the confessionalism that was the high-water mark of the Baptist experience. The confession of faith was never an excuse or an invasion. It was simply a way of saying, "This is who we are, and this is how we intend to communicate what we believe both to the world and to each other."

We have an opportunity to restore church discipline in the congregation. Without discipline, we have a half-covenant, not a whole one. In the same way, we must reenergize evangelism, recognizing the challenge we face in ethnic, metropolitan, and urban realties. This is the challenge of a national denomination with an international mission.

Lastly, we have an opportunity now to reach out to a world desperately in need of hope, help, and the gospel. We are the vessels of the gospel of the Lord Jesus Christ. Missions is the heartbeat of our denomination, precisely because we believe that "whosoever will may come," and that "all who call upon the name of the Lord will be saved." We believe that faith comes by hearing and hearing by the word of Christ, and therefore we go, for without a preacher they will not hear.

When John F. Kennedy was running for president in 1960, N. Y. Stevens, who carried the Democratic banner from 1952 to 1956, advised him concerning religion. He said, "Senator, a politician's best refuge is a vague faith strongly held, or a strong faith vaguely held." What God requires from Southern Baptists, however, is a strong faith strongly held. That alone points the way to the Baptist future.

CHAPTER TWO

SOUTHERN BAPTIST IDENTITY: A THEOLOGICAL PERSPECTIVE

R. Stanton Norman

"WHAT MAKES A BAPTIST A BAPTIST?" The seeming simplicity of the question often belies the complexity of the answer. Ask any Baptist this question and you will receive as many answers as there are Baptists. Baptists usually agree that they have a distinctive theological identity. They disagree, however, over the nature of this identity.

INTRODUCTION

The question of "what makes a Baptist a Baptist" typically occurs within debates over Baptist distinctives. Many different beliefs are cited as true "Baptist distinctives." Some stress broad principles such as the priesthood of all believers, believer's baptism, a regenerate church membership, the primacy of the Scriptures, or congregational autonomy. Others call attention to religious freedom, soul competency, or the lordship of Christ as defining criteria. A popular answer often heard in pulpits is that Baptists are the only Christians who believe in "the Book, the blood, and the blessed hope."

Another common approach to identifying Baptist distinctives is what I call "the appeal to the Baptist precedent." Statements such as "Baptists have always believed this" are often cited as the undisputed truth that will bring immediate resolution to the debate. One Baptist leader is fond of saying, "Mama taught me that this is what Baptists have always believed," as though "Mama's authority" removes all doubt. With all due respect to his mother, "Mama" may not be right. Although these appeals are intended to strengthen the credibility of someone's position, more often than not, what is offered as Baptist "precedent" is usually tainted by personal agendas and ignorance of Baptist history and theology. Emotional claims of historical continuity typically bring confusion rather than clarification.

I have examined almost every document that claims to be a work on Baptist distinctives, and my research has uncovered significant issues that have direct bearing on the "Baptist distinctive" debate. First, writings on Baptist distinctives share particular theological components that are common to all these works. I contend that these components are the defining criteria of what are "writings on Baptist distinctives." Second, these treatises reflect a distinctive theological method. Third, the theological components and the theological method that are found in these documents converge to form a Baptist confessional theology.

CONSTITUENT ELEMENTS OF BAPTIST DISTINCTIVES

Certain theological components are common among writings that claim to articulate the distinctive Baptist identity. An inductive analysis has identified these mutually shared doctrinal traits.[1] These constituent elements are necessary and determinative for classifying a work as a writing on Baptist distinctives.[2]

Epistemological Component

The first component present in all writings on Baptist distinctives is the epistemological basis for theological formulation.[3] Baptist distinctive writings reflect a serious commitment to establish the basis for religious authority. The goal of determining this foundation is to solidify the viability of the distinctive theological identity of Baptists. All treatises that qualify as distinctive writings contain some type of discussion regarding the source of religious authority.

The Bible as the Epistemological Foundation

The most prominently held epistemological basis for religious authority among Baptists is the Bible. Baptists, along with other Christian denomi-

---

[1]The following overview of common components among writings on Baptist distinctives is representative and not exhaustive. The primary sources used throughout this work all comply with the components stipulated and thereby qualify for the designation of a "writing on Baptist distinctives."

[2]For purposes of brevity, the term "Baptist distinctives" will be used as a synonymous expression for any and all books, monographs, pamphlets, sermons, etc., that can rightfully be classified in this theological genre.

[3]Paul D. Feinberg defines epistemology in its religious expression as the inquiry into the nature of knowledge about God and the justification of claims to religious knowledge ("Epistemology," in *Evangelical Dictionary of Theology* [Grand Rapids, MI: Baker, 1984]). The objective basis for knowing religious claims will be the definition employed herein.

nations, appeal to the Bible as their ultimate or sole source for religious authority. Baptists distance themselves from other denominations, however, by claiming a complete dependence upon Scripture as the principal foundation for their beliefs and practices. Whereas certain other Christian groups incorporate extra-biblical sources such as tradition for religious authority, Baptists in their distinctive writings contend that they alone consistently and exclusively hold to the Bible exclusively as their religious authority.[4]

Some Baptists narrow biblical authority to the New Testament.[5] This sub-grouping emphasizes that the New Testament as the source of religious authority is that which distinguishes Baptists from all other Christian denominations.[6] Some Baptists go so far as to teach that doctrinal developments that are neither supported nor taught in the New Testament disqualify those beliefs from being considered "baptistic."[7]

The assertion of the Bible as the source of religious authority is of paramount importance to the distinctive theology of Baptists.[8] Baptists categorically oppose any authoritative human imposition between God and man. Such intrusions interfere with the essence of the faith relationship between the Creator and his creation. Because of this aversion, Baptists

---

[4]John Quincy Adams writes, "Baptists aim to restore the order of the primitive churches. They make no appeal to tradition, the Fathers, or expediency. They simply ask, 'What do the Scriptures teach?' They follow the New Testament model of a church, and invite all to test them by it. It is not strange, therefore, that they confidently appeal to God's Word for proof of the correctness of all they do. They take it all from the Bible, and therefore they know it can all be found there. Take any Scripture account of the course pursued by the apostles, or of the practice of gospel churches, and you will find the counterpart in a Baptist church" (*Baptists, the Only Thorough Religious Reformers*, rev. ed. [New York: Sheldon & Co., 1876], 162).

[5]Henry Cook, *What Baptists Stand For* (London: Kingsgate Press, 1947), 18. It is this emphasis on the supremacy of the New Testament in all matters of the church's faith and practice that constitutes the basis of the Baptist position. It is to the New Testament we must go for direction, and it is by the standards of the New Testament that we must seek to regulate our convictions and conduct.

[6]Benajah Harvey Carroll states, "When Baptists say that the New Testament is the only law for Christian institutions they part company, if not theoretically at least practically, with most of the Protestant world, as well as from the Greeks and Romanists" (*Baptists and Their Doctrines: Sermons on Distinctive Baptist Principles*, comp. by J. B. Cranfill [New York: F. H. Revell, 1913], 11).

[7]James Madison Pendleton, *Three Reasons Why I Am a Baptist, with a Fourth Reason Added on Communion*, 13th ed. (Nashville: Graves, Marks & Co., 1857), 5–6. See Pendleton, *Distinctive Principles of Baptists* (Philadelphia, PA: American Baptist Publication Society, 1882), 11, where Pendleton seems to contradict himself when he appeals to the entire Bible as the "supreme standard of faith and practice."

[8]The notion that the Bible is the source of religious authority for Baptists is regularly illustrated by the manner in which Baptist distinctives are developed. Vast amounts of material and time are devoted to some type of exposition of the Scriptures in order to develop or validate some particular doctrinal point. E.g., *Baptist, Why and Why Not* (Nashville: Sunday School Board, Southern Baptist Convention, 1900), 169–78; Jeremiah Bell Jeter, *Baptist Principles Reset*, (Richmond, VA: Religious Herald Co., 1902), 14, 16, 18–26; Philip L. Jones, *A Restatement of Baptist Principles* (Philadelphia, PA: Griffith and Rowland Press, 1909), 35, 52–53; William Richardson White, *Baptist Distinctives* (Nashville: Sunday School Board, Southern Baptist Convention, 1946), 28–34; P. Lovene, *Distinctive Baptist Principles*, 2nd ed. (Chicago: Baptist Conference Press, 1950), 39–43; Cook, *What Baptists Stand For*, 85–90. Joseph Burnley Moody not only develops an elaborate biblical exposition for his formulation of Baptist distinctives but also argues for a typological hermeneutic; see Moody, *The Distinguishing Doctrines of Baptists* (Nashville: Folk & Browder, 1901), 7–83.

typically reject the use of creedal statements.[9] They instead appeal to the Bible as their authoritative creed for all matters of doctrine and practice.[10]

Individual, Autonomous, Religious Experience as the Epistemological Foundation

Another epistemological expression is individual, autonomous, religious experience.[11] Although the majority of writings on Baptist distinctives begin with some assertion of biblical authority, some Baptist distinctives contend that religious experience is the epistemological basis. This premise is asserted as a necessary stipulation in order to have a valid understanding of the role of the Bible and the process of conversion in Baptist thought. The argument for religious experience as the primary epistemological foundation is a twentieth-century development in the history of Baptist distinctives.[12]

Polemical Intention Component

The second component found within Baptist distinctives is "polemical intention." Polemical intention is the notion that the author is purposefully expounding those theological traits that distinguish Baptists from other Christian denominations. This element critiques the theological distinctiveness of other Christian denominations in light of their differences with Baptists.

Part of the overall Baptist theological identity are those doctrines that they share with other Christian denominations. Theological conceptions, such as Christology, the Trinity, and eschatology that are common among Baptists, can typically be found in other Christian groups. Theological treatises or doctrinal explications written by Baptists are intentionally dif-

---

[9]Timothy George notes that Baptists have always rejected two expressions of creedalism. Baptists have opposed forms of creedalism in which governmental authorities seek to regulate or coerce religious life. Baptists have also opposed all forms of creedalism in which man-made doctrinal constructs are elevated above the Bible. George does suggest, however, that aversion to these forms of creedalism is not the same as the voluntary, conscientious adherence to explicit doctrinal statements. Baptists, according to George, have advocated such theological formulations and have even employed the term "creed" to describe the process (*Baptist Confessions, Covenants, and Catechisms* [Nashville: Broadman & Holman, 1996], 2–4).

[10]Cook, *What Baptists Stand For*, 18; Charles W. Gilkey, "The Distinctive Baptist Witness," *The Chronicle* 8 (July 1945): 102.

[11]Although the phrase is quite lengthy, each term is carefully and intentionally selected to convey what this component means. The word "individual" is selected to designate the emphasis upon the uniquely personal nature of religious experience. "Autonomous" suggests that the experience must be of the person alone. The notion is intended to reject ideas of imposed-faith or proxy-faith. "Religious" suggests that the discussion is not of all human experiences, but only those that are uniquely and distinctly religious. Within the current discussion, these religious experiences, but are Christian in expression. For purposes of brevity, the phrase "religious experience" will be used herein to designate this broad concept.

[12]Edgar Young Mullins, *The Axioms of Religion: A New Interpretation of the Baptist Faith* (Philadelphia, PA: Griffith & Rowland, 1908), 59–69.

ferent from writings on Baptist distinctives. These types of writings do not in and of themselves seek to articulate the distinctive theology of Baptists. Polemical intention is significant in that it is a primary component that distinguishes the distinctive genre from other types of Baptist theology. Polemical intention is theologically oriented and can have several differing expressions. It can critique the theological foundations or explications of other Christian groups in comparison with Baptists.[13] Polemical intention can target specific denominations[14] or certain religious movements.[15] Baptists have even criticized themselves in the way they formulate their own distinctive identity.[16] The purpose of the polemic is to highlight the supremacy and uniqueness of the Baptist position in contrast to the theological deficiencies of other positions.

Ecclesiological Component

The third component of these writings is the Baptist doctrine of the church. Those elements which distinguish Baptists theologically from other

---

[13]For Baptist polemics against pedobaptism, see Adams, *Baptists*, 25, 81–83; Herbert Gezork, "Our Baptist Faith in the World To-Day," in *Baptist World Alliance Golden Jubilee Congress, London, 1955* (London: Carey Kingsgate Press, 1955), 44; Henry Wheeler Robinson, *The Life and Faith of the Baptists* (London: Kingsgate Press, 1946), 71–74; Robinson, *Baptist Principles*, repr. 4th ed. (London: Carey Kingsgate Press, 1966), 60–61; Jeter, *Baptist Principles Reset*, 34–56; Pendleton, *Distinctive Principles of Baptists*, 80–89; *Baptist, Why and Why Not*, 153–62; James S. Kirtley, *The Baptist Distinctive and Objective* (Philadelphia, PA: Judson Press, 1926), 15–16; against state-church concepts, see Lovene, *Distinctive Baptist Principles*, 45; Jeter, *Baptist Principles Reset*, 124–25; Gezork, "Our Baptist Faith in the World To-Day," 44; Kirtley, *The Baptist Distinctive and Objective*, 20–21; James Donovan Mosteller, "Basic Baptist Principles and the Contemporary Scene," *Southwestern Journal of Theology* 6 (April 1964): 75–81; against sacramentalism, see George Edwin Horr, *The Baptist Heritage* (Philadelphia, PA: Judson Press, 1923), 88; Kirtley, *The Baptist Distinctive and Objective*, 9–15; against sacerdotalism and religious tradition, see Carroll, *Baptists and Their Doctrines: Sermons on Distinctive Baptist Principles*, 21–23; Kirtley, *The Baptist Distinctive and Objective*, 16–20; Jones, *A Restatement of Baptist Principles*, 16–17; Emlyn Davies, "Our Historic Baptist Distinctives," *The Chronicle* 16 (October 1953): 191. George Peck argues against the way Baptists have done things in the past and seeks to preserve a fluidity and viability to the Baptist identity for future ministry ("The Baptist Heritage: Practice, Polity, and Promise," *Andover Newton Quarterly* 19 [March 1979]: 215–22). In a sense, Peck is arguing against a "Baptist tradition." For Baptist polemics against Episcopal and/or Presbyterial church polity, see Mullins, *The Axioms of Religion*, 227–33.

[14]For Baptist polemics against Roman Catholicism, see Walter Rauschenbusch, *Why I Am a Baptist* (Philadelphia, PA: Baptist Leader, 1958), in *Rochester Baptist Monthly* 20 (1905–6), 2–3; Moody, *The Distinguishing Doctrines of Baptists*, 86–87, 135–39; Robinson, *Life and Faith*, 20; Lovene, *Distinctive Baptist Principles*, 23–24; Cook, *What Baptists Stand For*, 20–26; *Baptist, Why and Why Not*, 51–80; against Episcopalianism, see *Baptist, Why and Why Not*, 83–108; Moody, *The Distinguishing Doctrines of Baptists*, 140; against Congregationalism, see Lovene, *Distinctive Baptist Principles*, 45; against Methodism and Presbyterianism, see *Baptist, Why and Why Not*, 111–25, 129–36; against Lutheranism, see Mullins, *The Axioms of Religion*, 109–13; and against Campbellism, see *Baptist, Why and Why Not*, 139–50.

[15]See White (*Baptist Distinctives*, 57–63), where he specifically targets the National and World Council of Churches. Although White does critique doctrines and denominations, he does so within the confines of his assault upon the National and World Council of Churches. The articulation of White's understanding of Baptist distinctives is framed within a discussion of why Baptists, particularly Southern Baptists, should not become members of these councils.

[16]E.g., Eric H. Ohlmann levels his polemic against the way in which all other writings on Baptist distinctives have been formulated ("The Essence of the Baptists: A Reexamination," *Perspectives in Religious Studies* 13 [Fall 1986]: 83–92).

Christian groups are often most visible in the manner in which Baptists "do church."[17] Whenever Baptist distinctives are being developed, the work will in some capacity address Baptist ecclesiology. Although the types of church issues may vary in specificity or quantity, the presence of ecclesiastical issues is certain.

One common expression of this component is the mode of baptism. In distinctive writings, Baptists maintain that the only New Testament mode of baptism is immersion. Baptists have consistently affirmed the theological significance of baptism by immersion.[18] Some Baptists have elevated the mode of baptism to such status that the Lord's Supper was denied to those not baptized by this mode in a Baptist church.[19] The issue of baptism is also found within the ecclesiological component under the topic of believer's baptism. The baptism of conscious believers is a significant differentiation between Baptists and paedobaptists. Although Baptists have insisted that baptism is not necessary for salvation, they have contended for its importance for church membership.[20]

A regenerated, or believers', church is another feature of the ecclesiological component. Baptists maintain that a visible, local congregation should be constituted only of those who have experienced God's grace through faith, have been baptized, and have voluntarily associated themselves so as to participate in the mission of that local church. This notion stands in contradistinction to the inclusive state-church concept. For Baptists, such religious conceptions undermine the very heart of the gospel and a regenerated church membership. Due to the prevalence of the state-church position found among many Christian groups, Baptists contend that a regenerated church membership is unique to their distinctive ecclesiology.[21]

Congregational polity is also frequently discussed. Baptists readily admit that congregational polity is not their sole "theological property." They do claim, however, to make unique contributions to the doctrine by

---

[17]William Thomas Whitley, *A History of British Baptists* (Philadelphia, PA: J. B. Lippincott, 1923), 4.
[18]Ohlmann, "The Essence of the Baptists," 90–91.
[19]Pendleton, *Three Reasons*, 32–137.
[20]James Leo Garrett Jr., "Baptist 'Distinctives': Endangered Species" (sermon, Southwestern Baptist Theological Seminary, Fort Worth, TX, September 4, 1991), 1–3; Thomas Treadwell Eaton, *The Faith of the Baptists* (Louisville, KY: Baptist Book Concern, 1903), 20–41; Jonathan Gaines Bow, *What Baptists Believe and Why They Believe It* (Nashville: Sunday School Board of the Southern Baptist Convention, 1906), 25–31; Frederick L. Anderson, *Historic Baptist Principles* (Buffalo, NY: American Baptist Historical Society, 1920), 15; Cook, *What Baptists Stand For*, 118–38; Jones, *A Restatement of Baptist Principles*, 51–58; Kirtley, *The Baptist Distinctive and Objective*, 53–54; George, *Baptist Confessions*, 163–79; Lovene, *Distinctive Baptist Principles*, 33–34; Horr, *The Baptist Heritage*, 48–50; Adams, *Baptists*, 150–51; White, *Baptist Distinctives*, 29–30; Jeter, *Baptist Principles Reset*, 13; Carroll, *Baptists and Their Doctrines*, 33; Robinson, *Baptist Principles*, 11–28; Robinson, *Life and Faith*, 78–85 (although not rejecting immersion as the mode of baptism, Robinson is not as adamant about the form of baptism as he is about the theological meaning of baptism).
[21]Cook, *What Baptists Stand For*, 17, 32.

joining believer's baptism together with soul competency in order to form a peculiar expression of church government. This arrangement of these particular doctrines permits Baptists to claim their formulation as peculiar to them.[22]

Volitional Component

A fourth trait common within the distinctive genre is the "volitional" component. This element is expressed in two concepts that are somewhat distinct yet share common ground. These two expressions are religious liberty and soul competency.[23]

The first expression of the volitional component is religious liberty.[24] Baptists lived as a disadvantaged and persecuted sect for hundreds of years in England and in colonial America. Due to these circumstances, they constantly cried out for the freedom to follow their religious convictions and beliefs without external interferences.[25] The postulation of religious liberty by Baptists was quite revolutionary during the first centuries of Baptist life.[26] The reason for their insistence of religious freedom is attributed to their understanding of the gospel as requiring a voluntary, intentional response without any external coercion. As a distinctive expression of their

---

[22]E.g., Carroll, *Baptists and Their Doctrines*, 27–31; White, *Baptist Distinctives*, 38–39; Adams, *Baptists*, 121–26; Lovene, *Distinctive Baptist Principles*, 19–20; Kirtley, *The Baptist Distinctive and Objective*, 52–53; Jones, *A Restatement of Baptist Principles*, 43–51; Mullins, *The Axioms of Religion*, 55; Cook, *What Baptists Stand For*, 74–84; Eaton, *The Faith of the Baptists*, 17; Robinson, *Life and Faith*, 97–110.

[23]The designation of religious liberty and soul competency under the concept of volition follows that established by Mullins (*The Axioms of Religion*, 150–67). Although Mullins does give two separate discussions of the topics, the notions share similarities in their expressions within writings on Baptist distinctives. Mullins joins the concepts of freedom and responsibility together. For Mullins, every individual is made in the image of God and is therefore competent, responsible, and accountable to deal personally with God. This individual, or "soul," competency further implies for Mullins an unhindered access to receive or to reject a personal, individual relationship with God. Each "soul" has a volitional obligation to address his spiritual standing before God. Further, society has a volitional obligation to provide an unhindered or unobtrusive environment to allow persons the freedom to deal with God in this way. This rationale is why Mullins includes both soul competency and religious freedom together in his discussion (ibid., 150–57). Because Mullins gave these two ideas an overlapping treatment within the general confines of his discussion, the concepts are adopted herein to embrace both ideas within this one component.

[24]E.g., Adams, *Baptists*, 43, 90–97; Rauschenbusch, *Why I Am a Baptist*, 6, 9; Robinson, *Life and Faith*, 123–34; Robinson, *Baptist Principles*, 63; White, *Baptist Distinctives*, 13–16; Pendleton, *Distinctive Principles of Baptists*, 185; Lovene, *Distinctive Baptist Principles*, 75–77; Kirtley, *The Baptist Distinctive and Objective*, 20; Horr, *The Baptist Heritage*, 93–95; Jones, *A Restatement of Baptist Principles*, 73–78; William D. Nowlin, *Fundamentals of the Faith* (Nashville: Baptist Sunday School Board, 1922), 48–49; Davies, "Our Historic Baptist Distinctives," 195–96; Cook, *What Baptists Stand For*, 165; Carroll, *Baptists and Their Doctrines*, 23–24; *Baptist, Why and Why Not*, 269–78; Jeter, *Baptist Principles Reset*, 120–27.

[25]Ohlmann, "The Essence of the Baptists," 87. He further notes that although Baptists agree with other Protestants on many points, the notion of religious liberty has radically distinguished the Baptists from other denominations.

[26]See H. Leon McBeth, *English Baptist Literature on Religious Liberty to 1689* (New York: Arno Press, 1980). Not only did Baptists include their sentiments on this subject in their distinctive writings, but they also wrote extensively on it in separate treatises and confessions of faith.

unique theological identity, Baptists contend that faith must be a free and voluntary response to God.[27]

Another expression of the volitional component is soul competency.[28] Because of the inherent connection between the two ideas, when Baptists contend for religious freedom in their distinctive writings they normally discuss soul competency or vice versa. Baptists adamantly hold to the notion that the individual alone must approach and relate to God directly without any human intermediaries.[29] Soul competency can refer to the innate ability of each individual to relate to God, the responsibility of each person to know and serve God (or to reject God), or the initial experience of "doing business with God." Soul competency has proven a useful weapon against sacerdotalism, sacramentalism, pedobaptism, and state churches. In American Baptist life, soul competency has penetrated deeply into the distinctive theological identity of Baptists.[30]

Baptist distinctives share common theological components that define the criteria for this theological genre. Epistemological, polemical, ecclesiological, and volitional components are all found in some form in these works. Although arrangement and expression of these components can be somewhat diverse, these traits are the criteria that categorize a theological work within the genre of Baptist distinctives.

THE THEOLOGICAL HERMENEUTIC OF BAPTIST DISTINCTIVES

The next issue I will address is the theological hermeneutic employed in Baptist distinctives. Authors of Baptist distinctive writings develop a primary, or defining, distinctive that is more prevalent than the others. This "defining" or "organizing" distinctive serves as a foundational premise for the other distinctive doctrines.

---

[27]Adams, Baptists, 96–97.

[28]E.g., Rauschenbusch, Why I Am a Baptist, 3; Robinson, Life and Faith, 19; Robinson, Baptist Principles, 20–27, 68–69; Mullins, The Axioms of Religion, 59–69, 150–67; White, Baptist Distinctives, 12–15; Pendleton, Distinctive Principles of Baptists, 185; Lovene, Distinctive Baptist Principles, 57–62; Jones, A Restatement of Baptist Principles, 16–18, 81; Nowlin, Fundamentals of the Faith, 17, 49–50; Davies, "Our Historic Baptist Distinctives," 195–96; Carroll, Baptists and Their Doctrines, 15–18, 34; Kirtley, The Baptist Distinctive and Objective, 7–8; Horr, The Baptist Heritage, 92–97; James Burton Gambrell, "Obligations of Baptists to Teach Their Principles," in Jeter, Baptist Principles Reset, (Richmond, VA: Religious Herald Co., 1902), 250–51.

[29]William Roy McNutt, Polity and Practice in Baptist Churches (Philadelphia, PA: Judson Press, 1935), 21–25; Robinson, Life and Faith, 19, 24; Mullins, The Axioms of Religion, 53–57.

[30]Ohlmann asserts that soul competency in American Baptist life is shaped by three factors: rationalism's insistence on religion as a personal matter between the individual and God, revivalism's emphasis on a personal decision of faith, and the American enchantment for civil and religious liberty ("The Essence of the Baptists," 88).

I recognize that Baptists are too diverse and complex to be reduced to one central characteristic. The complexity of Baptist distinctives can best be understood, however, via an analysis that involves locating an organizing principle. My research has uncovered the explicit presence of such a methodology within the writings themselves.[31]

Biblical Authority as the Primary Distinctive

One group of writings on Baptist distinctives contends for biblical authority as the defining distinctive. The other distinctive components are the logical application of the core distinctive. Biblical authority is therefore the foundational premise; all the other distinctive components are the theological outflow of this core tenet.

Some distinctive writings stipulate that the existence of Baptists is the result of faithful obedience and submission to the authority of Scripture:[32]

> The fundamental principle of the Baptists is their belief in the supreme authority and absolute sufficiency of the Holy Scriptures; and their separate existence is the practical and logical result of their attempt to apply this principle in all matters of faith and religion.[33]

> The Baptists have been distinguished for their close attachment to the Scriptures. They, and they alone, have never appealed to any thing else for proof of any portion of their faith and practice, as Christians. . . . The simplicity of this principle has been favorable to their success.[34]

> The one fundamental principle of Baptists, and the foundation stone on which they rest as an effective Christian group in the world today, is their belief in the supreme authority and absolute sufficiency of the Holy Scriptures, especially the New Testament, as the complete and infallible guide in all matters pertaining to their faith and practice, and every other peculiarity which characterizes them is the practical outcome of this principle.[35]

---

[31]Contra Ohlmann, who, while affirming that such a prioritizing of Baptist traits exists, does not see any intentionality on the part of the Baptist writers in the delineation of characteristic Baptist emphases or the location of a central tenet of Baptist thought or foundation ("The Essence of the Baptists," 84). Ohlmann simply affirms the fact that these writings contain a core thesis. The evidence indicates, however, that many of the writers on Baptist distinctives did intentionally formulate a central thesis that interpreted or shaped the other distinctives.

[32]Joe T. Odle, *Why I Am a Baptist* (Nashville: Baptist Sunday School Board, 1972), 94–95; Robert A. Baker, *The Southern Baptist Convention and Its People* (Nashville: Broadman, 1972), 3; Davies, "Our Historic Baptist Distinctives," 193–95.

[33]*Baptist, Why and Why Not*, 26.

[34]Cited in R. Stanton Norman, *The Baptist Way: Distinctives of a Baptist Church* (Nashville: B&H, 2005), 11ff.

[35]William Holmes Rone, *The Baptist Faith and Roman Catholicism*, rev. ed. (Kingsport, TN: Kingsport Press, 1952), 3.

Baptist distinctives for these authors are the "natural" conclusion to the fundamental distinctive of biblical authority.[36]

Other distinctive writings apply biblical authority to Baptist ecclesiology.[37] With regard to the authority of the Bible and ecclesiology, "in his doctrine of the church, the Baptist [sic] rejects all that is not required by scripture and so the two primary principles harmonize, the second being an extension of the first."[38] Following a brief discussion regarding the significance of Baptist ecclesiology, Cook states that "this is the fundamental Baptist position. With this belief in the primacy of the New Testament Baptists always begin, and from it they draw all their conclusions."[39] Based upon their distinctive biblical authority, the procedure of Baptists is "to draw inferences for the practice of the church."[40]

The practice of baptism is also considered a theological derivative from biblical authority. The "search for Scriptural baptism" is nothing more than the application of biblical authority. Baptism by immersion is the consistent application of the all-sufficiency of the Scriptures.[41] Infant baptism is rejected on the basis that biblical authority propounds believer's baptism.[42]

Others derive soul competency from the distinctive of biblical authority. Based on this fundamental principle, Baptists are compelled to "enumerate some of the inferences that Baptists have deduced," the first of which is the competency and immediacy of the soul in communion with God.[43] The concept of soul competency is viewed as such an integral expression of biblical authority that "when one is denied or explained away, the other usually suffers like fate."[44] God's Word as the religious authority suggests that each person has the right and responsibility to approach God and appeal to Scripture.[45] Issues of individual responsibility and duty are stipulated as necessary corol-

---

[36]Eaton identifies the primary distinctive of Baptists as absolute submission to the "Scripture teaching." From this principle he derives the corollaries of soul competency, the church, baptism, and the Lord's Supper (*The Faith of the Baptists*, 4).

[37]Nowlin, *Fundamentals of the Faith*, 22–23; Moody, *The Distinguishing Doctrines of Baptists*, 7–8.

[38]Jack Hoad (*The Baptist: An Historical and Theological Study of the Baptist Identity* [London: Grace Publications Trust, 1986], 14–15) contends that the second principle, the Baptist understanding of the church, is "an extension" of the first, namely, the sole authority of the Bible in all matters of faith and practice.

[39]Cook, *What Baptists Stand For*, 19.

[40]Winthrop S. Hudson, *Baptist Convictions* (Valley Forge, PA: Judson, 1963), 6–7.

[41]Jeter, *Baptist Principles Reset*, 252; P. Lovene, *Distinctive Baptist Principles* (Chicago: Baptist Conference Press, 1950), 12–13; Pendleton and White also contend for a regenerate church membership in addition to baptism (Pendleton, *Distinctive Principles of Baptists*, 12–13; White, *Baptist Distinctives*, 4–7).

[42]Bow, *What Baptists Believe*, 4; Lovene, *Distinctive Baptist Principles*, 11.

[43]F. Anderson, *Historic Baptist Principles*, 16–17.

[44]Whitley, *A History of British Baptists*, 28–29.

[45]Adams, *Baptists*, 33–37.

laries of biblical authority.[46] Soul competency is construed as a viable and logical expression of the contention of the Bible as the absolute authority for faith and practice.[47]

A Shift in Methodology

Baptist distinctive writings prior to the twentieth century all shared the core distinctive of biblical authority. A shift in this expression occurred early in the twentieth century. Although many Baptists continued to assert biblical authority as the primary distinctive, others began to argue for the authoritative role of individual, autonomous, religious experience prior to the authority of the Bible. The first major work to argue for a "redefining" of the primary distinctive of Baptists was E. Y. Mullins's *The Axioms of Religion*.[48] Mullins elevated religious experience to an authoritative role that had previously been reserved in these writings on the Bible. This is not to say that issues of religious experience did not exist as a theological component within this distinctive genre; it certainly did. Mullins rather elevated this trait to a prominent role of religious authority, thereby infusing into the distinctive theological process a new, "interpretative" distinctive. *The Axioms of Religion* marked a significant shift in the prevailing understand-

---

[46]Carroll, *Baptists and Their Doctrines*, 15.

[47]Gezork, "Our Baptist Faith," 42.

[48]The first writing that mentioned religious experience as the characteristic distinctive of Baptists was Rauschenbusch, *Why I Am a Baptist*. Rauschenbusch's work was a precursor to Mullins's writing, but Mullins's work was far more pivotal and influential in the development of religious experience as the core distinctive in Baptist life. Two reasons support this assertion. First, Rauschenbusch's writing is more personal and testimonial. Unlike Mullins, Rauschenbusch gives no reasoning or basis for his claim. Although using personal religious experience as the foundation for the explication of other Baptist distinctives, Rauschenbusch only acknowledges the fact of personal religious experience and its implications as it pertains to his own personal spiritual pilgrimage. Mullins, however, provides careful argumentation for the philosophical and biblical basis for religious experience as expressed in soul competency and argues for its primacy as the primary Baptist distinctive. Second, others often cite Mullins's arguments and reasoning as the basis for the rationale of soul competency as the primary Baptist distinctive. For example, see Robinson, *Life and Faith*, 18; Jones, *A Restatement of Baptist Principles*, 15; McNutt, *Polity and Practice*, 21–25.

The influence of Mullins in shaping Baptist thought in general and religious experience in particular is noted by others (e.g., J. Clyde Turner, *Our Baptist Heritage* (Nashville: Baptist Sunday School Board, 1945), 37; Cook, *What Baptists Stand For*, 9, 216; Lovene, *Distinctive Baptist Principles*, 58; Ohlmann, "The Essence of the Baptists," 88; Mosteller, "Basic Baptist Principles," 60; F. Anderson, *Historic Baptist Principles,* 6; Garrett, "Major Emphases in Baptist Theology," 44). Harold Bloom has characterized Mullins as "the Calvin or Luther or Wesley of the Southern Baptists . . . not the founder of the Southern Baptists but their re-founder, the definer of their creedless faith" (Bloom, *The American Religion: The Emergence of the Post-Christian Nation* [New York: Simon and Schuster, 1992], 199). Mullins himself seemed aware that he was postulating a shift of emphasis in Baptist distinctive writings and reflects this intention in the title *The Axioms of Religion: A New Interpretation of the Baptist Faith*. Mullins continues to exert influence, especially on the popular level, through Herschel H. Hobbs, *The Axioms of Religion*, rev. ed. (Nashville: Broadman Press, 1978), which is a revision of Mullins's earlier work. Mark Whitten observes that Mullins's influence, due to his roles as seminary president, theology teacher, author, and denominational statesman, extended beyond the perimeters of Southern Baptist life to encompass all Baptists to some degree (Whitten, "Philosophy of Religion," in *Has Our Theology Changed? Southern Baptist Theology Since 1845*, ed. Paul Basden [Nashville: Broadman & Holman, 1994], 271).

ing of the theological distinctives of Baptists and thereby provided an impetus for a second defining distinctive from which some Baptists would elaborate their unique theological identity.[49]

Experiential Authority

Certain Baptist distinctives writings advocate an experiential authority as the primary, or defining, distinctive. The works that argue for religious experience as the primary distinctive also view the other distinctive components as the logical application of this core distinctive. Religious experience is for them the foundational premise. All other distinctive doctrinal formulations are the natural, theological outflow of this tenet. This phenomenon is intentional in expression and is often explicitly stated as such.

Walter Rauschenbusch illustrates the derivation of other Baptist distinctives from religious experience. After stipulating individual religious experience as the core distinctive theological trait of Baptists, Rauschenbusch applies this principle by asserting that the baptism of believers is the application of the prior principle of religious experience.[50] The baptism of believers is the consistent application of Rauschenbusch's understanding of religious experience. This notion is also determinative for his understanding of congregational polity, ministry, evangelism, and the Lord's Supper.

A contemporary example is Walter B. Shurden's work on Baptist distinctives.[51] Following Martin Marty, Shurden asserts that the notion of individual freedom is the "stackpole around which Baptist convictions develop."[52] He then uses the notion of individual freedom to address the topics of Bible freedom, soul freedom, church freedom, and religious freedom.

Other distinctive works apply their multifaceted expressions of religious experience in various ways. Soul competency is one expression of religious experience. Soul competency is posited as the "unifying

---

[49]The notion of a theological shift occurring with Mullins has been asserted by others. Tom Nettles posits that Mullins's theological methodology "began the inimitable influence" of Southern Baptists away from what Nettles contends was an SBC Calvinistic orthodoxy (Nettles, *By His Grace and for His Glory: A Historical, Theological, and Practical Study of the Doctrines of Grace in Baptist Life* [Grand Rapids, MI: Baker, 1986], 246–57). Although Nettles is addressing the issue of election in Southern Baptist theology, he is perceptive in identifying the influence which Mullins exerted not only on Southern Baptists but also, in many ways, on Baptist thought in general. Others who have made similar observation are Dwight A. Moody, with regard to Baptist understandings of the nature of the Bible (Moody, "The Bible," in Basden, *Has Our Theology Changed?* 12–13); Basden, with regard to Baptist understandings of predestination (Basden, "Predestination," in Basden, *Has Our Theology Changed?* 50–54); and Walter D. Draughon, III, regarding Baptist understandings of the atonement (Draughon, "Atonement," in Basden, *Has Our Theology Changed?* 84–96).

[50]Rauschenbusch, *Why I Am a Baptist*, 2.

[51]Walter B. Shurden, *The Baptist Identity: Four Fragile Freedoms* (Macon, GA: Smyth & Helwys, 1993), 1–4.

[52]Martin E. Marty, "Baptistification Takes Over," *Christianity Today*, September 2, 1983. It is interesting that Shurden looks to an American Lutheran church historian for his understanding of Baptist distinctives.

principle" for all distinctive aspects of Baptist theology.[53] No doctrine is more "baptistic" than soul competency, and no doctrine is more determinative of the theological peculiarities of Baptists than this concept.[54] Soul competency "is the principle which has shaped our [Baptist] history, dictated our attitude toward the Scriptures, formulated our conceptions of the Church, interpreted for us the meaning of the two New Testament ordinances, made us champions of soul [religious] liberty, sent us everywhere as missionaries of the cross, and given us a peculiar fitness to meet the spiritual needs of the age in which we are now beginning to live."[55] The believers' church is the theological application of soul competency.[56] Soul competency necessitates the correlative of biblical revelation, thereby deriving an understanding of Scripture from the notion of soul competency.[57] The Baptist distinctive of religious experience as expressed in soul competency provides the focal point around which all other doctrines are developed.[58]

Religious experience as expressed in Christ's lordship and in religious freedom is also determinative for other Baptist distinctives. With regard to the former, the lordship of Christ is "the root principle from which all the others evolve."[59] The distinctive doctrines are then construed as "emanating" ideas that flow from this doctrinal tenet.[60] With regard to the latter, religious freedom is the distinctive by which the other distinctives of the authority of the Bible, the believers' church, believer's baptism, and church/ state relations are understood.[61]

---

[53]James H. Rushbrooke, *Protestant of the Protestants: The Baptist Churches, Their Progress, and Their Spiritual Principle* (London: Kingsgate, 1926), 70. Mullins states that "the six axioms, taken in connection with the fundamental general principle out of which they spring—the competency of the soul in religion under God—may be regarded as the platform of human rights in religion" (*Axioms of Religion*, 77).
[54]Jones, *A Restatement of Baptist Principles*, 16–17.
[55]S. F. Skevington, *The Distinctive Principles of Baptists* (n.p., 1914), 9–10.
[56]Brooks Hays, *The Baptist Way of Life* (Englewood Cliffs, NJ: Prentice Hall, 1963) 38-47.
[57]Kirtley, *The Baptist Distinctive and Objective*, 7–8.
[58]Wayne E. Ward, "What Is a Baptist? Personal Religious Freedom," *Western Recorder*, April 4, 1970, 2. Although there is much variety of theology and practice among Baptists, certain emphases do characterize Baptists all over the United States and around the world. It is often said that Baptists have as many different viewpoints as there are Baptists—and even that quip points to the most basic characteristic of Baptist life, the religious freedom of each individual believer in his personal relationship to God. Almost all of the other Baptist distinctives flow from this basic one: their great stress upon religious liberty for all men; their rejection of any official hierarchy or bishop; their affirmation of the direct lordship of Jesus Christ over the church congregation without any church officer to mediate it; emphasis upon a personal experience of regeneration and faith in Christ; their requirement of a personal confession of faith in Christ before baptism; and their emphasis upon a personal call of God as the basic credential for the ministry.
[59]Mosteller, "Basic Baptist Principles," 61.
[60]F. Anderson, *Historic Baptist Principles,* 6.
[61]Earle G. Griffith, *Baptists: Their History, Principles, and Polity* (New York: Interstate Evangelistic Association, 1935), 39; G. Thomas Halbrooks, "Why I Am a Baptist," in *Being Baptist Means Freedom,* ed. Alan Neely (Charlotte, NC: Southern Baptist Alliance, 1988), 1–8; Cecil E. Sherman, "Freedom of the Individual to Interpret the Bible," in Neely, *Being Baptist Means Freedom,* 9–24; Richard E. Grove, "The Freedom of the Local Church," in Neely, *Being Baptist Means Freedom,* 25–36; Norman Cavendar, "Freedom for the Church in a Free State," in Neely, *Being Baptist Means Freedom,* 83–96.

Conclusion: A Baptist Hermeneutic

The evidence from the materials examined reveals several aspects of Baptist distinctives. First, identification and establishment of a core, or primary, distinctive is an essential part of developing Baptist distinctives. The writings typically distill the peculiarities of Baptist theology to one determinative theological concept. Second, Baptist distinctives are the application of the core distinctive to Baptist theology. This organizing tenet is applied logically and consistently by the formulators in order to shape the other distinctive components. This phenomenon demonstrates that "Baptist distinctives" are as much a "method of theology" as a defined body of literature.[62]

The evidence therefore suggests that writings on Baptist distinctives reflect a theological hermeneutic. These writings begin with a primary distinctive that is used to formulate certain other theological components. Although diversity of arrangement and nuance of application exist, Baptist distinctive writings reflect shared components that are common to all distinctive writings and are determinative for the "distinctive genre." The theological components, while similar in their overall content, also contain differing nuances of emphasis. These writings reflect a concern for the process of theology as much as the result. The employment of this approach has produced a thread of theological continuity throughout the distinctive theology of Baptists. When deviation from this approach occurs, then the thread of theological continuity is broken, and the result is a theological formulation foreign to the Baptist identity.[63]

Two Distinctive Traditions

The theological components and hermeneutics of this genre disclose further revelations in the quest to discover the distinctive doctrinal identity of Baptists. Two understandings, or "traditions," of Baptist distinctives have emerged within Baptist life, particularly within the SBC. Both of these traditions have existed side by side throughout most of the twentieth century. In recent years, however, the differences between the two have grown so great that they no longer appear able to coexist.

---

[62]Bernard Ramm argues that the true essence of Baptists is not in their unique theological components but rather in their unique and consistent method of doing theology ("Baptist Theology," *Watchman-Examiner* 43 [November 24, 1955]: 1070–73). Although contending for the primary distinctive of religious freedom via soul competency, Ramm argues that Baptists must produce their theology within certain theological boundaries. Doctrines that are formulated outside these established perimeters result in theological constructions that transgress the distinctive theological identity of Baptists. Ramm contends that the boundaries for Baptists are the evangelical doctrines of the Protestant Reformation.

[63]Ramm, "Baptist Theology," 1070–73.

These differences exist due to the manner in which the core distinctive shapes the development of theological identity. Works that affirm the primacy of biblical authority as the core distinctive develop and interpret the other distinctives in light of this organizing principle. This method reflects the Protestant Reformation tradition of *sola scriptura*. In fact, many of the authors of these writings believed that the Baptists and their distinctive theology were the logical outcome of the Reformation assumption of the preeminence of biblical authority. Those distinctive works that affirm the primacy of biblical authority can be categorized as "Reformation Baptist distinctives."

Writings on Baptist distinctives that affirm religious experience as the core distinctive embrace the Enlightenment assumption of individual autonomy. This profound emphasis upon the individual is often expressed in terms of individual freedoms, individual rights, and individual morality. This strand of distinctives can be called "Enlightenment Baptist distinctives." This tradition was birthed in Mullins's *The Axioms of Religion: A New Interpretation of the Baptist Faith*. As indicated by the title, Mullins intentionally sought to redefine the existing Reformation Baptist distinctive tradition. He wanted to stress that both religious experience and biblical authority are equal and necessary for developing Baptist distinctives. He did not, in my estimation, achieve this balance. His understanding of religious experience overshadowed his understanding of biblical authority. Religious experience became for Mullins the core distinctive that shaped his understanding of biblical authority. Baptist distinctive writings that evolved in conjunction with this tradition continued this emphasis.

Writings on Baptist distinctives have a unique ordering that affects the theological process. The Reformation tradition first asserts the primacy of biblical authority. These works construct a Baptist doctrine of the church based upon biblical authority. Religious experience in its various expressions is a necessary by-product of having a New Testament church built upon biblical revelation. The Reformation distinctive tradition affirms the role of individual accountability and responsibility. It does so, however, within the broader scope of the overall life and teachings of the church.

The Enlightenment distinctive tradition has, over a period of time, inverted this view. Following Mullins, this tradition moved from a "biblical authority core distinctive" that shaped church life and religious experience to a "religious experience core distinctive" that shaped biblical authority and church life. The defining distinctive in this tradition became a form of individual, autonomous, religious experience. On this foundation, a doctrine of the church developed that strongly emphasized the individual, sometimes to the neglect of the corporate life of the church. The Bible became a repository of information for individual spiritual blessings, individual Christian living, and individual religious freedoms, rather than an authoritative revelation for a community of born-again believers working together for the extension of God's kingdom. Religious experience replaced biblical authority as the core distinctive that interpreted the other Baptist distinctives.

In the earliest stages of Baptist life, the only distinctive tradition that existed was the Reformation Baptist distinctive tradition. At the beginning of the twentieth century, the Enlightenment Baptist distinctive tradition was birthed. These two traditions initially shared similar theological convictions. Over time, however, the two distinctive traditions grew further apart in their convictions and emphases.

These two distinctive traditions still thrive today. The Reformation tradition continues to demonstrate theological stability and historical continuity. Based upon its past historical continuity and theological stability, the Reformation tradition of Baptist distinctives will likely continue to flourish and to formulate a distinctive theological identity for many Baptists in the future. This tradition provides a large segment of Baptists with a theological connection to their past and strong theological identity for the future. If the past is any indication, this tradition will continue to exist and provide a theological identity for many Baptists yet to come.

The Enlightenment Baptist distinctive tradition has in recent days experienced a loss of theological stability and historical continuity. The exaggerated emphasis on individual, autonomous, religious experience makes theological cohesiveness almost impossible. Further, the Enlightenment distinctive tradition appears to be fragmenting within itself. Writings in this tradition not only have decreasing similarities with the Reformation tradition, but they also have fewer similarities with other works in the same Enlightenment tradition.[64]

The future prospects are not so bright in my assessment for the Enlightenment tradition of Baptist distinctives. Based upon its growing fragmentation, this tradition will likely either digress into theological oblivion or birth a new theological perspective, continuing its drift from a historic Baptist identity. It will eventually either reject any connection with Baptists or further try to redefine the distinctive identity of Baptists

---

[64]Examples of two such works include Shurden, *The Baptist Identity*, and Neely, *Being Baptist Means Freedom*.

in "un-baptistic" terms. Such a redefinition would, however, eliminate any historical or theological claim to the name "Baptist."[65]

These divisions within Baptist distinctives explain, to some degree, the current controversy within the SBC. Those who are often theologically described as "conservatives" tend to represent the Reformation tradition's emphasis of biblical authority. "Moderates," or those who are more comfortable with some form of religious experience as the foundational distinctive, tend to represent the Enlightenment distinctive tradition. Although these two distinctive traditions cannot account for all the divisions within the controversy, they help explain in part a major source of the controversy.

Confessional Theology

Different definitions exist for the concept of "confessionalism/confessional theology."[66] Martin Cook has developed a paradigm that permits classifying writings on Baptist distinctives as a form of confessional theology. He states that confessional theology is that endeavor that seeks to derive its core insights and its theological starting point from a perspective that is unique to a particular Christian religious community. This form of confessional theology may or may not be an interpretation of the formal creedal statements of particular denominations.[67]

Cook identifies three primary ingredients that define confessionalism. First, confessional theology is that theological discipline which has a "cognizant awareness" of a particular theological community in which a theological position is constructed. A confessional theology intentionally formulates its doctrinal expression within a specific community of faith.

---

[65]Such an enterprise is already underway. See the plea for a new Baptist identity in Curtis Freeman and others, "Re-Envisioning Baptist Identity: A Manifesto for Baptist Communities in North America" (unpublished paper submitted to various Baptist leaders, 1996). This paper argues for a postmodern Baptist identity.

[66]George notes that confessionalism is the production of confessions of faith that seek to provide a doctrinal identity and to promote denominational unity (*Baptist Confessions*, 1–5). Confessionalism in this sense also strives to identify common areas of belief among differing communities of faith. Alan Richardson defines confessionalism in the Reformation context as the formal presentation of beliefs produced by Protestants that provide interpretive guides to Scripture and/or creedal traditions (Richardson, "Confession[s], Confessionalism," in Alan Richardson and John S. Bowden, eds., *The Westminster Dictionary of Christian Theology* [Philadelphia, PA: Westminster, 1983], 116–17). Confessionalism in this sense produced formal theological treatises labeled as confessional theologies. These confessions usually (but not always) sought to profess a Protestant understanding of the faith in opposition to Roman Catholicism. H. Richard Niebuhr employs the term "confessional theology" to articulate a theological method that accepts the cultural and historical relativism of modern social sciences and yet affirms a distinct Christian revelation (Niebuhr, *The Meaning of Revelation* [New York: Macmillan Co., 1941], 38–42). Theology does its proper work when it articulates the language and view of the world that characterizes the Christian faith in all its particularity. Niebuhr contends that self-defense is the most prevalent error in all thinking and perhaps especially in theology and ethics. He is therefore most concerned to advocate a theology that finds communally shared affirmations of Christians.

[67]Martin Cook, *The Open Circle* (Minneapolis, MN: Fortress Press, 1991), 2–3.

This intention may be explicitly stated or implicitly assumed. Statement of intention is not as important as its actual presence.

Second, a confessional theology is "analytic." It identifies the epistemological basis for its own distinctive theology and the epistemological basis for other faith communities. The analytic is akin to a "theological diagnostic." It grapples with the inner workings and perspectives of its own theological heritage as well as diagnosing the doctrinal inner workings of other theological communities.

Finally, a confessional theology is "dialectic." The process contrasts and critiques the theological premises of other religious communities in light of its own. The results of the process vary. The dialectic may result in descriptive observations void of critical judgments. It may conclude by advocating the superiority of one confessional tradition over the theological deficiencies of another position. The endeavor may propose a synthesis of the two positions.

BAPTIST DISTINCTIVES: CONFESSIONAL THEOLOGY

Based upon these criteria, Baptist distinctives can rightfully be classified as one form of confessional theology. By use of Cook's definition, these writings do reflect a distinct awareness of the Baptist community in which they are constructed. The distinctive genre is formulated within the Baptist community. It speaks with a "cognizant awareness" of the Baptist heritage and attempts to preserve its distinctive theological identity. The intention may or may not be stated explicitly within this genre.

Distinctive writings also conform to the analytic dynamic of confessional theology. The analytic component investigates and identifies the epistemological basis, or the religious authority, for the Baptist position. This endeavor also identifies and critiques the epistemological basis of other Christian denominations.

These works are also confessional in their dialectic interaction with other denominations. The dialectic typically contrasts the unique theology of Baptists with that of other denominations. This aspect of the confessional method is typically found in the polemical intention component in this genre. In its theological interaction, the distinctive genre never seeks a synthesis. It instead expresses its confessional theology by advocating the superiority of the Baptist doctrinal position in opposition to other denominations.

"Everything That Glitters Is Not Gold"; or,
Not All "baptists" Are "Baptist"

The analysis lends itself to the conclusion that Baptists have a definitive, confessional theological tradition. This tradition is a clearly identifiable genre and is comprised of certain theological components that must be present in order to be classified as a distinctive writing. The components share doctrinal emphases that are present to some degree in all writings within this genre. The expressions "Baptist confessional theology," "Baptist confessional tradition," and "Baptist theological method" are accurate and appropriate phrases to use in reference to this genre.

The confessional theological tradition of Baptists may be used to identify and define the theological essence of Baptists. Being "Baptist" is more than just a name. They are known by clearly defined and historically established theological components. Baptists are more than just adherents of religious freedom, advocates of baptism via immersion, or practitioners of congregational polity. They are those individuals and churches that embrace to some degree all the core theological components that have been defined herein as common among writings on Baptist distinctives. For a person simply to advocate one or two of the theological components found within the distinctive genre does not designate that person as a Baptist. Deviation beyond these identified theological components is a deviation beyond the historically established boundaries that define Baptist distinctives.

Baptists do possess a continuity of theological identity. Our confessional tradition reflects diversity of emphasis in its doctrinal expressions. These differences may be shaped by various historical, contextual, and theological influences; they are transcended, however, by greater theological concerns. All distinctive writings share certain common theological conceptions as defined herein. In other words, Baptists in the twentieth century share certain common doctrinal convictions that were espoused by Baptists in previous centuries. When viewed from this perspective, Baptists can be said to have a common theological tradition that binds them all together around a common theological identity. Even persons like E. Y. Mullins, who sought to propose a new interpretation of Baptist identity, cannot escape the common theological components that are true of all Baptists. These persons may change the nuances of meaning or the arrangement of the components, but they cannot change the essential nature of the distinctives and still remain within the confessional tradition of Baptists. The fact that Baptists adhere to certain distinctive theological traits is an attestation to the doctrinal adequacy of these traits. These convictions transcend cultural and historical differences and bind Baptists around established theological components.

A third observation is that the theological commonality shared among Baptists in no way diminishes the great theological diversity found in Baptist theology. This continuous theological tradition strengthens the notion that Baptist distinctives provide a commonality of theological identity while simultaneously providing a sound theological basis from which to address the contextual, historical, and theological concerns that confront differing Baptists in differing times and contexts. A Baptist confessional tradition provides doctrinal continuity so that Baptists can formulate their doctrinal conceptions within the well-established parameters of the Baptist confessional tradition. This confessional tradition likewise provides enormous flexibility by allowing Baptists to address specific cultural concerns and contemporary issues theologically while permitting the formulators to remain within the confines of the Baptist confessional tradition.

The Final Word?

Two challenges face Baptists today. One is to be faithful to the heritage that is uniquely Baptist. Those who claim the name Baptist have a rich theological history. The tenets that we share with all Christians are part of our Baptist identity. Baptists should recognize that they are one part of God's overall kingdom work. As such, they should seek any and every opportunity to join together in God's kingdom work with those who believe in the great truths of the Christian faith. However, those truths that define us as Baptists are part of our heritage as well. We must appreciate the unique identity forged by those who discovered and refined these distinctives. As Baptists, we have an obligation to represent accurately and faithfully our confessional tradition. To misrepresent or modify the tenets that have historically represented the distinctive theological identity of Baptists is to belittle the labor and sacrifice of those who have gone before us.

The second challenge before present-day Baptists is the task of articulating our distinctive identity to our contemporary culture. This must be done with care and caution. On the one hand, if we are not careful, we can so accommodate our distinctives to current theological trends that we change the essence of the Baptist confessional tradition. On the other hand, if we are not sensitive to culture concerns, then we run the risk of preserving our distinctives in such a way that they are unintelligible to a contemporary audience; the present culture will neither understand nor appreciate the contribution that Baptist distinctives can make to current ministry and church concerns. As our Baptist forebears have taught us, our Baptist distinctives can do both. They can faithfully embody the great truths that have shaped us as a part of God's kingdom people, and they are dynamic enough that they can speak to any contemporary context and do so in a way that thoughtfully and critically engages the theological concerns of our time.

The distinctive theology of Baptists is still greatly needed today. It remains to be seen whether or not Baptists will rise to the occasion to reclaim their theological heritage in order to shape ministry and engage a culture that is both sophisticated and contemporary yet ancient and pagan. Only time will tell if the people distinctively called Baptists are up to the challenge.

CHAPTER THREE

SOUTHERN BAPTIST IDENTITY: A HISTORICAL PERSPECTIVE

Gregory A. Wills

IN THE INERRANCY CONTROVERSY that shook the SBC beginning in 1979, Southern Baptists divided over what it meant to be a Baptist. When Southern Baptist leaders polarized amid the conservative effort to make belief in inerrancy a condition of denominational service, their posture toward the inerrancy initiative derived in large measure from their understanding of Baptist identity. Conservatives believed that moderates had departed from the Baptist tradition and moderates felt the same way about conservatives. Each party in the conflict claimed to be true Baptists and claimed the imprimatur of Baptist tradition.

Conservatives believed that the true Baptist tradition consisted in maintaining New Testament faith and practice. They felt that they were responsible therefore to exclude false teaching. Those teachers and denominational leaders who held liberal doctrines departed from New Testament faith and practice. By their departure from the Baptist tradition they betrayed the trust of the denomination and relinquished their claim to their position. Sincere commitment to the traditional Baptist understanding of scriptural teaching, conservatives insisted, should be a condition of service in positions of denominational service.

Moderates held, on the contrary, that true Baptists did not exclude their fellow Baptists for divergent views of what the Bible taught. The denomination should not require seminary professors to believe some prescribed set of dogmas in order to serve the denomination, for that would infringe their freedom. When conservatives argued that seminary professors must be committed to Scripture truth, moderates effectively asked, "What is truth?"

Truth, they held, was a matter of individual interpretation. To exclude professors for divergent interpretations sincerely held would be un-Baptistic. The true Baptist tradition, moderates said, upheld individual freedom as the central Baptist commitment.

Conservatives and moderates thus responded differently to the question of the legitimacy of liberal professors based on sharply different views of what it meant to be a Baptist. But their views of Baptist identity had broader ramifications. It undergirded their responses to other issues of controversy in the denomination, from the ordination of women as pastors to affiliation with the Baptist World Alliance. It informed their views of the church, of the faith, and of denominationalism.

Conservatives held that being Baptist meant commitment to right doctrine and scriptural church order as the basis of denominational unity, Baptist identity, and cooperative endeavors. They held that adherence to scriptural faith and practice was a condition of fellowship and denominational leadership. Conservatives held that this was at the center of Baptist identity. It served as a fundamental presupposition of the conservative position.

On the contrary, moderate leaders argued that the Baptist tradition consisted in individual freedom. They expressed it variously as commitment to soul competence, religious freedom, liberty of conscience, the priesthood of the believer, regenerate church membership, and no creed but the Bible. But at the bottom of each of these expressions, as moderate leaders explained it, was commitment to the sanctity of individual freedom. This was a legacy of liberalism or modernism. Modernism sought to adapt Christianity to Darwinism and the naturalistic historical criticism of the Bible. Since the adaptation would require substantial redefinition of traditional Christian beliefs, modernists argued for a view of true Christianity that included toleration of divergent interpretations of Scripture. They placed the meaning of Christianity in some nondoctrinal essence and went about adjusting traditional doctrines to the new knowledge. Modernist Baptists developed their view of Baptist identity as part of this development.

During the inerrancy controversy, moderates bristled at the conservatives' premise that authentic Baptist identity included commitment to historic Baptist orthodoxy. Conservatives promoted commitment to inerrancy and the utility of confessions because they believed that scriptural faith and practice formed the basis for denominational cooperation and the boundaries of fellowship. Most pointedly, conservatives insisted that professors in Baptist colleges and seminaries should believe and teach in accordance with the views of Bible truth held by the churches. Conservatives held that many professors held liberal or neoorthodox views, starting from a rejection of inerrancy and culminating in such errors as the denial of the deity of Christ, the rejection of his substitutionary atonement, or opposition to salvation exclusively through faith in Christ.

Moderates responded in two ways. They first denied that there were any liberals teaching in the seminaries. In one of the most remarkable statements by a moderate leader, Roy Honeycutt, the president of The Southern Baptist Theological Seminary, stated in his 1984 convocation address that "one would be at a loss to discover a classical liberal among Southern Baptists, whether in the pulpit or classroom, college or seminary." The professors were committed to the church and held the Bible in esteem, moderates argued, and therefore were not liberals. Conservative leaders found the denials implausible. Although most professors were careful to keep their errors hidden from view, conservatives readily identified a number of liberals in the classrooms. And many rank-and-file Southern Baptists did not find Honeycutt's denials credible either. Many Baptists had sat in classrooms with these professors and had heard the liberal teaching first hand.[1]

Moderates argued second that even if there were liberal professors, it was un-Baptistic to deprive them of their positions on account of their beliefs. Roy Honeycutt explained the moderate view of true Baptist identity in the 1984 convocation address in which he called moderates to wage "holy war" against the conservatives. He explained that authentic Baptists would not exclude any person of good will. (Since conservatives wanted to exclude sincere Baptists based on doctrine, they were not persons of good will.) The Baptist tradition stood on one conviction above all others: the individual is free. And commitment to individual freedom meant "commitment to authentic pluralism." Honeycutt concluded then that "God calls us to exclude no one, but to include everyone" committed to cooperative missions. This pluralism, he claimed, was the basis of Baptist identity and "has characterized our denomination during its entire history."[2]

In fact, neither progressive nor traditional Baptists had ever practiced

---

[1] Roy Honeycutt, "Roy Honeycutt's 'Holy War' Convocation Address at Southern Seminary," in *Going for the Jugular: A Documentary History of the SBC Holy War*, ed. Walter Shurden and Randy Shepley (Macon, GA: Mercer University Press, 1996), 130. For some discussion of the spread of liberal (and neoorthodox) ideas among Southern Baptists, see David Stricklin, *Genealogy of Dissent: Southern Baptist Protest in the Twentieth Century* (Lexington: University Press of Kentucky, 1999); Wayne Flynt, *Alabama Baptists: Southern Baptists in the Heart of Dixie* (Tuscaloosa: University of Alabama Press, 1998); Wayne Flynt, "A Pilgrim's Progress through Southern Christianity," in *Autobiographical Reflections on Southern Religious History*, ed. John B. Boles (Athens: University of Georgia Press, 2001), 73–88; Gregory A. Wills, "Progressive Theology and Southern Baptist Controversies of the 1950s and 1960s," *The Southern Baptist Journal of Theology* 7, no. 1 (2003): 12–31.

[2] Honeycutt, "Convocation Address," 131.

that kind of inclusion. In the twentieth century, progressive Southern Baptist leaders aspired to wide inclusion, but even the most progressive denominational seminaries and colleges operated within their own theological boundaries. They did not welcome inerrantists and at times dismissed progressives, however reluctantly. And before the twentieth century Southern Baptists generally maintained definite boundaries of faith and practice in their institutions at various levels of denominational life. Baptist churches practiced a regular church discipline that expelled unrepentant members who embraced fundamental doctrinal errors. Baptist associations similarly expelled from fellowship any churches that departed from scriptural faith and practice. This traditional commitment to truth endured in the twentieth century as Southern Baptists opposed moderate leaders who tolerated the spread of error in their denominational schools.[3]

When progressive theology spread on the faculties of Baptist colleges and seminaries, many Baptists voiced objections. Even before the Second World War many Southern Baptist colleges experienced controversy over professors suspected of modernism, some of whom they dismissed after pastors and lay members demanded their removal. W. L. Poteat, president of Wake Forest College and the most prominent liberal among Southern Baptists, overcame two efforts to oust him. Others similarly survived the campaigns against them. Baylor, Furman, William Jewell, Mercer, and Limestone all dismissed professors, as did the New Orleans Baptist Bible Institute (now the New Orleans Baptist Theological Seminary).[4]

The progressive trend continued after the war. By the 1950s most Southern Baptists were convinced of the spread of liberalism in the colleges and seminaries and became increasingly vocal when denominational leaders responded to their demands for the expulsion of liberal professors with denials and temporizing. In 1960, SBC president Ramsey Pollard represented the views of most Baptists when from the platform of the annual meeting he insisted that the denomination's colleges and seminaries should

---

[3]For a discussion of church discipline and associational fellowship among nineteenth-century Southern Baptists, see Gregory A. Wills, *Democratic Religion: Freedom, Authority, and Church Discipline in the Baptist South, 1785-1900* (New York: Oxford University Press, 1997).
[4]Shailer Mathews, *New Faith for Old: An Autobiography* (New York: Macmillan, 1936), 80; Randall L. Hall, *William Louis Poteat* (Lexington: University Press of Kentucky, 2000), 130–55; Barry Hankins, *God's Rascal: J. Frank Norris and the Beginnings of Southern Fundamentalism* (Lexington: University Press of Kentucky, 1996), 28; James J. Thompson Jr., *Tried As by Fire: Southern Baptists and the Religious Controversies of the 1920s* (Macon, GA: Mercer University Press, 1982), 99, 79; unsigned, "The Action of the Board of Trustees," *Baptist Courier*, December 18, 1902, 4; Alfred S. Reid, *Furman University: Toward a New Identity, 1925-1975* (Durham, NC: Duke University Press, 1976), 95; Z. T. Cody, "Can It Be Justified," *Baptist Courier*, January 11, 1923, 2–3; Trustees of Limestone College, "Resolutions Adopted by the Trustees of Limestone College," *Baptist Courier*, July 5, 1934, 2–3; Flynt, *Alabama Baptists*, 386.

purge themselves of all liberal professors. Herschel Hobbs, who succeeded Pollard as convention president, felt assured that the "vast majority" of Southern Baptists supported Pollard's demand. Hobbs spoke for them when he stated that "any man who aspires to teach either in our Christian colleges or seminaries should either stay within the 'pasture' of what Southern Baptist[s] believe and teach or else he should hire his own hall. I am not for furnishing him a place to spout out his own views."[5]

Southern Baptists did everything they knew to do to persuade denominational leaders to exclude such professors. Sometimes they succeeded. The trustees of Midwestern Baptist Theological Seminary fired Ralph Elliott from his position as professor of Old Testament in 1962 after Elliott's *Message of Genesis*[6] ignited one of the most heated controversies in the history of the SBC. Other professors came under fire in subsequent years and a few lost their positions.[7]

Liberalism persisted nevertheless. Most Southern Baptists found the situation reprehensible and felt betrayed by denominational leaders who did not act to oppose liberalism except when the constituency compelled them. Rank-and-file Southern Baptists agreed with conservative leaders that orthodox faith and practice should be prerequisite to service as a denominational officer, missionary, or professor.

Throughout their history Southern Baptists have insisted that scriptural faith and practice formed the basis of their unity and identity. The shared commitment to that faith and practice also established boundaries of fellowship. Those who taught error departed from authentic Baptist identity and had no right to teach in the denomination's schools or hold positions of denominational service.

In the twentieth century the moderate view of Baptist identity coexisted with this conservative view. Theological progressives dominated denominational leadership in the twentieth century and they promoted the notion that being Baptist meant freedom. But the moderate version of Baptist tradition was essentially an invention of the twentieth century. Before the twentieth century, few Baptists urged that freedom was the essence of the Baptist tradition, but after 1900 or so, progressive Baptist leaders urged this view increasingly.

---

[5]Herschel H. Hobbs, letter to Ramsey Pollard, May 23, 1960, box 21, f. 5 (Herschel H. Hobbs Papers, Southern Baptist Historical Library and Archives, Nashville); Hobbs, letter to Ramsey Pollard, June 6, 1960, box 21, f. 5, Hobbs Papers.
[6]Ralph H. Elliott, *The Message of Genesis* (Nashville: Broadman, 1961).
[7]For a detailed narrative of the controversy, see Ralph H. Elliott, *The "Genesis Controversy" and Continuity in Southern Baptist Chaos: A Eulogy for a Great Tradition* (Macon, GA: Mercer University Press, 1992).

BAPTIST IDENTITY BEFORE THE
TWENTIETH CENTURY

For most Baptists prior to the twentieth century, Baptist identity derived almost entirely from the shared belief and practice of their churches. Eighteenth- and nineteenth-century Baptists held that their common theology and church polity made their churches Baptist. They expressed this in a number of ways.

In the first place, long before they formed any denomination-wide organizations, Baptists recognized that their churches formed a single fellowship united by their commitment to a common understanding of New Testament faith and practice. John Asplund, who traveled the nation gathering Baptist statistics in the 1790s, wrote that in order to be qualified to administer baptism, a minister "must have been baptized by a qualified minister of our denomination." Thus before there was a Cooperative Program, before there were mission boards, before there were any conventions at all, Baptists held that their churches constituted one denomination.[8]

The chief institutional expression of their denominational unity was their membership in the local association. The association required agreement in faith and practice as a condition of membership and enforced denominational boundaries based on that agreement. Associational membership was an essential part of Southern Baptist identity. Indeed, long after Baptists in the South organized the SBC, large numbers of churches did not participate in the convention or contribute to convention agencies, but they were still Southern Baptist churches. In 1882, for example, 55 percent of Virginia's Southern Baptist churches gave nothing to any of the denomination's boards. But Virginia was a picture of cooperative participation compared with much of the South. In 1903 the editor of Missouri's *Central Baptist* estimated that less than one-third of Southern Baptist churches contributed to the mission boards. But they were Southern Baptist churches nevertheless. They maintained the same faith and practice, and expressed it in associational fellowship.[9]

This sense of denominational identity appeared in other ways. When Baptists discussed religious groups, they identified them by their faith and practice. There were many groups that were Baptist in the sense of practicing believer's baptism, but they did not all belong to the orthodox or regu-

---

[8]John Asplund, *The Universal Register of the Baptist Denomination in North America* (Boston: John Folson, 1794), 5.
[9]A. Chiel, "Studies of the Minutes, Per Capita Income," *Religious Herald*, November 16, 1882, 1; J. C. Armstrong, "Baptist Affairs in the South," *Central Baptist*, May 21, 1903, 1.

lar Baptist denomination. The main body of Baptists in the United States did not recognize the Seventh Day Baptists, General Baptists, Free Will Baptists, Tunkers, Mennonites, and Brethren as having authentic Baptist identity. They did not hold fellowship with them because they differed in significant ways from the faith and practice of the regular Baptists.

Thus John Leland, the revered Baptist evangelist and defender of religious freedom, declared in 1790 that the Tunkers and Mennonites, although they practiced believer's baptism, were distinct sects from the Baptists. He also declared that the Anabaptists generally were not orthodox or regular Baptists. Leland held, for example, that the practice of immersion was one essential of Baptist identity. The Anabaptists practiced baptism by pouring. They differed at other important points also, and thus, they were not Baptists. Leland concluded finally that Baptists and Anabaptists were as different as Presbyterians and Roman Catholics. But the many regular Baptists, Leland said, were "united in their sentiments," for they interpreted the New Testament the same way. This union of faith and practice was the basis for the "free correspondence and communion" that circulated among them. They were one denomination united by their common faith and practice. [10]

T. P. Tustin, editor of the *Southern Baptist*, argued similarly in 1856 that orthodox Baptists had no fellowship with other groups just because they had the name of a Baptist. Although Primitive Baptists, Advent Baptists, and Mennonites practiced believer's baptism, Tustin wrote, they embraced errors in other important areas. Regular Baptists could not therefore hold them in fellowship. There could be no denominational identity with them.[11]

But the Separate Baptists and Regular Baptists in the South pursued a different course. They relinquished their separate identities because they believed the same things in essential areas. And by 1801 they declared their mutual fellowship and identity. When Shubal Stearns and Daniel Marshall began establishing Separate Baptist churches throughout the South in the eighteenth century, they differed in some ways from the Regular Baptist churches that already occupied the South. The Separates had withdrawn from the legally established churches of New England and had become Baptists. Their heritage was distinct from that of the Regular Baptists. But when preachers of the two movements met, they recognized

---

[10]"Virginia Chronicle," in *The Writings of the Late Elder John Leland*, ed. L. F. Greene (New York: G. W. Wood, 1845), 121.
[11]T. P. Tustin, "Schismatics—Hard-Shell Baptists," *Southern Baptist*, July 1, 1856, 2.

one another as holding the same interpretation of New Testament faith and practice. They were agreed in all essentials and should constitute one denomination. Separate Baptist preacher John Taylor, whose preaching ignited revival in Kentucky, united in fellowship with Regular Baptist preachers because, he said, "we found no difference as to doctrinal opinions." They worked out their minor differences, dropped their different names, and formally declared their union based on a common confession of faith and practice.[12]

Baptist churches expressed their commitment to unity of faith and practice as the source of Baptist identity also by insisting that those who departed from Baptist doctrine disqualified themselves as Baptists and could no longer remain members in their churches. Baptist churches sought to correct and reclaim those who strayed, but they excluded from fellowship those who refused to repent. Baptist churches excluded members who embraced doctrinal or ecclesiastical aberrations of all sorts: Deists, annihilationists, universalists, unitarians, certain Arminians, open communionists, and the like. Persons excluded from the church were no longer true Baptists.[13]

The motto for Baptist identity came from Amos 3:3: "Can two walk together, except they be agreed?" (KJV). Since Baptist identity was rooted in believing and practicing the same things, Baptist churches held that members who introduced false doctrine divided the denomination and relinquished any valid claim to being Baptist. Baptist churches expelled them from membership as schismatics and errorists. Texas leader B. A. Copass summed up the Baptist position: "To withdraw fellowship from one who differs in matters of faith is not an attempt to stifle freedom, but only getting rid of one who does not belong to that body. Why should the body tolerate in its fellowship one who is teaching heresy? Such a thing would be moral suicide."[14]

When modernism began to spread among Baptists in the late nineteenth century, most Baptists asserted that those who embraced modernist beliefs were no longer legitimate Baptists. For example, when J. E. Roberts, pastor of First Baptist Church of Kansas City, Missouri, began preaching modernist views in the 1880s, even Virginia's *Religious Herald*, which at times gave progressive Baptists space in its columns, declared that he was

---

[12]John Taylor, *A History of Ten Baptist Churches*, 2nd ed. (Bloomfield, KY: Will. H. Holmes, 1827), 30.
[13]Wills, *Democratic Religion*, 90–91. This is not to say that the standard of discipline was Baptist identity, but rather that they held that Baptist faith and practice instantiated New Testament principles. So departures from Baptist identity were in fact departures from Christian discipleship, and those who rejected Scripture, truth, or morality sinned against Christ, jeopardized their souls, and endangered the church.
[14]B. A. Copass, "Concerning Our Confession or Declaration of Faith," *Baptist Standard*, June 4, 1914, 2.

no longer a Baptist. The editors spoke for the denomination: "Baptists rather stoutly insist that those who wear the Baptist name shall maintain the Baptist doctrines."[15]

In the twentieth century likewise, a majority of Baptists insisted repeatedly that the rejection of certain doctrines was a rejection of Baptist identity. James B. Gambrell, who with E. Y. Mullins was the most influential leader of his era, taught that Baptist identity derived from unity of faith and practice. Denominationalism, he said, represented the fellowship that existed "among churches of the same faith and order, leading to cooperation in building up interests common to all."[16] As long as Baptists agreed on matters of faith and practice, Missouri editor J. C. Armstrong wrote in 1903, there was little danger of a division of fellowship. He held that the denomination's Baptist identity was remarkably strong because "in the main, there is perfect uniformity in doctrine and practice among the churches."[17]

Because Baptist identity derived from orthodox faith and practice, Baptist leaders argued that persons who departed from that faith and practice should have the integrity to seek fellowship with the denomination with which they most agreed. To the consternation and confusion of orthodox Baptists, liberal Baptists generally sought to remain in the Southern Baptist fellowship. The editors of the *Religious Herald* tried to explain the behavior of modernist Baptist preachers:

> As soon as he found that he was not a Baptist, the thing for him to do was to hand in his credentials, wish his brethren well and quietly walk out of their ranks. . . . But not so. About the last thing that one of these unhinged and noisy men who have an attack of omniscient liberalism will do is to quit us. He holds on to his place, draws his salary, and makes a brilliant effort to "reform" the Baptists. So long as he can find a few shallow and blustering supporters, he will cling to his position. He goes only when it becomes impossible for him to stay. His staying may upheave and disrupt the church or school which employed him under the mistaken notion that he was a Baptist; but what cares he for that?[18]

Liberal Baptists rejected this logic. They sought to remain in the denomination because they developed a different view of Baptist identity. For them, being Baptist was not about doctrines. It was about commitment

---

[15]Unsigned, "One More of the Same," *Religious Herald*, November 27, 1884, 1.
[16]James B. Gambrell, "The Growth of the Denominational Idea," *Biblical Recorder*, April 15, 1903, 2.
[17]J. C. Armstrong, "Baptist Affairs in the South," *Central Baptist*, May 21, 1903, 1.
[18]Unsigned, "One More of the Same," 1.

to a formal principle inherent in religious experience, the principle of individual freedom. In their new understanding of Baptist identity, they could reject the inerrancy of the Bible, the deity of Christ, the substitutionary atonement, and much more, and still be authentic Baptists.

BAPTIST IDENTITY IN THE
TWENTIETH CENTURY

This new understanding of Baptist identity bloomed in the twentieth century as progressive leaders and cultural trends promoted the redefinition. Progressive Baptists subordinated doctrine and practice to some spiritual principle or eternal essence which they generally called the "Baptist idea" or the "Baptist principle." They embraced the historical idealism of German philosophy as reflected in the thought of Hegel, Strauss, and Feuerbach. Many German religious leaders embraced historical idealism as a way to rescue Christianity from the assaults of scientific empiricism. The new religion they constructed is generally known as Liberal Christianity. The essence of Christianity, the liberals from F. D. E. Schleiermacher to Harnack argued, was not in its doctrines and practices, but in its lived experience. Underneath its various historical forms was an abiding essence that was the life and experience of religion. Doctrines were only temporary expressions of religious experience. Belief was extrinsic.

Baptist progressives embraced the liberals' historical idealism and defined Baptist identity in terms of an abiding essence or genius. This Baptist principle, they argued, was the source of all the various doctrines and practices of the Baptists, but the doctrines and practices were temporary expressions suited to specific historical needs. Different historical needs would lead to different doctrinal expression. The abiding essence could therefore adapt its faith and practice to every age in order to be relevant. For Baptist progressives, this meant adapting the traditional beliefs to accommodate the new learning represented by Darwinism and the historical criticism of the Bible. True Baptists altered their doctrine to keep up with the times. Thus Baptist modernists could modify their beliefs without ever losing their Baptist identity.

What then was the essence of Baptist identity for progressive Baptist leaders? Using Schleiermacher's idealist method, they concluded that it was individualism. Baptists, they said, had discovered the truth of the sovereign individual. Individualism meant freedom from extrinsic authority in all matters of the heart and mind, especially religion. This was the

Baptists' gift to the world. This was their genius. This was what it meant to be Baptist.

This new understanding of Baptist identity bloomed in the twentieth century as progressive leaders and cultural trends promoted the redefinition. Progressive Baptists subordinated doctrine and practice to some spiritual principle or eternal essence which they generally called the "Baptist idea" or the "Baptist principle." They embraced the historical idealism that undergirded the thought of Hegel and German philosophy generally. Many German religious leaders embraced historical idealism as a way to rescue Christianity from the assaults of scientific empiricism. The new religion they constructed became known as liberal Christianity. Liberals from Schleiermacher to Adolf von Harnack argued that the essence of Christianity was not in its doctrines and practices, but in its lived experience. Underneath its various historical forms was an abiding essence which was the life and experience of religion. Doctrines were only temporary expressions of religious experience. Doctrine was extrinsic.

Baptist progressives embraced the liberals' historical idealism and defined Baptist identity in terms of an abiding essence or genius. This Baptist principle, they argued, was the source of all the various doctrines and practices of the Baptists, but the doctrines and practices were temporary expressions suited to specific historical needs. Different historical needs required the development of different doctrines. The abiding essence could therefore adapt its faith and practice to every age in order to be relevant. For Baptist progressives, this meant adapting their traditional beliefs to accommodate the new learning represented by the new historical criticism of the Bible and especially by Darwinism. True Baptists, the progressives said, altered their doctrine to keep up with the times. Thus Baptist modernists could modify their beliefs without ever losing their Baptist identity. Progressive Baptist leaders discovered the essence of Baptist identity using liberalism's idealist method. Schleiermacher described the method: "The only pertinent way of discovering the peculiar essence of any particular faith and reducing it as far as possible to a formula is by showing the element that remains constant throughout the most diverse religious affections within this same communion, while it is absent from analogous affections within other communions."[19] When Baptist liberals sought the essence of Baptist identity this way, they discovered that it was individual-

---

[19]F. D. E. Schleiermacher, *The Christian Faith*, trans. H. R. Mackintosh and J. S. Stewart (Philadelphia, PA: Fortress Press, 1976), 52.

ism. Baptists, they said, had developed the truth of the sovereign individual. Individualism meant freedom from extrinsic authority in all matters of the heart and mind, especially religion.

For example, George A. Lofton, a prominent Southern Baptist pastor in Atlanta, Memphis, and St. Louis, argued that "the Baptist idea" was "personal freedom in all matters of religion."[20] A. J. S. Thomas, editor of South Carolina's Baptist paper, held similarly that freedom is "the very soul of the Baptist faith."[21] This was Baptists' gift to the world. This was their genius. Commitment to this was what it meant to be Baptist.

Progressive Baptists recognized that the Baptist heritage was nevertheless thick with doctrine. But the theological heritage posed little threat to their new approach to Baptist identity, because theology was merely a historically conditioned by-product of religious experience. J. W. Bailey, editor of North Carolina's *Biblical Recorder*, argued that although Baptists do have some definite beliefs, these beliefs are subordinate to the true Baptist idea. "The Baptist Principle, is, therefore, in its root—Individualism," Bailey said. "Their Principle, not their doctrine, marks them."[22]

Charles S. Gardner, professor at The Southern Baptist Theological Seminary, argued similarly that "Liberty is of the very essence of Baptist polity and life." Gardner acknowledged that Baptist identity must entail some definite beliefs. "There clearly must be a limit beyond which a man cannot go and retain any just claim to denominational fellowship," Gardner claimed, though his principles did not seem to support this contention. He in fact advocated preserving a "Baptist type or expression of Christianity which is easily felt," but he insisted that "hard and fast lines can not be drawn" and no one could "mark out the limits of our fellowship."[23]

The essence of the Baptist faith, as Baptist liberals viewed it, was not in its doctrines, but in its life, its spirit. And that spirit, most progressive Baptists felt, was individual freedom. The unique mission of the Baptists is to inculcate individualism, which, as Bailey put it, is the "very secret of all progress" and the "great motive for the rise of the race." This meant that no person or institution had a right to encroach upon the conscientious beliefs of any individual. Although Bailey held that each local church is

---

[20]George A. Lofton, "Baptist Position Stated and Contrasted—The Purely Personal Idea," *Christian Index*, August 20, 1896, 2.
[21]A. J. S. Thomas, "Are Baptists Calvinists?" *Baptist Courier*, February 16, 1911, 4.
[22]J. W. Bailey, "The Baptist Principle," *Biblical Recorder*, November 12, 1902, 8.
[23]Charles S. Gardner, "Southern Baptists and Theological Liberty," *Biblical Recorder*, February 18, 1903, 2.

perfectly sovereign, he held also that not even the church could reproach an individual on account of doctrine.[24]

Ironically, Bailey held that Baptists should constrain any individual who reproached another for erroneous beliefs. He inconsistently called upon Baptists to be vigilant against the "slightest trenching" upon the Baptist principle of individualism. There was no room among the Baptists for persons who held that right doctrine was essential to Baptist identity. The least encroachment of individual freedom, he urged, should be "ended forthwith."[25] They were not true Baptists, in his view, if they insisted that a common faith and practice was essential to Baptist identity.

THE EMERGENCE OF SOUTHERN BAPTIST ETHNICITY

This new understanding of Baptist identity fit well with an additional source of identity that emerged largely after the Second World War. Postwar Southern Baptist leaders successfully enlisted Southern Baptist churches to establish and maintain uniform Baptist programs. The proliferation of these programs and the rapid growth of Southern Baptist churches in the postwar period together produced a powerful Baptist subculture in the South. The wide participation in these programs coincided with efforts to subordinate doctrine to experience and fostered an ethnic or tribal source of identity. Participation made one Baptist.

Participation in the cooperative endeavors and programs of the SBC played an important role in supporting the new approach to Baptist identity that emerged in the twentieth century. W. O. Carver, widely influential professor at The Southern Baptist Theological Seminary, connected Baptist identity to participation in convention programs. He argued that cooperative missionary efforts created Baptist denominationalism and formed the foundation of Baptist unity. "Before the beginning of the missionary movement among us, there were Baptist churches, but there was hardly a Baptist denomination." Participation in the SBC's missionary program

---

[24]Bailey was inconsistent on this point. When arguing against the right of the mission board to evaluate orthodoxy, he stated that "only the church can challenge a Baptist's faith" ("The Right of Challenge in Matters of Faith," *Biblical Recorder*, November 26, 1902, 8), but elsewhere argued that the church could not challenge individual conscience: "The ordinary Protestant conception of Religious Liberty is freedom of the church from interference by the State. The Baptist conception is freedom of the believer from interference by State or church or anything else whatsoever touching conscience" ("The Baptist Principle," 8). To vary from Baptist beliefs, Bailey conceded, was "to cease to be a Baptist." But only baptism is "the creed of the Baptists." And baptism is just a form of individualism. "It is in baptism that the Individual and the Democracy meet and plight their faith" ("The Creed of the Baptists," *Biblical Recorder*, December 10, 1902, 8).

[25]J. W. Bailey, "Some Fruits of the Baptist Principle," *Biblical Recorder*, November 19, 1902, 8.

created the denomination's identity. "It took missions to give us a sense of oneness." Carver said that missions also drove Baptist progress in doctrine, education, culture, and Christian piety. Without the cooperative endeavors, Carver seemed to say, there could be no authentic Baptist identity, no unity, no denomination. Participation created Baptist identity.[26]

But Carver's interpretation was historically inaccurate. Mission boards added a new dimension to Baptist denominational identity: that of voluntary agreement to cooperate broadly to send preachers of the gospel to the four corners of the earth. But Baptists conceived of themselves as a denomination before mission boards. They established their unity on the foundation of a common faith and practice and maintained membership in the local association as the chief institutional expression of identity. Participation in a mission board did not make them one denomination. Mission boards were important, and as more churches recognized that they could accomplish the Great Commission more effectively through them, they joined the effort. But even the cooperation with boards depended on their commitment to a stronger and older view of Baptist denominationalism, in which Baptist unity and identity consisted in their common faith and practice. Under the influence of liberalism and its historical idealism, Carver abandoned the traditional basis of Baptist identity and sought to attach the principle of freedom to that of participation in cooperative missions as the sole bases of Baptist denominational identity.

Carver's views found wide acceptance, especially among the denomination's progressive leadership. By attaching the principle of individual freedom to cooperative missions, the progressive view gained considerable influence. In the twentieth century, denominational leaders initiated a wide array of programs in addition to cooperative missions to further bolster this source of Baptist identity. And for about two generations, the approach seemed to work, as participation in denominational programs dominated local church experience and forged a Southern Baptist identity based on participation and belonging.

It worked in large part because in the postwar period Southern Baptist programs proliferated widely and established deep roots in most churches. These programs produced a powerful Southern Baptist subculture that fostered tribal identity. Churches made Southern Baptists by careful nurture. They were born into the group, nurtured in the rituals and practices of the

[26]W. O. Carver, "Why Baptists Grow: The Importance of Missions in Relation to Baptist Progress," *Baptist Argus*, June 25, 1903, 6.

group, and completed the certified rites of passage. Belief became subordinate to belonging and participation.

Many contemporary moderate leaders have reflected on this source of Baptist identity in recent years. Their experience has been remarkably consistent. Cecil Sherman, the founding executive officer of the Cooperative Baptist Fellowship, the moderates' alternative denomination, said that he was Baptist because his parents were.[27] Donna Forrester, who refused to leave Southern Baptists despite opposition to her ordination, considered her Baptist identity a birthright similar to nationality: "I could no more be a Methodist than I could be from Wisconsin."[28] She was born a Baptist in the same way she was born an American and a southerner. Molly Marshall, a prominent moderate theologian and former professor at the The Southern Baptist Theological Seminary, said that she had always been a Baptist; it was her heritage and was the same as being alive.[29] Gary Parker, former coordinator of Baptist Principles at the Cooperative Baptist Fellowship, concluded that many are Baptists because they were born and nurtured in it: "We breathe Baptist air and drink Baptist water and eat Baptist chicken."[30] Nancy Sehested, a leading moderate pastor, recognized the ethnic or tribal character of her Baptist identity: "I was born into the tribe of Baptists. . . . My siblings and I were all schooled in the tribal ways from the Texas branch of the house of Southern Baptists."[31] Moderate scholar and publisher Cecil Staton Jr. summarized the experience of so many postwar Southern Baptists: "I am Baptist born and Baptist bred . . . it would be almost impossible for me to be anything other than a Baptist."[32]

When postwar Baptists said that they were "born" Southern Baptist, they meant that they were nurtured in a distinct Southern Baptist vision of life, values, and society. The elements that shaped this identity included such experiences as walking the aisle and receiving baptism by immersion, attending Baptist youth camps, participating in the Baptist Young People's Union or its successor, the Baptist Training Union, attending a Baptist college or seminary, and receiving a weekly dose of ethnic indoctrination in Sunday School classes that taught the curricula sent down from Nashville's Baptist Sunday School Board. Perhaps more than any other program, how-

---

[27]Cecil Sherman, "Hard Times Make for Hard Thinking," in *Why I Am a Baptist: Reflections on Being Baptist in the 21st Century*, ed. Cecil P. Staton Jr. (Macon, GA: Smyth and Helwys, 1999), 135.
[28]Donna Forrester, quoted in "Women Leave Baptists to Minister," *Spartanburg Herald-Journal*, October 21, 2002.
[29]Molly Marshall, "A Baptist by Conscience; A Baptist in Hope," in Staton, *Why I Am a Baptist*, 89.
[30]Gary Parker, "The Four 'C's of Being Baptist," in Staton, *Why I Am a Baptist*, 103.
[31]Nancy Sehested, "This Is My Story, This Is My Song," in Staton, *Why I Am a Baptist*, 131.
[32]Cecil P. Staton Jr. "A Personal Journey to England and Back Again," in Staton, *Why I Am a Baptist*, 157.

ever, the Woman's Missionary Union contributed to this Baptist identity. The organization enrolled the youth of each church in such weekly training programs as the Girls-in-Action (formerly the Girls' Auxiliary) and the Royal Ambassadors. Here they trained children in the Bible, discipleship, world missions, history, and culture. They required them to memorize the structure and workings of the SBC. Here, above all, they created Baptists.

The educational program of the Woman's Missionary Union was indispensable. Baptist girls advanced through the stages of the Girls-in-Action missions education program: maiden, lady-in-waiting, princess, queen, queen-with-a-sceptre, and queen regent. Baptist boys did the same in the Royal Ambassadors: page, squire, knight, ambassador, ambassador extraordinary, and ambassador plenipotentiary. The annual coronation ceremony traded somewhat on the pageantry of the southern cotillion, with the queens and attendants appearing in formal finery. Conversion, walking the aisle, saying the sinner's prayer, receiving baptism, and believing a few Baptist-like ideas were important, but authentic Baptists had to advance through the other Baptist rites of passage. Queen regent and ambassador plenipotentiary were as authentic as one could get.

Adult converts can scarcely achieve Baptist identity in this sense. But those who had completed its rituals of conversion and rites of passage achieved authentic Baptist identity. And it was hard to shake off. Those who joined other denominations could not avoid taking their Southern Baptist ethnicity with them. Former Southern Baptist Sam Hill, noted historian of southern religion, recognized that although he had defected from the SBC, he had become a Southern Baptist Episcopalian. And those who went on to graduate from a Baptist college or seminary and attained the highest levels in the tribe assumed the responsibility of protecting the boundaries of Baptist identity.[33]

On my ordination council sat a man who had served many years as a denominational official. He knew what it meant to be a Baptist and he doubted that I was one. He probably felt that I was too conservative on inspiration and inerrancy and atonement, but this probably represented a deeper problem. I clearly believed that commitment to traditional Baptist views of New Testament faith and practice would qualify someone as a Baptist. I did not realize that I could never really be Baptist. Although I had belonged to Southern Baptist churches for about six years at the time, I was not ethnically Southern Baptist. I was not born Baptist. I was not

[33]Samuel S. Hill, "Southern Religion and the Southern Religious," in Boles, *Autobiographical Reflections*, 15.

nurtured in the ways of the tribe. When Baptist boys were attending Royal Ambassador meetings, I was taking ceramics class with liberal Methodists. When good Baptists matriculated at Baptist colleges, I went to Methodist ones. Baptists who anticipated vocations in the church went to one of six Southern Baptist theological seminaries; after my conversion I went to a northern evangelical seminary. I had learned about the Cooperative Program and Lottie Moon through books instead of through the Woman's Missionary Union's educational programs. Ethnicity is nurtured within the group; I came from outside the tribe, and my misguided belief that I could be Baptist by joining a regular Baptist church and agreeing with orthodox Baptist doctrine corroborated my outsider status.

This tribal source of identity was not intrinsically harmful to theological sources of identity. Postwar conservatives advanced through the same programs and felt the same influences, but they drew on the older tradition and kept commitment to New Testament truth at the center of Baptist identity. When progressives tied the programs to their vision of a Baptist identity that substituted commitment to individual freedom for commitment to the same faith and practice, it caused harm, but it produced good as well. Many conservatives, who might otherwise have left the denomination over the refusal of its leaders to preserve orthodox faith and practice, remained in the denomination in large measure because they too had been nurtured into the tribe.

For much of the twentieth century, this Southern Baptist ethnicity was the glue that held the denomination together while growing theological diversity pushed it apart. Like the strong nuclear force that overcomes a molecule's natural repulsions, ethnicity held Southern Baptists with divergent beliefs and identities together. There were some defections. Some conservative churches withdrew and became independent or identified with one or another fundamentalist movement. Some modernists withdrew and joined the Episcopal church or some other denomination. But most remained. Whether conservative or moderate, they felt in their bones that they were authentic Southern Baptists and could not conceive of any other identity. Their identity was not chosen, it was given. They were born Baptist.

The one besetting problem for many progressive Southern Baptist leaders in the twentieth century was that this identity retained a thoroughly provincial cast. To be Southern Baptist meant being southern. Although some educated Baptists rejected their southern heritage outright, most felt a strong ambivalence toward it. Their identity was southern at its very center—they could not help it. But they felt that the South's provincial char-

acter— its heritage of fundamentalism, racism, and social backwardness—
was an embarrassment.

Conservatives tended to be less embarrassed by these aspects of southern identity and felt less ambivalence about their attachment to the South.
But since their Baptist identity had more to do with belief than with breed-
ing, the South's shortcomings did not necessarily challenge their comfort
with their Baptist identity.

Many moderates, and especially the more progressive among them,
felt that they had transcended the provincial aspect of the Baptist identity
in which the churches had nurtured them. When they left home for college they were fundamentalists who believed in inerrancy, dispensational-
ism, Landmarkism, and the general superiority of Southern Baptists and
southern society. In college or seminary, or through other experiences, they
learned to view many of their theological and social beliefs as the outmoded
dogmas of southern anti-intellectualism and cultural backwardness. There
was a broader, nobler tradition of which Baptist fundamentalism was ignorant. It was the scholarship of Protestant and Catholic liberalism.[34]

They remained in Baptist churches but they adopted a cosmopolitan-
ism that identified with the broad mainstream Protestant tradition of
Western Europe and the United States. They expressed this identification
by rejecting their region's cultural and theological orthodoxy. They generally sympathized with the civil rights movement, the women's liberation
movement, the Equal Rights Amendment, the *Roe v. Wade* decision, and
the ordination of women to pastoral office. In politics they rejected their
region's post-Carter preference for the Republican party. In theology they
embraced evolution and the historical criticism of the Bible that allowed
them to revere the Bible without claiming its inerrancy or plenary inspiration, to revere Christ without having to endorse a substitutionary atonement, God-ordained killing in the Old Testament, or fabulous legends.
They emphasized experience over doctrine and sought closer connection
with other religious traditions.

Moderates rejected the more-scriptural-than-thou boosterism in which
they felt they had been raised. Their cosmopolitan outlook meant that they
viewed conservative Baptist identity as a combination of parochialism (i.e.,
Baptists alone are faithful to the New Testament, have the biggest of everything, and were the first in everything) and anti-intellectualism ("Don't let

---

[34]See, e.g., Staton, "A Personal Journey," 158–60; Wayne Ward, "Wayne Ward," in *How I Have Changed My Mind: Essays by Retired Professors of the Southern Baptist Theological Seminary*, ed. John D. W. Watts (Louisville, KY: Review and Expositor, 1993), 88–96; J. Estill Jones, "J. Estill Jones," in Watts, *How I Have Changed My Mind*, 98–104.

college ruin you," the conservative pastors warned their youth). Moderates had outgrown this. The problem with conservative Baptist identity, they felt, was that it was parochial in its Southern Baptist boosterism and anti-intellectual in its insistence on inerrancy and its rejection of historical criticism. But being Baptist, moderates felt, had to be "more than arrogance and ignorance."[35]

The progressive redefinition of Baptist identity in the twentieth century afforded moderates with a way to remain Baptist and to reject the southern provincialism in which they were raised, including especially its theological fundamentalism. Since they taught that Baptist identity consisted in commitment to freedom, they could be Baptist without being fundamentalist. Their progressive college and seminary professors introduced them to this tradition that established Baptist identity on freedom and tolerance, and they embraced it. They valued religious liberty, individual freedom, and church autonomy as the essence of being Baptist. Walter Shurden summarized the moderate view: "The core value of the Baptist vision of Christianity is voluntarism. Freedom. Choice." Authentic Baptists privileged individual freedom above all.[36]

But they remained in the tribe. Indeed, the strong contribution of Southern Baptist ethnicity made the transition easier. They embedded the new version of Baptist identity into their native Baptist tribalism. This powerful strand of Southern Baptist identity that developed in the twentieth century was not therefore mere ethnicity. For moderates, the ethnicity had a meaning and a purpose. Being Baptist meant supporting and perpetuating the "Baptist idea" of individual freedom. Since progressive moderates held that Baptist identity inhered primarily in individual freedom, they concluded that conservatives who placed doctrinal limits on denominational service were "not true Southern Baptists."[37]

THE BURDEN OF BAPTIST IDENTITY

Although the progressives made extraordinary progress, they found it tough sledding. Most rank-and-file Baptists rejected the naturalistic historical criticism that seemed to deny much that the Bible taught. They rejected Darwinism, and they did not embrace the rather subtle historical idealism by which progressives claimed to reconcile the Bible with the criticism and evolution. Progressive leaders generally recognized that most Southern

---

[35]Staton, "A Personal Journey," 163.
[36]Walter Shurden, "Second Baptist Church, Greenville, Mississippi," in Staton, *Why I Am a Baptist*, 150.
[37]Cecil Sherman, quoted in "Denominational Loyalists Meet," *Baptist Courier*, November 13, 1980, 16.

Baptists rejected the new progressive view of Baptist identity. Liberal editor Josiah Bailey, for example, concluded that "not one Baptist in a thousand conceives the genius of the Baptist position."[38]

Conservative Southern Baptists came under many of the same powerful influences and were likewise nurtured into Baptist ethnicity. They too read the books and heard the Sunday school lessons that advanced commitment to freedom as the highest Baptist ideal. But they felt that being Baptist must also include commitment to certain fundamental doctrines like the inerrancy of the Bible, substitutionary atonement, and salvation only by personal faith in Christ. For conservatives, being Baptist was first and foremost about faithfulness to Christ as revealed in his inspired and inerrant Word. And if necessary, conservatives were prepared to leave the tribe in order to remain Baptists. They advanced commitment to New Testament faith and practice as the highest Baptist ideal. Conservatives made it a fighting point that neither tribal credentials nor commitment to freedom could suffice for Baptist identity.

The progressive trends of the denomination in the twentieth century nevertheless shaped the identity of conservatives in various ways. Moderates controlled what was taught in the college and seminary classrooms and in Sunday school. They wrote the books that told Baptists their history, their doctrine, and their identity. They taught Baptists how to function as churches, associations, and conventions. Conservatives quickly recognized the unscriptural character of some of that heritage, but much of that influence remains unrecognized. In some areas conservatives continue in the thoughts and ways that progressive leaders taught them.

Moderate leadership received assistance from another source. Trends in modern western culture aided and abetted moderate views of Baptist identity on the one hand, and constituted an independent source of influence that eroded traditional sources of identity on the other. Americans embraced a more expansive view of individual freedom as the twentieth century progressed, and conservatives have not escaped its influence.

Conservatives have pitched their tent on the ground of the traditional view of what it means to be a Baptist, the view that orthodox doctrine is central to Baptist identity. But Southern Baptists still labor under the burden of the moderate view of Baptist identity. Insistence on the full inspiration and inerrancy of the Bible, the deity of Christ, the necessity of the new birth for salvation, and the reality of miracles is essential, but if the resurgence stops there, it is incomplete. Authentic Baptist identity

---

[38]Josiah Bailey, "The Baptists and Periods of Transition," *Biblical Recorder,* May 6, 1903, 1.

stands or falls on the commitment to maintain the faith and practice of the New Testament.

Perhaps the most obvious area in which the recovery is incomplete relates to the Bible's teaching on the church. Baptists once insisted that to be a true Baptist one had to embrace the New Testament's teachings about the governance and ordinances of the church. This is what they meant by the term "practice" in the phrase "New Testament faith and practice." The extensive and enduring influence of the moderate view of Baptist identity appears clearly in this area of Southern Baptist life.

Our churches have in practice attenuated the New Testament standard of regenerate church membership. We are uncertain whether we should expect evidence of regeneration beyond consent to be led in a prayer of faith. Baptists once looked for the New Testament signs of repentance, humility, and a changed life. They judged in charity, but they accepted the responsibility to judge. We now tend to think it uncharitable to look for such evidence. One result is that in our churches there are many professed Christians who give no other evidence of regeneration. We have diminished the standard of evidence of conversion to repeating a prayer and expressing a wish to join the church. Our volume is increased but the value is reduced.[39] On average, less than one-third of our membership gathers together for the Lord's Day worship service. And judging by the decreasing ages at which we baptize children, we seem to practice what we do not preach—we are making Baptists by birth, not by faith. Our membership rolls, with their extensive lists of inactive members, testify against us in this area. On the last day we will give an accounting for many whose false hopes of salvation we endorsed and sustained.

In our administration of the Lord's Supper we show how much we have come under the influence of progressive views of Baptist identity and modern subjectivist views of morality. We are often disorderly in our administration of the ordinance and seem to reject Scripture's teaching regarding it. In the New Testament baptism is the first command of Christian discipleship and is therefore prerequisite to participating in the Lord's Supper. Those who count their infant sprinkling as baptism have not yet obeyed the Lord they profess. They are ineligible. This is what our Baptist forebears held and what our confessions teach. But in many churches we invite unbaptized professing believers to take and eat. In so doing we are endorsing their disobedience of Christ's command and we

---

[39]See H. H. Tucker's more extensive comments on the decline of commitment to truth ("Has the Time Come?" *Christian Index*, July 9, 1885, 8).

will share the guilt. Indeed, in some churches, we invite all persons, making no distinction and uttering no warning to those who do not even profess regeneration. In both of these circumstances, we invite persons to eat and drink judgment on themselves (1 Cor. 11:27–30).

Under the influence of moderate views of Baptist identity, many of our churches have abandoned or want to distance themselves from congregational church government. We have forgotten why Baptists established congregational government in the churches. Moderates taught us that we are congregational because it is the natural church expression of our commitment to individual freedom, but Baptists once believed that congregationalism was scriptural and could readily point out passages that supported it.[40]

Our churches have generally abandoned scriptural church discipline. We practice a thin discipline—church staff who sin are given paid leave, Christian counseling, and a generous severance package, and are declared cured. We then commend them to another church, where they repeat the same crimes. This is an area where most conservative pastors are aware of our disobedience as churches. The influence of moderate views of Baptist identity and of our individualist culture has convinced us that scriptural church discipline ought not and cannot be done. But Baptists once thought otherwise. They believed that if Christ commanded it, that settled it.

In other ways we show that we still labor under progressive views of Baptist identity. We are uncertain about the boundaries of our fellowship, because in some ways we have embraced the moderate belief that being Baptist means freedom. And so we continue to hold the hands of Baptist churches that endorse heresy and tolerate immorality. Baptist associations traditionally expelled member churches that departed from the beliefs and practices that the churches of the association professed as the foundation of their fellowship together. In recent years, some Southern Baptist associations have successfully moved to expel churches that departed from a New Testament belief or practice, but the offenses that attract attention are limited. Associations have expelled churches that have endorsed homosexuality, ordained a woman to the pastoral office, embraced Pentecostalism, or admitted members without believer's baptism. In many cases the expulsions overcame appeals to freedom only with great difficulty.

In other instances, aberrant churches have remained members in good

---

[40]For an example of the moderate approach, see Robert C. Balance Jr., "Baptist Born, Baptist Bred," in Staton, *Why I Am a Baptist*, 10–11. On traditional Baptist arguments for congregationalism, as well as for other aspects of church government, see the documents collected in *Polity: Biblical Arguments on How to Conduct Church Life*, ed. Mark Dever (Washington, DC: Center for Church Reform, 2001). Just a few of the verses teaching congregationalism are Matt. 18:15–17; 1 Cor. 5:5, 12–13; and 2 Cor. 2:6.

standing in their association. One Southern Baptist church has tolerated in its membership persons who unashamedly and publicly paraded their serial adultery. And yet the church remains a member in good standing in its Southern Baptist association. To permit such churches to remain in the association constitutes an endorsement of their errors as consistent with orthodoxy. The other member churches that remain in fellowship with them thus participate in their sins. Most of the churches repudiate such errors, but have no heart for expelling churches that have embraced heresy, immorality, or unscriptural forms of church order. To do so seems churlish and unkind because of modern sensibilities that privilege civility as the highest virtue. More important, even many conservatives, influenced by the moderate tradition that being Baptist means freedom, fear that such action would violate the autonomy and independence of the churches. Associations that expel aberrant congregations do not interfere with that church's autonomy. They only insist that the association is likewise autonomous and is free to expel from its membership any church that departs from New Testament faith and practice.

Let us say, once and for all, that true Baptist churches will not walk together with churches that discount the authority of the Holy Scriptures, deny the deity of Jesus Christ, give false hope of salvation apart from faith in Christ, or tolerate immorality. Let us insist on unity based on sound denominational principles, that is, on our commitment to the same faith and practice. And let us determine that our faith and practice shall be based on Scripture, not on modern sensibilities, not on misguided progressive interpretations of Baptist tradition, and not even on the beliefs and practices of some ostensible golden age of Baptist orthodoxy.

Participation in denominational programs and cooperative endeavors should contribute to our denominational identity, but it should be subordinate and complementary to the role of our common faith and practice. So let us stand on the traditional ground of denominational unity and remember that "on fundamental principles, agreement is necessary to fellowship."[41] Let us recover authentic Baptist identity in whole and not merely in part. Let us recover, that is, a fully biblical identity, for true Baptist principles are Bible principles. And this is the only solid foundation for faithful and effective cooperation in the fulfillment of the Great Commission.

---

[41]Jesse Mercer, "Address to the Baptists of Georgia," *Christian Index*, December 15, 1836, 774.

CHAPTER FOUR

IS JESUS A BAPTIST?

Timothy George

I WAS BORN IN Chattanooga, Tennessee, in 1950. I had never heard of the city of Jackson. For us, the world stopped at Nashville. Memphis was the Far West, and anything beyond that was the Old Frontier. I came from what we would call today a dysfunctional family. My father was an alcoholic and died in the city jail when I was twelve years old. My mother suffered from polio and was not able to care for me or for my younger sister, Lynda. Lynda was brought up in a Baptist Children's Home in Cleveland, Tennessee, and I was left to be raised by two great-aunts, neither of whom could read or write. I am the first person in my family to have received a college education. But even though my folks could not read or write, they could certainly talk, think, and argue. I am sure I received my calling as a theologian from endless hours of arguing with my Uncle Willie over the truth claims of Mormonism. Once I straightened him out, I took on the Unitarians down the street and the Roman Catholics across town.

We lived in a section of Chattanooga called Hell's Half Acre. It was an integrated neighborhood even back in the 1950s, not because we who lived there were uppity liberals trying to make a social statement but simply because none of us, neither whites nor African Americans, could afford to live anywhere else. I would have said that we were dirt poor, but we couldn't afford any dirt. I know what it is like to go to bed hungry, and how it feels to have kids make fun of your shabby clothes at school.

In that community there was a little Baptist church. I would call it a country church in the city, for although the church was located in the heart of the inner city, they worshiped as if they were still way out in the sticks (which is where most of them came from). They would shout and moan, and sometimes people got Holy Ghost fits. Brother Ollie Linkous preached with a holy whine and we sang old-fashioned Stamps-Baxter songs. One I remember to this day went like this:

> Here among the shadows, in a weary land.
> We're just a band of strangers passing through.
> Burdened down with sorrows, fears on every hand.
> But we're looking for a city built above.

If you had to place this church on the map of Baptist typology, it would be at the outer edge of the bubbling bilge of a rivulet washed up by the backwaters of Sandy Creek. And we *were* a band of strangers living in shadows, surrounded by fears. But when I later read about how the early Christians in Carthage were known to their neighbors by the love they had for one another, I knew what that meant, for this church embraced me and my folks with a love that was palpable. They didn't have much, but what they had they shared with us: picnic lunches in the summertime, and sacks of coal in the wintertime to keep us from freezing to death. There was an unfeignedness about their love that was unmistakable.

That little Baptist church taught me John 3:16, and "Jesus loves me this I know, for the Bible tells me so," and "This little light of mine, I'm gonna let it shine, let it shine till Jesus comes." They also taught me that I was a sinner and needed to be saved, that I couldn't save myself and that we were saved only by grace through faith, not of works lest anyone should boast (Eph. 2:8–9), a verse that was emblazoned in my mind from earliest days. On August 6, 1961, after I had heard a sermon on Psalm 116, I asked Jesus Christ to come into my life, to forgive my sins, and to be my Lord. Soon thereafter, I felt called to preach, and I began to preach. No one ever told me you had to go to college or seminary or anything like that. I just began to preach. I would preach to the kids at recess; I held "Lawn for the Lord" services in the neighborhood, and I became a youth evangelist. The height of my youth evangelism career came a few years later at a little congregation in Lynchburg, Virginia, called Thomas Road Baptist Church.

I am a Baptist because Sam Peek, my sixth grade teacher and a Baptist deacon, took me to an RA camp. I am a Baptist because Al Davis, a director of missions, introduced me to a Southern Baptist missionary from Ghana and explained to me how the Cooperative Program enabled Baptists to work together to fulfill the Great Commission. I am a Baptist because Sam D. Sharp, a fiery evangelist who is still going strong at age ninety-two, took me under his wing and, though he had had no opportunity to receive a formal education himself, said to me: "Timothy, read all you can, learn all you can, and don't be afraid of ideas. You can believe the tomb is empty without your head having to be!"

I am a Baptist because a Baptist preacher named Martin Luther King Jr. challenged the racism deep in my Southern Baptist soul in the name of the Christ I was taught to sing about in Sunday school: "Jesus loves the little children. All the children of the world. Red and yellow, black and white. They are all precious in his sight." I am a Baptist because, when I was a high school student, Herschel H. Hobbs came to First Baptist Church of Chattanooga and preached a marvelous expositional sermon on the deity of Jesus Christ based on the Greek text of John chapter 1. I am a Baptist because during seven years of graduate study at Harvard, what we used to call the Home Mission Board allowed me to serve as a church planter in an inner-city Baptist congregation in Boston. I am a Baptist because all during those seven years at Harvard, Dr. R. G. Lee wrote me letters on his famous green stationary from 508 Stonewall Avenue in Memphis, Tennessee, encouraging me to be faithful to the Bible, faithful to the gospel, and faithful to the call that God had placed on my life. I was a Baptist before I knew what being a Baptist was all about, because I came to know Jesus Christ through the witness of the people of God called Baptists. And in all my years of study, I have never found a more persuasive or more compelling way of trying to be a faithful, biblical Christian.

Given what I have said about my background, perhaps you will not be surprised that when I moved from Boston to Louisville in that historic year, 1979, I found myself a bit dazed and bewildered at the goings on in Southern Baptist life. I did not like the raucous tone and polarizing rhetoric generated on both sides of the Controversy in about equal measure, it seemed to me. But I was close enough to the center of gravity to know that there were legitimate concerns raised by conservative critics who, early on in the Controversy, were asking only for parity. I thought then, and I still think now, that had our denominational leaders at the time responded to this challenge with more discernment, constructively and proactively, the rupture in our Baptist fellowship which has strained our relationship to the point of breaking could have been avoided. Instead, a strategy of denial, and stonewalling, and then counter-insurgency was adopted. Perhaps I am wrong about that, but eventually when a more realistic direction was taken by the SBC seminary presidents in the Glorietta Statement of 1987, it was too little, too late. I have written perhaps more

than I should have about the Controversy, and I do not retract anything
I have said or written in this regard. I am glad this denomination no
longer welcomes leaders who deny the miracles of the Bible including the
virgin birth of Jesus, or who argue for abortion on demand as a tenet of
religious liberty, or who tout a host of other issues that are tearing apart
every mainline Protestant denomination in America today. But I have also
come today to say something else. *We will not meet tomorrow's challenge
by forgetting yesterday's dilemma, but neither will we win tomorrow's
struggles by fighting yesterday's battles.*

In 1990, David Dockery and I edited a volume, *Baptist Theologians*,[1]
which has been republished under the title *Theologians of the Baptist
Tradition*.[2] In the preface to that book, we said this: "We believe that how
we act and relate to one another within the Body of Christ is no less important than the theology we profess and the beliefs we champion. Indeed, they
are inextricably linked, for true revival and spiritual awakening will only
come in a context of repentance, humility, and forgiveness. We hope for
the miracle of dialogue, not a raucous shouting at one another, nor a snide
whispering behind each other's backs, but a genuine listening and learning
in the context of humane inquiry and disciplined thought." That was true
in 1990, and it is still true today.

With that in mind, I want to recommend three strategies, admittedly
rather broad, grand, sweeping strategies, as we stand on the cusp of this still
new century and seek to fulfill with fidelity the charge we have been given
in this world of 6,739,000,000 persons all made in the image of God, most
of whom have never heard the gospel of Jesus Christ for the first time.

RETRIEVAL FOR THE SAKE OF RENEWAL

When I was a student at Harvard Divinity School, one of my professors,
Harvey Cox, like me a former Baptist youth evangelist, published a book
entitled *Turning East*.[3] Harvey was then in his post-Secular City, pre-Pen-
tecostal phase and was much enamored with Buddhism and spiritualities
of the East. In that book he argued for what he called the "principle of
genealogical selectivity." In trying to work out a viable spirituality today, he
said, "There are two principal historical sources to which we should look.
They are the earliest period of our history and the most recent, the first

---

[1]Timothy George and David S. Dockery, eds., *Baptist Theologians* (Nashville: Broadman, 1990).
[2]Timothy George and David S. Dockery, eds., *Theologians of the Baptist Tradition* (Nashville: Broadman
& Holman, 2001).
[3]Harvey G. Cox, *Turning East: The Promise and Peril of the New Orientalism* (New York: Simon and
Schuster, 1977).

Christian generations and the generation just before us. . . . The ransacking of other periods for help in working out a contemporary spirituality is either antiquarian or downright misleading." Did you get that dialectic? Primitivism on the one hand (the first Christian generation), and presentism on the other (the most recent generation, *my* generation). This is the heresy of contemporaneity and it undergirds much of the liberalism and individualism that marks not only left-of-center theologians like Harvey Cox, but wide swaths of Baptist and evangelical life as well.

Against this "imperialism of the present" (as I have called it) and the ideology of self-importance that undergirds it comes the call for a Baptist retrieval of the Christian heritage as a source of renewal for the life of the church today. Retrieval for the sake of renewal—that was exactly the program of the Reformation. *Ad fontes*—back to the sources—was their motto. This was not a call to leapfrog over the intervening centuries back to some mythical, nonexistent pristine New Testament church as though Thomas Aquinas, Anselm, Bernard of Clairvaux, Augustine, Athanasius, and Irenaeus had never lived, or as though the fathers of Nicea and Chalcedon had never struggled with the doctrine of the Holy Trinity or the person of Jesus Christ. No, what they were about—and what the English Baptists of the seventeenth century, both Generals and Particulars, were about—was a critical appropriation of the Christian tradition ever subjecting itself, and themselves, to the normative authority of the written Word of God. This is why the framers of the *Second London Confession* of 1689 identified themselves with what they called "that wholesome Protestant theology" of the Reformation, and why the framers of *An Orthodox Creed,* a General Baptist confession of 1679, included the full text of the Apostles' Creed, the Nicene Creed, and the Athanasian Creed in their statement of faith. They declared that all three of these historic documents "ought thoroughly to be received and believed . . . for they may be proved by most undoubted authority of Holy Scripture and are necessary to be understood of all Christians." These were Baptists, mind you. This is retrieval for the sake of renewal.

Understanding our heritage will help us deal constructively with the issues and controversies we face today. This kind of retrieval will help us to place in perspective some of the questions that still generate more heat than light within our own Southern Baptist fellowship, such as (1) are Baptists a creedal people? and (2) are Baptists Calvinists? Let's look briefly at each one of these.

Are Baptists a Creedal People?

"No creed but the Bible" was a slogan of the Campbellite movement in the nineteenth century and it has become axiomatic in many circles as a marker of Baptist identity today. Yet prior to the twentieth century, most Baptist theologians, from Andrew Fuller to E. Y. Mullins, spoke very affirmingly of "the Baptist creed." They strongly rejected the idea that voluntary, conscientious adherence to an explicit doctrinal standard was somehow foreign to the Baptist tradition.

It is nonetheless true that Baptists have never advocated *creedalism*. In two very important senses Baptists are not, and never have been, a creedal people—that is, a creedalist people. First, Baptists of all theological persuasions have been ardent supporters of religious liberty, opposing sometimes to the point of persecution, imprisonment, and all kinds of degradations, state-imposed religious conformity, and the attendant civil sanctions associated therewith. Believing that God alone is the Lord of the conscience, Baptists deny that civil magistrates have any legitimate authority to regulate or coerce the internal religious life of voluntary associations, including churches.

Second, Baptists are not creedalist in that they have never agreed that any humanly constructed doctrinal statement should be elevated to a par with Holy Scripture, much less placed above it. As Baptist confessions themselves invariably declare, the Bible alone remains the *norma normans* for all teaching and instruction, "the supreme standard by which all human conduct, creeds, and religious opinions should be tried." Unlike Eastern Orthodoxy which elevates the conciliar decisions of the first seven ecumenical councils to an infallible status, and the Roman Catholic Church which does the same thing with all twenty-three ecumenical councils, as they count them (including Vatican II), Baptists have never "canonized" any of their confessions. Rather, we have held them all to be revisable in the light of the Bible, God's infallible, unchanging revelation.

It must also be admitted that within the Baptist family there is a minority report on confessions, a libertarian tradition represented in colonial America by John Leland, who rejected the use of the Philadelphia Confession of Faith by saying, "We need no such Virgin Mary to come between us and God." Yet when such a confession became a means of uniting the Regular and Separate Baptists of Virginia, even John Leland, perhaps the most anti-confessional Baptist in colonial America, could allow the usefulness of such a document so long as such a statement was not placed on the level of the Bible nor "sacredized" by those who adopted it.

Still, for all of their value, confessions must be used with great wisdom and care. Confessionalism, like creedalism and traditionalism, can stultify and choke as well as undergird and defend. When matters of secondary and tertiary importance are elevated to a level of primary significance and are placed right next to the doctrine of the Trinity or justification by faith alone, then we are veering away from orthodoxy to orthodoxism, or from tradition, which Jaraslov Pelikan famously defined as the living faith of the dead, to traditionalism, which is the dead faith of the living. Retrieval can lead to reversal as well as to renewal. If the *Baptist Faith and Message* becomes a grab bag for every problem or issue that arises, then it will cease to be a consensual statement of Baptist conviction. S. M. Noel, a Kentucky Baptist of the nineteenth century, has words of wisdom for us here. Our confession, he said, "should be large enough to meet the exigencies of the church by preserving her while in the wilderness, exposed to trials, in peace, purity, and loyalty. And it should be small enough to find a lodgment in the heart of the weakest lamb, sound in the faith."

Are Baptists Calvinists?

And now, an even briefer word on the question, Are Baptists Calvinists? Historically and empirically, the answer to this question is: some are and some are not, and it has been thus among Baptists for nearly 400 years. Now, understand that I am not neutral about this subject. I was born an Arminian, as everyone is. I came only slowly, through much study and reflection, to a Reformed understanding of the doctrines of grace as taught by such notable Baptists as John Bunyan, Benjamin Keach, Roger Williams, John Clarke, Isaac Backus, Andrew Fuller, William Carey, Richard Furman, Jesse Mercer, James P. Boyce, John A. Broadus, B. H. Carroll, Charles H. Spurgeon, John L. Dagg, R. B. C. Howell, Patrick Hues Mell, and Augustus Hopkins Strong, to go no further. I know of nothing that has happened in the history of salvation since these great Baptist theologians wrote about God's grace that makes what they said outdated or irrelevant to our contemporary concerns. I commend their theology to my fellow Baptists today, not because it is theirs, or mine, but because it seems to me to reflect the underlying and overarching storyline of God's redemptive love revealed in the Bible from Genesis to Revelation. *But brothers and sisters, we need not kill one another over such issues today!* I like what our SBC president, Dr. Frank Page, has said about this matter. Our differing opinions over the details of Calvinism are a family discussion and should not be a source of division and acrimony among us.

I don't know who does more damage to our Baptist fellowship: the rabid anti-Calvinists who slander and stereotype all Reformed theology as hyper-Calvinism, or some of the Calvinists who want to tweak the leaves of the tulip so tightly that in their desire to defend the doctrines of grace, they have forgotten to be gracious. At Beeson Divinity School we regularly offer a course on John Calvin and another on John Wesley. Baptists have something to learn from both of these great leaders, but we are bound to neither.

I have a word of caution to my friends who lean in an Arminian direction. Beware lest your exalting of human capacity lead you past Arminianism into rank Pelagianism. Arminianism is an error; Pelagianism is a heresy. And it will surely lead us, as H. Richard Niebuhr pointed out some years ago, to a truncated view of "a God without wrath bringing men and women without sin into a kingdom without judgment through a Christ without a cross." John Wesley would doubtless turn over in his grave to see what passes as Arminianism in some circles today!

And I also have a word of caution to my friends who lean in a Calvinistic direction. Beware lest your exalting of divine sovereignty lead you into the heresy of real, as opposed to merely alleged, hyper-Calvinism. The original founders of the SBC were well aware of this danger, for the anti-mission movement was red hot at the time the SBC was organized in 1845. They established this denomination to be a missionary and evangelistic enterprise, committed to sharing the good news of Jesus Christ with everybody everywhere in the world. What passes as Calvinism in some circles today would make Andrew Fuller turn over in his grave and even John Gill take a spin or two!

I have a proposal: let us banish the word "Calvinist" from our midst. It has become the new "N-word" for some, and an unseemly badge of pride for others. It does us no good. A Calvinist in the strict sense is a person who follows the teachings of John Calvin and, while John Calvin was surely one of the greatest theologians who ever graced the Christian church, no true Baptist agrees with Calvin on infant baptism, or presbyterian polity, or the establishment of the church by the state, however much we may learn from him in other respects. Let us confess freely and humbly that none of us understands completely how divine sovereignty and human responsibility coalesce in the grace-wrought acts of repentance and faith. Let us talk about these matters and, yes, let us seek to persuade one another, but let this be done with gentleness and respect as we are admonished in 1 Peter 3:15. Let us speak the truth to one another in love, for truth without love is not really truth. It is rather a perverted form of puffed-up pride, just as love without truth is not really love, but mere mushy sentimentality. Above all, let this discussion not hinder our joining hands and hearts to work together as evangelists and as Baptists across our theological differences. Let us join together with Charles Haddon Spurgeon, perhaps the greatest Baptist preacher who ever lived, in his open, unfettered appeal to the lost, as seen in his wonderful sermon on John 6:37, "Him that cometh to me I will in no wise cast out":

> Him that cometh to me: that is the character. The man may have been guilty of an atrocious sin, too black for mention; but if he comes to Christ he shall not be cast out. I cannot tell what kind of person may have come into this hall tonight; but if burglars, murderers and dynamite men were here, I would still bid them come to Christ, for he will not cast them out. No limit is set to the extent of sin: any "him" in all the world—any blaspheming, devilish "him" that comes to Christ shall be welcomed. I use strong words that I may open wide the gates of mercy. Any "him" that comes to Christ though he comes from slum or taproom, boarding room, or gambling hall, prison or brothel—Jesus will in no wise cast out.[4]

Any him, and if Spurgeon were preaching that sermon today, he would also add, *any her*. Anyone, anywhere, anytime, anyway—any him, any her! Jesus will in no wise cast out. That is the tone we need, whether you lean one way or another on the decrees of God and how they are ordered from all eternity. Let us get this one thing right; when we get to heaven we can spend a few thousand years in the theology seminar room up there sorting through the details, and we will understand it by and by.

PARTICULARITY IN THE SERVICE OF UNITY

Several years ago I was going through my daily mail when (to my surprise) I found a personal letter from Rome, Italy. I looked a little more closely, for I do not get letters from Rome every day, and lo and behold, it was marked from the Congregation for the Doctrine of the Faith (which used to be called the Inquisition). I thought they were after me! But I opened it up and there I found a personal letter signed by Cardinal Joseph Ratzinger who now, of course, is Pope Benedict XVI. A few months before I received this letter, Ratzinger had issued a very controversial document called *Dominus Iesus* which created something of an uproar within the ecumenical world. In that document, Ratzinger not only asserted that Jesus Christ is the world's only

---

[4]"The Certainty and Freeness of Divine Grace," *Metropolitan Pulpit*, 1864.

Redeemer against certain pluralizing trends within Roman Catholic theology, but he also reasserted the traditional claims of the Roman Catholic Church against other Christian groups, referring to their view of the church as "seriously deficient." Contrary to almost everyone else who commented on the document, I had written a little piece commending it, saying that it represented the kind of candid ecumenism we needed more of—an ecumenism that did not paper over serious differences but faced them honestly in a common quest for truth. Ratzinger wrote to say that he appreciated my comments, and that I had indeed understood what he was trying to say.

What I advocated was an ecumenism of conviction, not an ecumenism of accommodation. This is what I mean by particularity in the service of unity. Yes, it is much easier to ignore theological differences and downplay doctrine, but that approach to Christian unity also results in a shallow, superficial togetherness that will not long endure. On this issue, I stand with Cardinal Ratzinger—I am a Benedictine. Theology matters because truth matters. Yes, we must speak the truth to one another in love, but speak the truth we must. I have always liked the statement from Simone Weil in her little book, *Waiting on God*. "Christ," she wrote, "likes us to prefer truth to him because, before being Christ, he is truth. If one turns aside from him to go toward the truth, one will not go far before falling into his arms."[5]

So, is Jesus a Baptist? Some people in our tradition have thought so, pointing out that Jesus was not baptized by John the Methodist, or John the Presbyterian, and certainly not by John the Episcopalian, but by John the Baptist. But surely, as they say in French, this is *un question mal posée*. The question is not, "Is Jesus a Baptist?" but rather, "Are Baptists Christians?" Jesus did not found a denomination; he established a church. In the broadest New Testament sense, the church of Jesus Christ includes all of the redeemed of all of the ages, as Hebrews 12:22–23 makes clear: "You have come to Mount Zion, to the city of the living God (the heavenly Jerusalem), to myriads of angels in festive gathering, to the assembly [*ecclesia*] of the firstborn whose names have been written in heaven" (HCSB). This is the church with a capital C, the *Ecclesia* with a capital E, the one, holy, catholic and apostolic church outside of which there is no salvation, as our historic Baptist confessions have all confessed. It is indubitably true that the vast majority of uses of *ecclesia* in the New Testament do refer to local, particular congregations, and this means something very important and very precious for Baptist Christians. But the New Testament also refers

---

[5]Simone Weil, *Waiting on God*, trans. Emma Crawford (London: Routledge & Keegan Paul, 1951).

to church in a universal, general sense. Jesus did it when he said, "Upon this rock I will build [not my churches but] my church" (see Matt. 16:18). Throughout the book of Ephesians, Paul consistently presents the church in a universal sense as the Building, the Body, and the Bride of Christ.

Yet here on earth, as St. Augustine reminds us, the church is on pilgrimage living amidst the vicissitudes of history, flawed, fallen, ever attacked from without, and divided within. And yet this church, the visible church—which for Baptists means local, particular congregations of covenanted, baptized believers—is called to pray for, work toward, and embody the unity for which Jesus prayed to the heavenly Father in John 17; not some overarching, one-world church organization that Carl McIntire and other ecumenophobes have screeched against for decades but the New Testament confession of one faith, one Lord, and one baptism.

Why is this important? Why am I arguing for particularity in the service of unity? Not just so we can all get together, hold hands, and be nice, but so that our witness to the world will be credible. "That they may all be one," Jesus prayed to the Heavenly Father, "just as you, Father, are in me, and I in you, that they also may be in us, so that the world may believe that you have sent me" (John 17:21, ESV). Jesus himself links Christian unity with world evangelization.

A few years ago, my friend John Woodbridge and I published a book entitled *The Mark of Jesus: Loving in a Way the World Can See.*[6] It is dedicated to the memory of Kenneth Kantzer and Francis Schaeffer, great evangelical leaders both of whom had a great influence on John and me. One of the last things Francis Schaeffer wrote before he died was a little book called *The Mark of the Christian.*[7] It was an exposition of Jesus' words in John 13:35, "By this all people will know that you are my disciples, if you have love for one another" (ESV). Dr. Schaeffer said that in that verse Jesus gave the world the right to decide whether or not we are true Christians based upon our observable love for one another. When I first read that, I thought, "Surely this can't be true?" But I read the text in John again, and I discovered that Dr. Schaeffer was exactly right. Jesus gives the world—unbelievers—the right to decide whether or not we belong to him based upon our *observable* love for one another. "By this shall all people know that you are my disciples, if you have love for one another." How else are they going to know? They cannot peer into our souls, or know what is in

---

[6]Timothy George and John D. Woodbridge, *The Mark of Jesus: Loving in a Way the World Can See* (Chicago: Moody Publishers, 2005).
[7]Francis Schaeffer, *The Mark of the Christian* (London: Inter-Varsity Press, 1970).

our hearts. But they can listen to our lips, and look at our walk, and see how we treat one another within the body of Christ, including those brothers and sisters in the Lord with whom we do not see eye to eye.

But Baptist ecumenism? Isn't that like talking about a pregnant rooster or a married bachelor? As the old country preacher said when confronted with a biblical teaching that he didn't like, "Well, it may be in the Bible, but it sure ain't Baptist!" But is that really true? Now, if you don't like the word *ecumenism*, throw it out the window. I have no interest in defending it, although, unlike Calvinism, it is a New Testament word which we encounter every time we read the Christmas story in Luke 2: "In those days a decree went out from Caesar Augustus that all the world (*oikumené*) should be registered" (Luke 2:1, ESV). Ecumenical simply means universal, referring to the whole inhabited world. But forget the word; what about the reality it represents?

The world Protestant missionary movement began when William Carey, an English Baptist shoemaker turned small-town pastor, encouraged his fellow Calvinistic Baptists to establish a society for "the propagation of the Gospel among the heathens." By 1793 Carey had arrived in India to begin his remarkable career, which included the planting of churches, the building of schools, the organization of an agricultural society, the establishment of India's first newspaper, a protest against the burning of widows, and the translation of the Scriptures into some forty languages and dialects. Now Carey was a Baptist, indeed a rather strict one, but in his missionary labors he worked with the Anglican missionary Henry Martyn, with Methodists, Presbyterians, and even, God bless them, Arminian Baptists, in the interest of extending the witness of the gospel to the peoples of India and the East.

In 1810, Carey set forth what has been called the "most startling missionary proposal of all times" by calling for a coordinating strategy for world evangelization. "Would it not be possible," he asked, "to have a general association of all denominations of Christians, from the four corners of the world, held once in about ten years? I earnestly recommend this plan. And I have no doubt but that it would be attended with many important effects." Exactly one hundred years later, in 1910, the first great International Missionary Conference was indeed held in Edinburgh, Scotland. However much we may deplore the fact that the modern ecumenical movement has been hijacked by advocates of a liberal left-wing agenda, which it certainly has been in many respects, we should never forget that it was born on the mission field and that a Baptist missionary was the midwife.

Particularity in the service of unity? Yes, by all means, let us maintain, undergird, and strengthen our precious Baptist distinctives—our commitment to a regenerate church membership, believer's baptism by immersion in the name of the triune God, our stand for unfettered religious liberty, and all the rest—but let us do this not so that people will say how great the Baptists are, but rather what a great Savior the Baptists have, what a great God they serve. May they be able to say, "Just look at those Baptist Christians, see how they love one another! See how they work together with other believers. See how they put others ahead of themselves. You know, I think I'll give a listen to what they are saying about all this Jesus Christ stuff."

HUMILITY IN THE PRESENCE OF THE HOLY

Retrieval for the sake of renewal, particularity in the service of unity, and humility in the presence of the Holy. I want to begin with two caveats. The first is simply to acknowledge how difficult it is to write about humility because once you think you have got it, you have already lost it. Humility is not a virtue to be cultivated. It is a by-product of the fruit of the Holy Spirit. In Galatians 5, we read that the fruit of the Spirit is manifested in the forms of love, joy, peace patience, gentleness, and so on, and the fragrance of the fruit of the Spirit is humility. Others are more likely to recognize it in us than we ourselves.

The second caveat I want to add is a somewhat contrarian word about the topic of Baptist identity. Is there not something a bit narcissistic about our focusing so intently on this issue? A familiar Baptist motto is "retrieval for the sake of renewal," and yet I want to suggest that there is a fine line between retrieval for the sake of renewal and the projection of a Baptistocentricity, a denominational egocentricity, and a perspective that is self-absorbing, self-justifying, and self-gratifying.

I am not preaching to anybody unless it is to myself, but I think this is something that needs to be said. Do you know what the corrective for this malady is? It is to get a vision of this world in which we live, the world for which Christ died. The most important book I have read in the last decade—if you haven't read it, go out and buy it and read it—is Philip Jenkins's *The Next Christendom*.[8] Jenkins points out the shift in the bal-

---

[8]Philip Jenkins, *The Next Christendom: The Coming Age of Global Christianity* (New York: Oxford University Press, 2003).

ance of the world Christian population, from the northern to the southern hemisphere. This has become almost a cliché, and yet there is increasing evidence to back up what he says. For example, God is doing an amazing thing in China. Much of it is not denominationally focused. But who can say that God is not at work in an extraordinary way in those churches, underground and aboveground and in all kinds of places? On the other hand, in the smallest province of Western China, there are more Muslims today than there are Southern Baptists in the whole world. I am simply saying that we must keep this in perspective. And when we talk about humility in the presence of the Holy, let us beware lest we all fall into this temptation to think of ourselves more highly than we should.

Several years ago, my wife Denise and I edited a series of twelve books for Broadman and Holman called *The Library of Baptist Classics*. Most of these volumes are still in print today. One of those books was called *Treasures from the Baptist Heritage*,[9] and we included in that volume a sermon preached on May 26, 1843, by Jacob R. Scott to the Portsmouth Baptist Association of Virginia which convened in 1843 in the Baptist church at Mill Swamp. In his address to that Association, Jacob R. Scott preached a sermon on "The Dangers of Denominational Prosperity." I will quote a few lines of it. Two years before the founding of the SBC, he said this:

> And when we, my brethren, show symptoms of elation, in consequence of the great prosperity with which the Lord has crowned us, when we, as a denomination, or as separate churches, begin to boast of the great numbers in our ranks, the wealth, the talents, the respectability, the influence, that have been added to our communion, when we begin to lose that spirit of simple, lowly, unsophisticated piety, which characterized us in the days of our fewness and contempt, it will be high time for us to begin to tremble also. We may expect the withering frown of Jehovah, and the tide of our prosperity will be turned backward. We may rejoice indeed, that the Lord has blessed us; and let us be glad; but let us exult only because in our success, we see the advancement of truth, which is the cause of God, and essential to the enfranchisement, the glory, and the felicity of our race. It cannot be doubted, brethren, that with the enlargement of our denomination, there has come a tendency to this vain-glorying. I say it with regret, I fear the indications of this tendency have already made their appearance. What means the boastful parade so often made in our publications, or our superiority in numbers over other denominations? And especially of any inroads we may chance to have made on their ranks? Let us beware

---

[9]Timothy George and Denise George, eds., *Treasures from the Baptist Heritage*, The Library of Baptist Classics (Nashville: Broadman & Holman, 1996).

of this spirit. Let us see to it that we be not puffed up with arrogance. The devil cannot be better gratified than to witness this. Let us take heed lest we make shipwreck here, and it be left for us merely to furnish a beacon to some remoter generation, who, thus warned of the rock on which they are most likely to split, shall safely bear the holy trust now in our hands, into the port to which we had had the honor of bearing it but for our folly.[10]

I commend that to your consideration. There must be humility in the presence of the Holy.

Some years ago, an eightieth birthday party was held for the theologian Karl Barth. Barth was asked to get up and make a speech, and this is what he said:

> If I have done anything in this life of mine, I have done it as a relative of the donkey that went its way carrying an important burden. The disciples had to say to its owner: "The Lord has need of it." And so it seems to have pleased God to have used me at this time, just as I was, in spite of all the things, the disagreeable things, that quite rightly are and will be said about me. Thus I was used. I just happened to be on the spot. A theology somewhat different from the current theology was apparently needed in our time, and I was permitted to be the donkey that carried this better theology for part of the way, or tried to carry it as best I could.[11]

Dear brothers and sisters, that is all we are: just a bunch of donkeys that happened to be on the spot at the right time and who are called in the providence of God to carry a burden for a while. But what a precious, invaluable, infinitely glorious burden it is. Our job as donkeys is to carry him who took upon himself the burden of our sins on the cross. We must carry him faithfully, steadily, humbly, proudly, unashamedly, joyfully, along that treacherous path which leads finally to Calvary.

Humility is not a virtue we can cultivate; it is a gift which comes to us as we focus on the object of our vision, on the precious cargo we are permitted to carry for a little while. I quoted H. Richard Niebuhr earlier. Let me close with another quotation from his brother, Reinhold Niebuhr:

> Nothing that is worth doing can be achieved in our lifetime; therefore we must be saved by hope. Nothing which is true or beautiful or good makes

---

[10]Jacob R. Scott, "The Dangers of Denominational Prosperity," *The Virginia Baptist Preacher* 2:7 (July, 1843).

[11]Karl Barth, "Speeches on the Occasion of His Eightieth Birthday Celebration," in *Fragments Grave and Gay* (London: Collins, 1971), 112–17.

complete sense in any immediate context of history; therefore we must be saved by faith. Nothing we do, however virtuous, can be accomplished alone; therefore we are saved by love.[12]

These are the three theological virtues: faith, hope, and love. When we get to heaven, we will not need faith anymore, because we will have sight. We will not need hope anymore, because we will have the thing hoped for. But even in heaven, we will still need love. Love is the one thing we can experience in this life that will last forever and ever and ever, in the eternity of God. This, I submit, is a summons to humility. It is also the implicit covenant of all our dialogues and, in its fullest sense, it is the vocation to which you and I, we Christ-bearing donkeys, have been called.

---

[12]Cited in Henry B. Clark, *Serenity, Courage, and Wisdom: The Enduring Legacy of Reinhold Niebuhr* (Cleveland: Pilgrim, 1994).

CHAPTER FIVE

LEARNING FROM NINETEENTH-CENTURY BAPTISTS

Russell D. Moore

DRIVING THROUGH RURAL ALABAMA a few years ago, on the way home from a preaching engagement, I noticed a sign for a small independent Baptist church off the highway. The sign promised a congregation that is independent, fundamentalist, Landmark, and committed to the 1611 King James Version and the "old songs." Noticing that it was nearly time for the evening service, I stopped the car, hid my newfangled Bible translation under the seat, and walked in the front door. The church was about what I expected. A rack of Jack Chick tracts greeted me in the foyer. The old songs indeed were sung, with "old" meaning 1950s gospel tunes. The people were warm and welcoming, and the pastor preached the gospel—combining a strong, biblical call for repentance from sin with a welcoming offer of forgiveness through the shed blood of Jesus. As I sat in the pew, however, something caught my eye that signified how hard it is to walk in what these brothers and sisters would consider the "old paths." What I saw was an offering envelope, with a Scripture reference on it, "Whoever sows sparingly will also reap sparingly." I lived through enough Sword Drills to know that King James isn't afraid to say the word "soweth." The church—committed to the 1611 KJV—was receiving its offering to the Lord in an envelope bearing what the pastor would probably consider a new-age Bible translation, the New International Version. Upon further investigation, I noticed that the envelope was printed in Nashville, by our own LifeWay Christian Resources church supplies division. The church—committed to being independent—would never send its money to what they would probably consider the hopelessly compromised bureaucracy of the SBC, but, nonetheless, was receiving that very money in a product of said bureaucracy. I noticed the congregation turning to look at me, to see why I was staring so intently at the envelope—probably hoping I was a quirky billionaire under conviction as to how much of my fortune I should leave to the church.

It's appropriate that an offering envelope should prompt my mind to the subject at hand—that of T. T. Eaton and the nineteenth-century Baptist tradition—since Eaton was, among other things, a pioneer of the technology of the offering envelope. Historian Ferris Jordan notes that Eaton, as pastor of the Walnut Street Baptist Church in Louisville, Kentucky, devised a system of offering envelopes to prompt church members to self-consciously set aside their giving to the cause of global missions.[1] Eaton (1845–1907) also served as a pioneer when it came to educational innovation. His father, Joseph Eaton, served as president of Union University in Murfreesboro, Tennessee, while the younger Eaton taught mathematics and science at Union. T. T. Eaton served as a trustee of the Southwestern Baptist University in Jackson, Tennessee. It was due to his influence that the university in Jackson took the name and the heritage of Union University, this happening the year of Eaton's death. Union University owes much to Eaton, including the donation upon his death of his library, considered to be one of the finest in the South (a fact for which Southern Seminary is only now ready to ask forgiveness for our envy).[2]

Eaton is not remembered primarily now for his pivotal role in the emergence of Union University, nor for his pioneering work in the field of offering envelopes, but instead for his role as denominational controversialist. Eaton served as pastor of the historic Walnut Street Baptist Church while also serving as editor of the *Western Recorder*, the state newspaper of Kentucky Baptists. It is from this post that Eaton passed through—indeed often ignited—some of the most incendiary debates of the SBC, as the denomination moved from a century of war and "Reconstruction" to the twentieth century and its promise of progress.

Eaton's controversies are not in the past, however. Many of them still burn, and some simmer under the surface. Eaton is not a hero; nor is he a villain. He was a hell-deserving sinner who often gave the world empirical proof of his theology of total depravity. He was also, however,

---

[1]C. Ferris Jordan, "Thomas Treadwell Eaton: Pastor, Editor, Controversialist, and Denominational Servant" (ThD diss., New Orleans Baptist Theological Seminary, 1965), 69.
[2]James Alex Baggett, *So Great a Cloud of Witnesses: Union University 1823-2000* (Jackson, TN: Union University Press, 2000), 83.

a man of the church—who, in the words of William F. Buckley in another context, "stood athwart history, yelling, 'Stop!' with a Bible in his hands." Contemporary Southern Baptists stand much where Eaton stood—a new century is before us. A civil war is behind us, not a national conflict but a denominational one, and as with Eaton's South it is not really as behind us as we choose to think. In many ways, being Baptist means controversy, and always has (that's why the Landmarkers call it the Trail of *Blood*). So what can we learn from Eaton's life in the middle of Baptist controversy?

EATON AND THE RECOVERY OF
BAPTIST IDENTITY

When T. T. Eaton was felled by the heart attack that would kill him at a train station in 1907, his first response was not to cry out, "Is there a doctor in the house?" or "Are there any Christians here?" It was instead, "Are there any Baptists here?"[3] That's fitting for a man who spent his life arguing for the perpetuity of Baptist churches from the Jordan River to the present day and for the local church, the local Baptist church, as the meaning of "church" in the New Testament. Strongly influenced by Landmark leaders such as J. M. Pendleton—also a Union University professor—Eaton did hold to the perpetuity of Baptist churches from the apostles until the present day. This is why he led the charge against the views of William Whitsitt, president of The Southern Baptist Theological Seminary, when Whitsitt wrote that Baptist churches discovered immersion in 1641 and that, perhaps even more jarring, Roger Williams, the celebrated American Baptist founder, was probably "baptized" by affusion. As Eaton wrote at the time, he believed that Baptists discovered immersion in A.D. 30 and had practiced ever since.

Eaton did not believe in the perpetuity of Baptist churches for historical reasons—nor did he seek to buttress his argument historically. He didn't trace a "trail of blood" from the first century to the present day. Indeed, he believed that such a project was dangerous to the faith. As Eaton put it in the *Western Recorder*: "For our part, we think Baptists have reason to be grateful to the Holy Spirit that the succession has not been accurately kept. If it had, tradition would have the same power over Baptists as it has over Catholicism. If the church at Jerusalem had continued in an unbroken line to this day, instead of going straight to the New Testament, as we ought to do, we should be inquiring anxiously what the Jerusalem church taught

---

[3]B. T. Kimbrough, *The History of the Walnut Street Baptist Church* (Louisville, KY: Walnut Street Baptist Church, 1949), 167.

about it."[4] Eaton believed that since Jesus promised that the "gates of hell" would not prevail against his church, and since the Lord's Supper is given as an ongoing proclamation "till I come," then one must infer that there were churches, rightly ordered, in every generation. Eaton was surprised that there would be controversy over such a notion: "We take it that no Baptist is opposed to others being Baptist, no matter in what age of the world they might have lived," he wrote. "We do not see how a man can be a Baptist and be opposed to the existence of Baptists in all ages."[5] Responding to Whitsitt's citation of a historian who knew of no immersions in England before 1641, Eaton simply responded, "Elijah was certainly a better witness as to Israel than was this unknown writer as to England; and Elijah said there were no true worshippers in Israel, while God said there were 'seven thousand.'"[6] Nor did Eaton believe in succession—that is an unbroken chain of Baptist churches, with each congregation giving birth to another. He simply believed that somewhere at any given time since the ascension of Jesus, there was a body of regenerate believers, practicing biblical baptism, church membership, and the Lord's Supper—and preaching the authentic gospel of grace.

For some contemporary Southern Baptists, the Landmark debates seem irrelevant—because Landmarkism seems so far away. Most of us do not hold to Eaton's view of perpetuity or to the more traditional successionist view—and I reject both as well. But often we think of Landmarkism as patently ridiculous and completely unreasonable, as though Landmarkers held that somewhere in the medieval world there were Acteens, or perhaps a Centrifuge somewhere in the pre-Reformation Alps. On the other hand, some contemporary Baptists see Landmarkers everywhere, identifying as Landmarkism doctrines that almost everyone on either side of the nineteenth century arguments would have agreed with—such as the idea that Jesus was, in fact, immersed by John or that baptism is a prerequisite to the Lord's Table and church membership or that baptism is a church ordinance and not simply an individual profession of faith. We need to ask not only what Landmarkers and their critics believed, but why. At the center of the nineteenth-century Baptist concern was a conviction that the ordinances matter. Eaton offered a thousand dollars to anyone who could find an example of *baptizo* in any Greek text, biblical or nonbiblical, that meant

---

[4]T. T. Eaton, "Editorial," *Western Recorder*, May 7, 1896, 8.
[5]T. T. Eaton, "Editorial," *Western Recorder*, January 21, 1897, 8.
[6]T. T. Eaton, "Preface," in John T. Christian, *Did They Dip? or, An Examination into the Act of Baptism by the English and American Baptists before the Year 1941*, 2nd ed. (Louisville, KY: Baptist Book Concern, 1896), 11.

anything other than "immerse."[7] Moreover, he—like almost all Baptists of his day—believed that baptism was a pronouncement not just of the individual but also of the church itself. This is why he rejected, along with most other Baptists, the immersions of individuals baptized in Campbellite churches in which the baptism is seen as part of the salvation of the believer, or in paedobaptist churches in which the immersion is a condescension to the individual preference or conscience of the candidate, rather than the testimony of the church to the witness of baptism to the death, burial, and resurrection of Christ and the unity of believers in him.

Eaton was wrong on perpetuity, I think—although I can cooperate cheerfully with those who agree with him—but both he and his interlocutors understood that the relationship between the church and salvation, or the church and the ordinances in obedience to Christ were not minor issues, merely the equivalent of debates between pre- and post-tribulational rapture views. If we are to be Baptists, and not just a collection of community churches (SBC), we must recover baptism and church membership. Yes, this means restricting church membership to those who have been baptized. This means explaining to those visiting our churches that we invite only baptized believers to the table—just as does every other major wing of Christianity—and then explaining what we believe baptism to be. This means recovering the gravity of baptism. Rather than walking out into the water with a candidate and explaining what we don't believe about the ordinance, we instead should be pointing to the fact that this is a proclamation—to the individual, to the church, to the world, to the principalities and powers that accuse him—that we believe this person is crucified with Christ, buried with him, raised in union with him, and seated in the heavenly places. When baptism is that defining and that significant, one does not simply joke about the temperature of the water and then slosh the candidate in and out.

It also means recovering the Lord's Supper. Why do we take the joyous victory feast our Lord has given us—which points to his coming messianic banquet in celebration of the defeat of all of his enemies—and turn it into a funereal drudgery in which we chew tiny bits of what seem to be Styrofoam and cough back shot glasses of juice, while scrunching up our faces and trying to feel sorry for Jesus? Jesus doesn't want you to feel sorry for him; through his Supper he is giving a victory party in advance, and declaring that you're invited.

---

[7] T. T. Eaton, "Preface," in J. M. Martin, *The Little Baptist*, new ed. (Louisville, KY: Baptist Book Concern, 1904), 4.

The recovery of Baptist identity means that we must take seriously what all sides of the Landmark controversies understood—that being Baptist means a regenerate church membership. If church membership is a declaration of the church of a credible profession of faith, then the persistence on our church rolls of so many who do not attend or who openly reject the faith is not just a scandal to the gospel—it is anti-evangelism. We would not go door-to-door announcing to whoever opens the door, "Congratulations, you're going to heaven." But we do the exact same thing when we count as members those who do not, in the words of the apostle John, love the brethren. The admonition in Hebrews to forsake not "the assembling of ourselves together" (Heb. 10:25–31, KJV) is not an encouragement, a helpful slogan for Friend Day. It is a warning passage. Just as there is not a Greek word for "infant baptism," there is not a Greek word for "inactive member." Yes, there are some churches that handle discipline badly. Some separate baptism virtually endlessly from profession of faith. We all know of the churches whose pastors "purge the rolls" without ever leading the congregation in this direction—perhaps just sending a letter to members who haven't attended in a year with "expel the fornicator from among you" across the top of the page. Discipline is not given to pastors, but to congregations—and congregations must be led by pastors to hear the whole counsel of God on this. Otherwise, the debate will not be over whether there were any Baptist churches in the Europe of the tenth century, but whether there are any Baptist churches in the Alabama of the twenty-first.

Moreover, Eaton was concerned about a loss not just of the ordinances or of biblical membership, but also of love for the church itself. Many scholars pinpoint the tension between Eaton and Whitsitt not first over the historical controversy that cost Whitsitt his presidency, but over their conflict over such parachurch organizations as the Baptist Young People's Union and Woman's Missionary unions—organizations Eaton believed would replace the primacy of the church. Again, Eaton was wrong about the Training Union; it actually helped preserve Baptist identity through the twentieth century, and we are impoverished by its loss. But Eaton's fear was not wholly unfounded. Baptist identity has indeed plummeted as American culture has embraced a hyper-Protestant individualism, in which parachurch organizations often take the place of the churches in instruction, discipleship, and even community. This is increased by the vast array of parachurch organizations—often out of necessity, in flight from apostate denominations—that came with the post-war evangelical movement.

When Southern Baptist liberal Foy Valentine famously said that "evangelical is a Yankee word," he was referring to more than just Mason-Dixon Line tensions. He feared the rootlessness and the churchlessnes of a parachurch world that is accountable more to a donor base than to the churches to which Jesus has given all authority in heaven and on earth. More and more of the students at our seminaries—not just mine—are saved in campus ministries on secular college campuses and more and more of them are discipled by parachurch campus ministries. I praise God for the evangelistic and teaching zeal of these ministries. But why are so few of our young people being called to ministry because of the example of a godly pastor? Why do so few of our young Christians point to their churches as the place where they first grasped the awe and mystery of Christ? There are exceptions, but they are far too few. The decline of Baptist identity is not the fault of Joyce Meyer or Joel Osteen, Wheaton or Colorado Springs. It is the fault of local congregations who refuse to teach and mentor. If more churches taught Titus 2 women's discipleship, there would be less need for Beth Moore DVDs. If more churches taught men to keep their promises, there would be less need to rent stadiums. If more pastors preached the Bible with passion and insight, if more churches actually crusaded for Christ on the campuses in their community, there would be less need for Campus Crusade for Christ.

EATON AND THE RECOVERY OF EVANGELISTIC CONFESSIONALISM

Ironically, T. T. Eaton, despite all of his conviction, could hold to a covenant theology that would put the Westminster Confession to shame. In a book advising fathers about looking for suitors for their daughters to marry, Eaton advised that the father and the young woman look for "good blood." In this bizarre case of Baptist eugenics, Eaton argued that one should look for good stock, not of wealth or ability, but of one who has "the longest line of pure and upright forefathers." As Eaton put it, "That man has the best blood in his veins who comes of a race of men and women who have been alike stainless in purity and inflexible in truth and honesty." He wrote: "Bad training is more easily overcome than bad blood. It is far more important that people should be thoroughbred than that horses should be so. The laws of heredity are no mere theories, they are laws of nature, inexorable as death and sternly enforced to the third and fourth generations."[8] One must wonder whether the pagan ancestry of Abram or the pharisaical fore-

---

[8]T. T. Eaton, *Talks on Getting Married*, 2nd ed. (Louisville, KY: Baptist Book Concern, 1906), 37.

fathers of Saul, not to mention the Gentiles of Ephesus and Galatia, would be considered "thoroughbreds."

Despite this anomaly, Eaton combined a rigorous theology with a confrontational zeal for world missions and personal evangelism. He argued for verbal inspiration and biblical inerrancy, seeing the winds of Darwinism and German higher-criticism heading for the South. Eaton challenged the liberal scholars, in light of the view that the truth of the Bible is "so mingled with the wrong and the crude notions of those times, that only a twentieth-century critic can distinguish the true from the false" to "eliminate all they regard as false from the scripture and add such things as have been inspired since the canon closed, so as to furnish an up-to-date Bible."[9] One can only wonder if a Jesus Seminar participant dug up this statement in some Baptist archive, and then attempted to take Brother Eaton up on his challenge.

Eaton was a Calvinist who, along with his sister, (in the words of one observer) reverenced the Philadelphia Confession next to the Bible itself[10] and who said, "I believe with Spurgeon that the Bible is soaked through and through with Calvinism, and take that out and you have very little of the Scriptures left."[11] But, like Spurgeon, Eaton did not abstract his view of God's sovereignty or of individual election from the context of the Great Commission. Theology was not a hobby for Eaton or for his nineteenth-century contemporaries, nor was it a quest for partisan identity. The theology fueled the mission, and the mission fueled the quest to know God. Despite all the flaws of T. T. Eaton, there is something that crackles with Book of Acts fervor when one reads a letter from the great Southern Baptist theologian James P. Boyce telling his colleague John Broadus in a letter that Eaton "objected to my speaking last Sunday because he was to take up Foreign Missions Collection, but agreed to my having next Sunday morning."[12] There's something to be learned here by contemporary Southern Baptists, including those fond of debates over Calvinism.

There is room for a variety of views within the SBC on how divine sovereignty relates to human responsibility and freedom. As a weird hybrid—who believes in personal election and in a universal atonement, and who wants both the best of theological rigor and revivalism—I hope both sides win, but in different ways. There would be fewer objections to

---

[9]T. T. Eaton, *Faith and the Faith* (Louisville, KY: Baptist Book Concern, 1906), 66–67.
[10]This observation came from the unedited typescript that was later published as the edited *Memoirs of John R. Sampey*. John R. Sampey, "Persons and Institutions I Have Loved: Memoirs of John R. Sampey," vol. 1, Archives and Special Collections, The Southern Baptist Theological Seminary, Louisville, 7.
[11]As quoted in Jordan, "Thomas Treadwell Eaton," 41.
[12]James P. Boyce, letter to John Broadus, December 23, 1887 (Broadus Papers, Archives and Special Collections, James P. Boyce Centennial Library, The Southern Baptist Theological Seminary, Louisville, KY).

the so-called "doctrines of grace" in our congregations if more Calvinist pastors spoke of election not in the abstract, but the way the apostle Paul speaks of it: to destroy human pride, to grant assurance, and to fuel our people to understand that there are no people groups or individuals who cannot be reached by the gospel, so therefore we must press the free offer on all of them. I wonder how many church members would be less inclined to fear the doctrine of election if they heard from a pastor they love and trust that election isn't about memorizing a catechism or joining an interest group. Instead, it's simply the words of "Victory in Jesus": "He sought me and bought me with his redeeming blood." I suspect a less abstract preaching of the biblical doctrine of election would result in more Calvinists in the SBC, not just among seminary students, but among pulpwood haulers and kindergarten teachers, too. I think Eaton would ask his fellow Calvinist pastors to preach John 3:16 *and* 1 John 2:2 (and there are many who do), sing "Just As I Am," and cancel the guest theologian one week in order to rally their people to take up a missions offering—even if the guest theologian is James P. Boyce.

At the same time, if more non-Calvinist pastors would preach how the Bible fits together, they would present a compelling vision of God's purposes that answers the deep questions of this and every age. If, in their pulpits, they would present a vision of a sovereign God and the purpose of history and of individual lives, there would be more non-Calvinists among the younger generation of Southern Baptists. There are many young people in this Convention who do not believe in unconditional election and who don't see how Calvinism fits with the free offer of the gospel. If they hear a compelling alternative from pastors they respect not just emotionally but intellectually, and if they see missions not just as being part of a good program but part of a vast global outworking of God's purposes from their non-Calvinist pastors, they will listen.

A good example of serious-minded, theologically rigorous Arminianism is to be found at the Free Will Baptist Bible College in Nashville. The first time president Matthew Pinson and I met, I sensed an immediate kinship. He is wrong, I think, on apostasy and libertarian freedom and conditional election, but our differences are subsumed by a common vision of ecclesial renewal and biblical literacy. And no one could accuse him or his faculty of being "man-centered" in their theology. In chapel, they sing the great old hymns of the faith right along with contemporary hymns from, of all things, the Sovereign Grace church movement of C. J. Mahaney. Pinson told me he agrees with almost all the lyrics of these songs, precisely because they exalt the grace of God in Christ. "Besides," he said, "no one writes apostasy hymns." I suspect if there were more SBC non-Calvinist pastors like Pinson (but without the apostasy stance, of course), they would gain a hearing among Baptists young and old.

Eaton held to a robust theology, but he was not afraid of impassioned, persuasive, invitational preaching. Take, for instance, this plea in his book to children: "What will be your fate, little boy? Little girl? It is for you to decide. No friend can get salvation for you; no enemy can prevent your being saved. You can and must decide for yourself, and decide ere the blast of death comes to take you away. Many of you will never see the summer of manhood, and many more will not come to the autumn of old age. When you do fade as a leaf, how will it be with you?"[13]

Eaton understood too that theology is not an intellectual exercise, nor is it the terrain of adults. Theology has everything to do with children. Eaton, one of the most recognized preachers and writers in the Convention, wrote a book for children. This was not a hyper-propositional catechism, nor was it a handbook of moralism. Eaton argued that anecdotes followed by Aesop's fable-style moral truths were not the means of conforming our children to Christ. His *Talks to Children* keep the narrative flow of the text. They engage what Russell Kirk called the "moral imagination." They sought to show how every passage points to Christ. They dealt with the whole counsel of God (including a children's lesson on the sacrifice of Jephthah's daughter!). And they grappled honestly with issues of sin, atonement, damnation, and reconciliation. To children, mind you, Eaton wrote the following words:

> Wicked men do not like to be told of their wickedness and to be asked to become good. They like to be praised and to be told what fine fellows they are. They do not like to be told how angry God is with the wicked and what terrible punishments are coming upon them. They prefer to hear pleasant things. Many people in this day are angry when preachers talk of their wickedness and tell them of the awful punishment in hell those must suffer who refuse to repent of their sins. They wish preachers to say nothing about such disagreeable things, but to tell how beautiful heaven is, as if it made any difference to a man who will not repent whether heaven is beautiful or not.[14]

Our forebears were often just as pitiful as we are at children's evange-

---

[13]T. T. Eaton, *Talks to Children* (Chicago: Fleming H. Revell, 1887), 184–85.
[14]Ibid., 133–34.

lism—see some of the maudlin, sappy children's novels of the nineteenth century. But Eaton seemed to understand what we must grasp, that a *VeggieTales* gospel cannot save. The message of the Bible is not "David was courageous; you be courageous" or "Noah cared for pets; you care for pets." The message of the whole Bible is the gospel of Jesus Christ. We teach our children to think of their forerunners in the faith, the types of Christ himself, as cartoon vegetables, and we wonder why we lose them in high school if they don't like youth camps, and in college, if they do.

What children are aware of, along with all persons made in the image of God, is that something is not right, with the cosmos and with themselves. Like all of us, they need to understand what this cosmic conspiracy is all about, what the mystery of all existence is, and that the point of everything isn't a "What" but a "Who." If we send our children to hell with True Love Waits cards clutched in their hands, or if we prepare them to be thrown into the outer darkness singing, "I am a C, I am a C-h, I am a C-h-r-i-s-t-i-a-n," then we have no business calling ourselves evangelical. The conservative resurgence in the SBC is not about the Evangelical Theological Society but about Vacation Bible School. This is why I would rather have a faculty member write a LifeWay Sunday school lesson that points to Jesus Christ as the pinnacle of all of Scripture and presents clearly the gospel to both believing and unbelieving children or teenagers, than to have him write another article for *Novum Testamentum.*

EATON AND THE RECOVERY OF COUNTERCULTURAL FAMILY

The issue of gender roles and family is now a persistent point of controversy in Baptist and evangelical life. Sometimes people imagine that those emphasizing such things are really longing for a more simple time, like the 1950s or even the nineteenth century when hierarchy and stability in family life were more recognized. And yet the life of T. T. Eaton shows us that the biblical witness on the family is always controversial, and always countercultural. The Whitsitt controversy itself had something to do with Ephesians 5. Eaton charged that Whitsitt had denigrated the church by suggesting that a Baptist woman married to a paedobaptist man should attend his church since the family was of more importance than the church. Eaton argued that genuine submission stopped where a command of God was concerned, a charge that Whitsitt apologized for in the trustee minutes published in the SBC Annual.[15] I suppose one can hear Conway Twitty and Loretta Lynn singing, "Southern Baptist woman / Paedobaptist man / We get together every time we can / The Jordan River can't keep us apart."

Despite this, Eaton was clear on male headship in the church and the home. He was also clear that this headship is not one of privilege. It is not, "Woman, get me my chips," but a self-sacrificial leadership that recognizes women, as Peter does, as both heirs of glory along with men, and as weaker vessels. Therefore, he warned women against marrying men given to drunkenness or to unfaithfulness or to indolence, precisely because of the wrecked lives it would bring. At the same time, he directly called men to account for their self-serving passivity and tyranny. He writes of a scene he observed in a hotel lobby in Louisville: a man saw the skirt of a woman at the top of a flight of stairs, and screamed, "Why in the world can't you get ready sooner?" When the woman descended enough for the man to see who she was, Eaton recounts, the man took off his hat and said, "I beg your pardon, madam; I thought it was my wife." Of this, Eaton writes: "Alas, alas, that a man should talk angrily to the one woman in the world who cannot help herself and must take whatever he chooses to say to her. If you have any manhood in you, and you want to talk insultingly to some woman, select one whose husband, or father, or brother can resent her wrong and protect her from your insults, rather than select the woman you have solemnly pledged yourself to love and protect, and who has confided her life to your keeping."[16]

Eaton saw the issue of the dual-income household as harmful to women and to children. While recognizing that there were single mothers or those in extreme hardship situations who needed to work, Eaton lamented the loss of male responsibility to provide for wife and children. As he put it: "It is because so many of our men are worthless, that so many of our women have to earn their bread. To glory over this fact, as some apostles of 'progress' are doing, is to glory in our shame. . . . It is a crying shame upon the men of any community, when any considerable proportion of the women are wage-earners."[17]

I have argued elsewhere that most Southern Baptists are intellectually in favor of a complementarity of gender roles as summarized in the *Baptist Faith and Message*, but they live practically more in conformity with *Ms. Magazine* and any given script of the television comedy *Everybody Loves*

---

[15]*Proceedings of the Southern Baptist Convention* (Atlanta: Franklin Printing and Publishing, 1897), 15.
[16]T. T. Eaton, *Wives and Husbands* (Louisville, KY: W. P. Harvey, n.d.), 26–27.
[17]Ibid., 4–5.

Raymond. There are going to be women—especially single mothers—in our communities who must leave their children in order to work, due to hardship and abandonment. Where are the pastors who will challenge churches to care for them, while challenging women to see the glory of motherhood and men to see that modeling provision and protection may mean doing without an extra car or living in a less desirable place, and that no Christian woman will say at the end of her life, "I just wish we had put the children in daycare"? It also means recognizing that the American economy that enables us to do so many commendable things for the sake of the gospel can also fuel a mammon-slavery that can only be confronted by straight—and controversial—biblical preaching. This sort of preaching moves beyond platitudes about happy homes to direct application that there are things more important to a man than the American Dream, and their pictures are right there in his wallet.

Eaton's example is also relevant when it comes to taking on the abuse and mistreatment of women—whether physical or emotional abuse, or abandonment. Right now in America a man who divorces his wife often ends up with a better income, a streamlined budget, and a younger trophy wife, while a woman more likely ends up in poverty and despair. And often they are sitting on opposite sides of our churches, with no word of discipline or warning. As Eaton would remind us, this is not "progress"; it is a foretaste of hell.

For Eaton, the self-sacrificial leadership of men extended, as in the Bible, to the church as the household of God as well as to the home. And, again, this was a matter of controversy then, as now. He addressed all the rebuttals one might find today from contemporary evangelical egalitarianism or cultural feminism. Also, he identified (rightly I think) the root of such a flattening of male and female roles: conformity to cultural rebellion against authority. Eaton writes: "I answer that the Scriptures are given to us for all time, that so far from changing Scripture teaching to suit the Nineteenth Century, it is our business to change the Nineteenth Century to suit Scripture teaching."[18] Then, as always, the argument centered over 1 Timothy 2, a passage that addresses not simply who has "Reverend" in front of whose name, but who is to teach men in the context of the church. Eaton spoke directly then against the practice of women teaching Sunday school. "Let it be remembered that the New Testament teaching is really binding on women—binding on them in church, in Sunday school, every-

[18]T. T. Eaton, *The Bible on Women's Public Speaking* (Louisville, KY: Baptist Book Concern, 1895), 23–24.

where—just as binding on them as on the men," Eaton wrote. "But it is said again that some of us are inconsistent. Well, suppose we admit it, what then? Does our inconsistency change the teaching or authority of Scripture? Suppose we are inconsistent, does that authorize us to violate the divine command? If we are inconsistent, the proper thing to do is to remedy the inconsistency, and not to make that inconsistency a plea for going contrary to Scripture."[19]

Contemporary Southern Baptists must address this issue. The *Baptist Faith and Message* statement on the male-only pastorate speaks to this issue because the New Testament does so in terms of teaching and of church authority. This militates against everything our culture teaches both girls and boys. The antithesis at this point will only increase. It is perhaps the gender issue more than any other that signals the collapse of Southern Baptist churches as southern culture at prayer, and that signals an opportunity to model a truly countercultural—indeed "retro-cultural"—model of community. We must be unafraid to preach what the Bible teaches here, and we must be ready to train young men to be preachers and leaders and to train women to disciple and teach women—and we had better be ready, perhaps in the near future, to find an attorney at our door, and perhaps even one day the police, when we do so.

EATON AND THE RECOVERY OF PRINCIPLED CONTROVERSY

The Whitsitt controversy in Baptist life wasn't just a contest between two ambitious and strong-headed men. Nor was it an academic debate. Eaton, after all, was Whitsitt's pastor at Walnut Street Baptist Church. Eaton baptized Whitsitt's wife.[20] On the Baptist Young People's Union debate, Whitsitt wrote in his journal that his wife sided with Eaton against her own husband when it came to the tactics employed.[21] A denomination was at stake; and with so many missionaries and the enormous Baptist presence in the South, in many ways the gospel itself was at stake. This is where Eaton's golden courage melts away into what seems to be wood, hay, and stubble. The *Western Recorder* was involved in various controversies, many of them about important matters, and on many of them Eaton was right. Nonetheless, he often resorted to innuendo, albeit restrained, and he allowed his sister, Josephine Peck, to write sometimes gossipy and often

---

[19]Ibid., 26.
[20]Kimbrough, *History*, 125.
[21]Charles Basil Bugg, "The Whitsitt Controversy: A Study in Denominational Conflict" (PhD diss., The Southern Baptist Theological Seminary, 1972), 93.

bombastic pieces in the newspaper, under the pseudonym of "Senex."[22] Eaton was nasty at times, but, for the most part, dealt simply with the issues involved—including in the Whitsitt controversy—and not with personal destruction.

The role of various media in Baptist controversy is a live issue at the turn of this century, as well as at the turn of the last. With several very notable exceptions, state newspapers are no longer the focal point of controversy. Some have suggested that the blogosphere has replaced the terrain of the *Western Recorder* and the *Baptist Standard* when it comes to Baptist brawling and bawling. In some important respects, that's true. It is also not as true as some of us might hope (or fear). Some Baptist bloggers speak in euphoric, revolutionary terms about the possibilities of blogging in building community, transforming the Convention, and so forth. Sometimes they speak of themselves almost as a caucus within the Convention. Southern Baptist leaders sometimes also think in the same terms, only with nervousness as to what "the bloggers" are up to. In reality, however, to paraphrase the Scripture, "they are not all bloggers who are called bloggers." Most blogs are not the widely read blogs saved on Bloglines accounts all over the Convention. Most consist of posts by young pastors or seminary students who are providing a forum for what they think about—for instance, a biblical text through which they are working, or how to apply the gospel to a specific situation in their churches or lives. Even among the widely read blogs, many of them are read specifically because of commendable content. There are others that criticize Southern Baptist leaders regularly— sometimes with good reason (like all leaders, Southern Baptist leaders occasionally do stupid things), but they do so without guile or malice. Even some of the most infuriatingly catty blogs have been known to mellow, as the bloggers themselves start to spend more time pastoring churches, raising families, and writing from the overflow from that. Some bloggers move from pastoring churches of only elderly people who aren't Internet savvy to churches in which people actually understand that Google can be a verb—the latter congregation would wonder why their pastor is sitting in a Starbucks in the middle of the day commenting endlessly about whether Bono is a five-point Calvinist, or whether Barack Obama is "the one to come" or should we wait for another, or whether Rick Warren is the False Prophet of Revelation 13. There's nothing venal there. The blogs, in this case, serve the function of a seminary cafeteria conversation. I am glad that the blog option didn't exist when I was at New Orleans Seminary in

---

[22]John R. Sampey, *Memoirs of John R. Sampey* (Nashville: Broadman, 1947), 79–80.

the mid-1990s, because I know exactly how viciously I would have lobbed criticisms at chapel speakers, late registration fees, and so forth. I did the same thing on the telephone and in hallway conversations that I might have done with a Blogspot account.

The difference between the blogosphere and the nineteenth-century Baptist world is one of accountability and responsibility. T. T. Eaton was restrained in his attacks against Whitsitt at the personal level, precisely because he had something to lose. In order to have a voice, he had to have subscribers. Churches had to continue to support the newspaper. A board of trustees would hold him to account, and over-the-edge gossip or character assassination would have ruined him. Like the state papers, the blogosphere can be an arena for every manner of sin, but the blogosphere brings with it unique temptations related to the immateriality of the Internet, the immediacy of the potential writings and response, and the Darwinian nature of the competition (the one with the most gossip or the most hateful rhetoric gets the most hits, both from the gossip-loving fans and from train-wreck observing onlookers). Most blogs are able to avoid this, precisely because the bloggers themselves see their primary accountability to their flesh-and-blood families and churches and communities. The rules of the blogosphere in denominational controversy ought to reflect the warning of the apostle Paul: "But if you bite and devour one another, watch out that you are not consumed by one another" (Gal. 5:15, ESV). The Whitsitt controversy was bad enough; it took the SBC years to recuperate, and churches and families were ripped apart. And yet T. T. Eaton was not consumed with hatred at William Whitsitt, or vice versa. Of course, there were impure motives and unfortunate moves on both sides. But there was not a personal vendetta, fueled by envy or covetousness or vengeance.

On the contrary, right now there are churches within the Convention with Internet sites devoted to compiling anonymous lists of grievances against their pastors and church leadership. This phenomenon is already moving to smaller churches, and what a whirlwind we will reap. Whatever our disagreements about Convention leadership or entity policies or even about blogging itself, we know that the Holy Spirit is not at work in anonymous letters or hauling lost people to business meetings in churches, and we certainly know that he is not at work in sites devoted to tearing apart with glee a man, a church, or a Convention. Within the conservative resurgence, there were occasional pugilists who came along, men who hated the leadership of the SBC more than they loved biblical inerrancy. The conservative resurgence would not have succeeded if these men and women had led the movement. Instead, the leaders were theologians such as Paige Patterson, pastors such as Adrian Rogers, men whom people in the churches saw preaching the Bible, evangelizing the lost, shepherding churches, and living lives. They didn't do so perfectly, but that wasn't the point. The people listened to them because they were believed to be men of God. They were not a coalition of everyone who had a grievance against Cecil Sherman.

The blogosphere is a perfectly acceptable place to discuss important issues—just as the state papers were the place for Eaton and Whitsitt to discuss Baptist origins and Baptist identity. We can debate, for example, whether or not the International Mission Board ought to have any policy at all on charismatic revelatory manifestations. If the churches want the SBC to move toward neo-Pentecostalism, that's what will happen. If not, it won't. We can survive the debate. What we cannot survive is a Baptist semi-cessationism, one that claims all the gifts of the Spirit are still operative, but that the fruits of the Spirit ceased with the apostolic age.

CONCLUSION

T. T. Eaton was right about many things, and wrong about some others. But I am still drawn to the offering envelopes. Before I knew about T. T. Eaton's role in the pioneering of the offering envelope, I found an old offering envelope in a Bible I hadn't used since high school. I would like to say I had jotted down diagrams of the last days or lists of the kings of Israel on it, but instead it was covered with tic-tac-toe games and questions back-and-forth with a friend about who was cuter, Melanie or Angel, in our home church youth group. On the other side was the logo of my church, Woolmarket Baptist, and the opportunity to give to all the things that made us Baptists. I thought of that offering envelope when I recently read Eaton's words to children, pleading with them to give up some candy or a toy to send money for the evangelization of the heathen. He wrote: "I haven't time to tell you of all the ways they suffer, about which you know nothing, but they lead hard, suffering, lives. The only thing which can make them happier in this world, is to teach them to trust Jesus and to love God. And that will not only make them happier here, but will make them happy in heaven. It will make little difference to them if they can be saved, how hungry and sick and poor and suffering they were in this world. And you can send them the Gospel if you will."[23]

That offering envelope I saved tells me a great deal about me, for better

---

[23]Eaton, *Talks to Children*, 59–60.

or for worse. The handwritten side reminds me that I'm human and fallen and frail. I'm able to write about nonsense while a man of God preaches of Christ and redemption and mercy. The other side reminds me that I'm a Baptist, and that I'm a part of a people who are human and fallen and frail. The offering envelope reveals something of our denominational braggadocio, something of the way we can make a program even out of reading the Bible. But it also reveals a people who, like Eaton before them, believe the Bible when it warns of hell, who believe the Father when he says he loves the world, who believe Jesus when he says to baptize the nations, and who believe the Holy Spirit when he says he will protect the church of Jesus—even from Baptists like us.

CHAPTER SIX

LEARNING FROM THE ANABAPTISTS

Paige Patterson

WE RECENTLY CELEBRATED THE 485th year of Leo Jud's triumphant consumption of Swiss sausages at the Froschauer's home in Zurich. Those gathered that fateful evening were mostly participants in Andreas Castleberger's lay Bible study groups, at least some of whom became Anabaptists in the months ahead. Jud, a frequent preacher at the Grossmunster, was hardly incognito when he brazenly defied the Lenten laws of the church on March 9, 1522, as he wolfed down his much-loved sausage.

Of course, the flavor of the pork was ancillary to the exhilaration of rebellion against the established practices of the Roman church. The act was both a declaration of religious liberty and a gesture of determination concerning the discovery of and obedience to the revelation of God rather than the canons of men. In a recent book-length article in *The Mennonite Quarterly Review*, C. Arnold Snyder reexamines the events accompanying the Zwinglian reformation in Switzerland and the South German territories in the eventful years from 1525 to 1530.[1] The value of the article is found on multiple levels. Snyder's history is the first survey of these formative years to take advantage of recent discoveries and theories about these radicals. Snyder's suggestion, for example, that pacifism may not have initially been as prominent a part of the movement as appears in the Schleitheim Confession, was an unexpected declaration. Other scholars, including Thomas Finger and Abraham Friesen, respond to Snyder's conclusions in shorter essays.

---

[1] C. Arnold Snyder, "The Birth and Evolution of Swiss Anabaptism, 1520-1530," *Mennonite Quarterly Review* 80, no. 4 (October 2006): 501–645.

Whatever one may conclude from these deliberations, the reading of this issue of *The Mennonite Quarterly Review* is a cogent reminder to Free-Church people in general and to Baptists in particular that the freedom-loving men and women who preached, debated, suffered, and died for their convictions were a remarkable lot and have much to teach contemporary Baptists. This is the case regardless of the question about the origins of Baptists. Those who argue for a foundation in English separatism are demonstrably correct. Those who see a connection to continental Anabaptism have not yet established indisputable evidence of such, but they can still suggest that similarities between the Swiss and South German Biblicists and Baptists are adequate to attract the interest of Baptists and sufficiently compelling to engender not only admiration but also in many cases imitation of their commitments and convictions.

Reconsideration of Anabaptists, particularly those in the south of Germany and in Switzerland, has significant value for the future of Baptists in America. The purpose of this chapter is to suggest several perspectives widely endorsed by these radicals, which Baptists facing the next decade would do well to reconsider, especially those that are confessionally codified though perhaps little practiced.

A REDEEMED, DISCIPLINED CHURCH

The model of the Magisterial Reformation was the *Volkskirche* or the *Landeskirche*. Children, regardless of personal faith, born into families with church affiliation were considered a part of the faith community. Anabaptists signed on to the major emphases of the Reformation. But while they believed Luther and others to be correct in the notion of justification by faith, they openly wondered why the implications of such a declaration were not nurtured and developed. As Franklin Littell noted in his 1958 monograph *The Anabaptist View of the Church*, these lonely reformers doubted that the magisterial reformers had escaped the fallen state of the Roman church.

The church in her fallen state seemed to the Anabaptists far different from the community of true believers, the brotherhood of spiritual athletes. We must remember that they counted the fallen condition of the church from the days of Constantine until the beginning of their own movement. The Reformers also belonged to the period of the Fall. The Anabaptists said that the revival began with Luther and Zwingli, but when the Reformers clung to the old idea of Christendom, the Radicals counted them out. The criticisms directed against the imperial Roman religion were also directed against the Reformers: church and state were amalgamated, empty formalism and spiritual slackness prevailed, and infants were baptized into Christianity before their understanding could give the membership any content. The Anabaptists wanted a thoroughgoing restitution of the church as she had been before the Fall, and they criticized the nominal Christianity of the middle period in suggestive terms.[2]

A restitution of the primitive church called for the church to be both redeemed and disciplined. In 1524, Balthasar Hubmaier's *Eighteen Theses* were published. The first two of these call attention to the necessity of faith:

1. Faith alone makes one holy before God.
2. This faith is the acknowledgment of the mercy of God, which he has shown to all in the offering of his only begotten Son. This excludes all sham Christians, who have nothing more than an historical faith in God.[3]

Pilgram Marpeck, the civil servant turned theologian, wrote in 1531:

1. Those who thus believe in Christ Jesus are made alive from all dead works of the law and circumcision, for Christ has made the consummation on the cross and finished what was promised to Abraham (John 19:30).
2. From now on, therefore, faith in Christ can do and produce what pleases God; disease and death are undone; life and health are at hand. The salvation of all men is accomplished, ignorance is excused, and, to children and all who have true simplicity [of spirit] the kingdom of God is given.[4]

However, the Anabaptists also realized that only God could know the human heart. People might profess faith in Christ and even be baptized without experiencing regeneration. Others might have genuine faith and yet, because of the weaknesses of the flesh, develop attitudes or exercise themselves in a way that reproaches Christ and embarrasses the church. Just as personal faith was essential to salvation, a disciplined church was essential to witness.

The Schleitheim Confession of 1526, apparently the work of Michael

---

[2]Franklin Littell, *The Anabaptist View of the Church* (Boston: Star King Press, 1958), 64–65.
[3]"The Eighteen Theses—Balthasar Hubmaier (April, 1524)," in *Anabaptist Beginnings 1523-1533*, ed. William R. Estep Jr. (Nieuwkoop: B. De Graaf, 1976), 24.
[4]"Pilgram Marpeck's Confession of 1532," in *The Writings of Pilgram Marpeck*, ed. and trans. William Klassen and Walter Klaassen (Kitchener, ON: Herald Press, 1978), 110–11.

Sattler, provided eloquent testimony for what the document termed "the ban":

> We agree as follows on the ban: The ban shall be employed with all those who have given themselves to the Lord, to walk in His commandments, and with all those who have been baptized into the one body of Christ and who are called brethren and sisters, and yet who slip sometimes and fall into error and sin, being inadvertently overtaken. The same shall be admonished twice in secret and the third time openly disciplined or banned according to the command of Christ. Mt. 18. But this shall be done according to the regulation of the Spirit, Mt. 5, before the breaking of bread, so that we may break and eat one bread, with one mind and in one love, and may drink of one cup.[5]

Furthermore, the Lord's Table was to follow baptism in which the professing believer identified with Christ and with his body, the church:

> In the breaking of bread we are of one mind and are agreed: All those who wish to break bread in remembrance of the broken body of Christ, and who wish to drink of one drink as remembrance of the shed blood of Christ, shall be united beforehand by baptism in one body of Christ which is the church of God and whose Head is Christ. For as Paul points out we cannot at the same time be partakers of the Lord's Table and table of devils; we cannot at the same time drink the cup of the Lord and the cup of the devil. That is, all those who have fellowship with dead works of darkness have no part in the light. Therefore, all who follow the devil and the world have no part with those who are called unto God out of the world. All who are enmeshed in evil have no part in the good.[6]

Contemporary Baptists have most often been faithful to the proclamation of the gospel. But the bloated membership rolls of Southern Baptist churches, coupled with the worldliness apparent in the church, bear painful witness to failure at two basic levels. Lack of care with new converts and the virtual absence of church discipline have created fellowships that mirror the conditions in other Protestant churches, which tend to emphasize the necessity of conversion far less than Baptists do. Exacerbating this problem is the tendency in Baptist churches to become de facto paedobaptists themselves, baptizing significant numbers of children under nine years of age who do not have a clear understanding of conversion.

---

[5]"The Schleitheim Confession—Michael Sattler (February, 1527)," in Estep, *Anabaptist Beginnings*, 101.
[6]Ibid.

Passion for missions and for the evangelization of the lost is commendable. Accusations against some pastors that they are "just interested in numbers" strike me as judgments relating to the motivation of the heart, which only God can really see. My own experience with pastors whose churches regularly report large numbers of baptisms is that these men are usually profoundly concerned for the lost and diligently involved in finding ways to get the gospel message to a world preoccupied with materialism and prestige.

Regrettably, sincerity of purpose is not to be equated with either wisdom or the New Testament pattern. The evidence of the New Testament suggests that the early church had confidence in its converts, baptizing them promptly upon their confession of Christ. At least at Pentecost, three-thousand people were baptized in a day. Knowing, however, the weakness of the flesh, the church was given a method for addressing moral and spiritual failure among her members.

The Anabaptists, like their New Testament counterparts, baptized with confidence those who wished to profess their faith in Christ. But they also made certain that the new believer understood that he or she was acting out the death of the old man and the resurrection of a new man. If serious problems developed thereafter and repeated admonitions were disregarded, then the ban was exercised and the offender was not allowed to come to the Lord's Table.

Church discipline is never easy. Those with sensitivity to their own sinfulness find it difficult to adjudicate failure in others. Furthermore, in the midst of the almost insurmountable difficulties, to say nothing of the expenditure of time, to attempt to ascertain the truth in any situation breeds an understandable reluctance to proceed.

Nevertheless, if contemporary Baptists find a way out of the present malaise, they must discover, as did our Anabaptist fathers, a way to make church membership meaningful. Without curtailing zeal for the lost, Baptists must take more time to instruct carefully those being baptized concerning the significance of the declaration that the candidate is making. Neither can matters of church discipline be relegated to apply only to the gross fleshly sins of highly visible members. Integrity and concern for the well-being of fellow humans should dictate at the very least that those who refuse to attend and participate in the life of the body should experience the ban. Ecclesial vitality is dependent upon meaningful church memberships in which being a "congregation" is more than just a spectator sport.

FAITH-WITNESS BAPTISM AS INTENTION

This conclusion leads us to an assessment of the Anabaptist understanding of baptism. Two years ago at a meeting of the pastors of larger churches, David Jeremiah made an impassioned plea that pastors not delegate all the duties of baptism to associates. He pointed to the diminishing significance of baptism in many churches and suggested that the importance of baptism as confession was in need of recovering. In so doing, Jeremiah linked himself with Anabaptist concerns.

Hubmaier, for example, spoke of three baptisms: "I confess three types of baptism: that of the Spirit given internally in faith; that of water given externally through the oral confession of faith before the church; and that of blood in martyrdom or on the deathbed."[7]

Expanding the thought, Hubmaier noted that, "In receiving water baptism, the baptized confesses publicly that he had yielded himself to live henceforth according to the rule of Christ. In the power of his confession he has submitted himself to the sisters, the brethren, and the church, so that they now have the authority to admonish him if he errs, to discipline, to ban, and to readmit him. . . . Whence comes this authority if not from the baptismal vow?"[8]

Note the nature of the confession. The one being baptized has yielded himself to live according to the rule of Christ. In so doing, he has also submitted himself to the sisters and brothers, so that he is also in submission to the church. Here apparently the church administered baptism and was thus prelated directly to the confession of faith. Baptism is not only into Christ, the head of the church, but also into his body.

The same note is sounded in the Schleitheim Confession:

> Observe concerning baptism: Baptism shall be given to all who have learned repentance and amendment of life, and who believe truly that their sins are taken away by Christ, and to all those who walk in the resurrection of Jesus Christ, and wish to be buried with Him in death, so that they may be resurrected with Him, and all those who with this significance request it [baptism] of us and demand it for themselves. This excludes all infant baptism, the highest and chief abomination of the pope. In this you have the foundation and testimony of the apostles themselves. Mt. 28, Mk. 16, Acts 2, 8, 16, 19. This we wish to hold simply, yet firmly, and with assurance.[9]

[7]Walter Klaassen, *Anabaptism in Outline* (Kitchener, ON: Herald Press, 1981), 166.
[8]Ibid., 168.
[9]"The Schleitheim Confession," in Estep, *Anabaptist Beginnings*, 101.

Amendment of life is demanded of those who would seek baptism. By faith Christ is received and witness is given in the baptismal waters. In this confession, the believer expresses his intention to walk in the way of Christ and the admonition of the church.

The contemporary church is often guilty of making both baptism and the Lord's Table a "tack-on" to worship. The pastor of the church is increasingly marginalized from both catechetical, pre-baptismal instruction and participation in the baptismal event itself. For the Anabaptists, baptism into an Anabaptist church was a possible death-warrant. Baptism's natural association with death was highlighted for these congregations—and it should be for modern ones also. Pilgram Marpeck stated this clearly in his *Admonition of 1542*: "[I]nsofar as we can search the Scriptures and understand them, we find that baptism takes place when believers are baptized and leave the realm of the will of flesh, give themselves over totally into the will of God, and commit themselves to it. That means to be born again in Christ and to be baptized in the name of God, to bury the flesh, to be raised with Christ, to wash off sin, to put on Christ, and similar expressions which the Scriptures use with reference to baptism."[10]

For renewal to take place in Southern Baptist life, churches must once again underscore the significance of baptism. The one being baptized has died to himself. He intends to follow Christ in thought and action. Baptism must be more closely associated with public confession and responsibility in the church enjoined on the believer.

THE BIBLE AS THE SOURCE OF AUTHORITY

In his 1980 publication *The Anabaptists*, Hans Jürgen-Goertz assessed the extent to which the Swiss Radicals devoted themselves to the Scriptures: "Every farm is a school, in which the greatest masterpiece of all, the Old and the New Testament, can be read."[11] This Swiss report was certainly exaggerated, but was applicable to the new religious situation of the early years of the Reformation. The teaching authority of the pope and of the clergy had been shaken. The layman took hold of the Holy Scriptures and either read them himself or had them read to him, finding the nourishment for his faith and his devotion that had previously been withheld. He also discovered forms of human relationships and fraternal communication that contrasted sharply with the mass, with indulgences, and with the clergy's displays of power. The Bible became a source of streams of critiques of

---

[10]"Admonition of 1542," in Klassen and Klaassen, *The Writings of Pilgram Marpeck*, 193.
[11]Hans-Jürgen Goertz, *The Anabaptists*, (New York: Routledge, 1980).

church and society and alternative concepts of Christian community. In the hands of the peasant or in the knapsack of the itinerant laborer, the Bible was initially a pledge of the layman's liberation from spiritual servitude. Through calls for "divine justice," it was soon also used in the struggle against social and political oppression. It unleashed antiauthoritarian aggression.[12]

The availability of the Bible to the common man was a revolutionary idea. Thus the farmer armed with Scripture became a critic of the established church, not on the basis of his misgivings about the integrity of these systems but on the basis of the teachings of the Bible. Human ecclesiastical systems contradicted the Word of God.

Confidence in the irrefutable nature of God's Word is apparent in Hubmaier's lengthy hymn entitled *God's Word Stands Sure Forever*. Essentially a journey through the whole of Scripture from Adam to Paul, each verse concludes with the phrase, "God's word stands sure for ever." Typical of those stanzas but particularly focused on the role of Scripture are these two verses:

> *Ah, man, blind man, now hear the word,*
>   *Make sure your state and calling;*
> *Believe the Scripture is the power*
>   *By which we're kept from falling.*
> *Your valued lore at once give o'er,*
>   *Renounce your vain endeavor;*
> *This shows the way, no longer stray,*
>   *God's word stands sure for ever.*

> *Praise God, praise God in unity,*
>   *Ye Christian people sweetly*
> *That he his word has spread abroad—*
>   *His word, his work completely.*
> *No human hand can him withstand,*
>   *No name how high soever;*
> *And sing we then our glad Amen!*
>   *God's word stands sure for ever.*[13]

Constant Anabaptist appeal to the Scriptures during the various disputations made clear to their detractors that they were only going to change their minds if convinced by Scripture, the final court of appeal.

---

[12]Ibid., 48.
[13]"God's Word Stands Sure Forever—Balthasar Hubmaier," in Estep, *Anabaptist Beginnings*, 172.

Luther, Zwingli, and others recognized that the debate was not just about the nature of Scripture but also about the interpretation of Scripture. The Magisterial Reformers also cited the Bible, often appealing to Old Testament texts. This in turn pushed the Swiss and South German brethren increasingly to cite the New Testament as the final norm.

For Southern Baptists this emphasis on faithfulness to Scripture may seem to be carrying coals to Newcastle, but contemporary developments in the ecclesiastical world suggest otherwise. Following the relative success of the conservative renaissance in Southern Baptist life and the general hegemony of the evangelicals, most in evangelical circles subscribe to a high view of Scripture. But there is reason to wonder if experience is not actually a more operative authority than the Bible for many Christians. What is transpiring in a given church may shape the understanding of Scripture more than the authority of Scripture establishes the norm for belief and behavior. Consequently, there is much to be valued in the insistence of the Anabaptists that major doctrines occupying the central stage and that human desires and experience must all be subordinated to the teachings of Holy Scripture.

THE CHURCH LOOKS DIFFERENT FROM THE WORLD

Church discipline was for the Anabaptists partially to ensure the purity of the church. Also, the ban was practiced not merely to exclude but hopefully to awaken to repentance as well. The practice of the disciplined church was an indication that the community of Christ was to function quite distinctly from the community of the world.

In Bernhard Rothmann's *Restitution* of 1534, the nature and function of the church is accentuated:

> The true Christian congregation is a gathering large or small that is founded on Christ in the true confession of Christ. That means that it holds only to his words and seeks to fulfill his whole will and his commandments. A gathering thus constituted is truly a congregation of Christ. But if this is missing a gathering cannot in truth be called a congregation of Christ even if it has the name a hundred times. That this is true and that the proper knowledge of Christ is that he is the true Lord and only Saviour and Redeemer and that this is the basis of the Christian gathering, the Scriptures confirm in abundance. . . . It is necessary to remain on this foundation. That we adhere solely to the words of Christ and do his will, to this he himself witnesses when he said to his disciples: If you keep my

words you are truly my disciples, and again: You are my friends if you do what I command you. But whoever concerns himself with other teachings and commandments cannot be a disciple or friend of Christ, nor do they belong in the church of Christ. To it belong only the disciples and friends of Christ who keep his teaching and commandments. When Christ sent out his disciples to gather his church he spoke to them and gave them this commandment: Go and teach all nations, baptize them in the name of the Father, the Son, and the Holy Ghost, and teach them to observe everything that I have commanded you. The first teaching is that they present to them the basics of God's will in Christ. If then they accept the teaching and wish to become disciples of Christ they shall baptize them so that they may put on Christ and be incorporated in his holy church. Finally, in order that they may remain friends of Christ, the ones baptized should be taught everything that Christ commanded. All this can be clearly seen in the apostolic writings. Behold, this is the true church of Christ from the beginning and still is. For although many others claim to be the church of Christ, as for example the anti-Christian papal crowd do, it is a vain claim. Not all that glistens is gold.[14]

Ulrich Stadler wrote in 1537 of the distinction between the world and the church, saying,

But it, that is, such a community must move about in this world, poor, miserable, small, and rejected of the world, of whom, however, the world is not worthy. Whoever strives for the lofty things [of this world] does not belong. Thus in this community everything must proceed equally, all things be one and communal, alike in the bodily gifts of their Father in heaven, which he daily gives to be used by his own according to his will.[15]

This contrast with the values of the world can only result from redemption and, as Marpeck notes, begins with the baptismal confession:

We are then correctly consecrated into the Christian church, purified of sins, incorporated in to Christ, and clothed with Him; only then may we appear, without shame, at the wedding of the highest King in honorable clothing and adornment. If, at this time, the entrance to the church were to be correctly confessed and practiced, then we would surely sense a holy and unblemished church. However, when this entrance has been destroyed, and almost everybody is confused about it, the holy church has also been desecrated and disrupted. It is to be assumed that the holy

---

[14]Klaassen, *Anabaptism in Outline*, 106–107.
[15]Ibid., 107.

church will never come to its holiness unless this entrance to the church will again be rebuilt, reinstituted, and cleansed of all infamy.[16]

Contemporary Baptist churches are often quite different from the social order in which they are immersed. However, the subtlety of the inroads of the Evil One manifests itself in the worldliness of the churches. Greater concern for the gifts of the Spirit than for the fruits of the Spirit marks a different road from the love and sacrifice of most Anabaptist congregations. The moral failures and ethical misfortunes of pastors and leading clergymen is a blight on contemporary churches. Such tragedies doubtless occurred in sixteenth-century Germany, but among the Brethren they were rare.

Independent Baptists of a former generation may have been guilty of emphasizing "separation" to the point of legalism, but the trajectory of the contemporary church seems destined to miss the goal of holiness of life and thought. Entertainment choices of believers as well as habits of life are often indistinguishable from those of the world. The slanderous gossip and heartless accusations of some Christians, added to a willingness to involve secular authorities in disputes among brethren, would have posed an enigma for Anabaptists and should be shameful in contemporary Baptist assemblies. A thirst for the ability to distinguish that which is holy is essential for Baptist futures.

THE SUPPER AS FELLOWSHIP TRUST

A cursory reading of 1 Corinthians 11:23–24 suggests that the Lord's Supper is primarily a memorial designed to focus on the atoning work of Christ. Baptism and the Supper together entail emphases on the atonement and resurrection, the two most crucial aspects of the life of Christ. Additionally, Paul apparently includes the themes of thanksgiving, proclamation, eschatological promise, and fellowship.

This last emphasis, fellowship, was integral to the Anabaptist understanding of the purpose of the Supper. As such, following Zwingli, they ascribed no sacramental value to the Supper. But unlike Zwingli, they tended to see the Supper as the appropriate place for the exercise of "the ban" in those cases of discipline that did not terminate in a happier conclusion. Walter Klaassen notes:

> Anabaptists equally rejected the Protestant discussion about the nature of the presence of Christ in the bread and wine. They regarded the discussion

---

[16]"The Admonition of 1542," in Klassen and Klaassen, *The Writings of Pilgram Marpeck*, 201.

as totally beside the point, and switched the discussion to a consideration of the presence of Christ in the "body" of believers, for which there was clear scriptural warrant. The presence of Christ was viewed, not as sacramental, but expressing itself in the exercising of the "rule of Christ" and in ethical and moral terms.[17]

The Schleitheim Confession of Michael Sattler voices a similar concern.

So it shall and must be, that whoever does not share the calling of the one God to one faith, to one baptism, to one spirit, to one body together with all the children of God, may not be made one loaf together with them, as must be true if one wishes truly to break bread according to the command of Christ.[18]

Contemporary Southern Baptists have, as a rule, failed to grasp this element of the Supper. Ample emphasis on the memorial nature of the ordinance can be found in Baptist churches, but the virtual absence of the emphasis on fellowship or community can be illustrated rather poignantly from my own failure in my first pastorate. Arriving at Sardis (why didn't they call it Smyrna?), I was intent on preparing the elements of the first celebration of the Supper under my supervision as the new pastor. This prepatory task I had taken on myself, assuming that as with most everything else in the church, the pastor was expected to make these arrangements. Armed with Welch's grape juice and small pieces of communion bread in a neat box purchased from the Baptist Book Store, I started to work.

When my kingpin deacon arrived, he looked at the bread and, less than politely, asked, "What is that?" "That is the bread for the Lord's supper," I replied confidently. "No, t'ain't," he said with some determination. "T'ain't?" I questioned. "No, t'ain't. Grandma Warren bakes the bread for the Lord's Supper," he asserted.

Now, I'm sure that's somewhere in the Bible; but for the life of me, I couldn't remember seeing it. Enter Grandma Warren with a huge loaf of bread. "What's that?" she queried, pointing to the bread. Shaken, I quickly offered, "That's a mistake, Grandma Warren."

"Don't they teach you preacher boys nuthin' down at that school?" she pressed. "Not much," I said hoping against hope that confirming her suspicions would bring the West Texas Inquisition to a conclusion. But Grandma Warren was on a roll now.

---

[17]Klaassen, *Anabaptism in Outline*, 190.
[18]Ibid., 195.

"Young preacher, do you know for sure that all of those little broken pieces of bread you brought came from the same loaf? If they didn't, then you are not telling the story of the one body of Christ. Now when the time comes, you stand up there and break the loaf for everybody so that we all know we are part of one body."

"Yes, ma'am."

Years later at First Baptist Church of Dallas, Texas, my pastor, W. A. Criswell, told me to watch carefully how he officiated at the Lord's Table. I noted a basin of water and watched in amazement as he washed his hands before three-thousand participants and proceeded to break the bread before all. I instantly concluded that, somewhere, Dr. Criswell had also studied with Grandma Warren.

This incident impressed upon my mind the importance of the Lord's Supper as fellowship, which was revolutionary to me since I had long accepted the idea that fellowship occurred after church or Sunday evening in the "fellowship hall" and was primarily for the consumption of pimento cheese sandwiches. Unfortunately, I fear that I was not alone and that Baptist churches of the modern era have seldom grasped this aspect of the Supper.

Understanding the Lord's Table as a fellowship of the Lord's body would provide a much-needed emphasis to the contemporary scene. A few churches have now raised the question about whether 1 Corinthians 5 may provide evidence that the Lord's Table is the appropriate place for the exercise of church discipline. Whether or not the passage is thus interpreted, the concept of the fellowship of the Body of Christ is a noble precept that needs to be recovered.

COURAGE OF CONVICTION

Schools and churches are fairly realistic in preparing young people for a hostile outside world. Most of our students would profess readiness to die for Christ in a hostile land, and I am convinced through my walking with these kids that a high percentage of them mean business. Suffering for the Lord at the hands of religious groups that are not committed to religious liberty is now almost an expectation. But as someone long ago noted, sometimes dying for Jesus may be easier than living for him.

The Anabaptists not only had to face fire, torture, drowning, and imprisonment, but they also encountered the misunderstanding and misrepresentation of the communities in which they lived. Some abandoned

Anabaptism. Some, like Hubmaier, recanted and then recanted their recantation. Not a few were models of faith and courage. Felix Manz was permanently baptized in the Limmat River. Sattler was tortured with white-hot tongs and then burned at the stake. Hubmaier was stretched on the rack and finally burned, and Marpeck was among the few who, while threatened often, managed to die a nonviolent death.

Hubmaier confessed both weakness and determination when he said:

> The heart of man proposes, but God disposes and directs according to His just will. I had planned to remain alone in my cellar and cave, and not to creep out into the light. Not because I shun the light, but that I might remain in peace. But God had designed otherwise, and drawn me, against my will, to give, as much as in me is, to everyone who would hear, a reason for my faith, namely in the matter of infant baptism and concerning the true Christian baptism there til now I hoped another would have done it.[19]

To his assailants, Hubmaier, sounding like Luther, said,

> If I have taught incorrectly then I implore all Christians that they likewise give me a witness with the divine word and change my error into a ladder of truth that I might climb upon it with Jacob to heaven. Therefore, I may err, I am a man but a heretic I cannot be as long as I call for instruction. If man corrects an erring donkey or ox, how much more is he responsible for correcting the erring brother by Scripture.[20]

Speaking of his Anabaptist brethren, Pilgram Marpeck gave testimony to their courage:

> Not only through external ceremonies but also through the power of Christ and his authoritative teachings and of the apostles, these people bear witness both in death and blood. And they do so uncoerced—freely, deliberately, and joyfully through the abundant comfort and power of the Holy Spirit of Christ in this world. Thus, they seal and confirm the power of Christ. Many of them have remained constant, enduring tortures inflicted by sword, rope, fire and water, and suffering terrible, tyrannical, unheard-of deaths and martyrdoms, all of which they could easily have avoided by recantation.[21]

---

[19]"On the Christian Baptism of Believers—Balthasar Hubmaier (August, 1525)," in Estep, *Anabaptist Beginnings*, 66.
[20]"A Sincere Christian Supplication and Petitions—Balthasar Hubmaier (September, 1524)," in Estep, *Anabaptist Beginnings*, 45.
[21]"A Clear Refutation," in Klassen and Klaassen, *The Writings of Pilgram Marpeck*, 50.

In America, the probability of extensive martyrdom is small, at least in the short haul. However, increasing social pressures and government intrusiveness into the realm of the churches threaten ominously. The general feminization of the social order and the marginalization of men pose hazards to home and church. The litigious inclination of the populace and the injustices of the judiciary are sufficient to frighten many aspiring pastors. If this were not enough to intimidate, Christian leaders have themselves frequently lived materialistically, selfishly, and even licentiously. In a media-rich world such failures are instantly magnified. Add to this the prevalence of gossip, innuendo, and ascription of motives that only God could know, and the picture of the local congregation is tragically marred.

To face these kinds of situations, sorrows, and heartbreaks, churches will have to recover the Anabaptist vision of suffering as a part of what it means to follow Christ. A generation of pastors, Bible teachers, and missionaries will have to be equipped not only to face the Islamic terrorist but also to stand before the carnal and malicious accusations of the sheep of the local flock, to accept the sorrows and continue solely out of a love for Christ, for his flock, and for the lost.

CONCLUSION

Anabaptists of the sixteenth century were intent on preaching the gospel to all. They held that duty in tandem with the responsibility to maintain a pure church insofar as that was humanly possible. To achieve this goal, converts were baptized immediately as a profession of faith, but somehow those early restorationists made lucid the idea that baptism was a death to the old way of life. The Lord's Supper reemphasized the concept of fellowship in the body of Christ, the body carefully following the lead of Christ, the Head. The Bible was viewed as the word of Christ to define the actions and purposes of the churches. Church discipline was practiced with a view both to the purity of the church and to the correction of erring brothers. Remarkable courage, doubtless born of sincere conviction and enhanced by the power of the indwelling Holy Spirit, transformed suffering, sorrow, and even death into superlative witness. May God help twenty-first-century Baptists recover the sixteenth-century vision of the Anabaptists!

CHAPTER SEVEN

THE ROOTS OF
BAPTIST BELIEFS

James Leo Garrett Jr.

THE PEOPLE CALLED BAPTISTS have often identified their churches as
"New Testament churches" and have frequently insisted that they are not
a creedal people. Consequently, one may be prone to assume that they owe
nothing to the creeds, the church councils, or the theologians of the sixteen
centuries prior to the advent of the Baptist movement. But that assumption
needs to be challenged and tested.

THE COUNCILS, THE CREEDS, AND THE FATHERS

The four earliest ecumenical councils constituted efforts to resolve theological
controversies after the subsidence of the major persecutions and the advent
of favorable treatment of Christians in the Roman Empire. The Council of
Nicaea (AD 325) rejected the teachings of Arius (c. 250–c. 336), notably that
God is an unoriginate and non-communicable monad and that Jesus was a
creature having a beginning and, being subject to change and sin, was "less
than God and more than man."[1] Nicaea responded by affirming that Jesus
as "the Son of God" was "of the substance of the Father," "begotten, not
made," and "of one substance with the Father."[2] Baptists have repeatedly
affirmed the deity and eternality of Jesus as God's Son and his incarnation,
thus manifesting only on rare occasions any tendency to resurrect Arianism.[3]

Some of this material appeared previously in James Leo Garrett Jr., *Baptist Theology: A Four-Century
Study* (Macon, GA: Mercer University Press, 2009), 1–22.
[1]J. N. D. Kelly, *Early Christian Doctrines* (New York: Harper and Brothers, 1958), 226–31; Jaroslav
Pelikan, *The Christian Tradition: A History of the Development of Doctrine*, vol. 1, *The Emergence of
the Catholic Tradition (100–600)* (Chicago: University of Chicago, 1971), 193–200.
[2]"The Nicene Creed," in *Nicene and Post-Nicene Fathers,* ed. Philip Schaff (Grand Rapids, MI:
Eerdmans, 1956), 14:3.
[3]Deviations, as in the case of the early eighteenth-century General Baptists, were recognized as heresy
by other Baptists.

Apollinarius of Laodicea (c. 310–c. 390) refused to allow for a human mind in Jesus by holding that the Godhead and Jesus' body were fused into a single reality.[4] The Pneumatomachians, or Macedonians, opposed the full deity of the Holy Spirit, asserting rather that the Spirit was a creature or a being between God and creatures.[5] The Council of Constantinople I (381), building on the objections by Gregory of Nyssa and Gregory of Nazianzus,[6] rejected Apollinarianism and likewise, together with other heresies, condemned the teaching of the Pneumatomachians.[7] Baptists have affirmed the full or complete humanity of Jesus[8] and the deity of the Holy Spirit.[9]

Nestorius (c. 381–c. 451) was credited with advancing the view—whether he actually did continues to be debated by today's scholars—that the two natures of Jesus Christ, the divine and human, were veritably two persons and that these two persons, being unaltered, were only "conjoined," or loosely connected. Nestorius rejected the prevailing use of the term *theotokos* ("God-bearing") for Mary the virgin, arguing that "God cannot have a mother" and "Mary bore a man, the vehicle of divinity but not God."[10] The Council of Ephesus (431), after no little intrigue, rejected Nestorianism and its followers and deposed and excommunicated Nestorius.[11] Although modern Baptist confessions of faith have tended not to address this issue specifically,[12] there is no evidence of any Baptist effort to disavow the union of the two natures in the one person of Jesus Christ.

Eutyches (c. 378–454), taking the word "nature" to signify "a concrete existence" and denying that Christ's manhood was of the same substance

---

[4]Kelly, *Early Christian Doctrines*, 289–95.

[5]Ibid., 259–60.

[6]Ibid., 295–300.

[7]Canons of Constantinople I, 1, 7, in *NPNF*, 2nd series, 14:172, 185.

[8]"Short Confession of Faith in 20 Articles, by John Smyth," art. 6; "A Declaration of Faith of English People Remaining at Amsterdam in Holland," art. 8; "Somerset Confession," art. 13; "Second London Confession of Particular Baptists," art. 8, sec. 2; "Orthodox Creed of General Baptists," art. 6, 7; "Treatise and the Faith and Practices of the Free Will Baptists," art. 5, sect. 2, in William L. Lumpkin, *Baptist Confessions of Faith*, 1st ed. (Chicago: Judson, 1959), 100, 119, 206, 260-61, 300-301, 371; "Southern Baptist Convention Statement of Baptist Faith and Message (1963)," art. 2, sec. 2, in Lumpkin, *Baptist Confessions of Faith*, rev. ed. (Valley Forge, PA: Judson Press, 1969), 394.

[9]"A Short Confession of Faith" (1610), art. 2, 3; "First London Confession of Particular Baptists," art. 2; "Orthodox Creed of General Baptists," art. 8; "Principles of Faith of the Sandy Creek Association," art. 1; "Treatise and the Faith and Practices of the Free Will Baptists," art. 7; "Articles of Faith Put Forth by the Baptist Bible Union of America," art. 3, in Lumpkin, *Baptist Confessions of Faith*, 1st ed., 103, 156–57, 301, 358, 372–73, 385; "Southern Baptist Convention Statement of Baptist Faith and Message (1963)," art. 2, sec. 3, in Lumpkin, *Baptist Confessions of Faith*, rev. ed., 394.

[10]Kelly, *Early Christian Doctrines*, 310–17. See also J. F. Bethune-Baker, *Nestorius and His Teaching: A Fresh Examination of the Evidence* (1908; repr. New York: Kraus, 1969); Friedrich Loofs, *Nestorius and His Place in the History of Christian Doctrine* (1914; repr. New York: Burt Franklin, 1975).

[11]"The Twelve Anathematisms of St. Cyril against Nestorius," and "Decree of the Council against Nestorius" in *NPNF*, 2nd series, 14:206–19.

[12]"A Short Confession of Faith (1610)," art. 8; "A Declaration of Faith of English People Remaining at Amsterdam in Holland," art. 8; "Second London Confession," art. 8, sec. 2; "Orthodox Creed of General Baptists," art. 6, 7, in Lumpkin, *Baptist Confessions of Faith*, 1st ed. 104-5, 119, 260-61, 300-301.

as our manhood, taught the confusion of his natures so as to imply one nature. Under interrogation, Eutyches acknowledged that Christ was "of two natures" but insisted that this was before the union of the natures and that after the union there was only one nature.[13] After being vindicated at the Robber Synod of 448, he was deposed and exiled by the Council of Chalcedon (451). The confessional statement adopted by Chalcedon not only rejected Eutychianism but also Arianism, Apollinarianism, and Nestorianism and explicated the doctrine of two natures in the one person.[14] It would prove in later centuries to be common ground for Roman Catholics, Eastern Orthodox, and Protestants.[15] As was noted in respect to Apollinarianism, Baptists have consistently affirmed the genuine and complete humanity of Jesus and have in reality concurred in Chalcedon's definition even when not explicitly stating such.

Hence for Baptists the affirmations of the deity of Christ, the complete humanity of Christ, the one person of Christ, and the two natures of Christ imply some indebtedness to these early councils, whether or not that indebtedness is formally acknowledged. Moreover, concurrent with these councils—Nicaea I through Chalcedon—was the framing of certain widely used Christian creeds.

That which we call the Apostles' Creed, sometimes called "R" for Old Roman Symbol, developed during the second and third centuries, being expressed in various similar but not identical texts until finally there came to be a single common text. Framed in order to give instruction at baptism or to refute heresies or possibly for both reasons, R had a Trinitarian structure and an extended section on the Son of God.[16] The Nicene Creed (N), the product of the council in 325, was specifically anti-Arian.[17] That which is called the Niceno-Constantinopolitan Creed (C) has a more extended section on the Holy Spirit. It has traditionally been taken to be the product of the Council of Constantinople I, but it did not appear in official conciliar records until the Council of Chalcedon.[18] The Athanasian Creed, actually a formulation based on the Trinitarian theology of Augustine of Hippo, probably originated in southern Gaul in the fifth or sixth century.[19]

Baptists have not normally included the recitation of any creedal or con-

---

[13]Kelly, *Early Christian Doctrines*, 330–34.
[14]"The Definition of Faith of the Council of Chalcedon," in *NPNF*, 2nd series, 14:262–65. See also R. V. Sellers, *The Council of Chalcedon: A Historical and Doctrinal Survey* (London: S. P. C. K., 1953).
[15]See James Leo Garrett Jr., "A Reappraisal of Chalcedon," *Review and Expositor* 71 (Winter 1974): 31–42, esp. 42.
[16]J. N. D. Kelly, *Early Christian Creeds*, 2nd ed. (New York: David McKay, 1960), 100–166.
[17]Ibid., 211–62.
[18]Ibid., 296–357.
[19]J. N. D. Kelly, *The Athanasian Creed* (New York: Harper and Row, 1964).

fessional statement in their congregational worship. It is, however, worthy of note that the Orthodox Creed of General Baptists (1678) included the texts of the Apostles' Creed, the Nicene Creed, and the Athanasian Creed and declared that these "ought thoroughly to be received, and believed," may be proved from the Scriptures, ought to be understood by all Christians, and should be taught by ministers and "in all christian [*sic*] families."[20] Also, at the first world congress of the Baptist World Alliance in 1905, its president, Alexander Maclaren, in the midst of his presidential address asked all those assembled to rise and to repeat the Apostles' Creed.[21]

Baptists have consistently affirmed that the canonical Scriptures are always superior to and more authoritative than any or all postbiblical tradition. Such a fact does not prevent or preclude evidence that certain of the church fathers, especially the Latin fathers, seem to have influenced positively the beliefs of the later Baptists. Two examples may be noted. Tertullian, who was the first Latin Christian writer to use the term *trinitas*, pioneered in the use of what became technical terms for the Trinity (one in substance and three persons)[22] and for the person of Christ (two natures, which he preferred to speak of as "two substances,"[23] in one person).[24]

Augustine of Hippo, especially in his controversial writings against the Pelagians, clearly set forth the doctrines of the universality of sin and the necessity of divine grace as pardon and power. This would so greatly influence all Western Christians that espousal of strictly Pelagian views would be far less likely,[25] and this was true of most Baptists.

PRE-REFORMATION SECTARIAN AND REFORMING MOVEMENTS

The modern advocates of Baptist church succession,[26] notably the Landmark Baptists, have posited and sought to identify a chain of pre-

---

[20]Art. 38, in Lumpkin, *Baptist Confessions of Faith*, 1st ed., 326–27.
[21]*The Baptist World Congress: Authorised Record of Proceedings*, London, July 11-19, 1905 (London: Baptist Union Publication Department, 1905), 20. For a probing treatment of the dependence of Baptist confessions of faith upon patristic theology and possibly more future "interaction" with the patristic tradition, see Steven R. Harmon, "Baptist Confessions of Faith and the Patristic Tradition," *Perspectives in Religious Studies* 29 (Winter 2002): 349–58.
[22]*Unius substantiae; tres dirigens* (*Against Praxeas*, 2:4).
[23]*Utramque substantiam* (*On the Flesh of Christ*, 18:6).
[24]*In uno plane* (*Against Praxeas*, 27:14).
[25]Here we do not consider either Semi-Pelagianism or those aspects of Augustine's theology that pertain to predestination and irresistible grace.
[26]This is the theory that there existed from the apostolic era to the seventeenth century in unbroken fashion churches which in teaching and practice, although not in name, were conformable to Baptists. See, for example, George Herbert Orchard, *A Concise History of Baptists from the Time of Christ Their Founder to the 18th Century* (1838; repr. Lexington, KY: Ashland Avenue Baptist Church, 1956); David Burcham Ray, *Baptist Succession: A Handbook of Baptist History* (1870; repr. Rosemead, CA: King's Press, 1949); Willis Anselm Jarrel, *Baptist Church Perpetuity, or, The Continuous Existence of Baptist Churches from*

Reformation reforming and sectarian movements. Often the claims of identity between such groups and Baptists of the last four centuries have not matched the historical evidence. But the lack of total identity does not preclude a kinship in respect to particular teachings or a common rejection of teachings and practices prevailing in the dominant ecclesiastical system. Albert Henry Newman, a Baptist historian writing more than a century ago, could find no common ground between modern Baptists and such early movements as Montanism, Novatianism, and Donatism or such later movements as the Paulicians and the Cathari. But Newman saw in early reformers such as Aerius, Jovinian, and Vigilantius and in the ancient British church an emerging anti-ascetic evangelicalism which did not challenge infant baptism, and he found in the followers of Peter de Bruys and Henry of Lausanne, the Waldenses, the Taborites, Peter Chelcicky and the Bohemian Brethren, and the Lollards advocates of anti-sacramentalism, biblical authority, and primitivism, who stopped short of the full recovery of believer's baptism.[27] Baptists have had no interest in kinship with the mystical heresy of the Free Spirit,[28] with later mystics such as John Tauler, Henry Suso, and John Ruysbroeck,[29] or with late quasi-Evangelicals such as John of Wesel, Wessel Gansfort, and Cornelius Hoen.[30]

THE MAGISTERIAL PROTESTANT REFORMATION

Despite modern denials by certain Baptists that Baptists are Protestants,[31] the matrix of the Baptist movement had been powerfully shaped by the Protestant Reformation, and some have even claimed that the Baptists are the truly thoroughgoing Reformers.[32]

Martin Luther's doctrines of the supremacy of the Scriptures over

---

the Apostolic to the Present Day Demonstrated by the Bible and by History (1894; repr. Fulton, KY: Baptist Gleaner, 1900); James Milton Carroll, *The Trail of Blood* (1931; repr. Lexington, KY: Ashland Avenue Baptist Church, 1979).

[27]Albert Henry Newman, *A History of Anti-Pedobaptism from the Rise of Pedobaptism to A.D. 1609* (Philadelphia, PA: American Baptist Publication Society, 1897), 15–61.

[28]Gordon Leff, *Heresy in the Later Middle Ages: The Relation of Heterodoxy to Dissent, c.1250–c.1450* (Manchester: Manchester University; New York: Barnes and Noble, 1967), 1:308–407.

[29]*Late Medieval Mysticism*, ed. Ray C. Petry, The Library of Christian Classics (Philadelphia, PA: Westminster, 1957), 13:245–62, 285–320.

[30]A. H. Newman, *A Manual of Church History*, rev. ed. (Philadelphia, PA: American Baptist Publication Society, 1933), 1:620–21; Heiko Augustinus Oberman, *Forerunners of the Reformation: The Shape of Late Medieval Thought* (New York: Holt, Rinehart and Winston, 1966), 63–65, 252–53.

[31]William Owen Carver, "Are Baptists Protestants?" *The Chronicle* 14 (July 1951): 116–20. Carver was refuting those who had given a negative answer largely on the basis of Baptist church successionism. According to Carver, "Anabaptists and Baptists have not improperly been described as 'Protestants of the Protestants'" (117).

[32]John Quincy Adams, *Baptists, the Only Thorough Religious Reformers*, rev. ed. (New York: Sheldon & Co., 1876).

all—especially late—church tradition and of Christ as the center of the Scriptures, of declarative justification by God's grace through faith alone, and of the priesthood of all believers[33] were all affirmed by Baptists, even when no specific acknowledgment was made to Luther. Likewise, Ulrich Zwingli's doctrine of the Lord's Supper as a memorial or symbolic observance[34] proved to be the dominant, though not the sole, theme in the Baptist teaching about the Supper. Moreover, John Calvin's doctrine of predestination,[35] whatever its debt to Augustine of Hippo, Thomas Bradwardine, John Wycliffe, and John Huss, had an impact on the theology of many Anglo-American Baptists. Martin Bucer's teaching that discipline is a mark of the true church,[36] though perhaps routed through Calvin or through the Anabaptists, found acceptance among early Baptists. Among the confessions of faith produced by the magisterial wing of the Reformation, the mid-seventeenth century Westminster Confession of Faith (1647)[37] was by far the most influential on early Baptist confessions of faith.[38]

CONTINENTAL ANABAPTISM

The sixteenth-century Anabaptists on the continent of Europe have played a singular role in the interpretation of Baptist origins. Those advocating different views of origins[39] have treated the Anabaptists differently. Those

---

[33]Paul Althaus, *The Theology of Martin Luther*, trans. Robert C. Schultz (Philadelphia, PA: Fortress, 1966), 72–102, 224–50, 313–18; A. Skevington Wood, *Captive to the Word: Martin Luther, Doctor of Sacred Scripture* (Exeter, UK: Paternoster, 1969), 119–28; E. F. Klug, *From Luther to Chemnitz: On Scripture and the Word* (Grand Rapids, MI: Eerdmans, 1971), 51–75.

[34]W. Peter Stevens, *Zwingli: An Introduction to His Thought* (Oxford: Oxford University Press, 1992), 94–110, esp. 98–99.

[35]Francois Wendel, *Calvin: The Origins and Development of His Religious Thought*, trans. Philip Mairet (New York: Harper and Row, 1963), 263–84.

[36]D. F. Wright, introduction to *Common Places*, by Martin Bucer, trans. and ed. D. F. Wright, The Courtenay Library of Reformation Classics (Abingdon, UK: Sutton Courtenay, 1972), 4:31.

[37]For the text, see Philip Schaff, *The Creeds of Christendom*, (New York: Harper and Brothers, 1877), 3:598–704.

[38]Especially "Second London Confession of Particular Baptists" and "Orthodox Creed of General Baptists," in Lumpkin, *Baptist Confessions of Faith*, 1st ed., 241–95, 297–334.

[39]Here we follow the threefold classification of Robert G. Torbet, *A History of the Baptists* (Philadelphia, PA: Judson, 1950), 59–62. Those advocating Anabaptist influence on English Baptists in terms of teachings, if not an organizational nexus, included Ernest Alexander Payne, *The Free Church Tradition in the Life of England* (London: SCM, 1944), 25, 27–28; Payne, *The Baptist Movement in the Reformation and Onwards* (London: Kingsgate, 1947), 20; Payne, *The Anabaptists of the 16th Century and Their Influence in the Modern World* (London: Carey Kingsgate, 1949); Payne, "Who Were the Baptists?" *Baptist Quarterly* 16 (October 1956): 339–42; Alfred Clair Underwood, *A History of the English Baptists* (London: Carey Kingsgate, 1947), 21–27, 35–55; James D. Mosteller, "Baptists and Anabaptists," *The Chronicle* 20 (January 1957): 3–27; ibid. (July 1957): 100–114; William R. Estep Jr., "A Baptist Reappraisal of Sixteenth Century Anabaptists," *Review and Expositor* 55 (January 1958): 55–58; Estep, *The Anabaptist Story* (Nashville: Broadman, 1963), 200–222; and Glen H. Stassen, "Anabaptist Influence in the Origin of the Particular Baptists," *Mennonite Quarterly Review* 36 (October 1962): 322–48. Those advocating the English Separatist origin of English Baptists with little or no influence from continental Anabaptism included Winthrop Still Hudson, "Baptists Were Not Anabaptists," *The Chronicle* 16 (October 1953): 171–79; Hudson, "Who Were the Baptists?" *Baptist Quarterly* 16 (July 1956): 303–12;

who have sought to trace Baptists in succession back to John the Baptist and the Jerusalem church have regarded the Anabaptists as an essential link in the chain of succession but have usually done little research or exhibited no scholarly acumen in dealing with the Anabaptists. Those who have adhered to the "Anabaptist spiritual kinship" theory have posited on the basis of careful studies not only of sixteenth-century Anabaptists but also various pre-Reformation rebaptizing sects as kinspeople to the later Baptists. Those who hold, on the basis of research, that Baptists derived from English Separatist Puritanism usually have viewed Anabaptists as outside the story of Baptist origins and as not contributing significantly to Baptist theology.[40]

The classification of various types of sixteenth-century Anabaptists has been attempted by modern church historians who have specialized in this field. Their work is important in determining whether and which Anabaptists may have influenced Baptists. A. H. Newman posited a fivefold classification of Anabaptists: "the chiliastic" or millennial, "the soundly biblical," "the mystical," "the pantheistic," and "the anti-trinitarian."[41] George Huntston Williams, within the larger framework of a threefold classification of "the Radical Reformation" (Anabaptists, Spiritualists, and Evangelical Rationalists), identified three types of Anabaptists: "revolutionary," "contemplative," and "evangelical."[42] Newman's "chiliastic" Anabaptists and Williams's "revolutionary" Anabaptists, which included Melchior Hofmann and the Munster kingdom, were virtually identical but did not seemingly shape in a positive way the later Baptists, except at the point of Hofmann's Christology.[43] Williams's "contemplative" Anabaptists included Hans Denck and Ludwig Hetzer, as did Newman's "mystical" Anabaptists, but Williams did not include Newman's "panthe-

---

ibid., 17 (April 1957): 53–55; Norman H. Maring, "Notes from Religious Journals," *Foundations* 1 (July 1958): 91–95; Lonnie D. Kliever, "General Baptist Origins: The Question of Anabaptist Influence," *Mennonite Quarterly Review* 36 (October 1962): 291–321; Barrington R. White, *The English Separatist Tradition: From the Marian Martyrs to the Pilgrim Fathers* (London: Oxford University, 1971), 161–64; White, *The English Baptists of the Seventeenth Century*, A History of the English Baptists (London: Baptist Historical Society, 1983), 1:21–23; and H. Leon McBeth, *The Baptist Heritage* (Nashville: Broadman, 1987), 49–63.

[40]For a detailed account of the historiography of Anabaptist-Baptist relations, see Goki Saito, "An Investigation into the Relationships between the Early English Baptists and the Dutch Anabaptists" (ThD diss., Southern Baptist Theological Seminary, 1974), 11–58.

[41]Newman, *A Manual of Church History*, 2:156–200.

[42]Introduction to Part One, in *Spiritual and Anabaptist Writers*, ed. George Huntston Williams and Angel M. Mergal, The Library of Christian Classics (Philadelphia, PA: Westminster, 1957), 25:28–31. Williams also set forth a threefold classification of Spiritualists: "revolutionary," "rational," and "evangelical" (ibid., 32–35).

[43]George Huntston Williams, *The Radical Reformation* (Philadelphia, PA: Westminster, 1962), 328–32; William R. Estep Jr., *The Anabaptist Story: An Introduction to Sixteenth-Century Anabaptism*, 3rd ed. (Grand Rapids, MI: Eerdmans, 1996), 290–91.

istic" Anabaptists such as David Ions, and Williams considered Caspar Schwenkfeld to have been an "evangelical Spiritualist." None of these can be seen as having significant influence upon the later Baptists. The same may be said of Newman's "anti-trinitarian Anabaptists," who may be equated with Williams's "Evangelical Rationalists," whose only traceable influence may have been that of Socinianism on the Mennonite-oriented Rhynsburger community,[44] from which Particular Baptists seemingly derived the practice of baptism by immersion. Hence the focus must clearly rest upon those whom Newman denominated "soundly biblical" Anabaptists, namely, the Swiss Brethren, the Hutterites, and the Mennonites.

Who, then, were the theological writers among evangelical Anabaptists who may possibly have influenced the Baptists even indirectly? An excellent foretaste of Anabaptist teachings may be seen in George Blaurock's account of his meeting with two Swiss, Conrad Grebel and Felix Mantz: "They came to one mind in these things, and in the pure fear of God they recognized that a person must learn from the divine Word and preaching a true faith which manifests itself in love, and receive the true Christian baptism on the basis of the recognized and confessed faith, in the union with God of a good conscience, (prepared) henceforth to serve God in a holy Christian life with all godliness, also to be steadfast to the end in tribulation."[45]

Moreover, when Grebel and his associates wrote to Thomas Müntzer, a revolutionary Spiritualist and anti-paedobaptist, they urged him, "Go forward with the Word and establish a Christian church with the help of Christ and his rule, as we find it instituted in Matt. 18:15–18 and applied in the Epistles."[46] Reflective of the ecclesiological concerns of the early Swiss Anabaptists were the Schleitheim Articles (1527), probably the work of Michael Sattler, with their sevenfold emphasis: believer's baptism, excommunication, the Lord's Supper, separation from the world, the office of pastor, non-use of the sword, and non-taking of oaths.[47]

Balthasar Hubmaier wrote his 36-article "On Heretics and Those Who Burn Them," "the first text of the Reformation directed specifically

---

[44]On the Rhynsburgers, see Newman, A History of Anti-Pedobaptism, 321–22, 387.

[45]Excerpted from the Hutterite Chronicle, in Williams and Mergal, Spiritual and Anabaptist Writers, 43.

[46]Grebel and others, "Letters to Thomas Müntzer," in Williams and Mergal, Spiritual and Anabaptist Writers, 79.

[47]For the text, see Lumpkin, Baptist Confessions of Faith, 1st ed., 23–31, and John Howard Yoder, trans. and ed., The Legacy of Michael Sattler, Classics of the Radical Reformation (Scottsdale, PA: Herald, 1973), 1:34–43.

to the topic of the liberty of dissent,"[48] four major treatises on baptism,[49] a treatise on excommunication,[50] and a treatise entitled "On the Sword,"[51] which was directed against his more pacifist fellow Anabaptists. It is not a question as to whether early English Baptists read the German-language writings by Hubmaier; rather it is whether his concepts of religious freedom, baptism, church discipline, and the rightful use of the sword[52] may have so crossed the English Channel as to make their advocacy by English Baptists something less than an innovation.

Pilgram Marpeck's two major writings contain a recurrent emphasis on the differences between the Old Testament and the New Testament and a rather complete treatment of baptism as "witness" (*Zeugnis*) rather than as "symbol" (*Zeichen*).[53]

Among the numerous writings by Menno Simons were his *Foundation of Christian Doctrine*,[54] with its threefold "call to discipleship," refutation of Roman Catholicism, and "appeals for toleration," his *Christian Baptism*,[55] three treatises on church discipline,[56] and three writings expressive of his peculiar view of the incarnation.[57] The argument has been made that the First London Confession of Particular Baptists (1644) was indebted to Menno's *Foundation of Christian Doctrine*.[58] Whatever influence his writings on church discipline may have had on early English Baptists such as John Smyth, any such influ-

---

[48]Introduction to "On Heretics and Those Who Burn Them," in H. Wayne Pipkin and John Howard Yoder, trans. and ed., *Balthasar Hubmaier: Theologian of Anabaptism*, Classics of the Radical Reformation (Scottdale, PA and Kitchener, ON: Herald, 1989), 5:58. H. C. Vedder and William R. Estep Jr. have held that Hubmaier was espousing full religious freedom for all humankind (Vedder, *Balthasar Hubmaier: The Leader of the Anabaptists* [New York: G. P. Putnam's Sons, 1905], 84; Estep, *Revolution within the Revolution: The First Amendment in Historical Context, 1612-1789* [Grand Rapids, MI: Eerdmans, 1990], 30, esp. n. 11), whereas Torsten Bergsten held that Hubmaier was calling only for religious freedom for the Anabaptists in Waldshut (*Balthasar Hubmaier: Anabaptist Theologian and Martyr*, trans. Irwin J. Barnes and William R. Estep Jr., ed. William R. Estep Jr. [Valley Forge, PA: Judson, 1978], 131–32).

[49]"On the Christian Baptism of Believers," "Dialogue with Zwingli's Baptism Book," "Old and New Teachers on Believer's Baptism," and "On Infant Baptism against Oecolampad," in Pipkin and Yoder, *Balthasar Hubmaier*, 95–149, 170–233, 246–74, 276–95.

[50]"On the Christian Ban," in ibid., 410–25.

[51]Ibid., 494–523. This treatise helps to explain why for modern Mennonites Hubmaier is not such a hero, whereas for Baptists he is. Baptists have followed Hubmaier in holding that a Christian can be a civil magistrate and therein make proper use of the sword.

[52]See Bergsten, *Balthasar Hubmaier*, 382–98, esp. 385, 387, 397–98.

[53]"Confession of 1532" and "The Admonition of 1542," in *The Writings of Pilgram Marpeck*, trans. and ed. William Klassen and Walter Klaassen, Classics of the Radical Reformation (Scottdale, PA, and Kitchener, ON: Herald, 1978), 2:108–57, 160–302; Introduction to "Confession of 1532," Klassen and Klaassen, *Pilgram Marpeck*, 107.

[54]*The Complete Writings of Menno Simons, c. 1496-1561*, trans. Leonard Verduin, ed. J. C. Wenger (Scottdale, PA: Herald, 1956), 103–226.

[55]Ibid., 227–87.

[56]"A Kind Admonition on Church Discipline," "A Clear Account of Excommunication," and "Instruction on Excommunication," in ibid., 407–18, 455–85, 959–98.

[57]"Brief and Clear Confession," "The Incarnation of Our Lord," and "Reply to Martin Micron," in ibid., 419–54, 783–834, 835–913.

[58]Stassen, "Anabaptist Influence," 322–48, esp. 347.

ence stopped short of Baptist acceptance of "shunning," or the social ostracism of those excommunicated, including that of husband and wife.[59] Furthermore, Menno's views of the incarnation—namely, that since women supposedly produce no seed, the Word became a human being in Mary, but not of or from Mary,[60] being akin to the teaching of Melchior Hofmann[61] as to the celestial flesh of Jesus—posed a problem for the early English General Baptists but did not gain acceptance by them.[62] Dietrich (or Dirk) Philips in his *Enchiridion* identified seven "ordinances" of the true church[63] and its twelve "notes,"[64] the latter drawn from the New Testament Apocalypse. The early English Baptists would also identify and characterize the church as distinct from the eschatological kingdom of God. Baptists have not accepted the teaching about the community of goods set forth by Hutterite theologian Peter Rideman,[65] but some of his ecclesiological images[66] were employed by later Baptists.

What specific Anabaptist teachings, therefore, can be identified as possibly influencing, even indirectly, the English Baptists? In answering this question, we will utilize two Mennonite confessions of faith, the Waterland Confession (1580) and the Dordrecht Confession (1632).[67] First, there is believer's baptism as constitutive of a gathered or truly ordered church. The Schleitheim Articles[68] and the Waterland Confession[69] specified believer's

---

[59]"Short Confession of Faith in 20 Articles by John Smyth," art. 18; "A Short Confession of Faith" (1610), art. 34; "A Declaration of Faith of English People Remaining at Amsterdam in Holland," art. 18, in Lumpkin, *Baptist Confessions of Faith*, 1st ed., 101 , 111, 121. The only confession favorable to shunning seems to have been "Propositions and Conclusions concerning True Christian Religion," art. 80, in Lumpkin, *Baptist Confessions of Faith*, 1st ed., 139.

[60]Wenger, introduction to "Brief and Clear Confession," in *Menno Simons*, 420.

[61]See Williams, *The Radical Reformation*, 325–32. As to Menno's slight alteration of Hofmann's doctrine, see ibid., 395–96, 503.

[62]Thomas Helwys opposed all forms of denial that Jesus took his human body from Mary in his *An Advertisement or Admonition unto the Congregations, which Men Call the New Fryelers* (London, 1611) and "accused John Smyth of accepting the Christology of the Mennonites." See James Robert Coggins, *John Smyth's Congregation: English Separatism, Mennonite Influence, and the Elect Nation*, Studies in Anabaptist and Mennonite History (Waterloo, ON: Herald, 1991), 32:123–26; "A Declaration of Faith of English People Remaining at Amsterdam in Holland," art. 8, in Lumpkin, *Baptist Confessions of Faith*, 1st ed., 119.

[63]Pure doctrine, two sacraments, footwashing, evangelical separation, command of disciples to love one another, keeping of Christ's commandments, and endurance of persecution ("The Church of God," in Williams and Mergal, *Spiritual and Anabaptist Writers*, 240–55).

[64]The Holy City, the New Jerusalem, its having come down from heaven, a bride, the glory of God, high walls, twelve gates, without temple yet purified by tribulation, the gates being open, stream of living water and trees of life, inclusion of Gentiles and exclusion of the wicked, and servants seeing, serving, and reigning with the Lord, in ibid., 255–60.

[65]Peter Rideman, *Account of Our Religion, Doctrine and Faith*, trans. Kathleen E. Hasenberg (London: Hodder and Stoughton, 1950), 88–91.

[66]Especially holy people, bride, body, assembly of the true children of God, gathering by the Holy Spirit, light of the world, and community of saints (ibid., 38–44, 114).

[67]For the texts, see Lumpkin, *Baptist Confessions of Faith*, 1st ed., 44–66, 67–78.

[68]Art. 1, in ibid., 25.

[69]Art. 31, in ibid., 60.

baptism, and the Dordrecht Confession[70] related it to incorporation into the church. An early Helwys confession[71] was explicit both about believer's baptism and the constituting of churches, whereas other General and Particular Baptist confessions[72] only affirmed believer's baptism. A possible negation of such Mennonite influence comes from Irwin B. Horst's argument that so-called Anabaptists in pre-Elizabethan England did not practice believer's baptism.[73] But the Separatists retained pedobaptism, and John Smyth's congregation was in Amsterdam. For William R. Estep Jr., there was "little doubt that Mennonite influence played a role in Smyth's rethinking of the biblical teachings on baptism and the church."[74]

Second, there is church discipline as necessary to the life of the true church, especially on the basis of Matthew 18:15–17. Anabaptist confessions[75] clearly specified admonition and excommunication, or the ban, and the same was true of early English General and Particular Baptist confessions.[76]

Third, there is the elevation of the New Testament in authority over the Old Testament, especially in matters of ecclesiology. Marpeck had elevated the New Testament while retaining the canonicity and inspiration of the Old Testament.[77] Although this elevation of the New Testament is not specifically stated in the earliest Baptist confessions of faith, John Smyth's *Principles and Inferences concerning the Visible Church* (1607)[78] exhibits much greater reliance on the New Testament than the Old.[79]

Fourth, there is the advocacy of religious freedom for all human beings and the absence of persecution. Although the claim that Hubmaier advocated such freedom has been challenged,[80] the advocacy by Menno

---

[70]Art. 7, in ibid., 71.

[71]"A Declaration of Faith of English People Remaining at Amsterdam in Holland," art. 13, 14, in ibid., 120.

[72]"Propositions and Conclusions concerning True Christian Religion," art. 70; "First London Confession of Particular Baptists," art. 39; "Second London Confession of Particular Baptists," art. 29, sec. 2, in Lumpkin, *Baptist Confessions of Faith*, 1st ed., 137, 167, 291.

[73]*The Radical Brethren: Anabaptism and the English Reformation to 1558*, Bibliotheca Humanistica and Reformatorica (Nieuwkoop: B. de Graaf, 1972), 2:178.

[74]Estep, *Revolution within the Revolution*, 45. See also Estep, "On the Origins of English Baptists," *Baptist History and Heritage* 22 (April 1987): 19–26.

[75]"Schleitheirn Articles," art. 2; "Waterland Confession," art. 35, in Lumpkin, *Baptist Confessions of Faith*, 1st ed., 25, 62.

[76]"Short Confession of Faith in 20 Articles by John Smyth," art. 17; "A Short Confession of Faith" (1610), art. 33, 34; "A Declaration of Faith of English People Remaining at Amsterdam in Holland," art. 17; "First London Confession of Particular Baptists," art. 42, 43, in ibid., 101, 110–11, 121, 168.

[77]William Klassen, *Covenant and Community: The Life, Writings, and Hermeneutics of Pilgram Marpeck* (Grand Rapids, MI: Eerdmans, 1968), 105, 124–30; Estep, *The Anabaptist Story*, 193–95.

[78]In *The Works of John Smyth, Fellow of Christ's College, 1594-8*, ed. W. T. Whitley, tercentenary ed. (Cambridge: Cambridge University, 1915), 1:249–68. See also Estep, *Revolution within the Revolution*, 41.

[79]For a modern Baptist exposition of the supremacy of the New Testament, see Henry Cook, *What Baptists Stand For* (London: Kingsgate Press, 1947), 13–24.

[80]See n. 48 above.

Simons[81] is rather clear. Likewise, Smyth,[82] Helwys,[83] Mark Leonard Busher,[84] and John Murton[85] were advocates.

Finally, the fact needs to be noted that certain Mennonite teachings and practices, identifiably four, were specifically rejected by the early English Baptists. First, Baptists[86] rejected the Anabaptist teaching[87] that Christians ought not to serve as civil magistrates because they must use the sword, although John Smyth was an exception.[88] Second, Baptists[89] rejected the Anabaptist teaching[90] that Christians ought not to be soldiers but rather be nonresistant. Third, Baptists,[91] with the exception of John Smyth,[92] rejected the Anabaptist teaching[93] that Christians ought not to take civil oaths. Fourth, Baptists rejected, as noted previously,[94] the Mennonite practice[95] of shunning those who have been excommunicated.

ENGLISH SEPARATIST PURITANS

Separatists are understood to have been those English Puritans who, not being willing to continue to await thoroughgoing reforms in the Church of England, separated therefrom by constituting congregations or conventicles on the basis of a church covenant and congregational polity. B. R. White has insisted that their goal was not so much reformation of the existing church as restitution of New Testament Christianity.[96]

Certain precursors to the Separatists have been identified, although the extent to which the Separatists acknowledged them as their forerunners is

---

[81]"Foundation of Christian Doctrine," part 3; "A Pathetic Supplication to All Magistrates"; "Brief Defense to All Theologians"; "The Cross of the Saints," in Wenger, *Menno Simons*, 190–226, 525–31, 535–40, 581–622.

[82]"Propositions and Conclusions concerning True Christian Religion," art. 84, in Lumpkin, *Baptist Confessions of Faith*, 1st ed., 140.

[83]Thomas Helwys, *A Short Declaration of the Mistery [sic] of Iniquity* (1612), replica ed. (London: Kingsgate, 1935).

[84]"Religion's Peace; or, A Plea for Liberty of Conscience" (1614), in *Tracts on Liberty of Conscience and Persecution, 1614-1661*, ed. Edward Bean Underhill (London: J. Haddon, 1846), 1–81.

[85]"Objections Answered by Way of Dialogue" (1615) and "A Most Humble Supplication of Many of the King's Majesty's Loyal Subjects" (1620), in ibid., 85–231.

[86]"A Declaration of Faith of English People Remaining at Amsterdam in Holland," art. 24, in Lumpkin, *Baptist Confessions of Faith*, 1st ed., 122–23.

[87]"Schleitheim Articles," art. 6; "Waterland Confession," art. 37, in ibid., 27–28, 63–64.

[88]"A Short Confession of Faith" (1610), art. 35, in ibid., 111–12.

[89]"Second London Confession of Particular Baptists," art. 24, sec. 2, in ibid., 284.

[90]"Dordrecht Confession," art. 14, in ibid., 75–76.

[91]"A Declaration of Faith of English People Remaining at Amsterdam in Holland," art. 25, in ibid., 123.

[92]"A Short Confession of Faith" (1610), art. 36; "Propositions and Conclusions concerning True Christian Religion," art. 86, in ibid., 112, 140.

[93]"Schleitheim Articles," art. 7; "Waterland Confession," art. 38; "Dordrecht Confession," art. 15, in ibid., 29–30, 64, 76.

[94]See n. 59 above.

[95]"Waterland Confession," art. 36; "Dordrecht Confession," art. 17, in ibid., 63, 77.

[96]White, *The English Separatist Tradition*, xii, xiii, 2.

disputed. Sectarian "Freewillers"[97] in Kent and Essex during the reign of Edward VI (1547–1553) were cited by Champlin Burrage,[98] but White[99] discounted them as forerunners. The Strangers' Church—composed of foreigners, established by John a Lasco, expelled under Mary, and reconstituted under Elizabeth I—according to Timothy George, "with their own liturgy and discipline, was itself a source of envy on the part of some who found the pace of reformation in the established Church intolerably slow."[100] Secret conventicles, especially one in the London area, during Mary's reign (1553–1558), which seem to have been distinct from the earlier Freewillers,[101] "were sustained by the ministry of itinerant preachers" and practiced excommunication.[102] During the early Elizabethan era there were congregations that were distinct from the Church of England in their worship and met in private homes, but they left no evidence of any teaching or practice of a covenanted or gathered church.[103] From one of these, the Plumbers' Hall Church in London, Puritan rather than Separatist,[104] which claimed a biblical warrant for church reform and practiced church discipline,[105] some members departed and united with the Privy Church.[106] The latter, led by Richard Fitz, was clearly Separatist vis-à-vis the Church of England,[107] indeed "the first-known congregation in England which had a covenant." "To obey this covenant each member separately pledged himself and then took communion as a ratification of his consent."[108]

Major writings by Separatist authors gave expression to Separatist principles.[109] Robert Harrison (?–c. 1585) in *A Treatise of the Church and the Kingdome of Christ* (c. 1580) equated the church and the kingdom, enjoined the observance of Matthew 18:15–17, and defended a separated

---

[97]See O. T. Hargrave, "The Freewillers in the English Reformation," *Church History* 37 (September 1968): 271–80, who identified these as "Arminians *avant la letter*" (280).

[98]Champlin Burrage, *The Early English Dissenters in the Light of Recent Research, 1550-1641* (1912; repr. New York: Russell and Russell, 1967), 1:50–53; 2:1–6.

[99]White, *The English Separatist Tradition*, 2–3.

[100]Timothy George, *John Robinson and the English Separatist Tradition*, NABPR Dissertation Series, no.1 (Macon, GA: Mercer University Press, 1982), 16.

[101]W. M. S. West, "The Anabaptists and the Rise of the Baptist Movement," in *Christian Baptism: A Fresh Attempt to Understand the Rite in Terms of Scripture, History, and Theology*, ed. Alec Gilmore (Philadelphia, PA: Judson, 1959), 255.

[102]George, *John Robinson*, 17–23. White has treated these as precursors to the Separatists (*The English Separatist Tradition*, 6–14).

[103]West, "The Anabaptists," 258.

[104]Burrage, *The Early English Dissenters*, 1:79–86.

[105]George, *John Robinson*, 27–31.

[106]Estep, *The Anabaptist Story*, 278.

[107]Burrage, *The Early English Dissenters*, 1:86–93; 2:9–18; White, *The English Separatist Tradition*, 29–32; Estep, *The Anabaptist Story*, 179–80.

[108]West, "The Anabaptists," 258–59.

[109]McBeth has labeled Robert Browne's congregation "the pioneer church," Francis Johnson's "the ancient church," John Robinson's "the pilgrim church," and Henry Jacob's "the JLJ church" (*The Baptist Heritage*, 27–32).

and gathered church.[110] Robert Browne's (c. 1550–1633) *A Treatise of Reformation without Tarying for Anie* (1582) endorsed the civil duties of the magistrates but denied them the power to reform the church, conceived of the risen Christ as ruling covenanted congregations, and called on Puritans not to "tarry" for magisterial reform.[111] Henry Barrow (c. 1550–1593) in *Four Causes of Separation* (1587) identified the false manner of worshiping the true God, the ungodly members retained in churches, the anti-Christian ministry imposed on the churches, and the anti-Christian polity of churches.[112] Barrow and John Greenwood (?–1593) in *The True Church and the False Church* (1588) extended the list of marks of the false church to eleven,[113] and Barrow in *A True Description out of the Worde of God, of the Visible Church* (1589) prescribed a fivefold ministry (pastor, doctor, elders, deacons, widows).[114] Barrow's anti-Anglican polemic reached its full expression in *A Brief Discoverie of the False Church* (1590).[115] Henry Ainsworth (1571–c. 1622) answered the Oxford doctors in *An Apologie or Defence of Such True Christians as One Commonly (but Unjustly) Called Brownists* (1604),[116] whereas Francis Johnson (1562–1618) in *Certayne Reasons and Arguments Proving That It Is Not Lawfull to Heare or Have Any Spiritual Communion with the Present Ministerie of the Church of England* (1608)[117] set forth seven reasons.

The Separatist congregation in London of which Francis Johnson was pastor, but which was exiled in Amsterdam without Johnson and which then chose Henry Ainsworth as pastor, framed in 1596 a confession of faith entitled *A True Confession*. It expressed Calvinistic doctrine and congregational polity and would be used "as a model" by Particular Baptist churches in London when they framed their 1644 Confession.[118] Among its major doctrines were divine foreordination to salvation and to condemnation, the fall of Adam and its consequences, Christ's offices as mediator, prophet, priest, and king, the royal priesthood of the people of God, the identification of the church with Christ's spiritual kingdom, the fivefold ministry,

---

[110]For the text, see Albert Peel and Leland H. Carlson, eds., *The Writings of Robert Harrison and Robert Browne*, Elizabethan Nonconformist Texts (London: George Allen and Unwin, 1953), 2:31–69.

[111]For the text, see ibid., 151–70. See also White, *The English Separatist Tradition*, 58–62.

[112]For the text, see Henry Barrow, *The Writings of Henry Barrow, 1587-1590*, ed. Leland H. Carlson, Elizabethan Nonconformist Texts (London: George Allen and Unwin, 1962), 3:54–66.

[113]For the text, see John Greenwood, *The Writings of John Greenwood; 1587-1590, together with the Joint Writings of Henry Barrow and John Greenwood; 1587-1590*, ed. Leland H. Carlson, Elizabethan Nonconformist Texts (London: George Allen and Unwin, 1962), 4:98–102.

[114]For the text, see Barrow, *The Writings of Henry Barrow*, 2:4–23.

[115]For the text, see ibid., 263–673.

[116]Photocopy from Cambridge University Library.

[117]Photocopy from Bodleian Library, Oxford.

[118]Lumpkin, *Baptist Confessions of Faith*, 1st ed., 79–81.

congregational polity, and the duty of civil magistrates to suppress false religions and establish the true religion.[119]

What specific Separatist doctrines may have positively influenced the early English Baptists? First, there is humanity's Adamic disability. The First London Confession of Particular Baptists[120] employed language almost identical to that of *A True Confession*,[121] and the Second London Confession,[122] being a revision of the Westminster Confession of Faith, was even more specific as to humanity's being "in" Adam and Eve when they fell. Second, we take note of the Bible as the rule of faith and practice. *A True Confession* described the Bible as "the rule of this knowledge, faith and obedience,"[123] and the Second London Confession, modifying the Westminster's language, declared, "The Holy Scripture is the only sufficient, certain, and infallible rule of all saving Knowledge, Faith, and Obedience."[124] Third, the royal priesthood of all Christians seems to have come to the Baptists from Separatism. Whereas both Anabaptist[125] and Separatist[126] documents referred to the offices of Christ as prophet, priest, and king, only *A True Confession*[127] taught the universal Christian priesthood specifically and in detail. Fourth, there is congregational polity, about which the Separatists were very explicit. *A True Confession*[128] explains the congregation's duties respecting its ministers, excommunication and its careful use, and mutual counsel and help among congregations. A Helwys confession taught that no congregation should assert any "prerogative" over another,[129] the First London Confession spelled out the authority of each congregation to choose its officers,[130] and the Second London Confession taught that congregations have authority over their worship and discipline and for choosing and ordaining both bishops or elders and deacons.[131]

But there were some Separatist teachings that were rejected or at least not accepted by early English Baptists. First, there is double predestina-

---

[119]For the text, see ibid., 82–97.
[120]Art. 5, in ibid., 158.
[121]Art. 5, in ibid., 83.
[122]"Second London," art. 6, esp. sec. 2, 3, in ibid., 258–59; "Westminster," art. 6, esp. sec. 2, 3, in Philip Schaff, *The Creeds of Christendom*, 4th ed. (New York: Harper and Brothers, 1919), 3:615–16.
[123]Art. 7, in Lumpkin, *Baptist Confessions of Faith*, 1st ed., 84.
[124]"Second London," art. 1, sec. 1, in ibid., 248; "Westminster," art. 1, in Schaff, *The Creeds of Christendom*, 3:600–606.
[125]"Waterland Confession," art. 11, 12, 14, in Lumpkin, *Baptist Confessions of Faith*, 1st ed., 50–51.
[126]"A True Confession," art. 10, 12–18, in ibid., 85–88.
[127]"A True Confession," art. 14, 17, in ibid., 85–86, 87.
[128]Ibid., art. 22–25, 38, in ibid., 89–90, 94.
[129]"A Declaration of English People Remaining at Amsterdam in Holland," art. 11–12, in Lumpkin, *Baptist Confessions of Faith*, 1st ed., 120.
[130]Art. 36, in ibid., 166.
[131]Art. 26, sec. 7–9, in ibid., 286–87.

tion, which was clearly taught in *A True Confession*,[132] whereas the First London Confession[133] referred only to election to salvation and vengeance toward, not foreordination of, the nonelect. According to the Second London Confession,[134] the nonelect are "left to act in their sin to their just condemnation" in what some call the doctrine of preterition (passing over). Moreover, the Westminster Confession's references to foreordination "to everlasting death" and ordination to wrath were deleted.[135] The Orthodox Creed of General Baptists, building upon the Westminster, relocated and rewrote the doctrine of divine decrees so as to treat them as conditional.[136]

Second, the doctrine of double reconciliation was not retained. According to *A True Confession*,[137] not only are elect human beings reconciled to God through the death of Jesus Christ but also God is reconciled to elect humans through the cross. But the First London Confession[138] referred only to Christ's reconciliation of the elect, and the Second London[139] likewise affirmed single reconciliation.

Third, some functions of civil magistrates taught by Separatists were rejected by Baptists. As previously noted, according to *A True Confession*[140] magistrates have the power and function of suppressing false religions and establishing the true religion. On the other hand, the First London Confession[141] acknowledged subjection to king and parliament as to civil laws but declared that conscientious objection to some ecclesiastical laws may be necessary. The framers of the Second London Confession[142] deleted the Westminster doctrine of the suppression of false religions and generally emphasized obedience to and prayer for magistrates.

Fourth, whereas *A True Confession*[143] never questioned or deviated from pedobaptism, the earliest Baptist confessions of faith[144] clearly taught believer's baptism.

---

[132]Art. 3, in ibid., 82–83.

[133]Art. 5–6, in ibid., 158.

[134]Art. 3, sec. 3, in ibid., 254.

[135]"Second London," art. 3, sec. 3, 6–7, in ibid., 254–55; "Westminster," art. 3, sec. 3, 7, in Schaff, *The Creeds of Christendom*, 3:608–10.

[136]Art. 9–10, in Lumpkin, *Baptist Confessions of Faith*, 1st ed., 302–4.

[137]Art. 14, in ibid., 85–86.

[138]Art. 17, in ibid., 160–61.

[139]Art. 8, sec. 5, in ibid., 262.

[140]Art. 39, in ibid., 94–95.

[141]Art. 49, 52, in ibid., 169, 170.

[142]Art. 24, in ibid., 283–84; "Westminster," art. 23, in Schaff, *The Creeds of Christendom*, 3:652–55.

[143]Art. 35, in Lumpkin, *Baptist Confessions of Faith*, 1st ed., 93.

[144]"Short Confessions of Faith in 20 Articles by John Smyth," art. 14; "A Short Confession of Faith" (1610), art. 29; "A Declaration of Faith of English People Remaining at Amsterdam in Holland," art. 14; "Propositions and Conclusions concerning True Christian Religion," art. 70; "First London Confession," art. 39; "Midland Association Confession," art. 13; "Standard Confession of General Baptists," art. 11; "Second London Confession," art. 29, sec. 2; and "Orthodox Creed of General Baptists," art. 28, in ibid., 101, 109–10, 120, 137, 167, 199, 228–29, 291, 317–18.

In summary, Baptists have adhered to the Trinitarian and Christological doctrines formulated by the first four ecumenical councils and expressed in the earliest Christian creeds. They have shared with medieval sectarian and reforming groups anti-ascetical, anti-sacramental, and primitivist intentions. They seem to have been indebted to various magisterial Reformers: Luther for the supremacy of the Scriptures over tradition, justification by grace through faith, and the priesthood of all Christians; Zwingli for a memorialist understanding of the Lord's Supper; Bucer for church discipline as essential to the true church; and Calvin for predestination as a major doctrine. Continental Anabaptist influence can most clearly be seen in believer's baptism as constitutive of a truly ordered church, church discipline as necessary, the New Testament as superior to the Old Testament, and religious freedom for all humans. English Separatist influence can be most accurately identified in terms of humanity's Adamic disability, the Bible as the rule of faith and practice, the priesthood of all Christians, and congregational polity.

PART TWO

MINISTRY AND CONVENTION PERSPECTIVES

CHAPTER EIGHT

AXIOMS OF A COOPERATING SOUTHERN BAPTIST

Morris H. Chapman

IN THIS CHAPTER I will seek to address the subject of connectionalism versus cooperation within the context of the SBC. The subject concerns whether and how individual congregations of Baptists can work on Christian projects (missions, benevolences, moral issues, and education) with fellow Baptists without compromising local church autonomy. Through the years, this has been a major question for Southern Baptists.

DEFINING CONNECTIONALISM

Connectionalism is a term used to describe the relationship between local churches and other ecclesiastical bodies (e.g., other churches, associations of churches, and conventions). I should note that not everyone interprets the term uniformly. The founders of the SBC used the idea of connectionalism approvingly. For example, William B. Johnson, the first president of the SBC and the primary author of its first constitution, employed the term positively. He was interested in finding a "bond of union . . . for the promotion of righteousness."[1]

What shall we conclude about connectionalism and Southern Baptists?[2] Because connectionalism is widely understood as a violation of local church autonomy, it must be rejected as an acceptable polity for Southern Baptists.

---

[1] "Constitution of the First Baptist Convention, South Carolina, 1821" in Robert A. Baker, *A Baptist Source Book: With Particular Reference to Southern Baptists* (Nashville: Broadman, 1966), 75.

[2] In recent years, discussions regarding connectionalism and cooperation focused on the issue of Baptist entities and sole membership. Differing positions have been ably set forth by Dr. Chuck Kelley of New Orleans Seminary and Dr. David Hankins, state executive for the Louisiana Convention. Dr. Kelley's paper may be found on Baptist2Baptist.net under the category of "sole membership." Also, you will find Dr. David Hankins's response to Dr. Kelley's paper in the same category. I invite you to read both papers.

It is also probably wise not to attempt to rehabilitate the term to William Johnson's definition of non-controlling cooperation. To do so would lead to more confusion. However, this does not mean that Southern Baptists do not value ecclesiastical bodies beyond the local church or official relationships between churches. On the contrary, maintaining these relationships is a *core value* of Southern Baptists. It is called *cooperation,* the other word discussed in this topic.

DEFINING COOPERATION

As Southern Baptists, how should we feel about cooperation? Cooperation between congregations in the form of associations and conventions should be more highly prized and protected than ever as a necessary component of being Southern Baptist. From the beginning of our Convention, cooperation has been critical to our growth. Where there is no trust, there is no cooperation. Our Convention may be doctrinally pure, but without cooperation, without trusting each other, our Convention shall cease to have the dynamic missions enterprise that reaches to the far corners of the earth. In order to build upon the shoulders of our forefathers, our goal must be unwavering trust among ourselves. If trust is not possible, neither is cooperation. The consequence will be a diminishing witness around the world and a much smaller Convention. While this goal seems readily obtainable, it cannot be forgotten that trust is a trait to be earned; it is not a birthright. To earn trust, one must learn to trust.

As far back as the Philadelphia Association in 1707, Baptists began to form associations of churches. There were, of course, some Baptists who opposed the creation of *any* organized structures for missions. For some, the opposition stemmed from anti-missions theology (e.g., Daniel Parker, who began a predestinarian movement among Baptists, and Alexander Campbell, who fomented the Campbellite split from Baptists). For others, it was because they believed the local church was the only legitimate organization permitted by the New Testament (e.g., John Taylor in the early 1800s, and T. P. Crawford of the Gospel Missions Movement of the late 1800s).[3] Crawford expressed this sentiment when he wrote the following:

> Centralization and ring-government may suit the policy of other denominations. They do not suit ours, but are deadly hostile to it. Yet, strange to say, this dangerous element was first introduced among us with the first session of the Old Triennial Convention in 1814; and, stranger still,

---

[3]H. Leon McBeth, *The Baptist Heritage* (Nashville: Broadman, 1987), 373.

the Northern Baptist Union and the Southern Baptist Convention have continued it down to the present day. Their Boards are self-perpetuating, irresponsible central bodies with unlimited permission to grow in power by absorbing the prerogatives and resources of our churches, as the old Roman hierarchy grew by absorbing those in the early ages of Christianity.[4]

Most Baptists, however, did believe these organizations were permissible and beneficial and affirmed cooperative Christian missions beyond the local church. They were always extremely careful to insist authority resided in the local church and not in these ecclesiastical bodies. Baptists simultaneously employed two different approaches to the cooperative missionary work of the churches: (1) the societal model and (2) the associational model. The societal method reflected the views of those who believed cooperation by Baptists beyond the local church was permissible but that it could not be carried out as an extension of the churches. Therefore, societies for particular benevolences (missions, education, etc.) were organized and directed by interested individuals, not churches. The most prominent example of societal methodology in American Baptist history was the Triennial Convention organized in 1814, of which Baptists in the South were a part until the forming of the SBC in 1845.

The other approach to corporate missions work by Baptists in America is the association or convention model. Historian Robert Baker notes that the associational method usually involved a denominational structure fostering many benevolences, and had an interdependent and connectional relationship in all the benevolent work through the association.[5] The most remarkable example of the association model is the SBC (although it was not the first, since the South Carolina Baptist Convention was organized on this model in 1821).

At the organizing meeting of the SBC in 1845, William Johnson explained how the SBC would work: "In its successful operation, the whole Denomination will be united in one body for the purpose of well-doing, with perfect liberty secured to each contributor of specifying the object or objects, to which his amount shall be applied, as he pleases, while he or his Delegation may share in the deliberations and control all the objects, promoted by the Convention."[6]

Therefore, Southern Baptists purposefully formed a Convention built

---

[4]Baker, *A Baptist Source Book*, 280.
[5]Ibid., 99–101.
[6]Ibid., 165.

on the cooperation of the churches. Robert Baker writes: "Disdaining the possibility of overwhelming the authority of local congregations, Johnson was suggesting a more centralized body that would have control over all the benevolent objects projected by Southern Baptists."[7]

UNDERMINING COOPERATION

How important is the concept of cooperation to Southern Baptist identity? It is foundational. The "Rope of Sand" is James L. Sullivan's description of our cooperative polity. Since the rope has been in existence, it has proven in many ways to be as strong as steel. Conversely, the material used to weave the rope obviously is fragile, and remains strong only as long as it remains tightly woven, even strengthening under stress. When Southern Baptists are not bound tightly together, there can be only one anticipated result—a dismantling of the rope. At first, a few grains of sand may drop from the rope without much notice, but once the sand begins to move, one grain against another, the entire rope will disintegrate at warp speed. This does not mean the bricks and mortar will fall as did the walls of Jericho. Like the cathedrals of Europe, some semblance of structure may stand for generations, but they no longer will house a mighty force of God's people who came together with stouthearted biblical convictions, determined obedience to the Great Commission, a passionate love for the lost, and a compassionate heart for the hurting.

Is the issue of cooperation a contemporary concern for Southern Baptist identity? Very much so. In the current climate, there are practices and attitudes among vast numbers of Southern Baptists that have the potential for greatly reducing, if not destroying, the effectiveness of our churches and the Convention's ministries. I have identified three different emphases that might be termed "church worldviews." All of them, in their own way, are detrimental to the health of our common work because all of them undermine cooperation.

Undermining Cooperation by Decay

The first worldview is perfunctory performance. This approach to church life is marked by Spirit-less apathy, having a form of godliness but denying the power thereof (2 Tim. 3:5). This is not new to the people of God. It was a common sin of the Old Testament. In fact, while idolatry was the most common sin of the Israelites from the Judges to the exile, from the exile to

---

[7]Ibid.

the time of Christ their most common sin was perfunctory religion—just going through the motions, rule-keeping without regard for heart-change. Hundreds of our contemporary churches have fallen into this pattern. They value their human traditions over the movement of God. They spend their time and energy fighting for control of the congregation. Their motto is: "Come weal or woe, our status is quo." These congregations are in need of spiritual renewal, of revival. The Empowering Kingdom Growth (EKG) initiative was birthed with these congregations in mind. The mission statement of EKG states, "Empowering Kingdom Growth (EKG) is an initiative designed to call individual Southern Baptists to renew their passion for the Lord Jesus and the reign of His kingdom in their hearts, families, and churches from which God can forge a spiritual movement marked by holy living, sacrificial service, and global witness."[8]

Undermining Cooperation by Default

The second type of church worldview is pragmatism. These are the churches whose primary question for church life is: "Does it work?" The emphasis on quantifiable success (nickels and noses) can relegate such weighty matters as sound doctrine, spiritual heritage, and sacrificial service to the hinterlands of congregational life. I am concerned we have a generation of Southern Baptist pastors who do not know Joseph and who have uncritically embraced the trappings of nondenominationalism. Their congregations are not taught the great principles and the great people on which our denomination was founded and which caused it to flourish.

The churches are left to adopt secondary, less effective, even dangerous practices and methodologies by default. They simply are not being taught the value of Baptist heritage. These congregations could be helped by events such as the Baptist Identity Conference at Union University. They could be helped by becoming better informed biblically, theologically, and historically. They could be helped by studying research like Thom Rainer's *Surprising Insights of the Unchurched* before they discard Baptist identity and purpose.

Undermining Cooperation by Design

The third trend I will identify is simply politics. This church worldview is of particular moment to contemporary Southern Baptist life. While politics (the art of working with people) is always present in social structures,

---

[8]See http://www.empoweringkingdomgrowth.com.

including ecclesiastical ones, politics has played an unusually large and influential role in Southern Baptist denominational life for the last quarter of a century. In fact, at the 2004 annual convention, those of us who participated in leadership roles in what has been called the SBC conservative resurgence gathered for a Silver Anniversary celebration. And it was something to celebrate. Our beloved SBC was saved from the theological and numerical decimation known to most other mainline American denominations in the last half of the twentieth century because of the conservative resurgence. Thoughtful, aggressive, prayerful politics was an integral ingredient of its success.

However, one of the challenges we now face, in my opinion, is how to move beyond aggressive partisan politics to a model of denominational decision making that is more normative for Southern Baptists and more beneficial. While vigilance against heresy is always a task of faithful Christians, it appears to me that some Southern Baptists want to make every decision, even those not affecting doctrine and practice, based upon loyalty to friends, parties, or agendas. If this evaluation is true, and a "politics for politics sake" practice prevails, the SBC will be the poorer for it. It will result in narrower participation in denominational life, a shallower pool of wisdom and giftedness in our enterprises, and a shrinking impact upon the world. Those who may be in this aggressive political mode or party approach can be helped by understanding the vast potential for expanding God's kingdom that lies in the time-honored principles of cooperation that have marked our Convention's work.

So, in summary, it can be seen from these contemporary church worldviews, the deterioration may be caused by deliberately brushing away a few grains of sand here and there (to use Sullivan's analogy)—not enough for anyone to notice, but enough to begin the weakening process in the spirit of cooperation. In most instances the deterioration may be the unintended consequences of a pastor who has failed, for whatever reason, to grasp the reality that cooperation is the lifeline (albeit a rope of sand) of this Convention, or if so, the failure of that pastor to ask the question, "What difference does it make?" These unintended consequences may stem from (1) having a personal preference for an independent polity; (2) having mentors who never grasped the potential of cooperative missions, choosing to give little or nothing through the Cooperative Program; (3) perceiving, rightly or wrongly, that the Convention has become a nonessential in the health and growth of the church; (4) adopting the world's mantra for giving: "If I give I want to know precisely how it is spent"; (5) having a strong sense of personal motivation, believing that cooperation, like a church committee, is far too slow a process for doing missions; (6) having a tendency to launch satellite congregations loyal to the mother church rather than plant cooperating churches loyal to the Convention; or (7) viewing the Convention as a bureaucracy that is too big, too costly, and too uninformed to understand what the church is facing, and believing that even if the Convention understood, its response time would be too slow to be effective. Regardless of the reason, the unraveling of the rope of sand would be a tragedy in a Convention whose churches have networked their way to building enormous mission enterprises for God's glory and the salvation of the unsaved.

SEEKING A SOLUTION

How can we correct these trends and practices that threaten our cooperative identity? At the 1980 SBC in St. Louis, at the invitation of the Committee on Order of Business, I gave the Response to the Welcome.[9] The time allotted was ten minutes. In an effort to be a good steward, I decided I should seize upon at least nine of those minutes to define what I believed was Southern Baptist tradition. The discussion of inerrancy had erupted during the preceding year and I felt it was my responsibility to state my convictions, and hopefully to lay down a roadmap for the future. I asked the messengers the question: "What is Southern Baptist tradition?" Then I defined it as conservative theology and cooperative methodology.

In the first one-third of the response I spoke of our conservative theology:

> Our conservative heritage is based upon the belief that the Bible is the authoritative, inspired, infallible Word of God, inerrant in the original autographs. When men have stood unequivocally upon this truth, their teaching has been enriched and their preaching empowered because God is a God of Truth. Historically, when a denomination has failed to stand upon this truth, it begins, sooner or later, to fall for anything. We also know deep in our hearts that our enthusiasm for evangelism and missions will not exceed our convictions about biblical authority.

For the next two-thirds of the response I spoke about cooperative methodology:

---

[9]Morris H. Chapman, "Southern Baptist Tradition: What Is It?" (response to the welcome at the Southern Baptist Convention, St. Louis, MO, 1980).

Just as we are a people of the Book, we are also a people who are one in the bond of love. This tie that binds our hearts in Christian love has given birth to the cooperative program, cooperative missions, cooperative education, cooperative literature, and above all, a cooperative spirit. In our Convention there are some who tend to be conservative, but not cooperative, and there are others who tend to be cooperative, but not conservative. However, the rank and file of Southern Baptists is both conservative and cooperative. The world just waits for controversy to erupt among us, but what the world needs to see is the love of God explode within us. For without love, what we do and what we say will be as sounding brass or a tinkling cymbal. We may have the faith to remove mountains, but without love, God says, it is nothing. We are on the threshold of the mightiest movement in evangelism and missions in our history and with the love of God in our hearts, we can take this nation for Christ.

I reminded the messengers that the only living thing on which the curse of Jesus fell was a fig tree that bore no fruit. Then I quoted J. W. Storer of Oklahoma who was president of the Convention in 1954 when it met in the same city, St. Louis. He read Ephesians 4:16, "From him the whole body, joined and held together by every supporting ligament, grows and builds itself up in love, as each part does its work" (NIV). Then he said, "All joints (ligaments) are not alike, which illustrates our diversity, that voluntary principle which Baptists so correctly prize." To be sure, there are Baptists who seem dedicated to separatism, who refuse to play on the team, who prefer to return their own punts, call their own signals, do their own blocking, run their own interferences, and set off for a goal line diagonal with the field. They refuse, however, to recover their own fumbles. I concluded by saying, "The genius of Southern Baptist tradition is that we have been able to speak our minds without losing our heads. Our forefathers intended we are to be a denomination of convictions, not convenience. They determined we are to be a denomination of cooperation, not coalitions."

Allow me to expand on my remarks of 25 years ago and suggest some principles I will call Axioms of Cooperating Conservatives. There are six of them. The first three axioms speak to the conservative qualities of cooperating conservatives. The last three speak to the cooperating qualities of cooperating conservatives. These two sides must be held in tension.

Confession: The Theological Axiom

To confess is to confess the truth. We are a confessional people. Unity does not take precedence over truth. Consider the following: "If you must make a choice between heresy and schism, always choose heresy." This recent quote by Peter James Lee, the Episcopal bishop of Virginia who voted to approve the appointment of openly homosexual bishop V. Gene Robinson, is diametrically opposite of what cooperating conservatives practice. If we must choose between heresy and schism, we always, always, choose schism. Even when it is painful for us to separate from some beloved colleague, cooperating conservatives must always choose truth before unity. Early Southern Baptist leaders experienced this in the late ninteenth century when Crawford Toy was dismissed from the faculty of our oldest seminary because of his acceptance of European liberalism. We face the same sad reality now with the Baptist World Alliance. Our brothers in the Venezuelan Baptist Convention concluded in a resolution sent recently to the SBC that there cannot be a bigger problem in the midst of God's people than that of the lack of unity. Cooperating conservatives respectfully disagree. Failing to affirm the truth is a bigger problem than the lack of unity.

It should be noted that the Executive Committee voted to recommend to the SBC in June 2004 that the Convention withdraw from the Baptist World Alliance. As chairman of the SBC/BWA Study Committee, I was aware that this was an issue about which good Southern Baptists would disagree. After all, the SBC was a founding member of the organization and has been a member for the 99 years of its existence. In 1997, the chairman of the Executive Committee, James Merritt, at the request of SBC President Tom Elliff, appointed a BWA Study Committee. Increasingly, questions were being raised about the direction of the BWA and the feelings of many of its member bodies toward the SBC. These concerns were especially acute because the Convention was contributing $420,000 annually to the budget of the Baptist World Alliance, a large proportion of the BWA annual operating budget. The deliberations among the committee members led us to ask, "Is the SBC better represented in the world through the Baptist World Alliance or would the Convention better represent itself to like-minded Christians throughout the world?" We came to the conclusion that the latter of the two was true, partially because of our decreasing confidence in how we were being represented to other Baptists with regard to theological, ecclesiological, and missiological issues. While the committee is aware that the members will be criticized for making a decision that on the surface appears to be driven by isolationist views, nothing could be further from the truth. If the Convention withdraws its membership, we fully intend to begin immediately planning for ways to maintain friendships with our

Baptist brethren from around the world and build bridges to all conservative Christians, which is what has taken place.

In the early years of the recent conservative resurgence to which I
alluded earlier, Jimmy Draper, then president of the SBC, set out what he
termed "irreducible minimums of Southern Baptist doctrine."[10] Draper
rightly concluded that, without these common beliefs, Southern Baptists
could not remain vital nor should we remain unified. The *Baptist Faith &
Message*, through its various editions, is the effort of Southern Baptists to
define our commonly held beliefs. As cooperating conservatives, Southern
Baptists have insisted our unity is dependent on our common belief and
cannot be sustained apart from it.

Courage: The Societal Axiom

God honors the man who has not only convictions, but also the courage
of his convictions. What good is our faith if we hide it under a bushel? It is
not enough to believe the right things. We must give testimony to the right
things. John Revell and Ken Conner wrote a book entitled *Sinful Silence:
When Christians Neglect Their Civic Duty*.[11] Christians must engage the
culture regardless of personal sacrifice and rejection.

Jude wrote, "Beloved . . . it was needful for me to write unto you,
and exhort you that ye should earnestly contend for the faith which was
once delivered unto the saints" (Jude 3, KJV). I will give several quotes
in these axioms from Carl Henry's *The Uneasy Conscience of Modern
Fundamentalism*. Henry, in my opinion, embodied the axioms I am describ-
ing. His main thesis was that fundamentalism had neglected its responsibility to engage the world's ills: Christianity opposes any and every evil,
personal and social, and must never be represented as in any way tolerant
of such evil; it rejects the charge that the fundamentalist ideology logically
involves an indifference to social evils; an assault on global evils is not only
consistent with, but rather is demanded by, its proper world-life view.[12]
Cooperating conservatives attempt to please God rather than men. Peter
and John told the Sanhedrin they would continue to speak what they had
seen and heard (Acts 4:20) because they chose to obey God rather than
men. On the other hand, John tells of certain secret disciples of Jesus (John

---

[10]James T. Draper, *Authority: The Critical Issue for Southern Baptists* (Old Tappan, NJ: Fleming H. Revell, 1984), 105–6.

[11]John Revell and Ken Conner, *Sinful Silence: When Christians Neglect Their Civic Duty* (Nashville: Ginosko, 2004).

[12]Carl F. H. Henry, *The Uneasy Conscience of Modern Fundamentalism* (Grand Rapids, MI: Eerdmans, 2003), 45.

12:43) who would not confess their faith publicly because they "loved praise from men more than praise from God" (NIV). It is not our goal to unnecessarily alienate society. But if there is a choice on an issue between what God says and what men say, we choose to follow God.

Character: The Ethics Axiom

This axiom speaks to how we conduct our daily lives. Consistent character is a necessary component of the Christian life. No admonition is more useful to those of us who highly value sound doctrine than the phrase "practice what you preach." For cooperating conservatives, believing must be accompanied by ethical living; orthodoxy (right doctrine) must lead to orthopraxy (right practice). Simply holding the right doctrinal beliefs doesn't mean you are right about everything or that your behavior or relationships are righteous. Christianity should be known not only by its biblical convictions, but also by the life and testimony these convictions inspire. A mistake of some fundamentalist movements in the past has been the belief of the adherents that to be right with doctrine is to be right with the Lord. True righteousness was too easily discarded in favor of a type of dogmatism that was stifling and demoralizing to other Christians. In other words, right doctrine was equated to righteous living. They are not one and the same. A zeal for the Bible should result in a zeal for living for Christ, i.e., treating others with dignity, telling the truth, and insisting upon one's own integrity.

Collaboration: The Ecclesiastical Axiom

Our understanding of New Testament ecclesiology affirms the slogan "we can do more together than separately." We, as Great Commission Christians, elevate cooperation of Christians as a core value. We could call this good connectionalism—a combining of resources for ministry and missions. It's associationalism, the modus operandi of the founders of the SBC.

Cooperating conservatives reject the hyper-high church view of some who say *only* a local church may accomplish the kingdom's work. In fact, cooperating conservatives would insist that such an independent view is counter-productive to the work of the gospel. It is clear from the New Testament that the congregations in various regions understood they had an obligation to the ministry outside their own locale. The council at Jerusalem (Acts 15) in AD 50 indicates doctrinal concerns were to be considered by the larger Christian family. Another example of multi-congregational cooperation was the commissioning of missionaries. The famine in Jerusalem evoked the collection of a freewill offering from among the Gentile churches. Both John's epistles and the book of Hebrews insisted that hospitality for other Christians was a congregational duty. To reiterate, this axiom of collaboration (we can do more together than separately and God expects no less) is what makes Southern Baptists fundamentally different from independents or separatists.

Charity: The Attitudinal Axiom

Charity is the spirit of collegiality, generosity in spirit, no slander or malice, grace and mercy, no arguing or defaming over disputable matters or nonessentials, avoidance of legalism, not majoring on the minors. Again, I quote Carl Henry. He said, "Fundamentalists are quicker to oppose than to propose." He further stated, "What distressed the growing evangelical mainstream about the fundamentalist far right were its personal legalisms, suspicion of advanced education, disdain for biblical criticism per se, polemical orientation of theological discussion, judgmental attitudes toward those in ecumenically-related denominations, and an uncritical political conservatism often defined as Christian anticommunism and Christian capitalism that, while politicizing the gospel on the right, deplored politicizing it on the left."[13] Cooperating conservatives believe it is entirely possible, in fact necessary, to maintain an irenic spirit without bending one iota on basic doctrine. It is a matter of developing an attitude built on the fruit of the Spirit (Galatians 5) and the mind of Christ (Philippians 2). Charity includes compassion and civility, being kind always. Timothy George, commenting on Carl Henry, said, "His commitment to the orthodox Christian faith was solid as a rock, but I never heard him speak in a bitter or disparaging way about anybody, not even those with whom he disagreed."[14]

Co-belligerency: The Political Axiom

Cooperating conservatives cooperate where it is possible. Carl Henry wrote:

> The time has come now for Fundamentalism to speak with an ecumenical outlook and voice; if it speaks in terms of the historic Biblical tradition, rather than in the name of secondary accretions or of eschatological biases on which evangelicals divide, it can refashion the modern mind. But a double-minded Fundamentalism, one that veers between essential and

---

[13]Ibid., 45.
[14]Timothy George, "Inventing Evangelicalism," *Christianity Today* 48.3 (March 2004): 49.

inessentials, will receive little of the Lord, and not much of a hearing from the perishing multitudes.[15]

Henry promoted the ideals of unity, education, evangelism, and social ethics while maintaining the absolute truth claims of historic Christian orthodoxy.[16] The principle is we can join together with folks whose theology we do not share in order to accomplish good works, as long as we do not compromise our theology. Simply working with them is not a compromise in itself.

CONCLUSION

The SBC needs fine-tuning. In fact, the Convention may require an over-haul, not in its polity, but in its programming and the processes by which it functions daily. A major overhaul by the national Convention and the state conventions appears to be an absolute necessity, letting the facts speak for themselves lest the conventions discover too late they were blind and deaf to a delivery system that better serves the churches. Questions waiting to be asked and answered are stacking up by the month. There are pressures to establish more special offerings for Southern Baptists. This could unleash a horde of denominational entity fundraisers fanning out across the nation to make their appeals directly to the churches, reestablishing the failed practices of the societal system of denominational work from a bygone era. Furthermore, although Cooperative Program (CP) receipts continue for ten of the last eleven years to exceed the CP receipts of the prior year, the trend in the percentage of the total undesignated gifts given by the local church through the Cooperation Program slipped from 10.5 percent for a five-year period in the mid-1980s to 7.39 percent in 2001–2002. The slippage is trending toward becoming an erosion of the entire Convention landscape. If the erosion continues, it will erupt into a landslide, forcing an evaluation of our delivery system (how we relate and minister to the churches) and needed changes. The tragedy is that by the time we are forced to evaluate, it will be too late to recover the ground we have lost.

The SBC is a network of churches volunteering to work with other like-minded Baptist churches. Should this network fall apart, there is no Convention. You need only to look at the Southern Baptist landscape today to understand we are in an era of enormous flux.

The fluidity of the Convention is amazing. In some states we have two

---

[15]Henry, *Modern Fundamentalism*, 63.
[16]George, "Inventing Evangelicalism," 49.

organized state conventions. In a few more, we have two state conventions, one organized, the other unorganized. We have churches exercising their freedom to leave a geographical association and join an association that is more doctrinally compatible. We have a number of state Baptist colleges and universities that have broken free from relationship with the Convention. We have seminaries and colleges that have become Southern Baptist because they have chosen to do so, in contrast to institutions of higher learning that exist because a convention has chosen to establish, partially fund, elect trustees, and otherwise secure the existence of the school. Inclusive of Jackson, Tennessee, the vision for a newly configured association has been announced, called the Mid-South Baptist Association of Churches. The vision is to include parts or all of seven states: Tennessee, Alabama, Mississippi, Arkansas, Missouri, Illinois, and Kentucky. Not until this mega-association becomes more reality than vision will we be able to measure its effect upon the traditional configurations of state conventions and associations now in existence. Convention leaders must not fail to take into account that we are not driving the changes. Pastors and their churches are driving the changes from the perspective of field generals. We have the responsibility of offering our observations and our collective assistance to the churches. If our conventions are not careful to take into account a shift in the landscape, we shall find ourselves inessential after all. The conventions exist to serve the churches, not to insist that the churches fit into the Convention, a voluntary choice that is already their option. On the other hand, the churches must communicate their needs to the conventions. When they do, we are compelled to listen and, as far as possible, take action to meet the needs brought to the attention of the conventions.

As has been mentioned already, the importance of cooperation within the Southern Baptist environment cannot be overstated. Cooperation is enormously vital to the existence of the SBC and its cooperating state conventions. Enough words cannot be strung together to state adequately the danger that lurks in the shadows, waiting to break down communication and cooperation among us. Where it is intentional, individuals must reassess their own attitudinal axiom. Where the break down is unintentional, churches and conventions must reassess why the cooperative nature of our Convention is breaking down.

If the churches lose the vision and the understanding of the Cooperative Program, missions suffer. If missions suffer, the conventions suffer. If the conventions suffer, reorganization and reallocation of funding shall no longer be a choice. Now is the time for leaders of all conventions to concentrate upon priorities of their organization's very existence and determine that more shall be done for less. To fail to do so will bring the disadvantages of smaller budgets and reduced ministries. Now is the time to maximize our resources by creating leaner organizations and eliminating wasteful expenditures for failing and static ministries and programs. To put our money behind ministries that genuinely assist the churches who gave us a portion of their undesignated and designated offerings is a formula for fulfilling our Lord's command to "go ye therefore." Anything less must become unacceptable. It is incumbent upon chief executives and trustees to assure the very best use of resources by giving laser-like focus to those pursuits that most honor our Lord Jesus Christ and expand his kingdom on earth.

It is my prayer that the Axioms of Cooperating Conservatives can become a catalyst for discussing the basis of our denominational work and that this current generation of Baptists can learn to revalue our corporate ministries. May God allow us to embody the principles of our Convention founders—to maintain the proper balance between conservatism and cooperation—and, thus remain useful to the Lord Jesus until the end, when he shall have delivered up the kingdom to God (1 Cor. 15:24).

CHAPTER NINE

TOWARD A MISSIONAL CONVENTION

Ed Stetzer

THE TERM "MISSIONAL" is being employed with increasing frequency across the evangelical spectrum. Within the SBC, it also seems that many are working hard to incorporate the term into our denominational vernacular. But are we really a missional convention? If so, then what are the signs of our missional identity? If we are not, then how can we, as Southern Baptists, move from merely assuming a new buzz-word to assuming an identity and common practice commensurate with this recently popularized word?

In addressing the above questions, it is necessary to trace the origin of the term, as well as examine its use within the context of the SBC. To be clear from the start, and contrary to some reports, "missional" is not a new word. Its origin goes back at least one-hundred years. It is first mentioned in the 1907 *Oxford English Dictionary*, which cites W. G. Holmes's *Age Justinian & Theodora II*: "Several prelates, whose missional activities brought over whole districts and even nationalities to their creed."

The first Southern Baptist, and the first missiologist, to publish using the term "missional" was Francis DuBose, then a professor and director of the World Missions Center at Golden Gate Baptist Theological Seminary. DuBose wrote about the concept of missional theology in his book *God Who Sends*: "Where have we missed the meaning of our pilgrim faith? Why has the biblical meaning of mission so escaped us? Where did we abandon the legacy of the Jesus way? We live before the mystique of the missional vision. But we seem to be able to keep it a vision—a vision at a safe enough distance to keep us from being compelled by its power."[1] In May 1999, I preached at The Southern Baptist Theological Seminary chapel and contended that the entire church should assume a missional posture, explaining that "the normative expression of New Testament Christianity is missional."[2] I believe it even more strongly today.

Since that day, the word has been used with increasing frequency by an increasing number of Southern Baptist leaders, sometimes without regard for its etymological origins and twenty-first-century contextual meaning. Ignoring both the base definition and normative contemporary application of the term has resulted in confusion. Put more plainly, part of the problem regarding the debate over what it means to be "missional" is that the term has been used by many people in different ways.

HOW SOUTHERN BAPTISTS HAVE USED THE TERM "MISSIONAL"

"Missional" is used in most Southern Baptist contexts to describe the attitude of obedience to sharing the gospel around the world that all believers should possess. Such a concept is nothing new to the 160-year-old SBC. According to the first line of the final report from the Ad Hoc Committee on the Cooperative Program, "Southern Baptists have always been a missional people."[3] Statements such as these clearly reveal a common understanding of this term by many Southern Baptists as reflective of our historical commitment to the Great Commission and the Great Commandment.

While some have suggested that the "missional" concept is little more than a passing phase, the emphasis on being missional cannot be dismissed so easily. In numerous instances the term's use has become more prominent—and for good reason. Danny Akin's 2006 SBC nominating speech gave special emphasis to the fact that his second VP nominee was "missional." At the North American Mission Board (NAMB), the "Enlistment Team" has been renamed the "Enlistment and Missional Networks." The Southern Baptists of Texas now have a "Missional Leaders' Network"[4] (title is theirs) and recently tied the idea of "missional" to the Cooperative Program.

Southern Baptists have always been a missional people. From the

---

[1]Francis M. DuBose, *God Who Sends* (Nashville: Broadman, 1983), 14.
[2]Ed Stetzer (sermon at Southern Seminary, May 14, 1999); reported by *Baptist Press*, May 14, 1999, http://bpnews.net/bpnews.asp?ID=998.
[3]"'Missional' Focus Must Include Cooperative Funding, Report Says," *Baptist Press*, December 4, 2006, http://www.bpnews.net/bpnews.asp?ID=24519.
[4]"Missional Leaders' Network," Southern Baptists of Texas Web site, http://www.sbtexas.com/missions/mln.htm.

inception of the SBC in 1845, we have always rallied around the command of Christ to carry the gospel to the entire world. At the heart of our local churches, and of all organizations and agencies beyond the local church, is the desire to share the good news of the gospel of Jesus Christ. The Cooperative Program was implemented to give each Southern Baptist a way to be a part of reaching the world for Christ through their local church. Sadly, we too often have allowed our focus to become ingrown and diverted from our evangelistic responsibility. Most of the strategies and initiative in this report focus on telling the story of what we are currently doing through the Cooperative Program, but we must not fall into the trap of thinking we can reposition the Cooperative Program in the hearts of Southern Baptists by focusing only on what we are accomplishing: "It is vitally important that we also cast a new vision to Southern Baptists, a compelling vision that challenges them to use the immense resources God has placed in our hands to literally fulfill Acts 1:8 in our generation. We must place before our people, our pastors and our churches a challenge that is so big that it will require us to give sacrificially, pray passionately and become personally involved in reaching the world for Christ."[5]

Anthony Jordan, executive director for the Baptist General Convention of Oklahoma (BGCO), predicts a missional SBC based upon our past "missions-minded" orientation: "I am convinced we have set our course to be a missional people. We are dedicated to reaching people from every background. Every boy and girl ought to be able to hear about Jesus in their own language."[6] Jordan is right and courageous to say that we are not yet there, but have set our course to become missional.

Even some of our seminaries have begun to use the word "missional." Not surprisingly considering its origin, the word is common at Golden Gate. However, some might be surprised to discover that New Orleans Baptist Theological Seminary now has a class called "Developing a Missional Church,"[7] and Jim Millirons[8] recently led a conference at New Orleans Baptist Theological Seminary called "On Missional Resurgence." Missional church books are now required reading for evangelism students at Southeastern Baptist Theological Seminary.

---

[5]"Final Report of Ad Hoc Cooperative Program Committee," Baptist2Baptist, March 22, 2006, http://www.baptist2baptist.net/b2barticle.asp?ID=286.
[6]"Wedgwood Writes Words of Love on Sanctuary Floor," *Baptist Press*, October 14, 1999.
[7]"Specializations and Associated Classes: Ongoing Specializations" (class listed under "Church Planting/Missions"), New Orleans Baptist Theological Seminary, http://www.nobts.edu/ProDoc/DMin/Specializations.html.
[8]"Contend, Contextualize, and Cooperate" was birthed in a lunch conversation with Jim Millirons, who is leader of the "missional emphasis" at the Georgia Baptist Convention.

Seminary presidents and denominational executives are not the only ones within Southern Baptist life who see value in this term. Local church pastors are also calling for the implementation of the missional concept in one form or another. Ted Traylor, pastor of Olive Baptist Church in Pensacola, Florida, recently called for a missional mindset, remarking at the Alabama Baptist Pastors Conference that being missions-minded is not enough. "Praying for missionaries is great, but if you're just missions-minded and praying for someone else [when] you're supposed to go yourself, you're not being missional," Traylor said. "It's not a great thing to send people if God has told you to go." Traylor told the crowd that the time has come for churches to move past being simply missions-minded and become missional. "The problem at Olive Baptist Church is that many people don't really believe that half of our town is dying and going to hell," he said, adding that the same goes for Alabama Baptist churches. "One out of every two people is lost in Alabama. We as Baptists are not missional because we don't really believe that."[9] Statements such as these reveal a distinction between the historically "missions-minded" SBC and the need to be "missional," or to become missionaries ourselves and to lead our people into a clear mission. The question is whether or not Southern Baptists will take that mission up and, again, become a missional people.

HOW OTHERS ARE USING THE TERM

Southern Baptists aren't the only ones laying claim to the use of the word "missional." Nearly every group, evangelical or otherwise, is making frequent use of the term. Subsequently, some Southern Baptists are reticent to employ the term because of its use and endorsement by others outside evangelicalism.

For example, the General Commission on the United Methodist Men states that one of its goals is to promote "Programs of Mission in cooperation with all areas of the Church dealing with missional opportunities."[10] J. Bennett Guess in the February–March 2006 issue of the United Church of Christ News writes, "Since General Synod, and perhaps even before it, I've been feeling the need for a new missional emphasis, something energizing that draws us together—not apart—as we prepare to celebrate our 50th anniversary in 2007 and make our way beyond."[11] Even the Unitarian Universalists

---

[9]"Ala. Baptists Devote Time to Missions and Evangelism," *Baptist Press*, November 17, 2008, http://www.bpnews.net/bpnews.asp?ID=24417.
[10]See the United Methodist Men home page, http://www.gcumm.org/Resources%202001/UMM%20mission.html.
[11]J. Bennett Guess, ed., "United Church of Christ News," http://www.ucc.org/ucnews/febmar2006.

have made common use of the term. In their *A Manual for District Staff and Volunteers: New Congregation and Growth Resources, Congregational Services*, they write, "Missional strategies should be crafted to help define a congregation's identity through a process of spiritual discernment."[12]

Among Baptists, the moderate Cooperative Baptist Fellowship has also used the word to point their congregations in a specific direction. The Cooperative Baptist Fellowship (CBF) has a whole "missional church" emphasis that it encourages its partner churches to adopt and employ.[13] In March 2005, *The Biblical Recorder* ran an article entitled, "Moderates asked to embrace 'missional church' movement." In the article David Hughes, pastor for First Baptist Church Winston-Salem, N.C., is quoted saying, "A missional church is easier to describe than it is to define. It's not just a church that does missions." In the same article, Brent Greene, minister of spiritual formation at Hughes's church, said, "The missional church is about being on mission 24/7."

What we can clearly see is that from one end of the theological spectrum to the other, many are claiming to be on a missional track of ministry. That frightens some and causes some to conclude that a missional emphasis is a liberal one—seeping into the conservative SBC. But, not so fast . . .

CONSERVATIVE EVANGELICAL USE OF "MISSIONAL"

Conservative evangelicals are also employing this term. A few years ago, the Wesleyan Church asked me to keynote their first ever national meeting to help them become a "missional denomination." Randy Pope, pastor of the theologically driven and culturally engaged Perimeter Church in Atlanta, preached a message at this year's Presbyterian Church in America (PCA) General Assembly entitled, "The PCA: A Missional Church?" from 1 Corinthians 9:19–23. The Assemblies of God Department of U.S. Missions includes "missional" as one of their four values. The Evangelical Free Church held a "Missional Summit" for their leaders in 2007 and they have renamed their church planting leadership: "Missional Church Planting Team." The Nazarene Church's denomination has adopted "Missional" as their denominational goal, and they describe themselves as Christian, Holiness, and Missional.[14]

---

[12]"New Congregation and Growth Resources," http://archive.uua.org/cde/education.
[13]"Communities of Missional Practice," Cooperative Baptist Fellowship, http://www.thefellowship.info/Missions/Communities.
[14]"We Are a Missional People," official site of the International Church of the Nazarene, March 2006, http://www.nazarene.org/ministries/administration/visitorcenter/values/missional/display.aspx.

The evidence is therefore overwhelming that the missional concept is breaking out all over evangelicalism (and beyond). Several recent articles in *Leadership Journal* further confirm this trend; Eric Reed, the managing editor, spoke of missional as:

> . . . a philosophy of ministry: that followers of Christ are counter-cultural, on a mission to change the culture. Missional refers to the specific activity of churches to build the kingdom of God in all settings where church members are at work rather than building up the local congregation, its programs, members, and facilities. . . . Individual Christians in local congregations are taking new ownership of the mission. We are becoming missional.[15]

Some examples from *Leadership* that demonstrate this ecclesiastical metamorphosis include Northwood Church, an SBC church in Texas, a Chicago-area Baptist Association led by Keith Draper, and Perimeter Church in Atlanta. Each of these ministries is at the same time solidly conservative and unashamedly missional.

Still, not everyone within Baptist life is happy with the dissemination of the missional concept. One of the primary reasons for the hesitation of some to embrace being missional is that the term has long been associated with more ecumenical circles.

Missiologists David Bosch, Lesslie Newbigin, and Craig van Gelder wrote of the church's need to interact with and impact culture. To accomplish this, the church had to be appropriate to that culture and be focused on the mission of God. The terminology shifted, primarily because of Darrell Guder's popular book, *The Missional Church*. In fact, many outside evangelicalism who employ the term regularly come from ministries that were largely birthed out of the Gospel and Our Culture Network (involving Darrell Guder and others). Other organizations, such as Emergent Village, began to encourage the forging of cooperative partnerships between people and churches of vastly different theological vantage points. In doing so, some have created a dichotomy between the "doctrinal" and the "missional," suggesting that the point of unity for Christians is not theology, but mission. As a result, these groups defined the word in a different way from some of their predecessors.

Other writers, researchers, pastors, and missiologists from a conservative perspective followed suit, rallying around the missional cause with

---

[15]Reed, Eric, "Currents: A Leadership Report," *Christianity Today*, Winter 2007, 20.

the recognition that it was descriptive of the true church and therefore prescriptive of how the church should operate. Tim Keller of Redeemer Presbyterian Church in New York, along with a few others, challenged the church to reexamine its role in the world. Suddenly, missional books, blogs, conferences, and articles were almost everywhere.

The rapid and increasing use of the term "missional" caught the attention of still other evangelical groups such as 9Marks Ministries. Jonathan Leeman of 9Marks writes:

> My guess is that conservative writers and pastors in the emerging church movement like Mark Driscoll, after tromping through some of the same fields as their liberal counterparts, reached down, pulled up the missional plant by the roots, and then transplanted it into conservative soil . . .
>
> Ed Stetzer, for instance, frequently cites Newbigin, Bosch, and the GOC [Gospel and Our Culture Network] gang in his book *Planting Missional Churches*. Yet where a GOC writer will say something like "missional Communities are cultivated through participation in particular social or ecclesial practices," Stetzer will ask, "What does the Bible require for church?" It's probably unfair to say that conservatives like Stetzer want to build on a biblical foundation, whereas the ecumenicals don't. It's probably kinder to simply say that Stetzer sees *the Bible* as authoritative for the church's mission, where as someone like Newbigin, drawing on the fiduciary epistemology of Michael Polanyi, will say that *Jesus* is the authority for its mission. What does this mean? It means that Newbigin does not want to give the Bible unqualified approval as Jesus' inerrant word, so he pits Jesus and his word against one another.[16]

Leeman's analysis here is correct. In the ongoing discussion and development of the concept, I freely admit that conservative evangelicals did appropriate the term back from the ecumenical movement—even though Francis Dubose had used and defined the term earlier (as I learned from *God Who Sends,* required reading in my missions Ph.D. program at The Southern Baptist Theological Seminary).

It was Tim Keller, however, who "pulled up the missional plant by the roots, and then transplanted it into conservative soil." Keller's influence is hard to understate when it comes to evangelical engagement in missional

---

[16]Jonathan Leeman, "What in the World Is the Missional Church?" 9Marks, October 2006, http://sites. silaspartners.com/CC/article/0,,PTID314526%7CCHID598014%7CCIID2265778,00.html.

ministry (which may also explain why much of the "missional" talk in conservative circles comes from the Reformed tradition).

Still, all of the examples cited above sufficiently serve to illustrate that no one in Christendom has a monopoly on the term, including Ecumenicals. And it is a shame that in a time when we have lost an outward focus in Southern Baptist life, some of our theologians are reticent to lead us to a more missions-focused theology and missiology simply because the concept was also emphasized by our more liberal counterparts. "Missional" is not an ecumenical term and it is certainly not their truth. "Missional" is central to who we are and what God created his church to be. As previously alluded to, "missional" does not refer to an activity or a program, but rather to the very nature of a true, God-honoring, biblical, missions-focused, contextualized church. You cannot separate the concept from this reality. (I cannot address here the theological and missiological underpinnings of the term. Instead, see "The Missional Nature of the Church and the Future of Southern Baptist Convention Churches" in *The Mission of Today's Church*.[17])

Regardless of who has used the term and what they've meant by it, there can be no doubt that any Christian church that is true to its calling is thoroughly, consistently, and unapologetically missional. Therefore, the issues of who used the term first and who continues to invoke it are largely irrelevant and, I believe, a distraction from the bigger problem: we are far off mission.

Not all who use this term "missional" are missional. Some think of "missional" only as support of missions elsewhere in the world while neglecting their own neighborhoods. But missional churches seek to engage their immediate cultures as well as the *ethne* of the world. Giving to missions or going on short-term mission trips—as important as these are—do not fulfill our missional calling, nor does focusing exclusively on the church and its community while ignoring the rest of the world. Though the church's immediate context is vitally important, the churches that are missional also focus on opportunities beyond their doorsteps to make Christ known. They involve the members in the ministry and mission of church and gospel. As stated in the most recent *Leadership Journal*, "Missional churches activate laity to carry out God's mission in their various spheres of life."[18]

---

[17]Ed Stetzer, "The Missional Nature of the Church and the Future of Southern Baptist Convention Churches," in *The Mission of Today's Church: Baptist Leaders Look at Modern Faith Issues*, ed. R. Stanton Norman (Nashville: B&H Academic, 2007).
[18]Chad Hall, "Missional Possible: Steps to Transform a Consumer Church into a Missional Church," *Christianity Today*, Winter 2007, 35.

BEING MISSIONAL IS NOT ABOUT TERMINOLOGY, BUT FOCUS

Bringing the aforementioned observations to bear on the issue of "Baptist Identity" may be an uncomfortable process for some. Unfortunately, some Baptist leaders, like many others within the larger spectrum of evangelicalism, have a tendency to object to anything that someone else uses. If the liberals talk about "social justice," we cannot. If the mainliners talk about "the kingdom," we must not. If the emerging church speaks of "cultural relevance," we object to the term. But the appropriate way to address mainline and emergent error is not to avoid these terms, but instead to define them in light of our Scriptural mandate. In fact, if we are consistent in rejecting any terms employed by those outside our theological tradition, the unavoidable result will be the rejection of even biblical language.

Many non-evangelicals also use terms like "evangelism," "gospel," "kingdom," and, yes, "missional" in a way that we do not. But we dare not abandon such terms. Instead, we should be clear when defining terms to ensure their accurate usage. These terms were used originally by neither liberals nor conservatives. They were originally employed or commanded by Scripture. The problem is that we spend so much time objecting to terms, we never get around to changing our churches.

While "missional" may be a relatively new term, it is not a new concept. On the contrary, it is reflected in the pages of Scripture and seen, with varying degrees of clarity, throughout the ensuing centuries. Our Lord emphasized the strategic importance of a missional focus when he stated, "As the Father has sent Me, I also send you" (John 20:21, NASB). Earlier in his gospel, John speaks of the incarnation. In Eugene Peterson's paraphrase, he writes that the Lord "became flesh and blood, and moved into the neighborhood" (John 1:14, MESSAGE). Like our Lord, we are supposed to take up residence right among our neighbors. This is far from a new concept. In the ancient Epistle to Diognetus we find these words: "Christians are not distinguished from the rest of humankind by country, or by speech, or by dress. . . . They do not dwell in cities of their own, or use a different language, or practice a peculiar life. They live in countries of their own, but simply as sojourners; they share the life of citizens, they endure the lot of foreigners; every foreign land is to them a homeland, and every homeland a foreign land."[19]

For more than a century, we have embraced this idea as it relates to

---

[19]Duane K. Friesen, *Artists, Citizens, Philosophers: Seeking the Peace of the City* (Scottsdale, PA: Herald Press, 2000), 28.

the foreign mission field, while simultaneously failing to realize that "missional" is not only global, but also local. The missional mandate includes our own neighborhoods and communities. It is precisely the implementation of international missions strategy in North America that is causing much angst. Nevertheless, such a shift is absolutely essential, as the evidence of a declining church so clearly illustrates.

It is not exaggeration to say that evangelical churches (including SBC churches) are failing to impact the lost people of North America. New statistics from the Leavell Center at New Orleans Baptist Theological Seminary show that 89 percent of Southern Baptist churches are not effectively reaching unbelievers. According to the study, only 11 percent of the churches are experiencing healthy growth.

The Leavell Center's method of measuring church growth health was based on the following simple criteria:

- Ten percent total membership growth over five years
- At least one person baptized during the two years of the study
- A member-to-baptism ratio of 35 or less in the final year of the study (these churches needed 35 or fewer members each year to baptize one new convert)
- For the final year of the study, the percentage of growth that was conversion growth must have been at least 25 percent

New statistics also revealed the growing inability of North American churches to penetrate their cultural context and reach people with the gospel. The American Religious Identification Survey showed that every two years on average, an additional 1 percent of Americans identify themselves as having no religion: "One of the most striking 1990–2001 comparisons is the more than doubling of the adult population identifying with no religion, from 14.3 million (8%) in 1990 to the current 29.4 million (14.1%)."[20]

In addition, the number of unchurched people continues to increase, even with Barna's charitable definition of the unchurched. A Barna Group study explained, "Since 1991, the adult population in the United States has grown by 15 percent. During that same period the number of adults who do not attend church has nearly doubled, rising from 39 million to 75 million—a 92 percent increase!"

The above statistics demonstrate the struggle of SBC churches to be

---

[20]Chris Herlinger, "Number of Americans with No Formal Religion Increasing, Survey Finds," *Christianity Today*, January 1, 2002, http://www.christianitytoday.com/ct/2002/100/33.0.html.

evangelistically effective. Day after day, as the culture around us becomes more unfamiliar and even hostile toward Christianity, many Southern Baptist churches separate themselves further from the culture they are called to reach, with a self-affirming and predictable comfortable denominational subculture contributing to this widening distance. This chasm of cultural understanding makes it increasingly difficult for our "church culture" to relate to "prevailing culture." Without intentionality, churches become less contextual, less indigenous, and less evangelistically effective over time. The final result of this drift is that we eventually become the very thing we abhor—a church that is not faithful to its biblical mandate to engage and transform culture with the gospel.

Those who oppose a contextualized mission based on a fear of the very real danger of cultural syncretism may be surprised to learn that Baptists on the American frontier, so often cited as a role model today, were often accused of being too "close" to the culture. They wanted to be "of the people." They were accused of being—in today's terms—too "culturally relevant." Congregationalists, Presbyterians, and Episcopalians were scandalized by the earthiness and even worldliness of Baptists on the Western frontier in the early 1800s. In every sense of the phrase, Baptists, like the incarnate Christ, "moved into the neighborhood" as they evangelized the frontier. Over time, *we* (Southern Baptists) have become the *scandalized* while others have been more effective at penetrating the culture, and more adept at "moving into the neighborhood."[21]

But deep down inside, we really do believe that culture is a relevant consideration for missions. In fact, we demonstrate this belief every time we send new missionaries to foreign lands and, like Lottie Moon, expect them to don the clothes, live the customs, and be part of the community while proclaiming a faithful gospel. Therefore, we should not forbid North

---

[21]For more information, see such works as William H. Brackney, ed., *Baptist Life and Thought, 1600-1980: a Source Book* (Valley Forge, PA: Judson Press, in cooperation with the American Baptist Historical Society, 1983); Charles Chaney, *History of Missions in America* (South Pasadena, CA: William Carey Library, 1976); Roger Finke and Rodney Starke, *The Churching of America: Winners and Losers in Our Religious Economy* (New Brunswick, NJ; Rutgers University Press, 1992); Colin Brummitt Goodykoontz, *Home Missions on the American Frontier: With Particular Reference to the American Home Missionary Society* (Caldwell, ID: The Caxton Printers, Ltd., 1939); Nathan O. Hatch, *The Democratization of American Christianity* (New Haven and London: Yale University Press, 1989); Victor I. Masters, *Baptist Missions in the South* (Atlanta, GA: Publicity Department of the Home Mission Board, 1914); H. Leon McBeth, *The Baptist Heritage* (Nashville: Broadman, 1987); William Warren Sweet, *Religion on the American Frontier, 1783-1840*, vol. 4, *The Methodist* (Chicago, IL: The University of Chicago Press, 1946); Francis Wayland, *Notes on the Principles and Practices of Baptist Churches* (New York: Sheldon, Blakeman & Co., 1857); Gregory A. Wills, *Democratic Religion: Freedom Authority, and Church Discipline in the Baptist South, 1785-1900* (New York: Oxford University Press, 1997); Judson Boyce Allen, "Westward Expansion, Southern Baptist," in *Encyclopedia of Southern Baptists* (Nashville: Broadman, 1982); Penrose St. Amant, "Frontier, Baptists, and the American" in *Encyclopedia of Southern Baptists* (Nashville: Broadman, 1982).

American missionaries, pastors, and laity from doing the very thing we train and expect international missionaries to do.

BEING MISSIONAL IS ABOUT MISSIOLOGICAL THINKING, NOT JUST MISSIONARY SUPPORT

As mentioned previously, missiological thinking is not the same as missionary support. Simply put, being "missions-minded" alone does not mean that we are "missional." Many churches that support cross-cultural missions do not carefully apply strategic missiological thinking or focus on the mission of God within their own context. Unfortunately, some have confused missionary support—an important concern that needs more attention—with paying someone else to do missional ministries like evangelism and church planting, albeit on a foreign field. But this thinking precludes obedience to our Lord's commission in our local context. Church members are unable to experience fruitful service through participation in *missional* work within their own community.

Many churches will go to great lengths and tremendous expense to involve members in "missional" activities far from home, yet fail to fully engage their own neighborhood. Perhaps one of the contributing factors to this seeming inconsistency is the ability for us to behave "missionally" for a short period of time in a "far country" where coworkers and neighbors can't see us. In these short-term/long-distance missions events, we are able to experience the passion of missional living without really becoming incarnational to our own context.

This approach to missional work is perhaps the unfortunate outcome of a separation between missions and evangelism in popular thinking among Southern Baptists and other evangelicals. To many, missions is something done "elsewhere" by "someone." Thus, some churches that are "far-thinking" and "far-reaching" in terms of international missions are failing to reach the people in the shadows of their steeples. North America is not viewed as a mission field. In fact, many believe it to be a "reached" field only in need of an evangelism strategy, not a true missional engagement.

What is needed is not merely an understanding of missiological thinking, but a commitment to missional thinking. While missiology concerns itself with study *about* missions and its methodologies, missional thinking focuses on *doing* missions in every geographical location. Such thinking is needed if the SBC is to remain faithful in its calling to serve churches by equipping them to impact their surrounding communities.

Perhaps this is why fewer rising leaders look to Southern Baptists as the source for missionally effective strategies. Instead, they will often downplay their theological convictions to learn and implement the strategies of those who do not hold our biblical distinctive. They do so because they see the need for new indigenous expressions and they have not seen Southern Baptists, as a whole, engage in the necessary theological and missiological thinking to develop such strategies. Why has this shift taken place?

Perhaps one reason is that those who are most effective in the "old" culture are unable to contextualize in the new. Those who were most successful in the last paradigm often have the most difficulty in the next. Such one-time innovators have seen certain cultural expressions of effective Christianity, and are unable to consider methods and models different from their own. They "know" what works. They have seen it work before (perhaps in 1954). They "know" if they just try, pray, and go as fervently as they did back then, it will work that way again. The problem is that with the exploding diversity taking shape on our continent, many present-day North American contexts are increasingly less like North America, and more like other parts of the world. Consequently, what was once effective in reaching those North American communities is no longer effective. We simply have not recognized that the "how" of ministry is, in many ways, determined by the "who," "when," and "where" of culture.

"Missional" means building upon what we have been and is not a rejection of what we have been doing. To avoid confusion, let's be clear: when a "missional" leader states that we must "engage and transform the culture for the cause of the gospel," that is not a rejection of the "soul-winner" who states that we must "win the lost to Jesus." They may be communicating the same objective. The objective is the glory of God through a kingdom focus that results in the salvation of the lost. We must realize that our move toward a missional denomination is one that embraces the best of our identity, celebrates the missional work of the past, and catapults us toward a cultural engagement upon the North American continent that will see the salvation of Christ extend to the people groups of our communities.

Churches and denominations whose ecclesiology is partially defined by a particular cultural expression often lock themselves into that culture, remaining in that era's music, methods, and strategies. This is where many Southern Baptists currently find themselves—trying to reach the 2000s with the formerly successful methods of the 1950s (or 1890s). Additionally, Baptists did best when they were locked into one corner of the nation geographically. Even when we broke out of the geographic South, we took a southern monoculture with us. We were successful because we had unlocked the missional code for early twentieth-century southern culture, wherever that culture existed. While this approach is still successful in a few areas, it is a methodology that is increasingly found to be disconnected to its present cultural surroundings.

What is the alternative? Southern Baptist churches must begin to think and act "missionally" in their settings. Presently, we are struggling with the challenge of finding the proper balance between cultural relevance and biblical fidelity. Churches need to realize that the United States and Canada are in fact mission fields and, as a result, begin to fulfill their missional heritage. To accomplish this, they must discern how best to connect with the current culture without compromising the gospel message.

This struggle is, of course, ongoing, as has been the case throughout the history of the church. From Tertullian to Calvin to Niebuhr, there has always existed a tension regarding how the church should interface with culture—a tension regarding the appropriate intersection between theology, ecclesiology, and missiology. With this reality in view, we should dialogue with the awareness that being Southern Baptist is about theology and cooperation, not a certain methodology. To be Southern Baptist means that we believe certain things and cooperate together to build God's kingdom.

WHAT A MISSIONAL SOUTHERN BAPTIST CHURCH LOOKS LIKE

If Southern Baptists are to be, once again, the vibrant body that we have been in the past, we need *not* return to the *methods* of the past. G. K. Chesterton explains, "We are learning to do a great many clever things. Unless we are much mistaken the next great task will be to learn not to do them."[22] It would appear Southern Baptists have not yet done so.

God has blessed three-week revivals, radio preaching, Sunday school enrollment campaigns, and bus ministry. God used these indigenous and contextual methods in their time. But our task is not to pine for methods. Instead, our focus must shift from the *methods* of those times to the *motives* of those times—which involved reaching the lost with the best practices of the day.

Today, Southern Baptists must stop treating North America as a monocultural continent. Every culture and subculture that now exists on this

---

[22]Dale Ahlquist, "Lecture III: Twelve Types (and Varied Types)," The American Chesterton Society, http://www.chesterton.org/discover/lectures/3twelvetypes.html.

continent needs the gospel to be explained fully, each at a different starting point but with the same ending point. Milfred Minatrea explains it this way: "At the core, it is not the number of activities a church is involved in that defines success, but whether those activities result in accomplishing God's mission for His church."[23]

Missional churches in our day are different from churches that choose to enshrine the methods of past cultures. They are also frequently different from one another. Joe Thorn observes, "The more similar the context, the [more] similar the churches will look incarnationally, but each community is somewhat different and requires the gospel and kingdom to be preached/demonstrated in different ways. As I see it a missional church must therefore be at least three things: sent, engaged, and incarnated. The 'missional church' is almost a redundant expression. The people of God are inherently a sent people. It is who we are, and that gives birth to what we do. We just tend to forget this."[24]

Tim Keller gave the following five elements of a missional church:

1) Discourse in the vernacular.
2) Enter and retell the culture's stories with the gospel.
3) Theologically train laypeople for public life and vocation.
4) Create Christian community which is countercultural and counterintuitive.
5) Practice Christian unity as much as possible on the local level.

The reason missional churches look different is that they are willing to take a risk to engage their culture. There is always risk in contextualization, and many churches are unwilling to take that risk. Some choose not to risk the condemnation of those who are comfortable within the crumbling walls of a Christendom that is more informed by modernity than by Scripture. Some cannot understand because they choose to equate contextualization and missional thought with compromise. Some cannot understand because they love their "church" culture too much. Some cannot understand because they value the paradigms of the past more than they value people of the present age, and as a result will gladly lose their children, their children's friends, and an entire subculture of their community in order to preserve their traditions.

We see this same emphasis in Southern Baptist life. Many voices call for a "return" to something to answer the problem of denominational decline. Influential voices confidently assert that a return to certain cultural

---

[23]Milfred Minatrea, *Shaped by God's Heart* (San Francisco: John Wiley & Sons, 2004), xvi.
[24]http://www.joethorn.net/2005/07/18/the-missional-church.

expressions of ministry, preaching, and evangelism will cause the church to reclaim its effectiveness. In fairness, some of these emphases are needed and helpful. Others, however, are simply a reaction against the culture by reemphasizing the models that were successful in the past.

I don't want anyone to "come back" to a specific paradigm of church beyond that which is commanded in Scripture. Instead I want them to, in the words of Adrian Rogers, "come to Jesus." For when they do, Jesus speaks lovingly to them and sends them to people who live in culture.

Misinformed and fearful persons will always resist what they do not understand or what does not blend with their preferences. However, if the church is willing to be missional, and its theologians and thinkers are willing to assist it, the kingdom will advance to new tongues, tribes, contexts, and cultures. It is important here to note that most of the theologians in Southern Baptist life have been, and continue to be, generally absent from the important conversations about the intersection of church and culture among young leaders (though, thankfully, there are a handful of notable exceptions). While many in the theologian class are still unsure about Rick Warren's Hawaiian shirts and PowerPoint projector, young leaders are struggling with how to be, do, and tell the gospel in homosexual communities, transitioning inner cities, and vast suburban wastelands—and they look to others for the answers. It should not be so.

As the church rediscovers its missional mandate, it can receive a renewed passion to be a people on mission—taking the contextualized message and unchanging gospel into cultures and to people untouched by existing churches. Solid missional and theologically sound churches can be planted, revitalized, or grown—if we will choose to engage our culture and be part of the solution, not continue to lob grenades of half-truths and caricatures into missional church contexts.

If the theologian class can partner with best-practice leaders, the end result can be theologically sound, missionally vibrant churches that engage the culture while remaining true to the "faith once delivered to the saints." Perhaps we need a conversation to discuss how we can engage cultures with biblically faithful and culturally relevant ministry, and affirm all different kinds of biblically sound churches. At first glance, the result may look culturally different, but to God, the result is the same. From his perspective, the Word has become flesh in a new setting, as these new churches express that missional mind-set. And it is no less valid than if they were new indigenous churches in Africa or Asia.

How can this happen? How can we find that balance? It will require at least three things: missional churches must (1) contend for the faith, (2) contextualize their ministries, and (3) cooperate with other churches for the kingdom of God.

CONTEND (JUDE 3)

Many Southern Baptists have already given their opinions on what the missional church should be. I suggest that it should be "incarnational" (deeply connected to the community), "indigenous" (reflect to some degree the culture of the community), and "intentional" (use methodologies that focus on the mission and purposes of God). It is this balance of biblical fidelity and cultural relevance that helps the missional church shape a cohesive strategy for reaching its lost community. The North American Mission Board (NAMB) has officially adopted this language to define a missional church: "A missional church is a biblically faithful and culturally appropriate reproducing community of disciples sent on mission by God to advance his kingdom among all peoples."

NAMB included the words "biblically faithful" for an important reason. The missional church will always contend for the gospel in its setting, because that is its nature. It is being obedient to its calling. It not only sees its obligation, but also recognizes its opportunities. On the other hand, when a church withdraws or isolates itself from its culture, it can no longer represent the Lord effectively—even though it has the words of life. Many churches withdraw by default. They do not understand their culture, nor do they know how to engage it.

Two hindrances often occur when churches try to contend for the gospel without engaging their society. First, they are seen as irrelevant, and consequently, their message is also viewed as irrelevant. Second, the church does not really know the needs, desires, or concerns of those around them, nor do they see the possibilities that exist to act upon these opportunities and speak to people's hearts. Missionaries all over the world have to learn the culture in order to engage it. If we viewed ourselves as missionaries, thinking and acting "missionally," we would have greater success in contending for the gospel. In short, we must contend for a high view of Scripture and for what we believe as biblically shaped Christians. The Scriptures are always relevant in this and every culture—but we are not the Scriptures and we would do well to remember that.

CONTEXTUALIZE (1 CORINTHIANS 9:22-23)

Some approaches to mission strategy, such as colonial and institutional missions, did not work in the past because they had the wrong focus. During the colonial era for example, the intent of western missionaries was not only to make converts, but also to conform the converted into good westerners. When we realized the error of colonial missions, we began to plant indigenous churches that looked different from culture to culture and from generation to generation. They developed their teaching from the unchanging biblical text and their methods from the ever-changing cultural milieu. A definition from 1938 might be helpful:

> An indigenous church, young or old, in the East or in the West, is a church which, rooted in obedience to Christ, spontaneously uses forms of thought and modes of action natural and familiar in its own environment. Such a church arises in response to Christ's own call. The younger churches will not be unmindful of the experiences and teachings which the older churches have recorded in their confessions and liturgy. But every younger church will seek further to bear witness to the same gospel with new tongues."[25]

If Southern Baptists could simply adopt this attitude in our current denominational environment, an unstoppable synergy would result in the conversion of souls, the transformation of lives, and the revitalization of entire areas by the power of the gospel. Such has been, and should continue to be, the essence of Baptist cooperation.

When speaking of "contextualization," I mean to describe a concept once known as "indigenization." The conceptual shift from the latter term to the former is this: the definition of *indigenous* is "born within the culture." Apart from Jewish culture, the Christian faith manifestly is *not* born within a culture and thus is not indigenous. The faith cannot become genuinely indigenous to a culture from which it is not born. This becoming a part of the culture—blooming where it is planted—is a process called "contextualization." Modern missiologists, then, espouse the contextualization of the gospel within every culture on earth.

Evangelicals continue to struggle with presenting the unchanging gospel in an ever-changing cultural setting. Contextualization often feels to them like cultural compromise. In a Southern Baptist culture still recovering

---

[25]International Missionary Council, *The Growing Church: The Madras Series* (New York, International Missionary Council, 1938), 2:276. Cited in Mark Terry, Ebbie Smith, and Justice Anderson, eds., *Missiology* (Nashville: Broadman & Holman, 1998), 311.

from a battle over truth and liberty, diverse expressions of church seem to lose biblical truth in an expression of methodological liberty. It just does not feel right.

Every culture is imperfect and thus at times hostile to the gospel. However, cultures remain the context where Jesus Christ meets persons by grace.[26] We must pay attention to the culture if we are to be truly missional.[27] Preaching against culture shows misunderstanding of what culture is—preaching against it is like preaching against someone's house. There are good things and bad things in it, but it is where people live and where we need to meet them. Just as we exegete the biblical text, we must exegete the culture where we seek to proclaim that biblical text.

Reggie McNeal, until recently the director of leadership development for the South Carolina Baptist Convention, was quoted saying, "One of the hallmarks of the missional church is its move to connect to the community. We have been trying for years to get the community to connect with us. Now the church is connecting to the community."[28] This contextualizes the church's ministry—and many Southern Baptist churches are engaging the culture for the cause of the gospel.

Yet while kingdom work like this continues, the fight about contextualization goes on within the SBC. Like a giant tug-of-war, each side is pulling hard. One side sees these missional expressions as culturally relevant dangers. The battle lines soon become clear: Cultural relevance versus biblical faithfulness, a classic tyranny of the "OR."

To be sure, cultural relevance can be confusing. On one hand, the church can be so focused on cultural relevance that it loses its distinctive message and ceases to be salt and light; this is a very real threat, and it has happened to countless churches and denominations. On the other hand, the church can also decide that culture does not matter. Such a perspective will lead to a church whose message is indiscernible and obscure to those who are "outside."

Let me propose an alternative, one that actually describes both the "missional" concept as well as the essence of Baptist identity through the centuries. Our churches need to be *biblically faithful, culturally relevant, counter cultural* communities. For my full treatment of that short sentence,

---

[26]Donald R. Jacobs, "Contextualization in Mission," in *Toward the 21st Century in Christian Mission,* ed. James M. Phillips and Robert T. Coote (Grand Rapids, MI: Eerdmans, 1993), 236.
[27]George Hunsberger, "The Newbigin Gauntlet," in *The Church Between Gospel and Culture* (Grand Rapids, MI: Eerdmans, 1996), 24.
[28]Amanda Thompson, "Missional Thinking Embraced by Hartsville Church," *Baptist Courier,* March 8, 2006, http://baptistcourier.com/303.article.print.

see my article in the *Catalyst Monthly*.[29] In short, we must recognize that we must do more than just contend; we must contend and contextualize as a counterculture. Without such, our Convention has no future outside of its cultural and geographic confines. But we do have a future, and that means that SBC churches can and should look different from one to another. But looking different makes it harder to cooperate.

COOPERATE

We must be known as the Convention that believes in biblical fidelity *and* engaging people in the culture. And we must learn to do it together. I recognize that many churches have not yet moved from inerrancy to sufficiency, but as a Convention we have settled the theological issues and have developed a clear confession. The Protestant Reformers had a saying that well describes our current challenge: *ecclesia simper reformanda*, "the church, always reforming." Now that we have experienced a necessary theological resurgence and reform, we must move toward a missional resurgence and reform of our churches. We have our theology settled. Now let us get our mission together.

Make no mistake: I am not one who says, "Let's just cooperate around missions and not worry about theology." (See my article on the subject at SBCLife.[30]) Theology matters—and this is precisely why we had a resurgence of conservative theology. But a theological renaissance that is not followed by biblical evangelism and mission is odd indeed. Yet that, according to Thom Rainer as cited in *Baptist Press,* is exactly what has occurred:

> Between 1950 and 2003 annual total baptisms remained basically the same, a "classic plateau." In 1950 Southern Baptists baptized 376,085, while 377,357 were baptized in 2003. Throughout the period, the highest level of baptisms was 445,725 in 1972 and the lowest was 336,050 in 1978, the year before the beginning of the conservative resurgence. More troubling, Rainer asserts, is the spike in congregational baptism ratios— "How many members does it take to reach one person for Christ in a year?"—which he regards as the preferred "measurement of evangelistic health since it takes into consideration church size." In 1950, one person was baptized for every 19 members of SBC churches. In 1978, the baptismal ratio increased to 36 to 1, and by 2003 the number had climbed to 43 to 1. A lower ratio is desired. "The trend in total baptisms in the Southern Baptist Convention thus depicted a clear pattern of plateau. But the more

---

[29]http://www.catalystspace.com/content/monthly/detail.aspx?i=1198&m=01&y=2006.
[30]Ed Stetzer, "Can We Do Missions Without Doing Doctrine?" SBC Life, February 2003, http://sbclife. net/Articles/2003/02/Sla4.asp.

revealing measurement of baptism ratios reveals consistent evangelistic deterioration," Rainer argues. "The baptismal ratio since the onset of the conservative resurgence has worsened. The trend is negative and disturbing. Though numbers are not ultimate measures of spiritual realities, the data we do have indicate a denomination in evangelistic crisis," he adds.[31]

A couple of things should be noted regarding these figures. First, there has been an enormous population increase since 1950, so the "flat" baptism totals actually reflect a dramatic decline when observed against the backdrop of a growing U.S. population. Second, the Annual Church Profiles report that Southern Baptist membership has grown substantially, and though many who are reported as members cannot be located, a larger membership should mean that we have more members evangelizing the lost. But it doesn't.

My own analysis found that from 2004 to 2005, all but one baptism age category went down. The category that went up? Preschoolers—those under five years of age. That makes me nervous. Though I am not one to say that a five year-old cannot trust Christ, it is hard to see the march toward infant baptism as good news.

Total annual baptisms by Southern Baptist churches also show alarming trends. In 2005, 11,740 churches reported zero or one baptism. This is an increase of 5.6 percent of churches who baptized no more than one person. Over 55 percent of churches baptized no youth (twelve- to seventeen-year-olds) in 2005, up from 52 percent the previous year. The number of churches baptizing ten or more declined to 10,062 in 2005. This is down from 10,598 in 2004.[32] And the trends have continued in recent years.

To quote Calvin Guy: "We apply the pragmatic test to the work of the theologian. Does his theology motivate men to go into all the world and make disciples? Does it so undergird them that they, thus motivated, succeed in this primary purpose? Theology must stand the test of being known by its fruit."[33] Our theological resurgence was necessary and important, but to date it has not passed the "Cal Guy" test. The time has come for biblically faithful believers to take the message to people in the culture. And we must learn to do that together.

Cooperatively fixing this problem will not be easy. We have no historical precedent in denominational life for cooperating with such incredibly

---

[31]James A. Smith Sr., "SBC in 'Evangelistic Crisis,' but Would Be Worse Off without Resurgence, Study Says," *Baptist Press*, May 4, 2005, http://www.bpnews.net/bpnews.asp?ID=20723.
[32]Ed Stetzer, "Disturbing Trends in Baptisms," North American Mission Board, October 25, 2006, http://www.namb.net/site/apps/nl/content3.asp?c=9qKILUOzEpH&b=1594357&ct=3198417.
[33]Classroom notes, missions class, Southwestern Seminary.

diverse expressions of church and ministry. On the contrary, it is telling
that the discipleship arm of the SBC was called the "Baptist Sunday School
Board" until just a few years ago. For decades, Baptists had Sunday school
(with attendance pins), nine-verse invitation hymns, suits, and King James
Bibles, and everyone knew what a Southern Baptist looked like. Judson
Allen explains it well in the 1958 *Encyclopedia of Southern Baptists*: "A
Southern Baptist tends to remain a Southern Baptist, whether he lives
in Virginia, Georgia, California, Ohio, or Montana. He needs not easily
adjust to a church fellowship in which methods and practices are different
from those to which he has been conditioned. Churches which are methodologically different are automatically suspect."[34]

Today it is still true: "Churches which are methodologically different
are automatically suspect." At the NAMB Center for Missional Research,
we completed a study of over 2,200 SBC seminary graduates from 1998 to
2004. One question dealt with the issue of what Allen calls "methods and
practices." The results speak to Allen's comments. Graduates were asked
to choose the church ministry paradigm that best fit their church. The
most common answer, chosen by 39 percent, was traditional-progressive:
"churches that rely on programmatic structure to address the spiritual
needs of the community. These churches often use Sunday School, but may
not exclusively use SBC programs."

The second most common approach is the choice most similar to the
1958 version referred to by Allen. Twenty-four percent of the graduates
chose traditional programs: "Churches that rely on traditional SBC programs (e.g., Sunday School, Discipleship Training, Brotherhood, WMU,
and Music) to address the spiritual needs of their community." We should
rejoice and be thankful for their ministry.

Next, with 17 percent, was Purpose Driven: "Churches that deliberately align their activities with the PDC five purposes of church (worship,
fellowship, discipleship, ministry, and evangelism) identified by Rick
Warren."

Additionally, 9 percent chose relation-based churches with structure
and growth driven by face-to-face relationship (e.g., house church, cell
church, and international Christian communities). Emerging, postmodern
churches (4 percent) and affinity churches targeting a particular affinity or
ethnic group (3 percent) rounded out the responses.

Since only 24 percent would look like the kind of church described in
Allen's article, we need to decide if we want to give the others the reception

---

[34]Lynn May, ed., *Encyclopedia of Southern Baptists*, 4 vols. (Nashville: Broadman, 1958).

that Allen described. Although it is no longer 1958, it certainly can feel that way for churches with diverse methodologies when they attend many denominational events. If we continue to treat these methodologically diverse pastors as "automatically suspect," they will choose a different path—and our Convention will be weaker. We need to find ways to cooperate.

Although over 98 percent of those graduates who responded agreed that they believed in inerrancy, they tended to differ on other issues or to hold positions contrary to those held by those churches that Allen mentions. For example:

- Seventy-eight percent of those graduates also believe that "a culturally-relevant style is important for a church to be evangelistically effective."
- Twenty-six percent are verse-by-verse preachers (to be more specific, 26 percent of the respondents indicated that they preached "Primarily explanation or commentary on the biblical text . . . " more than 90 percent of the time).

These are our graduates and young leaders; we need them, even if they do things differently in their context than we do in ours. We've already told a whole generation of "Purpose Driven" pastors that they're really not needed or wanted in today's SBC. Are we intent on communicating this same message to the next generation? Is it our intent now to go on to the next generation who dare to call themselves "emerging," even when some disapprove of the term?

Cooperation is a God-sized task, and it will take all of us in missional cooperation to build the kingdom of God. But we have learned from history, theology, and the best of missional practitioners that as we engage our local community, we will become better partners with others who wish to reach their community for Christ, and will certainly be more energized to support the Cooperative Program to make a global impact for Christ.

For too long we've cast a suspicious glance (and sometimes even verbal assaults) at others in our denomination who don't dress like we do, who enjoy different music, who use projectors and praise bands, who don't include the word "Baptist" in the name of their churches, who preach differently, who have small-group ministries outside the church facilities, who don't use the same curriculum we do, who don't have evening services, who don't utilize an "altar call," who are reaching people with whom we do not feel comfortable, and who differ with us on secondary issues. (And, yes, sometimes those comments have been directed the other way as well.)

Southern Baptists may have concerns and suspicions about "new ways," but from our inception in 1845, we have been deeply committed to reaching our communities. A growing number are now beginning to realize that this commitment requires a missional engagement of culture accompanied with a proclamation of the timeless, unchanging gospel. This requires new expressions, strategies, and systems. Such a shift will be difficult over the noise of those who oppose the contention that we can be both biblically faithful *and* culturally relevant. However, our task is not to listen to those who love church culture more than they love Christ's commands. Christ will build his church through pastors and churches that engage the culture in a biblically discerning manner.

The real question is this: Will the SBC and its entities be seen as partners in the process of raising up new indigenous expressions of Southern Baptist churches? If we can embrace diverse forms of scripturally sound church and ministry, we can again see the kingdom impact that I believe God wishes to renew in us. Can we cooperate? Or will our contending be in vain as those who have contextualized to different communities no longer work with us, not because of their theology but because of their ministry expression?

CONCLUSION

We can no longer continue trying to reach North America with "one-size-fits-all" methods and an inward denominational focus. The shift toward a missional SBC will consequently necessitate a change from the way many churches are doing ministry. Baptists have a choice: we can argue about whether we'll use the noun *missionary* or the adjective *missional*, or we can recognize that a lost world needs us to stop arguing about nomenclature and obey Christ's commands. Simply put, it does not matter what you call it, it matters that you do it. And we are not doing it.

Within the wider world of evangelicalism, the issue is settled; most evangelical denominations have decided they need change and they want to be "missional." At the same time, we may not be ready. Too many of our denominational and church leaders are still objecting to casual clothes in worship, while other churches and organizations are reaching people in diverse cultures—including those who wear casual clothes.

Furthermore, many young leaders who have been alienated and marginalized are not pining away, hoping that the SBC will welcome them back. Many of them have moved on to networks and other partnerships where they can get on with missions instead of getting into an argument.

The result of this phenomenon has become the "elephant in the room" for Southern Baptists. There is a reason so many churches are forming networks—they are doing so because they do not see ours as their best investment of time and energy. If our seminaries do not teach cultural engagement, if our agencies primarily espouse strategies from a past era, and if our associations reject anything that does not look like a tent revival, it will be little surprise that our young leaders consider us "out of touch."

The first step in organizational decline is the loss of our creative people, who decide to go on to more entrepreneurial settings. We have already lost most of this number; in fact, we have actively pushed many of them out by teaching and preaching against them in many SBC contexts and venues. The next step in decline is that the most competent among us begin to leave. Although I do not think we are yet at this point, we are rapidly approaching it. This is apparent to me as I observe the best and brightest among us who do not consider denominational involvement helpful or a good use of their time, and thus put their time and resources elsewhere. The most competent denominational leaders are two generations away from emerging leaders. I ask in this context: where are the 40- to 50-year-old versions of greats like Adrian Rogers, Jimmy Draper, Ed Young, or W. A. Criswell?

When Jimmy Draper was planning the first national "young leaders" meeting, he asked me for suggested speakers. I told him what we needed most was a nationally known pastor who had credibility with young pastors, and who was also still clearly connected with the denomination. His voice went up in excitement as he asked, "Exactly, who?" With sadness, I replied, "That's my point."

Many young leaders have chosen other paths and networks—and as a result we have lost both their influence and the chance to influence them. If we want to keep the creative and competent among us, we need courage to speak to fringe elements within our Convention—those who have been given a platform in an earlier struggle and are now empowered by the Internet and e-mail. Our message to them should be that we want, need, and affirm all kinds of scripturally sound churches.

In reflecting on this exodus of young leaders, I must confess that I have grown both weary and encouraged at the same time, a feeling that many tell me they share. However, let's not get lost in the terminology. That's not the issue. I think J. I. Packer's wisdom, when addressing renewal terminology, is quite appropriate here when discussing the term "missional." He writes:

We should not make an issue of this or any other verbal preference. As Thomas Hobbes observed long ago, words are the counters of wise men ("they do reckon by them"), but they are the coinage of fools, in the sense that unless certain words are used—the right buttons pressed, as we say— fools cannot recognize that the thing to which they apply the words has been spoken of at all, however many equivalent words may have been employed in place of their beloved shibboleths. We should take to heart Hobbes's warning and remember that two people can use different words and mean the same thing, just as they can use the same word and mean different things.[35]

It is critical that we now come to a point of heeding the use, and more importantly, the meaning of the term "missional" as used by DuBose in 1983. Though none of us has been as bold, DuBose accurately summarized it in this manner when speaking about the cross of Christ and its use of ornamentation in our building and thought: "The ornamental beauty of a bejeweled cross in comfortable Christendom is not the biblical meaning of the beauty of the cross. The New Testament meaning of beauty is the beauty of missional purpose—the vicarious and redemptive suffering of Jesus which was the climactic act of the mission of God through his Son."[36]

Let me close with this. "Missional," in the end, is simply a word. In fact, it is not even a word that matters. It is irrelevant. But in a declining denomination, a missional *emphasis* does matter. Can we allow some of our brothers and sisters to use one word and others of us to use another? Can we also agree that we are *off* mission and need to get back on? Factions will not help, and I have no interest in creating another one based on the "missional" label. Still, we need to recognize the importance of missional ministry in all kinds of churches. Traditional churches can and should be missional as well, which is why we affirmed such churches in *Breaking the Missional Code.*[37] I'd simply ask, "Can the biblically faithful traditional church join hands with the boomer Purpose Driven church and partner with the scripturally sound emerging church?" I hope so.

Does that mean any and every theological position or practice can and should be part of the SBC? No, certainly not! I am a Baptist, not because I was reared or redeemed at a Baptist church, because I was not.

---

[35]J. I. Packer, *Keep in Step with the Spirit: Finding Fullness in Our Walk with God* (Grand Rapids, MI: Revell, 1993), 195–196.
[36]DuBose, *God Who Sends*, 95.
[37]Ed Stetzer and David Putnam, *Breaking the Missional Code: Your Church Can Become a Missionary in Your Community* (Nashville: B&H, 2006).

I am a Baptist because I am a Biblicist. Based on my best understanding of Scripture, "Baptist" and "biblical" are, and should be, synonyms. And problems are created when they are not. Problems come when we place history, tradition, or even consensus over the authority of Scripture (something which I believe the *Baptist Faith and Message 2000* adeptly avoided). But the SBC is a Convention with which we joyfully affiliate and partner for a cooperative mission from a common theological persuasion (the current *Baptist Faith and Message*). It is not a church, like a Lutheran Church, with which we align in a common or required paradigm of ministry.

I am ready to see Southern Baptists united by our common, already agreed-upon theology and mission. Personally, I am ready to cooperate, even with those who are different from me. I won't ask Paige Patterson to become as Reformed as I am. I won't ask Al Mohler to sing the music I sing with his shirt untucked. I won't ask Morris Chapman to don my silly glasses, or utilize video clips to illustrate his sermon.

I won't ask them to do it like me and will expect them not to ask me to do it like them. I want to be in a Convention where we agree on enough to get back on mission. If we can't do that, we should start preparing for our inevitable denominational demise today. But if we can, the future is as bright as our churches—all of them, from many different paradigmatic background, cooperating together to reach a lost world through a missional effort that represents the essence of our history and identity. Listen to the invitation DuBose laid out almost a quarter-century ago: "Through the biblical concept of the sending, we have come to see the Christian life as a missional pilgrimage, a journey in mission—more, a journey *into* mission—an odyssey that will end only in the eschaton."[38]

Southern Baptists began the Cooperative Program for the purpose of "eliciting, combining, and directing the energies of the whole denomination in one sacred effort, for the propagation of the Gospel."[39] I'm ready to *contend* for theologically sound ministry, *contextualize* in different contexts, and *cooperate* for the sake of the gospel. That sounds like "one sacred effort" to me, and I am ready to join hands in a new, missional SBC. Will you join me?

The fire of controversy can and will burn us all, as well as hinder the spread of the gospel. The nations—ours and those around the globe—are waiting for that gospel. To use a metaphor, let's not fiddle and fuss

---

[38]DuBose, *God Who Sends*, 160.
[39]Michael K. Whitehead, "Why Cooperate?" Baptist2Baptist, http://www.baptist2baptist.net/b2barticle.asp?ID=37.

as Nashville burns. That fire of controversy is a fire that will spread to Alpharetta, Richmond, state conventions, associations, and our own churches. We have all smelled the smoke. As we fight the fire, a lost world continues to wait for the saving message of Christ. Let's get on mission—and let's do it together.

CHAPTER TEN

THE FUTURE OF THE TRADITIONAL CHURCH

Jim Shaddix

THE STORY IS ALL TOO REAL. Hear it well . . .

There was a traditional Baptist church that had two members. And the younger of them said to his church, "Church, give me the share of heritage that is coming to me." And it divided its heritage between them. Not many days later, the younger member gathered his King James Bible and notes from his pastor's weekly evangelistic sermons, and took a journey to a far university. There, he squandered his Baptist tradition, less-than-captivating worship experience, borderline legalism and overall superficial Christianity in reckless postmodernism. By and by, someone came along and took him to an emerging church, where together they burnt candles, smelled incense, celebrated the perceived mystery of the Bible, and deconstructed what little theology the young Baptist had. The speaker verbally assaulted the church, whacked away at all the stuff the young Baptist thought was dumb about his background, and systematically shredded his religious experience. And the young Baptist said, "Yeah, yeah—that's exactly right! I hated that organ, the gospel quartet, the robed choir, those old hymns and responsive readings. They never made any difference in my life!"

RECOGNIZING THE NEEDS OF THE NEXT GENERATION

I want you to meet a young Baptist. He hails from a rapidly evaporating pool of young people in Southern Baptist life. In 1980, we baptized more than one-hundred thousand eighteen- to thirty-four-year-olds in our churches. Twenty-five years later that number dipped to slightly more than sixty thousand, a frightening figure when you consider that the United States population climbed above three-hundred million.[1] Only 31 percent of twenty-somethings attend any kind of Christian church, although more than half of them attended church weekly in high school. That's a 42 percent drop from high school graduation to age twenty-five and a 58 percent decline from graduation to age 29. If the stats hold up, our young Baptist friend—who was an active churchgoer as a teenager—won't be involved in anybody's church by his thirtieth birthday.[2]

This young Baptist is supposed to be our future, but his rapid disappearance is a painful reminder that the future of the traditional church in our denomination is really not an issue of the future of *traditional* Baptist churches, but of the future of *young* Baptists. If our young people disappear, then our churches disappear. And if our churches disappear, then our future disappears. So if we're going to understand anything about the future of our traditional churches, I submit that we must look more closely at our young people than we do our churches.

There's no doubt that numerous alternative spiritual venues are deceiving many young Baptists just like the one in our parable. If they're not dropping out of organized churches altogether, they're being captured by philosophies like the emerging church. Both venues—nonchurch and emerging church—champion a belief in nothing! That ought to tell us something: our young people are not running *to* something; they're running *away* from something. The question that begs an answer is, "What are they running away from?"

The standard answer we give is that young people are running away from our style, our music, our form, and our tradition. While the emerging church movement is not the only non-Baptist philosophy capturing scores of young people, it may be the best indicator we've had in a long time that this apostasy from the church is *not* really about style and form. Think about it—candles and incense and mystery and formlessness. Many of those things not only don't carry a contemporary techno-driven aura, but they actually have striking similarities to dead, ritualistic religions of the past.

As we approach the subject of the future of the traditional church, we can't afford to oversimplify this issue as if it were a choice between the "contemporary" and the "traditional." The definitions of these words

---

[1] Libby Lovelace, "LifeWay Research Examines the New View of Young Adults." http://www.lifeway.com/ lwc/article_main_page/0%2C1703%2CA%25253D164570%252526M%25253D200725%2C00.html.
[2] "Twentysomethings Struggle to Find Their Place in Christian Churches." *The Barna Update*, September 24, 2003, http://www.barna.org/FlexPage.aspx?Page=BarnaUpdate&BarnaUpdateID=149.

are elusive at best. I would consider Riverside Baptist Church in Denver somewhat contemporary, with a blended style of music. We sing a mixture of praise and worship choruses, Passion songs, Brooklyn Tabernacle music, and some hymns, and we put the words up on big screens with PowerPoint. We clap and raise our hands, and periodically some of our people even sway as they sing. And we have a choir and a praise team, as well as a band and an orchestra. We don't have a Sunday evening service, and we have only one business meeting each year.

Some time ago I had two interesting conversations about our worship in the same week. The first conversation was with one of our senior adults, who made the profoundly original suggestion that we needed to sing more hymns, the ones we "grew up with." "After all," she said, "the hymns were what got us through difficult times."

"More than the Bible?" I asked, immediately wishing my mouth had an "un-send" button on it.

"Well, we really don't know much about the Bible," she replied. "But we know the hymns."

A few days later I was talking with one of our young twenty-somethings about musical worship styles, and he hesitantly informed me that a lot of his contemporaries were somewhat frustrated with our "traditional" music style. When I asked him to be specific, he said that while they resonated with the biblical teaching, the choir turned them off—especially the robes. Thus, I've got one group that thinks we're over-the-edge contemporary, and another group that thinks we're stuck-in-the-mud traditional (along with a whole lot of sub-preferences in between). What's a pastor to do?

If we generalize this trend as simply a choice between the "contemporary" and the "traditional," we will surely evaluate and analyze only the things we can see and touch and hear (music styles, architectural forms, pews, pulpits, and suits). Mark it down: our children are not running from our lifeless style and form; they're running from something intangible, something that's more difficult to get their arms around. They're running from a lifeless Christianity. And they're so turned off by it that they're running to *nothing* as an alternative. But the tangible—what we can see and touch and hear—always takes the rap. That's why style and form get blamed for it.

Evidence of this reality lies in the fact that the emerging church, seeker- and purpose-driven ministries, religious cults, and other alternative spiritual venues aren't nearly as appealing to nonchurched young people as they are to marginally churched young people. One noted Bible scholar observed that most of the architects of the emerging church movement are guys who grew up in a traditional church that didn't have a lot of depth and breadth, and who reacted to the superficiality and legalism of it.[3]

But there's plenty of evidence lying around that what our young people are really reacting to is not our styles and forms. Consider the hymns, for example. I submit to you that our young people are not opposed to the hymns, even if they don't realize it or are not willing to admit it. Dave Crowder, Charlie Hall, Chris Tomlin, Kristian Stanfill, and Matt Redman are just a few of the contemporary Christian artists who are reviving the hymns among the younger generations. The *Passion* movement among Christian singles, college students, and young couples has even produced a CD entitled *Hymns: Ancient and Modern*. No, our young people are not opposed to hymns. They're opposed to the lifeless and heartless way we often sing them!

Additionally, the twenty-somethings are finding fresh meaning in the ordinances of baptism and the Lord's Supper, as well as in ancient icons like stained glass. Do you realize that today the organ is played more at professional baseball games than it is in Baptist churches? When was the last time you went to a professional baseball game and saw people get up and walk out, resolved never to return, because they played an organ at the seventh-inning stretch? And don't you think it's interesting that the twenty- and thirty-somethings will spend their time and money to hear Jay Leno and David Letterman give their monologues . . . in a suit and tie? Nobody leaves mad or offended, and nobody writes them off as irrelevant.

The reality is that much of the reaction to traditional church forms today comes from a fabricated Christian culture within our own camp, not from a secular world that thinks we're irrelevant. And the reason it's fabricated is that neither we nor our young people have stopped to process the real thing from which they're running. We're not taking the time to identify the real problem, so the only thing either one of us can do is place the blame on what we can feel, touch, and see—the styles and forms. The future of the traditional young Baptist is not as simple as replacing our organ with his keyboard and acoustic guitar, nor is it as simple as contrasting my suit and tie with his untucked shirt. We must look deeper than the external.

Here is the first assessment I would make about the future of the traditional church. The traditional church will survive and thrive *if* it under-

---

[3]John MacArthur with Phil Johnson, "What's So Dangerous About the Emerging Church?" *Grace to You*. Interview conversation on CD 107.

stands that young people are leaving, not because of what we're giving them, but because of what we're not giving them.

FILLING THE NEED FOR TRUTH AND SUBSTANCE

Now, that begs the question, *What is it we're not giving them?* "The Parable of the Young Baptist" continues . . .

> And when the young Baptist had spent everything, a severe spiritual famine arose in the postmodern culture, and he began to be in need. So he went and hired himself out to one of the pastors of the seeker church, who sent him into his faddish fields to feed faddish trends. And he was longing to be fed with the faddish pods that the faddish trends offered, but no one gave him anything of substance. But when he came to himself, he said, "How many of my home church's members have more than enough bread, but I perish here with hunger! I will arise and go to my church, and I will say to it, 'Church, I have sinned against heaven and before you. I am no longer worthy to be called your member. Treat me as one of your yokefellow deacons.'" And he arose and came to his church. But while he was still a long way off, his home church members saw him and felt compassion, and ran and embraced him and kissed him. And the young Baptist said to his home church members, "Church, I have sinned against heaven and before you. I am no longer worthy to be called your member." But the church members said to one another, "Bring quickly the best choir robe, and put it on him, and put a quarterly in his hand, and wingtips on his feet. And bring the fattened chicken and fry it, and let us eat dinner-on-the-grounds. For this our young member was dead, and is alive again; he was lost, and is found." And they began to have fellowship.

I want you to hear something encouraging. There's a very good possibility that our young Baptist friend will at least consider coming back. Like the biblical story of the prodigal, our parable finds the young man returning to the very roots he had previously abandoned. In both parables, the young man came to the realization that there actually was value in the home that he left, especially when it was compared to the reality of the life he thought he wanted. I would suggest to you that the return of the young Baptist—and in part the future of the traditional church—is dependent on two factors. One factor is certain and the other is yet to be determined.

Factor One: A Firm Foundation

The factor we can be sure about is that every nontraditional philosophy and movement built on unbiblical premises will expire. It will run its course and peter out. Postmodernism and its child, the emerging church, are faddish. Go back to the Christian psychological preaching of Harry Emerson Fosdick, which gave birth to the power of positive thinking championed by Norman Vincent Peale. Follow it through to the new neo-orthodoxy of Robert Schuller, and then to the seeker sensitivity of Bill Hybels. It won't take you long from there to trace the influence into our own denomination and pulpits. But neither will it take you long to identify each one's day in the sun and each one's setting on the horizon of evangelicalism.

And the more recent the movement or mindset, the shorter its existence will be. Each one will have a shorter shelf life than the one preceding it. The reason is that everything exhausts itself faster in our explosive media environment because we run everything to its limit at a more rapid pace. We exhaust everything faster through television, radio, cell phones, PDAs, iPods, the Internet, and blogs. This world experienced thousands of years of premodernism, but only hundreds of years of modernism. We'll have a few years of postmodernism, and then something else will come along (if it hasn't already). But they'll all be short-lived, and their constituents will move on to something else in hopes that it will satisfy the longing in their souls. And some of them will come back home.

Personally, I believe this is one place we must tip our hats to the traditional church. The traditional church is not built on passing styles and forms. The healthy traditionalist knows these things change faster than Terrell Owens changes football teams. And there are an infinite number of stylistic and programmatic preferences that make perceived "relevance" impossible to keep up with. The church that trusts its future to its willingness, ability, and success in reinventing itself every time a new cultural wind blows is in for a long road of paranoia, schizophrenia, and frustration. From a stewardship standpoint alone, the Christian church—with its volunteer financial base—cannot sustain the re-creation process necessary to keep up with all the variations in musical styles and technological advances, not to mention the infinite number of personal preferences among individual constituents. And any effort to do so will certainly result in spending the bulk of our resources on our preferences and whims as opposed to advancing the gospel among the nations.

Yes, there is a quality of traditionalism that has served us well. Many traditional churches have an admirable reverence for the past. They honor the past in a healthy way. Churches that are just grabbing every new fad that comes down the pike are more committed to methodology than they are to theology and more concerned about being successful than being faithful. There are numerous traditional churches in our convention that make changes very slowly because they revere the good traditions, and their changes are conformed more by those things than they are pragmatic methods.

Factor Two: The Response of the Church

That brings us to the factor yet to be determined regarding the return of our young Baptists. While the certain demise of unbiblical philosophies and movements is only a matter of time, the question mark is what exactly our young people will find waiting for them at home. They will return to their roots—*if* their roots are strong and deep. They will return to their roots—*if* their roots can truly satisfy that longing in their souls.

Do you know the common denominator in all those faddish movements I mentioned earlier (psychological preaching, positive thinking, new neo-orthodoxy, seeker-sensitivity)? John MacArthur observed that the common trend amongst these fads is the down-playing, depreciating, diminishing, and sometimes absolute disappearance of sound theology, classic doctrine, the centrality of Scripture, and the expositional preaching and teaching of the Bible.[4] When you take those things away, you remove any possibility of a right understanding of God and, subsequently, a right relationship with him. That's why their neglect leaves voids and unfulfilled longings in people's lives.

Now the easiest thing for us to do at this point is to say, "Well, that couldn't be the problem in our Baptist churches because we're already doing those things." After all, we did have the conservative resurgence and got all of our churches back on track. In fact, most people would say that the traditional church is actually defined and characterized by things like a high view of Scripture, good theology, and expository preaching. But is that really the case, practically and functionally?

Of the forty-thousand plus churches in our denomination, most of them are traditional congregations that still follow the LifeWay program, still associate with the local and state and national conventions, still follow the thematic emphases of the denominational calendar, and still sing

---

[4]MacArthur, "What's So Dangerous About the Emerging Church?"

gospel songs from the hymnal, and the preacher still preaches a 30-minute evangelistic message every week followed by an altar-call invitation. We know that. But what we fail to realize is that many of the people in these churches often have no more spiritual discernment than the members of an emerging church. Why? Because things like Baptist affiliation, denominational loyalty, Cooperative Program giving, and traditional ecclesiology are not substitutes for substantial theology and faithful exposition of the Bible with integrity. And just giving lip-service to these elements simply fosters people's susceptibility to falling prey to deceptive movements.

I was intrigued by a recent study within our own circles based on interviews with eighteen- to thirty-four year-olds from all over the United States. Some were unchurched, some were regular church attendees, and some were even church leaders. The research indicated that one of the things that characterizes this generation is the search for "authentic answers." The study went on to report that both the churched and the unchurched said "they desired to participate in Bible study that minimizes finding pat answers in the exploration of Scripture." One of the researchers concluded, "The lost and the saved in this age group are looking for just what the church can provide in Biblical community. They want absolute truth but they embrace the struggle of finding it themselves. They don't want it to be spoon-fed to them." Respondents cited "the combined knowledge and experiences of the group" as well as "a climate of honesty" as appealing characteristics of small-group meetings in the church.[5]

I might be alone in my assessment, but I would submit several cautions before buying into that research too quickly and building one's new church program around it. First, the opinions expressed are couched in lingo that sounds frighteningly similar to that coming from the postmodern, emerging church. Second, any time you listen to the combined voice of both the regenerate and the unregenerate, you're going to come away with a skewed—if not adulterated—opinion. The very suggestion that the regenerate and unregenerate are saying the same thing ought to tell us that we've got a problem. Third, you don't provide authentic answers to a starving generation by minimizing objectivity in Bible study, democratically polling the group to determine truth, and leaving the conclusions in the hands of those championing for self-discovery. Our all-too-frequent approach to Bible study of going around the room and asking, "What does this verse mean to you?" will be our death! There may be more relativism and existentialism in our camps than we're willing to admit. Several years ago, Dr.

---

[5]Lovelace, "LifeWay Research."

Chuck Kelley of New Orleans Seminary wrote an article in which he suggested that many Southern Baptists were "functional universalists." While we would never admit to embracing the idea that everyone is eventually going to heaven, we indicate such a belief by the infrequency with which we share our faith. Well, I wonder sometimes if many of our churches are not also filled with "functional relativists" and "functional existentialists."

Above our relativism and existentialism is our pragmatism, and the tragedy of our pragmatism is that differences in stylistic appeal are the only things tangible enough for us to blame for our abandonment of traditions. While we're arguing about how to give the traditional Baptist church a cosmetic make-over with regard to styles and forms, our people are going out into the world without a mastery of the Bible, without a solid foundation of systematic and biblical theology, and without roots deep enough to withstand the winds of false doctrine that blow their way every day. Much of the fault lies in the fact that the only things they hear in some of our churches are weekly Roman Road sermons aimed at people who aren't even present, and self-help Sunday school lessons targeting Christians who are just trying to survive daily life.

We must understand that verbal or written assent to the *Baptist Faith and Message* is not the same as being rooted and grounded in biblical doctrine and theology. And we must understand that reading a passage of Scripture and then spring-boarding off of it into a revivalistic message or a thirty-minute diatribe on the evils of abortion, homosexuality, and drunkenness is not necessarily faithful, biblical exposition. I've known many Southern Baptists—who never share their faith—to confuse the terms "evangelistic" and "evangelical." They call themselves "evangelistic" when they're really just claiming a loose association with evangelicalism. Many preachers do the same thing with the word "expository." They call themselves "expository preachers," when all they really do is read a text longer than a verse or two, and then proceed to totally abuse its meaning. We've got to check the integrity between the labels we claim and what we really do.

The young Baptist in the parable is not the victim of an out-of-date musical style or an institutionalized denominational form, however faulty those things sometimes may be. He is the victim of not being grounded in historic sound doctrine, right theology, and the intentional and faithful exposition of God's Word. Just look at any kind of movement, past, present, and future. If those elements don't characterize it, you've got problems, even if it looks like a traditional Baptist church.

Here is my second assessment about the future of the traditional church. The traditional church will survive and thrive *if* it intentionally disciples its people with sound doctrine through the exposition of Scripture.

A RETURN TO RELEVANT, PASSIONATE FAITH

But that alone won't do it. We have yet another problem. "The Parable of the Young Baptist" concludes . . .

> Now the elder Baptist was out on visitation, and as he came and drew near to the church, he heard music and dancing (well, maybe not dancing). And he called one of the deacons and asked what these things meant. And he said to him, "Our younger member has come, and the staff has killed the fattened chicken, because we have received him back safe and sound." But he was angry and refused to go in. The church members came out and entreated him, but he answered them, "Look, these many years I have served you, and I never disobeyed your traditions, yet you never gave me a fried chicken, that I might celebrate with my friends. But when this young member of yours came, who has devoured your tradition with prostitutes, you killed the fattened chicken for him!" And the church members said to him, "Elder Baptist, you are always with us, and all that we have is yours. It was fitting to fellowship and be glad, for this your younger member was dead, and is alive; he was lost, and is found."

Sitting in any church service, traditional or non-traditional, will be quite different within the next ten years. One of our denominational servants predicts that when a pastor speaks of some current world event, many members will have the ability to quickly access a digi-cam from the referenced area to observe what's happening in real time. It's not unlikely that when a pastor shares a statistic, several members will quickly access the original research to see if his citation is accurate. A member who discovers the pastor exaggerated the actual facts might even text his Sunday school class scattered across the congregation, leading group members to quickly exchange online opinions about the need to censure the pastor because of his tendency to stretch the truth.[6]

In the more progressive churches, the difference will likely be even more magnified. Operators in the booth may give the congregation a whiff of Johnson's Baby Oil at a baby dedication, or they may provide a vanilla scent to accompany the lighting of candles during a candlelight service. It's not outside the realm of possibility that a missions pastor will pres-

---

[6]Richard Ross, "Youth Ministry and the Church in Ten Years," *Network Magazine*, Winter 2006, 6.

ent the congregation with a challenge to fund a new church building in a third-world country, and at the end of his challenge, all members realistically could take out their PDAs and move funds to the church account. In less than a minute, the large video screens could report the grand total of contributions, followed by a live shot from the site where the building will be built. The sponsoring church then gets to be blessed immediately as the groundbreaking ceremony begins.[7]

Certainly, all churches will not be equally as aggressive. And it's true that many traditional, nonadapting churches will get left in the dust, not because they're unwilling to compromise their doctrines and traditions, but simply because they're stubborn and prideful. They will refuse to do things as simple as adding a nontraditional instrument or incorporating an occasional contemporary song in order to connect with a broader range of age groups. Other churches will actually be led by sincere leaders who genuinely want to reach people for Christ, but who simply fail to understand the times and make practical and logical adjustments to a more "up-to-date" church life. Their visions, too, will go unrealized. All kinds of churches resist change and new forms. The numbers show that these congregations— which comprise 60–70 percent of all churches—are plateaued or slightly declining in membership. For many of them, staying this course will simply result in the inability to pay the electric bill. One researcher posits that their buildings will be sold to church plants anxious to start a new kind of church or to Muslims who will transform them into mosques.[8]

But the real problem may be deeper than being close-minded to innovative church forms and styles. Like the elder son in the Bible and the elder Baptist in our parable, many traditional Baptists have a heart problem. We have some symptoms that may cause us to turn up our noses not only at our own kind when they return to their Baptist origins, but also at those we're responsible for reaching. I've met good Baptists who would rather see their daughters marry a pagan white drunk than a godly black man. We're more stirred by western patriotism than we are by historic evangelicalism. If I've seen it once, I've seen it a hundred times—a traditional Baptist congregation sits in lethargy and complacency, half-heartedly mumbling the words to songs of glorious praise and even great hymns of the faith, only to rise to their feet with hands over their hearts and tears in their eyes when a soloist begins to sing Lee Greenwood's "I'm Proud to Be an American." We've got a heart problem when we're more passionate about the flag than we are the

---

[7]Ibid., 7.
[8]Ibid.

Father, and when we pay more allegiance to "Old Glory" than to his glory! We've got a heart problem when pastors don't stay longer than a couple of years at any given church, and when they're constantly looking for the next place with a higher salary and "better situation." We've got a heart problem when our church rolls are filled with unregenerate members who never darken the doors unless it's to weigh in on dismissing the pastor or derailing the proposal to relocate. And the future of the traditional church is dependent upon whether those things get fixed, not whether we change our styles and forms.

Our irrelevance doesn't come from forms and styles. Our irrelevance comes from a hollow, lifeless religion that is devoid of the Holy Spirit's presence and power and absent of biblical direction. Our irrelevance comes from paying lip-service to the Great Commission when our budgets and our programs give absolutely no indication that we care in the least about taking the gospel to the nations. Our irrelevance comes from spending God's money to build facilities that look more like high-tech amusement parks than places to worship and study the Bible, especially when our brothers and sisters in Christ in China, Indonesia, Uganda, and the Sudan don't have food, clothing, medical supplies, and shelter.

Our younger Baptists are of great value to Christ's church, and they do have something to bring to our table. We had better wake up and realize that with all their faults and shortcomings, God has given them a measure of grace in discerning authenticity in the church. They know that learning about missions and giving to missions is not the same as *doing* missions. This younger generation wants to *do*, not just study and give. They can see through our hypocrisy, and they won't put up with our saying we love God and his mission while all the time showing disdain for people of different races and lower income levels. They're keenly aware that we preach and talk a lot about prayer, and they know that we share a lot of prayer requests. But they also take note of the fact that we never give any significant time in our church program to getting on our faces before God and crying out to him in desperation. They can see right through our haphazard, emotionless, cold expressions of what we call worship, and they know that it just doesn't jibe with true love for and allegiance to our Creator and Savior.

Bob Coy, senior pastor and founder of the 18,000-member Calvary Chapel in Fort Lauderdale, Florida, identifies this as the crisis of relevancy. It's not an issue of the younger generation's search for contemporary forms and styles, but their search for real truth and reasons for actions. "The emptiness of yesterday's liturgy has got to become relevant," Coy says. "The next generation is screaming for a relationship with God."[9]

If, in fact, these young Baptists are the future of the traditional church, then perhaps it's wise for us to listen to those who study their generation. Richard Ross, professor of student ministry at Southwestern Seminary and originator of *True Love Waits*, describes churches that are just now becoming visible in the U.S. but likely will grow and proliferate in the next ten years:

- They're built on a biblical model of church life, focused on completing the Great Commission, and centered on relationships with God and among his followers.
- They're desperate for God, for revival, for the transformation of culture, and the evangelization of the lost—both locally and globally.
- They're permeated by pervasive, extended, and sacrificial callings to prayer that take priority over sleep, eating, or creature comforts.
- Their senior pastors and other core leaders demonstrate genuine brokenness and humility before God, and that spirit makes them warm and accepting of all peoples, including racial groups with historic anger toward each other.
- Believers discover intimacy with God, vibrant relationships with others, and the capacity for great faith. Out of desperation they listen closely for prophetic instructions about how to move forward to impact the world for Christ. Once they get their marching orders, they get off their knees and move forward with unstoppable confidence. Their own love for the heart of God makes them want to announce his glory among all people groups.
- They ask God to show them an acceptable lifestyle of simplicity in order that they might free resources for kingdom activity. They're always preparing financially for family members to take the gospel to new places—and to support others who will go where they cannot go.
- When believers gather at church, the issue is the same: How can the church function in the most frugal manner possible in order to release resources for kingdom activity?[10]

None of those things are dependent upon musical style, denominational involvement, or any other element by which we normally characterize the traditional church. Mark it down, fellow Baptist, and especially those among us who are in the traditional arena. When our young Baptist brethren come home, we'd better make sure they find us engaged in God-centered worship, sacrificial prayer, vibrant and holy Christian living, and

---

[9]Rebecca Barnes and Lindy Lowry, "The American Church in Crisis," http://www.outreachmagazine.com/library/features/06mayjuneftramericanchurchincrisis.asp.
[10]Ross, "Youth Ministry."

a passionate and sacrificial abandonment to the mission of Jesus Christ. If they don't find it, they won't stay. If they do, they'll embrace us again. And our attrition rate will go down, regardless of our musical styles and denominational forms.

Here is the third and final assessment I would make about the future of the traditional church. The traditional church will survive and thrive *if* its people have a change of heart about their God, his worship, and the people for whom he died.

CONCLUSION

The thing that has always intrigued me about our treatment of the parable of the prodigal son in Luke 15 is that we often miss the point. We most frequently gravitate toward the strong gospel message of the prodigal, and sometimes tip our hats in disgust to the coldness of the elder brother. The key to unlocking its message is found in what it has in common with the two parables that precede it—the parables of the lost sheep and the lost coin. In all three parables, somebody longs to find something, and somebody throws a party when something is found. That's just like heaven when lost sinners come home. And the three parables in succession build to a crescendo of indictment against the hypocritical, traditional religionists of the day who actually opposed God's agenda, while all the time thinking they were for it.

Southern Baptists, we must not miss the point. I'm neither an Old Testament prophet nor the son of an Old Testament prophet, but I am bound to offer a response to a similar question that an Old Testament prophet was asked: "Son of man, can these *traditional* bones live?" I believe that our traditional churches can survive and thrive with hymns and organs and choirs and denominational loyalty *if* they are grounded in sound doctrine and faithful exposition of God's Word, and *if* they have a hot heart and desperation for God and his agenda. But we're not good for many more days of surface theology, topical preaching and teaching, hypocritical living, lifeless and heartless worship, and token involvement in God's mission of making disciples of all nations—in neither the traditional nor the nontraditional church.

CHAPTER ELEVEN

EVANGELISM AND CHURCH GROWTH IN THE SBC

Thom S. Rainer

I ONCE CHECKED INTO AN Albuquerque hotel to speak at the New Mexico Baptist Convention evangelism conference. I followed my typical road-warrior pattern of turning the shower on full blast with hot water. My purpose in this ritual is to allow steam to build in the bathroom and hang my clothes so that most of the wrinkles are removed. It's the lazy man's way of ironing.

On this occasion, however, my plans went awry. When I thought sufficient time had passed, I opened the bathroom door to retrieve my clothes. The heavy steam escaped immediately and made its way to the smoke detector. Ear-piercing alarms began to sound throughout the hotel. People flooded into the hallways. But I remained in my room standing on a chair fanning the smoke detector in desperation.

The alarm finally stopped. I thought I was in the clear. Then a knock sounded at my door. It was the night clerk, an elderly lady of obvious German descent.

"Is there a fire in this room?" she demanded.

"No ma'am," I responded meekly.

"The computer said there was a fire in this room," she insisted.

"Ma'am, you can see there is no fire in this room," I retorted.

My new acquaintance squinted her eyes and then opened them at a moment of revelation. "Did you take a shower?" she asked excitedly.

"Uh, yes I did." I knew I had been caught.

She looked at me sternly as she began to walk away. "You have brought much attention to yourself," she concluded.

WARNING BELLS

Alarms are sounding loudly. Our convention is not focused. Various voices of concern are being heard in local churches, in academic settings, on blogs, in essays, in books, and in agencies. Perhaps one of the clearest numerical indicators of concern is the measurement of baptisms in the SBC during the past half-century.

We must acknowledge the limitations of numerical data such as baptisms. Such measures are imprecise at best. Spiritual realities cannot be accurately quantified. Still, a look at our baptisms in recent history should indeed sound alarms. In 1950 Southern Baptist churches recorded 376,085 baptisms. In 2005 the number was 371,085, a numerical decrease from 1950 despite the fact that our membership had more than doubled from just over seven million to over sixteen million. Please hear clearly this statistical reality. We are baptizing today less than we did in 1950, though we have today a membership that is 130 percent larger than it was over a half century ago!

A few years ago I wrote an article in *The Southern Baptist Journal of Theology* entitled "A Resurgence Not Realized: Evangelistic Effectiveness in the Southern Baptist Convention Since 1979."[1] My thesis was straightforward. Despite the theological reformation that has taken place in our denomination, we have seen no measurable impact on evangelistic health. Indeed, many hoped and prayed that right theology would lead to right church practices, and thus to evangelistic health. Such has not been the case.

SOURCES OF APATHY IN THE SBC

Why is the SBC evangelistically apathetic in the whole? Why are the trends discouraging at best and dismal at worst? I will attempt to answer those questions. Some of my responses have objective research behind them; others are more subjective and anecdotal in nature. But all the responses are mine, and I take full responsibility for any erroneous conclusions.

For simplicity, my analysis falls into five categories: eschatology, ecclesiology, sociology, responsibility, and humility. I will be brief with the first four items, and spend a bit more time on the fifth.

Eschatology

If there is an eschatological belief driving baptisms downward, it is the denial of a literal hell. Throughout church history, those denominations

---

[1] Thom S. Rainer, "A Resurgence Not Realized: Evangelistic Effectiveness in the Southern Baptist Convention since 1979," *The Southern Baptist Journal of Theology*, 9.1 (Spring 2005).

that have compromised this doctrinal truth have been the quickest to decline. The impetus for evangelism is weakened when our views are pluralistic, universalistic, or annihilistic.

Surely Southern Baptists have not abandoned the doctrine of a literal hell, you might retort. *After all, we are inerrantists. We believe the Bible.*

Prior to my coming to LifeWay Christian Resources, I consulted with many churches. We asked members of those churches to complete a survey, and one of the questions asked about their belief in a literal hell. The results were surprising. Each year we saw a greater number of Southern Baptists in so-called conservative churches who could no longer embrace a theology that included a literal hell. Could the SBC be following mainline churches on this path?

Ecclesiology

On a given Sunday, only about seven million persons attend a Southern Baptist church. We have over sixteen million members. It would appear that our church rolls are filled with nonmembers and, likely, unregenerate members. While time will not allow me to delve into possible reasons for this strange ecclesiology that is comfortable with unregenerate membership, I do know this: that which is dead cannot tell another dead person how to have life.

It is also curious to me that two camps seem to exist on this issue. In one camp are those who are calling for more intentional evangelism, while in another camp are those who are calling for regenerate membership. Must the two be mutually exclusive? Is not intentional evangelism that results in regenerate church members the best of biblical ecclesiology?

Sociology

While no study has tracked the socioeconomic status of Southern Baptists since 1950, it appears that we are more materially comfortable. And material comfort may very well diminish evangelistic enthusiasm. The prophet Haggai declared: "Is it a time for you yourselves to dwell in your paneled houses, while this house lies in ruins?" (Hag. 1:4, ESV). Israel was more concerned about its material comfort than building the house of God.

When my youngest son, now twenty-two years old, was a high school senior, he gained a reputation in football as a monster on the field. On one occasion, he asked me, "Daddy, does God mind if I hurt people?" I assured him he could tackle the opponents with abandon for the glory of God.

Imagine my surprise when, one Saturday morning (after a particularly bru-
tal Friday evening on the football field), I found the 6' 3" middle linebacker
sprawled on the sofa, watching HGTV (for the uninitiated, Home and
Garden Television).

I asked the obvious question: "Son, why are you watching HGTV?"

With an incredulous look on his face, he responded: "'Cause . . . the
remote control is broken."

I responded in a loud voice: "Son, when I was your age I walked bare-
foot through the shag carpet and had to change one of the three channels
by hand! You get up and get moving!"

Comfort. Is it possible that we are more comfortable building our own
houses rather than building God's house?

Responsibility

In a survey we conducted, over one-half of pastors in the SBC admitted they
had neither developed a relationship with a lost and unchurched person,
nor had they personally witnessed to someone in the past six months. And
over three-fourths of Southern Baptist laity confessed they had made no
intentional evangelistic efforts in the past year. Apparently evangelism is
no longer the responsibility of the individual Christian. Indeed it is often
relegated to a program in which very few participate, or it is expected that
the staff will shoulder that responsibility, or it is exhorted from the pulpit
but not practiced in life. But when evangelism is not my responsibility, it
does not happen. When I expect others or programs or pastors to be sole
purveyors of the Great Commission, it simply won't happen.

Bear with me a moment and follow this statistical excursion. Our
denomination has fewer than four-hundred thousand baptisms each year.
But suppose one person, just one, was used of God in each church to reach
one person for Christ every two weeks. If each church had only one such
evangelist, our baptisms would more than triple in the SBC to 1.2 million.
And such results also assume that no one else is reaching people for Christ.

But it's no one's responsibility.

Evangelism has become the ministry that is always someone else's
responsibility.

Humility

Ultimately evangelism is the overflow of our relationship with Christ. We
are only effective when we yield our way to the filling of the Holy Spirit.

But my problem is that I am too often filled with my own pride and my own will rather than the Holy Spirit.

In Acts 4:8 we learn that Peter was filled with the Spirit. Then in verse 20 he confronts his adversaries, the Sanhedrin, and boldly declares: "We are unable to stop speaking about what we have seen and heard" (HCSB). That is evangelism: to be so filled with the Spirit that you cannot help but speak about Jesus. Such evangelism requires that I become dependent on the Spirit and exhibit a humility that lets go of self. It is ironic that my most effective evangelism takes place when I realize how ineffective I am in my own power.

I know that I am part of the problem in the SBC. Why? Because I too often lack the humility that demonstrates my total dependence on God. The greatest disappointments in my own ministry came when I did not manifest the fruit of the Spirit: patience, or love, or kindness, or gentleness . . . those times when I did not demonstrate humility. And my work was then fruitless, blown away like chaff, dry straw in hurricane-force winds.

Please hear this plea for a more humble ministry. Such a ministry does not mean we compromise the Word; we simply live the Word to a greater degree. It does not mean we become soft in our theology; it means that we realize that one of the greatest theological truths is that love is the greatest of these. It does not mean we never disagree; it means that we disagree with patience and kindness and gentleness. It does not mean that we fail to bring light to sin; it means that we also have an awareness of our own sin, that the splinter we are addressing may be smaller than the log in our own eyes.

The failures and acrimony are wearying, in evangelicalism in general and the SBC in particular. But I know if a true evangelistic revival is to come, it must begin with God, and I must let him begin with me.

It is therefore my commitment to seek God's power to move in the following direction:

- That I might become a man who spends more time in the Word.
- That I might become a man who spends more time in prayer.
- That I might become a man who seeks to serve before seeking to be served.
- That I might become a man who first recognizes my own sinfulness before I point to the sins of others.
- That I might become a man who seeks not only to know more about God, but to know God more fully and personally.
- That I might become a man who realizes that I do not always have the answer, and that there are many wiser voices than my own.

- That I might become a man who is more open, less judging, more caring, and more humble.
- That I might become a man who not only talks about the gospel, but also faithfully shares it.

When my wife was diagnosed with cancer two years ago, I could never have expected the path we would travel. Nellie Jo and I prepared ourselves for the surgeries, the chemotherapy, and the radiation. And to some extent, my wife prepared herself for the hair loss and the sickness that the treatments brought. But we were unprepared for the emotional toll such disease brings. We could have not anticipated the side of this disease that you hear about but cannot comprehend until it happens. However, we are now beginning to see how God has blessed both of us in the midst and aftermath of this terrible time. We are more dependent on God; we are closer to God; and we have a great humility, recognizing that we had no say in this ordeal and that it was all in the hands of an omnipotent, omniscient, and omnipresent God.

May we live out the rest of our lives in the humble awareness that we are but clay in the Potter's hand. May our ministries be filled with conviction *and* compassion, certitude *and* servanthood. May we repent of sins of arrogance, self-centeredness, superiority, and lovelessness.

May we have a more humble ministry, and thus, according to the will of our Sovereign, see a greater harvest of souls for him.

CHAPTER TWELVE

THE FUTURE OF STATE CONVENTIONS AND ASSOCIATIONS

Michael Day

LOCAL BAPTIST ASSOCIATIONS and state Baptist conventions are a critical component of cooperation in Baptist life, generally, and Southern Baptist life in particular. The birth of the first Baptist association in America at Penepek, Pennsylvania, in 1707, the establishment of the first "southern" Baptist association in Charleston in 1751, and the organization of the first state Baptist convention in South Carolina in 1821 set the stage and became the model for subsequent associations, state conventions, and national entities that would design, develop, and deliver the cooperative ministries and methodologies for which Baptists are traditionally known. Therefore, it is appropriate that any discussion that focused upon the future of cooperation in Southern Baptist life should include a discussion of the future of local Baptist associations and state conventions.

My personal engagement in that conversation, however, must be preceded by several qualifying statements. So, please allow me to issue a disclaimer or two before moving ahead with the discussion. First, I am a *traditional* Southern Baptist. A "denominational X-ray," if there were such a thing, would probably not reveal one contemporary Baptist bone in my body. As a popular evangelist is fond of saying, "I was Southern Baptist nine months before I was born." As for me, I was cradle-rolled, toddler-ed, beginner-ed, primary-ed, junior-ed, and intermediated in Southern Baptist Sunday school. I own every Sunday school pin known to man. I was in Sword Drill, Speaker's Tournament, and Royal Ambassadors. I would have been a GA and an Acteen if it had been allowed.

I learned to sing from the only hymnal Southern Baptists will ever really need—the 1956 *Baptist Hymnal*. That was a hymnal you could count on. You could count on "Holy, Holy, Holy" being hymn #1, just as it should have been and perhaps as it ought to be now. (Do you know that in the 1975 and the 1992 versions of the *Baptist Hymnal*, the publishers had the audacity to make "Holy, Holy, Holy" hymn #2? That is just wrong— for a traditional Baptist "such as I.") You could count on #93 ("The Old Rugged Cross") and #240 ("Just As I Am"). You could count on "Jesus Loves Me" at #512, even though we never used the hymnal for that song and only sang the first verse. Most of all, you could count on the hymnal containing all the verses and all the stanzas of every hymn, even though Southern Baptists were going to sing only the first, second, and fourth— because that is the way we do it in the traditional Southern Baptist church. Those are the traditional Southern Baptist roots from which grows much of my understanding and thought about the future of associations and state Baptist conventions.

Second, I must confess to you that I am not a scholar, but merely an observer of Southern Baptist life. Most of what is contained herein could not be classified as an academic treatise, but is best considered an examination of what has changed and what is changing in our denomination. Specifically, I come to this discussion as a participant in and observer of the rapid and overwhelming theological, ecclesiological, and denominational shifts that have occurred, and continue to occur, in the SBC for nearly three decades.

Finally, I must also confess my denominational heritage and experience. The thoughts and understandings contained here were planted in traditional Baptist soil, nurtured in contemporary Baptist experience, and have come to fruition within the context of denominational service. I served for twelve years with the former Brotherhood Commission, SBC, as an editor, program specialist, project consultant, administrator, and denominational liaison. I was also privileged to serve eight years on the executive staff of the North American Mission Board, SBC. Now, I am working as director of missions for a regional Southern Baptist association of churches based in Memphis, Tennessee. My denominational experience represents no claim to fame, but does adequately describe the environment in which my opinions, thoughts, concerns, and conclusions in regard to the future were shaped. I will work hard to avoid being negatively reactive or blindly loyal to the "way we've always done things," while admitting that the "way I've seen things done" does influence the construction of this view of the future. With those disclaimers aside, let us begin our discussion of the future of Baptist associations and state conventions.

THE PATHWAY FROM THE PAST

On the Monday prior to the Thursday presentation of these thoughts at the *Baptist Identity II Conference*, we received in our office a packet from the North American Mission Board containing promotional materials for the annually calendared SBC Associational Emphasis Week. The theme for that particular year, which celebrated the birth of the first Baptist Association in America in 1707, jumped from the top of the first page: "The Baptist Association . . . Then and Now." My assistant, aware of the state of my preparation for the conference at that point in time, altered the title ever so slightly, and tossed me a page that read: "The Baptist Association . . . Then and Now . . . And Just In Time!" I could not help but be reminded that while serving at the North American Mission Board, I had led an unsuccessful effort to "kill" the publication of annual associational emphasis materials based on their very high production and distribution costs and their very low production of desired results. On Monday, I immediately gave thanks that the effort had been unsuccessful and began to scour the promo materials for help in preparing for the presentation.

Context is amazingly influential upon how we act and feel, isn't it? As we consider the future of associations and state conventions, it is important to understand the context in which associations and state conventions were birthed and shaped. This journey down the pathway from the past will help us discover where we came from and how we got to where we are today.

The starting line for the pathway from the past is a period that we will call the "Beginnings of Baptist Cooperation." The period is dated from 1707 to 1814 and is marked by the establishment and development of 125 local Baptist associations in the colonies. The first of those, the Philadelphia Baptist Association, birthed in 1707, established the essence of associational cooperation in their determination to "select the most capable in every congregation" and to meet yearly "to consult about such things as were wanting in the churches, and to set them in order."[1]

The first association also nailed down important concepts in terms of how cooperative associations and churches would relate to one another. In 1749, the association asked Benjamin Griffith to write an article on the authorities and duties of an association of churches. Griffith's response

---

[1] Walter B. Shurden, "Minutes of the Philadelphia Baptist Association," The Center for Baptist Studies, Baptist Classics, http://www.centerforbaptiststudies.org/resources/philadelphia.

set forth principles still held dear to cooperative Baptist bodies today. He affirmed that "the association is not a superior judicature" holding any power over the churches, that the association "has no superintendency over the churches," and that, in fact, the association is "subservient to the churches."[2] Griffith's essay also asserts that the association is autonomous, just as the local congregation is autonomous, and retained the right and responsibility to exclude churches found to be "defective in doctrine and practice."[3] The essay also made clear the association's prerogative to counsel the churches in matters of faith and practice, while maintaining the church's prerogative to accept or reject such counsel. With these strong statements, Benjamin Griffith and the Philadelphia Baptist Association cemented the foundations of mutual autonomy and mutual cooperation that have characterized cooperative Baptist bodies from that day forward.

The beginning days were also important in another sense. According to Paul Stripling, "subsequent associations multiplied and apparently functioned much like the Philadelphia Association."[4] But Stripling also points out that the Philadelphia Association, along with the Charleston Association (1751) and the Sandy Creek Association (1758), was extensively involved in missionary outreach by 1770, predating the commonly held beginning of the modern missions movement by twenty-two years. "The fervent spirit for missions," says Stripling, "made the number of Baptist churches in America multiply quickly, from fewer than 20 churches in 1700 to more than 2,000 one hundred years later."[5]

What can we conclude from this brief review of the beginnings of Baptist cooperation? It is clear that in the beginning days the local association nailed down both what it would be and what it would do. It would be an autonomous body of autonomous individuals and autonomous churches voluntarily cooperating in the mission of God's church. Bill Agee of the North American Mission Board suggests that associations were highly effective in both their being and doing for their first one-hundred years. He concludes: "They fostered fellowship, maintained uniformity in faith and practice among the churches, gave support and counsel, and provided a vehicle for churches to cooperate in a broader ministry."[6] Not a bad start at all!

---

[2]Ibid.
[3]Ibid.
[4]Paul Stripling, *Turning Points in the History of Baptist Associations in America* (Nashville: B&H Publishing Group, 2006), 9.
[5]Ibid.
[6]Bill Agee, "The Baptist Association . . . Then and Now: The Beginning Days," preparation materials for 2007 Associational Emphasis Week (Atlanta, GA: North American Mission Board, SBC).

Let's move to the second major mile marker along the journey from the past and call it "Transitions in Baptist Cooperation." This span of years, stretching from 1814 to 1920, is marked by the development of additional local associations, missionary societies, state Baptist conventions, and the SBC in 1845. It does not seem that local associations perceived these particular entities as a threat to their identity or mission—at first. Rather than view these new organizations as competitors, the existing local associations became actively involved in their creation. Nevertheless, the emergence of these larger cooperative bodies created an identity crisis for the previously effective associations. Following the creation of the South Carolina Baptist Convention in 1821 and the Southern Baptist Convention in 1845, the association could no longer define itself as a freestanding unit, but had to define itself in relation to those two new entities.

The redefinition was dramatic and challenging. Charles H. Ryland, addressing the Dover Association of Virginia in 1900, bemoaned the shift and asserted, "The district association has been diverted from its original purpose, and has become a mere reproduction on a small scale of the state convention."[7] Glynn Ford's study of associations in Virginia is a bit more objective, perhaps, than Brother Ryland's passionate plea, but still notes a dramatic shift during this period. Ford says: "The changes involved shifting from a doctrinally based fellowship of churches to an implementing agency of the denomination; shifting from a guardian of the fellowship to a denominational promoter; and shifting the initiative for mission from the churches to the state convention and national convention."[8] Thus, we can affirm, the transitional period from 1814 to 1920 was just that—a period of significant change marked by the creation of state conventions and the first redefinition of the local association. It is even more significant as a period in which there emerged a perception that the state conventions and the national convention might take the *initiative for mission* away from the local church.

The third major mile marker in our pathway from the past, dating from 1920 to 1978, may best be called the "Boom in Baptist Cooperation." Though there were challenges in defining the denomination and all its components, this was "boom-time" for Southern Baptists. The end of the First World War brought an unprecedented spirit of optimism and cooperation. As a matter of fact, "cooperation" became the watchword for Baptists during this period. The Seventy-Five Million Campaign, from 1919 to

---

[7]Ibid.
[8]Ibid.

1924, produced more pledges than it did profits, but it set the stage for the establishment of the Cooperative Program in 1925. In that same year, SBC adopted the *Baptist Faith and Message*, which included an article regarding cooperation, as our confession of faith. This particular period saw the beginning of confessed cooperation and intentional cooperation among the churches.

It will never be a bad thing for Southern Baptists to affirm cooperation and determine *how* we will cooperate. But it should be noted that the cooperative foundations poured in the mid- to late 1920s created an interesting dynamic for state conventions and local associations. First, in 1928, the SBC established a definitive role for the state conventions. The *1928 Southern Baptist Convention Annual* affirms, "The cooperative relations between this Convention and state bodies as now established are limited to the one matter of collecting funds for South-wide and state objects in conjunction with a unified appeal for the objects. The state convention boards are at present recognized by this Convention as collecting agencies for South-wide as well as for state funds. This arrangement, however, is not an essential in Baptist organization, but is made simply as a matter of convenience and economy, and may be changed at any time."[9]

Though the action of the Convention in 1928 seemed to prop open a door of possible change in regard to the receipt and disbursement of cooperative program dollars, it should be noted that, to this day, no such change has occurred. The state conventions are still the receivers and distributors of those monies that are officially considered cooperative program funds. In general, that action served to solidify both the cooperative and financial position of the state conventions.

On the other hand, the inception of the Cooperative Program created a different dynamic for local associations. Paul Stripling notes: "Following the creation of the Cooperative Program, actual debate arose as to whether the local association had any legitimate place in Baptist life."[10] That quandary was affirmed by E. P. Aldredge, the editor of the *Southern Baptist Handbook*, whose *Reappraisal of the District Association* in 1933 suggested the possibility that the local association might have served its purpose and may no longer be a necessity in Baptist life.[11] Fortunately, at least as far as the self-image of the associations was concerned, Aldredge concluded, "The one way of enlisting our great mission causes and bring-

---

[9]*Southern Baptist Convention Annual, 1928*, 32–33.
[10]Stripling, *Turning Points*, 96–97.
[11]Bill Agee, "The Baptist Association . . . Then and Now: The Modern Era," preparation materials for 2007 Associational Emphasis Week (Atlanta, GA: North American Mission Board, SBC).

ing them back to the day of power and triumph . . . is to carry the battle for these great causes to the associations . . . I believe there is but one great agency among us that can solve this great problem of churches not giving to Southern Baptist causes . . . I believe our only possible relief lies in the Baptist Associations."[12]

It is evident that this period we are calling the "Boom in Baptist Cooperation" is characterized by the evolution of Southern Baptists' understanding of what cooperation means in a convention that is experiencing unprecedented health and growth. It is an era in which we brought cooperation down to a matter of dollars and cents, on one hand, while ascribing inestimable value to the results accomplished through the practice of cooperation, on the other. And, it is the period in which we realized that our multi-level conversations about the hows and whys of cooperation were just beginning.

Let us refer to the final mile marker along the pathway from the past as the "Re-formation of Baptist Cooperation." This period began with what we know as the conservative resurgence, and has not yet ended. It has been marked by massive restructuring of the SBC, major leadership changes within SBC entities, major cultural and theological challenges to which the SBC is pressed to respond, and the issuance of a revised *Baptist Faith and Message*. History will view this period in Southern Baptist life as rough, necessary, fruitful, and dramatically defining. I count it a privilege to have experienced and participated in Southern Baptist life during this period. That does not mean the time-frame is free of frustration, particularly for state conventions and associations. Both have experienced some pain in the process. Both have dealt with financial issues ensuing from those who choose nontraditional methods of support for the work of the convention. Both have wrangled with the theological stress that has accompanied the re-formation. Both are wrestling with the dilemma of maintaining or creating a denominational affinity in a post-denominational age. Both are struggling with how to relate (and perhaps even be relevant) to the traditional church, the emerging church, the missional church, the purpose-driven church, and the younger leaders. This is a period in which we have been dramatically re-formed and are reluctantly re-forming, and that is where we stand today.

The pathway from the past for state conventions and local associations, as well as for other denominational entities, is a wonderful maze of faithfulness, blessing, growth, complexity, and struggle. A less-academic summary of our history may go as follows:

---

[12]Ibid.

- We were *birthed by biblical Baptists* who embraced biblical models of the church and the mission of God in the world;
- We were *nurtured by believing Baptists* who were certain the mission of God in the world was too large for a single body and demanded cooperation among the many;
- We were *shaped by bureaucratic Baptists* who have worked long and hard to guide and administer what have become large and often bulky organizations;[13]
- We have been *defined by battling Baptists* who have fought most often for the right things, occasionally for the wrong things, but always toward producing the refinement and redefinition necessary in cooperative bodies; and,
- We are *questioned by befuddled Baptists* who are confused and concerned about the future of our cooperative efforts. As Frank Page (past president of the Southern Baptist Convention) said at a chapel address at Union University, "There is a lot of what we have been practicing for a long time that needs to be questioned."[14]

The questions may make us uncomfortable because our answers will determine our future. I am convinced that our current status and our current position on the pathway from the past leave us uncomfortable, but also leave us in a position to positively and proactively face and resolve the predicaments of the present while shaping a paradigm for the future of Baptist associations and state conventions.

THE PREDICAMENTS OF THE PRESENT

Following the annual meeting of the SBC in 2006, Dr. Timothy George summarized the spirit and actions of the Convention in an article entitled, "Southern Baptists after the Revolution." George describes the grassroots-driven, theologically based controversy that resulted in the re-forming of the SBC, but suggests, "In recent years, however, there has been a growing anxiety within the Southern Baptist Convention."[15] His ensuing description of the theological, structural, and relational anxieties attached to current-day Southern Baptist life is by no means negative, but by every indication, realistic.

Realistically, we Southern Baptists, at all levels of denominational life, have backed ourselves into some corners. We have walked ourselves out

---

[13]I know that some will struggle with, and perhaps be offended by, the characterization of associations, state conventions, and the SBC as bureaucratic. However, apart from the absence of a "stated hierarchy," our organizations meet all the criteria for such a label.

[14]Chapel address, Union University, February 14, 2007.

[15]Timothy George, "Southern Baptists after the Revolution," *First Things*, 165 (August/September 2006): 17–19.

to the edges of some cliffs. We have perched ourselves on some precarious spots. Basically, we have created some predicaments that must be delicately and decisively managed and resolved in order for us to find a future that is productive and effective in terms of cooperative ministry. We must face the following predicaments of the present.

The Duplicated-Effort Syndrome

We do good things in Southern Baptist life at a lot of different levels. The truth is we do the *same* things in Southern Baptist life at a lot of different levels. Permit me just one example. If you were to approach the Mid-South Baptist Association today, desiring to plant a church in our area, we would direct you to a staff member who can assess your church planting capacity and passion, process your request for financial support as a church planter, train you to be a more effective church planter, connect you to a network of church planters, and turn you loose to plant a church. All of those services are available through the Mid-South Baptist Association. Those services are also available through the Tennessee Baptist Convention. Those services are also available through the North American Mission Board. It is wonderful to know that we have such great denominational capacity for processing church planters, but it is frustrating to think that Southern Baptists are financing and supporting three different staffs in three different places to facilitate one task. Such duplication of effort is certainly not intentional but is a result of the largeness and complexity of our denomination. It should not surprise us that many faithful Southern Baptists see the duplication of effort and become concerned about the multiple dollars necessary to duplicate those efforts. Nor should it surprise us that many of those Southern Baptists lose faith in and cease support of associations, state conventions, institutions, and the denomination. It is a predicament we must manage as we negotiate the future.

The Institution-First Syndrome

The Baptist boom that preceded the conservative resurgence ushered in a proliferation of Baptist institutions at the associational and state convention levels. These institutions—colleges, academies, seminaries, children's homes, hospitals, camps, student centers, ministry centers, assemblies, etc.—were conceived and designed as tools for ministry. Over the years, the ministry conducted through various Baptist institutions has been fruitful and worthwhile. In recent years, associations and state conventions have begun to wrestle with the concept of ownership of institutions. Part of the struggle is financial—it takes a lot of money to operate a variety of institutions. Part of the struggle is political—as institutions grow they sometimes become concerned about self-governance or self-proliferating boards of directors. Part of the struggle is contextual—the world today is not the same as it was when Baptist institutions came into being. Part of the struggle is strategic focus—new ministry methodologies compete for the energy and focus previously reserved for institutional ministries.

Regardless of its source, the struggle is real. When were you last at a state convention or association meeting where the institutions attached to that state or association were not the hottest topic? The need to take care of all the business attached to the ownership of institutions is often the primary point of focus for state conventions and associations. We did not intend to be overwhelmed and consumed by these things, but our Baptist desire to provide ministry and to educate ministers landed us in the institutional business. The prevalence of institutions was brought on by perceived needs and the desire to meet those needs. In these days most state conventions are working as hard as they can to get out of the institutional business. I do not believe that local associations, state conventions, and the SBC ever intended for the ownership of institutions to become a controlling factor in the way they conduct their ministries. It is a reality and a predicament, however, that we must deal with today if we are going to move efficiently and effectively toward the future.

The Autonomous-Hierarchy Syndrome

In Southern Baptist life, every entity including the church, the association, the state convention, and the SBC will declare that autonomy is a sacred and necessary principle. Southern Baptists have historically and repeatedly affirmed that declaration. Every Southern Baptist entity would also disavow any presence of hierarchical structures or systems in Southern Baptist life. In theory, we make the assumption that the affirmation of autonomy has successfully warded off the emergence of hierarchical structures in Southern Baptist life. In practice, however, we must acknowledge the presence of a hierarchical system as a reality and predicament of current Baptist life and polity. Yes, we are autonomous, but we are also hierarchical. It is an implied hierarchy that is accepted voluntarily by participants in the system. In other words, though we will affirm autonomy and reject hierarchical, top-down structures, we often behave as if we require the approval of others, or we behave as if we think we have the right to direct, approve, or disapprove the actions of other entities within the system. Let me illustrate as follows.

Suppose that the autonomous member churches of an autonomous local association autonomously decide to direct their Cooperative Program monies to the autonomous association, rather than to the autonomous state convention that autonomously decides what portion stays in the state and what portion is sent to the autonomous SBC. The autonomous state convention says, "You can't do that. That is not how the system works." The autonomous association replies, "Yes, we can do it. We are autonomous." So the autonomous association makes a call to the autonomous SBC, and happily communicates their autonomous decision to send Cooperative Program funds directly from the autonomous association to the autonomous SBC. The autonomous SBC will likely make two autonomous responses. First, they may say, "You can't do that. That is not how the system works. The business and finance plan dictates that Cooperative Program monies are received through state conventions." Second, the autonomous SBC may reply, "Yes, you can send monies designated for autonomous SBC causes directly to Nashville, but they will not be considered 'Cooperative Program' monies." Regardless of the response, the somewhat beleaguered, but still autonomous, association returns to the autonomous member churches and says, "We cannot do it. Our plan does not fit the system." And the churches respond, "Okay, if you say so—but are we still autonomous?"

Persons who have spent their lives working within Southern Baptist systems will often speak of autonomy as both blessing and curse. It is a "can't live with it, can't live without it" conundrum. Perhaps this implied hierarchy has emerged as our way of accommodating the challenges of autonomy. Maybe it is just a naturally occurring phenomenon in the kinds of organizations we are trying to be. Perhaps it is a by-product of cooperative Baptist life. It is probably something we could learn to live with, or ignore, or leave for future generations to resolve, if not for one pressing issue: the real problem is that in the Baptist hierarchy, the church winds up at the bottom of the pile. If I read Scripture correctly, the church, the body of Christ, should be on top, well ahead of any denominational entity in any shape or any form. For this reason, we must now address and manage the predicament of autonomous-hierarchy.

The Codified-Cooperation Syndrome

Cooperation is a watchword for Southern Baptists. It is the principle upon which the work of local associations and state conventions is founded. Thus, it becomes very important for us to understand what we mean when we say we are cooperative bodies. Southern Baptist history is dotted with attempts to clarify the concept of cooperation for churches, local bodies, and state and national entities. Our challenge is to clarify without codifying. The *Baptist Faith and Message* issues a strong set of parameters for all faith and practice, and contains a very clear and adequately open statement of how we as Southern Baptists cooperate. Is it good enough? Is it strong enough? It seems that almost daily we attempt through our institutions, our entities, our state conventions, and our associations to further define what it means to cooperate as a Southern Baptist. We have to decide, what is enough? Most would say that the success of the conservative resurgence and the revision of the *Baptist Faith and Message* made those battles worth fighting. And yet, having those matters settled, we tend to want to move forward even more and draw the lines even tighter. I cannot judge if that is right or wrong, good or bad, but I am certain it is a dilemma and a predicament that must be managed as we go forward.

The Thinly Spread Missions Dollar Syndrome

A first glance at reports of Cooperative Program giving over the last eleven years is encouraging. In ten of the last eleven years, Cooperative Program receipts exceeded the prior year. In ten of the last eleven years, Southern Baptists gave more than they did the year before to support global ministries. That is good news. However, a closer look reveals some disturbing trends. A look at a five-year period in the mid-1980s reveals that CP receipts equaled 10.5 percent of the total undesignated receipts of the churches. A similar examination of 2001–2002 reveals CP receipts equaled 7.39 percent of the total undesignated gifts received by the churches. By 2003–2004, CP receipts equaled 6.68 percent of the total undesignated receipts of the churches. The missions dollar is thinning out. As a percentage of total receipts, churches are giving less through the Cooperative Program, which impacts state convention receipts. They may be giving more to local associations, but you wouldn't know that by listening to conversations at most associational meetings. Perhaps they are giving more directly to SBC causes, or perhaps more of the missions dollar is going toward para-church missions ministries. As the SBC Funding Study Committee reported in 2003,

A more disturbing trend, however, is the decline in the percentage of contributions by church members to the churches, and of the churches to missions. While total contributions have been increasing in previous years, the rate of growth has not been keeping up with growth in spending caused by rising costs and by growing ministries. During recent periods of strong economy, the increasing contributions have been taken by many as a signal of financial health. But the percentage of available income that has been contributed has been falling at an alarming rate.[16]

The truth is, we live in a day where fewer missions dollars must be spread over a larger scope of cooperative ministries. The thinning missions dollar is a predicament that local associations, state conventions, and national entities must acknowledge and address.

The Lost-Influence Syndrome

"Southern Baptist baptisms are at their lowest level in well over a decade! The number of churches planted by Southern Baptists has not increased significantly over the last ten years! Seventy-three percent of Southern Baptist churches are plateaued or declining!"[17] The numbers are in the news. Southern Baptists read them and wonder, "What in the world could be wrong?" Some read the numbers and assume the church is losing its influence in the world. They conclude that culture has overwhelmed the church's capacity to deliver the gospel and start new churches. I look at the numbers and wonder if the denominational entities have lost their influence in the churches. Are we providing resources that assist the churches to engage the culture? Are we providing resources to equip the church to share the gospel? Are we providing support that allows the church to fulfill its God-given vision? Are we encouraging the churches to influence the world, or are we attempting to influence the churches to support denominational activities and ministries?

As the church continues to lose influence in the world, local associations and state conventions should be asking, "What in the world is going on?" We must work hard to avoid contributing to any loss of influence the church may experience in today's world. We must constantly assess our relationships with the churches to ensure we are providing what they need to be a viable force in a postmodern world. The lost influence of the church in the world and the lost influence of local and state Baptist bodies combine

---

[16]SBC Funding Study Committee, "Report of the SBC Funding Study to the SBC Executive Committee," Baptist2Baptist, October 23, 2003, http://www.baptist2baptist.net/printfriendly.asp?ID=274.
[17]Statistics provided by North American Mission Board and LifeWay Christian Resources.

to pose one more predicament that Southern Baptist associations and state conventions must face as we forge our future.

A PARADIGM FOR THE FUTURE

Thus far, we have traveled the pathway from the past and discovered the major milestones in the history of local Baptist associations and state Baptist conventions. We have gained at least a partial sense of where we stand today through our examination of a few of the predicaments that local associations, state conventions, and the SBC in general must begin to manage and resolve. What should we do in response to all of that information?

Some might suggest that leaving the Convention and affiliating with another group is the best solution. Many have done just that. Others might suggest remaining affiliated with the Convention, but beginning some new type of association or convention that is free from the traditional challenges of Baptist life. A proliferation of affinity-based associations, theologically-based conventions, and functionally based fellowships gives evidence that many have done just that. Still others may affirm their desire to remain affiliated with the Convention, maintain their traditional alignments with traditional associations and state conventions, and work hard to positively and proactively effect the changes necessary for the fruitful future of local, state, and national Baptist bodies and the successful ministries of the churches. Morris Chapman, president of the Executive Committee, SBC, speaking at the first Baptist Identity Conference in 2004, suggested the following: "The Southern Baptist Convention needs fine-tuning. In fact, the Convention may require an overhaul, not in its polity, but in its programming and processes by which it functions daily. A major overhaul by the national convention and the state conventions appears to be an absolute necessity, letting the facts speak for themselves lest the conventions discover too late they were blind and deaf to a delivery system that better serves the churches."[18]

Chapman's remarks are profound, encouraging, and directly on target. It appears that the "overhaul" is underway as many local and state Baptist entities engage in the work of "re-creating" the local association or state convention with an eye toward creating cooperative bodies that are clearly focused on the work of the churches and clearly committed to assisting churches in the accomplishment of their work.

A new paradigm for cooperation is visible over the horizon of Southern Baptist life. A new operational model for state conventions and local asso-

---

[18]See Morris H. Chapman, "Axioms of a Cooperating Southern Baptist," chap. 8 in this volume.

ciations is emerging. It is certainly not fully developed as of today. In fact, it is in the stage of development at which it will probably be embraced and touted by the few and discussed and dismissed by the many. Nevertheless, there is a new paradigm developing in our denomination, primarily within the context of local Baptist associational life. It can be seen, in part, in the Tulsa Metro Baptist Association (Oklahoma), the Mid-South Baptist Association (Tennessee), the Austin Baptist Association (Texas), and the Extended Missions Network of Northwest Mississippi, to name a few. Parts of this new paradigm are also visible in the restructured Pennsylvania/ South Jersey State Baptist Convention, now known as the *Baptist* Resource Network of Pennsylvania/South Jersey.[19] The entities mentioned above are but a few among a growing number of Southern Baptist associations and cooperative bodies that are seeking a paradigm for cooperation that faces the realities of Southern Baptist life, builds the relationships necessary for cooperative ministry, and validates the relevance of associational work to the ministries of the churches. What are the characteristics of this new type of association or cooperative entity?

Church-Driven

This new paradigm for cooperation begins with affirmation that the church is the living expression of God's mission in the world. The Great Commission and Acts 1:8 were spoken to the nucleus of the church and not to local associations or denominational entities. Therefore, the work of an association or convention of churches must be driven by and focused upon the work of the churches. The "strategy" of the association or convention of the future will not begin with the development of centralized mission and vision statements, but with a prayerful and careful view of the vision, mission, and "strategies" God has established within each of his churches. This association of the future will not evaluate itself on the basis of "annual meeting" attendance or participation in associational events, but upon the extent to which it assisted the churches in the accomplishment of their God-given vision. It is a church-focused and church-driven vehicle for cooperation.

Priority-Based

A church-driven association, or cooperative entity, is not loosely guided by the whims or wants of its member churches, but is consistently controlled

---

[19]Baptist Resource Network: Baptist Convention of Pennsylvania/South Jersey, http://www.brnonline.org.

by the biblically based priorities of the church. The priority of the church, living as the body of Christ, is to behave and minister as Jesus did in establishing the church, proclaiming the good news, caring for people, and developing leaders and disciples. The priority-based association of the future will make every effort to focus its prayers, its efforts, and its resources upon the scriptural priorities of the church—starting and strengthening churches, developing leaders, and mobilizing the church to care for people and preach the gospel.

Resource-Focused

If the work of an association, or any cooperative body, consists of the work of the churches, then the ministry of that cooperative body must be focused upon providing the human, financial, and material resources that assist the church in accomplishment of their mission. The association of the future will work hard to resist developing associational programs and ministries. It will resist the ever-present impulse to become a "substitute" for the church. It will resist inviting the churches to support the programs of the association. Instead, it will work hard to generate support and resources that will assist the churches in fulfilling the mission that God has given to them.

Institutionally Free

If the cooperative association, or entity, of the future is truly focused on providing resources to assist the churches, it will work very hard to avoid owning anything or obligating itself to the maintenance of institutions that reduce the resources available to the churches. As associations give up ownership of community ministry centers, conference centers, campus facilities, etc., they will find they have increased financial resources with which to support churches that have a vision and strategy for such ministries. Instead of initiating, building, and developing such ministries, the association of the future will encourage and assist churches who engage in those ministries. This particular aspect of a new paradigm for cooperation will be a tremendous challenge to existing Baptist entities, structures, and institutions, but is worthy of the hard work required to determine how cooperative Baptist entities can gain institutional freedom while maintaining appropriate support of existing institutions that are viable for the expansion of the kingdom through the work of the churches.

Strategically Managed

The long and varied history of associations and state conventions in America has mandated a variety of roles for those who serve in leadership and staff positions. In the emerging model, the associational leaders' long-respected role of "Pastor-to-the-Pastors," "Baptist Mediator," or "Associational Administrator" will give way to a catalytic and facilitative leadership role. The value of staff and leadership in an association will be measured, not by how efficiently they conduct business and "direct" the work of the association, but by how effectively they facilitate and support the work of the churches. The management role so evident in Baptist structures of today will fade away and the missionary role so necessary for the leadership of cooperative Baptist churches will emerge.

Regionally Located, but not Geographically Bound

The twenty-first century brought with it the staggering realization that our world is a small world, after all. Through devices that most of us wear on our hip or carry in our pocket or purse, we have instant access to the entire world. With that kind of global access, why would we compel ourselves to operate within outdated Baptist boundaries? We live in an age when it is no longer necessary, nor productive, for us to affiliate solely within county or state lines. The new paradigm for cooperation is producing regional Baptist associations inclusive of churches from a number of counties in more than one state. The new model is also producing regionalized state conventions where the work of several existing associations is consolidated into a new association. The regionally located, but not geographically bound dimension of this new paradigm is largely unexplored. Perhaps the cooperative units of Southern Baptist life will one day be configured within the Metropolitan Statistical Areas (MSA) of America's 50 largest cities, or 100 largest cities, as opposed to the current configuration of 42 state conventions and more than 1,200 local associations.

Denominationally Connected, but not Traditionally Bound

The emerging paradigm for cooperation will test the patience, stretch the limits, and challenge the imagination of traditional Southern Baptist structures and organizational models. For example, associations will desire connection with national entities like the North American Mission Board, but will be hard-pressed to understand why that connection must be delivered through a state convention. Associations will want to promote, support, and contribute to the Cooperative Program but may become impatient with an SBC Executive Committee that limits the methods by which Cooperative Program monies may be received. The development of new models will stretch us indeed. Further, as it grows and develops, the new model will eventually overwhelm many current structures. If this model is fully developed, it is likely that local associations and state conventions, as we know them today, will cease to exist, giving way to new regional bodies that will focus on applying denominationally generated resources to the needs of the churches.

Kingdom-Conscious

We have a very committed and very effective pastor in our association who is fond of saying, "I'm too old to play games; I want to be about the work of the kingdom." That statement may well be the watchword for the association, or cooperative Baptist body, of the future. The effective association of the future will remain conscious of its heritage, its traditions, and its denominational connections—but not at the expense of its kingdom-consciousness. It will support and encourage kingdom-focused churches within the context of their particular denomination and outside of that context. It will work unceasingly to forge new relationships and partnerships with a variety of churches of like faith and practice. Why? Not in order to grow bigger or better, but so that God's kingdom might come on earth as it is in heaven. May God grant us the courage to cooperatively "seek his kingdom."

CONCLUSION: THE CLOCK IS TICKING AND THE PRESSURE IS ON

Our pathway from the past, our predicaments of the present, and the emergence of new paradigms for Baptist cooperation should alert us to the fact that the pressure is on and the clock is ticking for local associations and state conventions. It is time for us to pay attention to our past and ensure that our focus is upon "such things as are wanting in the churches."[20] It is time for us to push aside our present predicaments so that our focus might be upon the work of the churches, and not the structures of the Convention. It is time for us to pave new pathways for cooperation that focus upon facilitation and support of the accomplishment of a church's God-given vision.

    The pressure is on existing local associations to consider erasing exist-

---

[20]Shurden, "Minutes of the Philadelphia Baptist Association."

ing geographic boundaries and becoming regional resources for the work of the church. The pressure is on state conventions to consider downsizing or resizing into regional groupings that better identify with and better meet the needs of the churches. The pressure is on both local associations and state conventions to consider merging their efforts into one cooperative body as opposed to maintaining two entities and multiple systems. The pressure is also on local associations and state conventions to propose solutions for how institutions that are viable to the work of the churches are supported and institutions that may have outlived their mission are laid to rest. The pressure is on the SBC to consider accommodating, encouraging, and supporting the emergence of new models for cooperation at local and state levels. The pressure is on *all* cooperative Baptists to work together to effect necessary change in our systems, structures, entities, and churches for the future. As Morris Chapman reminds us,

> Convention leaders must not fail to take into account that we are not driving the changes. Pastors and their churches are driving the changes from the perspective of field generals. We have the responsibility of offering our observations and our collective assistance to the churches. If our conventions are not careful to take into account a shift in the landscape, we shall find ourselves inessential after all. The conventions exist to serve the churches, not to insist that the churches fit into the convention, a voluntary choice that is already their option. On the other hand, the churches must communicate to the conventions their needs. When they do, we are compelled to listen and as is possible take action to meet the needs brought to the attention of the conventions.[21]

The clock is ticking! The pressure is on! How will we respond?

---

[21]Chapman, "Axioms"

CHAPTER THIRTEEN

A FREE CHURCH IN A FREE SOCIETY

Richard Land

I BELIEVE THE BEST IS YET TO COME for Southern Baptists. We do face severe challenges, but we've faced severe challenges before. And it seems to me that we have more cause to be optimistic than pessimistic as we enter the twenty-first century. I believe that we will look back on the first two decades of the twenty-first century and we will say that these have been the greatest decades yet in Southern Baptist life. I truly believe that—I don't know how you could think otherwise when you're exposed to the students on our seminary campuses. I have the opportunity to be on almost all of our seminary campuses on a regular basis; our churches are providing our seminaries with students who are being trained to go out, not as occupation troops but SEAL teams, or those Green Berets who are going to go behind enemy lines and take new territory. Our students are committed, indeed. They are sold out to the Lord Jesus Christ. As a baby boomer, I am awed by their commitment, dedication, and willingness to go forth and sacrifice for our Savior.

I am also part of the tribe that has been described as "the Southern Baptists of the 1950s and the 1960s." I know this strains credulity, but I was a Sunbeam. In fact, I once preached at the First Baptist Church in Houston, and after I had finished, an elderly lady walked up to me and said, "Richard, I am Dorothy Elam." And when she told me her name, I knew who she was, because she kicked me out of Sunbeams. She said, "I was your first Sunbeam teacher, and you were a pill." I've actually been told this on numerous occasions. Complete strangers have come up to me and reminded me of how I was expelled from junior camp, or how I was kicked out of Vacation Bible School, in spite of the fact that my mother was the superintendent. But I was a Sunbeam; I was a Royal Ambassador. I came from one of those Baptist families that believed if the church was having an event, it was your spiritual duty to be there. I've been to every mosquito-infested youth encampment that Texas Baptists keep on the Gulf Coast. I dated GAs, I even dated a couple of queens with scepters, and I'm married to a woman who's the daughter, the granddaughter, the great-granddaughter, the niece, and now the wife and mother of Baptist preachers.

I really am grateful for my Southern Baptist heritage. I was reared in a Southern Baptist home, in a Southern Baptist church. I was baptized Easter Sunday, 1953, and I was six and a half years old. There's been a lot of abuse in the past, regarding baptizing small children without making certain they knew what they were doing. But I would plead with you, don't ever overestimate what a child can understand, and don't underestimate it, either. When I was six and a half years old, I knew I was a sinner, and I knew I needed to be saved. In fact, I don't know if anyone has ever embraced the doctrine of salvation by grace with more alacrity than did I, because I knew at six and a half I was never going to make it on a works-based salvation.

I once was introduced at a right-to-life rally by a Roman Catholic in the upwoods part of Michigan. He was a medical doctor, and he said, "I'm going to introduce Richard Land by reading parts of the preface from his book *For Faith and Family*, because I think it says who he is." I had never really thought about it that way before—introducing my topic by explaining my background—but in this particular context, discussing a free church in a free society, I want to do somewhat of the same thing.

I grew up in a devout Christian home, in a working-class neighborhood in Houston during the 1950s. I was the first person in my family to go to college, and I'm very grateful for my traditional upbringing, which taught me many valuable, foundational truths. First, I learned that the Christian faith is not a religion, but a personal relationship between Jesus and each individual who trusts him as Lord and Savior. Second, I learned that the Bible is God's holy word, fully authoritative, without mistake or error, and sufficient for doctrine, reproof, correction, and instruction in righteousness. I didn't know what the word "inerrant" meant until I got to college, but I was taught the principle of inerrancy when I was a mere youth.

Unfortunately, growing up in Baptist churches of that era, I was also taught that Baptists believed in a spiritual gospel that did not deal with social issues (with certain exceptions, of course: liquor and gambling).

To get involved in social issues was considered a violation of separation of church and state. Of course, that was when we were in our racial Babylonian captivity. This church—this Baptist tribe that we remember with such affection—was an all-white tribe, by the way. No persons of color need apply. Fortunately for me, I was always taught, growing up, that racial prejudice was not only wrong, it was sinful, and that I should never treat anybody as less than myself because of the color of their skin. But, of course, that didn't keep us from living in a segregated neighborhood and going to a segregated school and attending a segregated church. Thank God we've been liberated from that.

As R. Albert Mohler Jr. so accurately pointed out, we still don't fit the demographic reality of the country, but we've made extraordinary strides in the last twenty years with intentionality and at great cost. Southern Baptists have gone from a virtually all-white denomination in 1970, to a denomination where, at present, 20 percent of its members are of ethnic descent—African-American, Hispanic, Asian, and others. We've gone from zero to twenty in about twenty-five years. That is a significant demographic revolution, a significant spiritual revolution, and it at least gets us onto the launching pad for what should be our goal—practicing colorblind evangelism in every nook and cranny of the United States until our church membership reflects the demographic reality of the nation. I don't want to hear any of this nonsense: "Well, we have different worship traditions. We have a different sermon tradition. We have a different music tradition." A lost person doesn't have a worship tradition; if we go out and win the lost to Jesus, they're going to sing a lot like we sing, and they're going to hear preaching a lot like our preaching. We need to be about the business of winning people to Jesus and putting the truth to what I was taught: "Red and yellow, black and white, they are precious in his sight. Jesus loves the little children of the world." That means the little children of our neighborhoods, and our inner cities, too.

Over the years since then, I have learned better. I now understand that Christ's command to be salt and light demands that as his disciples we go out into the society and seek to make a difference for what is right and good. I now have a better perspective.

I grew up in Texas with a fifth-generation Texas father who sounded like Lyndon Johnson—he used words like "rench," "pench," "ench," "iice," "riice," and "niice"—and a mother from Boston, Massachusetts. I received a unique gift from my "bicultural" upbringing: I was given Texas with perspective. On one hand, I received this wonderful, never-give-up

heritage of the Alamo and the sheer possibility of things from big sky country; on the other hand, I had a Bostonian mother whispering in my ear that
biggest was not always best, and loudest was not always wisest. And like
the balanced perspective I received as a child, I've learned to understand
the tremendous, born-again personal salvation foundation of the Christian
faith with a vitally important additional perspective—the command of the
Savior for each of us to go forth and be salt and light in society.

My focus in this chapter is "A Free Church in a Free Society." And that
is the beginning of things for us as Baptists—a free church. Now, in actual
fact, we have three articles in our *Baptist Faith and Message* that deal with
the three broad issues that I want us to examine. The first is the church.

BAPTISTS AND THE CHURCH

I used to play a little trick on my students at Criswell College. I taught a
required course called "Baptist Distinctives," and I started off by saying,
"How many of you believe that belief in the inerrancy of the Bible is a
Baptist distinctive?" After they all raised their hands, I'd say, "Well, that
would be real news to John Calvin, Martin Luther, and Huldreich Zwingli,
not to mention B. B. Warfield." Baptists have, in almost all places and
at almost all times, given unwavering commitment to the full authority
and accuracy of Scripture. All Scripture is given by God. It is a perfect
treasure. But what has separated us from the beginning from most of our
Christian brethren is our doctrine of the church. Article VI, "The Church,"
in the *Baptist Faith and Message* separates us from almost everybody: "A
New Testament church of the Lord Jesus Christ."[1] Our forefathers went
to jail, and sometimes worse, telling both their Catholic and Protestant
persecutors they wouldn't be bound by proof texts fetched from the Old
Testament. We lived in the new covenant, through the blood of Christ. And
the manual for faith and practice for believers in the new covenant was the
New Testament. A New Testament church of the Lord Jesus Christ is an
autonomous, local congregation.

That simple statement—"A New Testament church of the Lord Jesus
Christ"—separates us from all those who have synods, bishops, and pres-
byteries. It separates us from Congregationalists, and it separates us from
a lot of Bible churches, too. Baptist churches are associated by covenant
in the faith and fellowship of the gospel, observing the two ordinances of
Christ, governed by his laws, exercising the gifts, rights, and privileges

---

[1] "Article VI: The Church," in "The Baptist Faith and Message" (2000), http://www.sbc.net/BFM/
bfm2000.asp.

invested in them by his Word, and seeking to extend the gospel to the ends of the earth. Each congregation operates under the lordship of Christ through democratic processes, and each church decides for itself whether it wants to be a Southern Baptist church. One of the things we seem to have often forgotten is that every Baptist associational group is autonomous, and it decides for itself with whom it will fellowship and with whom it will not. Each association is autonomous. It decides which churches it will have within its association and which ones it won't, by a democratic process.

The state convention makes its decision without regard to what the association says. It's so much fun to try to explain to a New York Times reporter that all organizational structure in Southern Baptist life is horizontal, and that the headquarters of the SBC is the local church. We are run by forty thousand-plus Southern Baptist churches. They decide how much they're going to give to the Cooperative Program, how much they're going to allot as a goal for their missions offerings, and how they are going to allocate the money that is entrusted to them. They also remind us periodically that *they* will decide how they're going to do it.

BAPTISTS, THE CHURCH, AND THE STATE

Now, on to the state. What we're discussing is a threefold issue—the church, the state, and society. It's important to note that the state and society are different. Article XVII, "Religious Liberty," discusses the matter of church and state: "God alone is the Lord of the conscience, and He has left it free from the doctrines and commandments of men which are contrary to His Word or not contained in it."[2] Church and state should be separate. The state owes to every church protection and full freedom in the pursuit of its spiritual ends. In providing for such freedom, no ecclesiastical group or denomination should be favored by the state more than others. Because civil government is ordained by God, it is the duty of Christians to render loyal obedience thereto in all things not contrary to the revealed will of God. The church should not resort to the civil power to carry on its work. The last thing we should ever want is government-sponsored religion. It's like getting embraced by a python. It squeezes all the life out of you and you fall over dead; just look at the empty cathedrals of Europe. It's our privilege, our duty, our obligation, and our responsibility to preach, teach, and spread the gospel—not the government's. We shouldn't seek the government's assistance, and we shouldn't accept the government's assistance

---

[2] "Article XVII: Religious Liberty," in "The Baptist Faith and Message" (2000), http://www.sbc.net/BFM/bfm2000.asp.

because, unless you're the National Endowment for the Arts (which seems to be the single exception to the rule), with the government's shekels sooner or later come the government's shackles.

When we as believers win people to Jesus—when we disciple them and they begin to come to a new core set of values, and when they begin to understand, from a new spiritual perspective, the truths and values of life and what should be done and what shouldn't be done in society—they have a right, and we have a right, as citizens, to bring our convictions to bear on public policy. Article XVII states that "the gospel of Christ contemplates spiritual means alone for the pursuit of its ends." The state has no right to impose penalties for religious opinions of any kind. The state has no right to utilize taxes for the support of any form of religion. A free church, in a free state, is the Christian ideal, and this implies the right of free and unhindered access to God on the part of all men, and the right to form and propagate opinions in the sphere of religion without interference by the civil power.

BAPTISTS, THE CHURCH, AND SOCIETY

We've heard what Baptists say about the church; we've heard what Baptists say about the church and the state; how about Baptists, the church, and society? That exact issue is covered in the *Baptist Faith and Message*, Article XV, "The Christian and the Social Order."[3]

All Christians are under obligation to seek to make the will of Christ supreme in our own lives and in human society. Means and methods used for the improvement of society and the establishment of righteousness among men can be truly and permanently helpful only when they are rooted in the regeneration of the individual by the saving grace of God in Jesus Christ. I was amazed the first time I read this. I don't think I ever heard one sermon about Article XV the whole time I was growing up in Baptist churches.

In the spirit of Christ, Christians should oppose racism . . . That statement was added in 2000; it should have been added at the 1963 convention, but it would have been difficult to get it passed then.

. . . *every form of greed, selfishness, and vice, and all forms of sexual immorality including adultery, homosexuality, and pornography.* In 2000, those last three categories were added—adultery, homosexuality, and pornography. Had Baptists changed their minds about those issues since 1963? No. But many Americans had. And one of the functions of a confession of

---

[3]"Article XV: The Christian and the Social Order," in "The Baptist Faith and Message" (2000), http://www.sbc.net/BFM/bfm2000.asp.

faith is not only to teach our own people what we believe but to speak and witness to society about what we believe is grievous immorality. And we as Baptists made it clear that we believe that homosexuality is immoral. It is against God's will, as are adultery and pornography.

We should work to provide for the orphan, the needy, the abused, the aged, the helpless, the sick. We should speak on behalf of the unborn and contend for the sanctity of all human life from conception to natural death. This statement was added in 2000. Why? Because we weren't killing babies every twenty seconds in 1963. We are today; we have been for 31 years, and Baptists have been outraged by it.

Albert Mohler and I have talked about this before, and I think that he is absolutely right: The moderates and the liberals—and there is a difference—have never really understood the degree to which the abortion issue drove the debate in the SBC. When Southern Baptists were appalled by the tidal wave of innocent blood that engulfed the nation after the *Roe v. Wade* decision, and they found out that their agencies and institutions were sometimes ambiguous and sometimes unfortunately *not* ambiguous about a woman's right to kill her unborn baby, they were shocked, they were embarrassed, and they were galvanized to action.

Every Christian should seek to bring industry, government, and society as a whole under the sway of the principles of righteousness, truth, and brotherly love. In order to promote these ends, Christians should be ready to work with all men of good will in any good cause, always being careful to act in the spirit of love without compromising their loyalty to Christ and his truth.

THE THREE PILLARS: CHURCH, STATE, AND SOCIETY

There are the three pillars—the church, the state, and society—that I want to address in this final section. The beginning point, the impetus, is the Baptist understanding of the biblical nature of the church and ultimately its relationship to the state.

Beginning in the sixteenth century, the Swiss Brethren, later known as the Anabaptists, struck at the very foundation of Western civilization for over a thousand years when they separated church membership from membership in the society. In that society your baptismal certificate was your birth certificate, and thus their rejection of infant baptism was seen as completely radical. The Constantinian synthesis had so warped the

Western Christian understanding of the church and its relationship to the state that even spiritual giants like Calvin, Luther, and Zwingli couldn't comprehend church and state not being in tandem together. The idea of the church as a visible, gathered assembly of born-again believers in the Lord Jesus Christ, baptized by immersion as an act of testimony and obedience, and the church not having any connection, relationship, or subservience to the state, was literally beyond the cognitive grid of John Calvin and Martin Luther. Just look at Geneva, or Luther's Germany. It was also beyond the cognitive grid of most of the Protestant reformers in Britain for many, many, many years. Although the Puritans wanted to "purify" the Church of England of the remaining vestiges of popery, they still wanted a state church; they just wanted a "pure" state church.

I'm the same age as George W. Bush, Bill Clinton, and Laura Bush; we were all born in 1946. One of the experiences of being a school-age child in the mid-1950s is that the government was going to give all of us dog tags—identification tags—so that when the nuclear attack came they could identify the cinders. (You know, the old "duck and tuck.") It was well known in Houston that we were five miles from one of the top five targets of the Soviet missile system, the oil refineries in eastern Houston and Pasadena. We knew full well that if there was ever a nuclear exchange, "duck and tuck" wasn't going to do us much good. Regardless, they sent home a form to have your dog tag made. They asked for your name and your address, and they also wanted you to indicate your religion. Because this was a simpler time in America, we had three choices: Catholic, Protestant, and Jewish. Although she knows better now, my mother was raised on the trail of blood (the belief of many 19th century Landmarkist Baptists that the line of Baptists could be traced all the way back to the "first baptistic expressions" in the early church), and thus her reaction was, "We're not Protestants. We're Baptists. I'm not going to put down Protestant. I'm not going to let your little brother and you have 'P' on your dog tag." She went down to see the principal, and she told him, "I want my boys to have 'B' for Baptist." Well, we got a "P" for Protestant. But you know what? I think the best term for Baptist is "Completed Protestant."

The impetus of the Protestant Reformation was to get back to the primitive pattern of the New Testament church. Guess what? We're the only ones who didn't fall off the wagon along the way. We made it all the way back. For example, take any church in the New Testament. Drop it down in the middle of western Tennessee, describe the characteristics, beliefs, and practices of that church, and then ask, "Now what kind of a church is that?" The answer would be, "That's a Baptist church." (The sole exception would be the church at Corinth; it used to be a Baptist church but it got kicked out of the association for speaking in tongues.)

When Roger Williams founded Providence Plantation in 1636, he established the first government anywhere in the Western world for over a millennium where you were free not only to worship as you please without fear of penalty, but free to stay home and shuck peas on the front porch on Sunday morning without fear of government interference. It took that long. And even then the victory wasn't won. The Puritan revolution in England foundered on this issue of the church and the state. They were united in what they didn't want: they didn't want a king trying to rule by divine right, and they didn't want an Episcopal church with bishops. However, once they got rid of the king, and once they got rid of the bishops, they couldn't decide what was going to take their place. In fact, Cromwell's army sat down for six weeks in Putney, in England, and had a debate about it: the Presbyterians wanted a Presbyterian state church; the Congregationalists wanted a Presbyterian Congregational state church that would allow Baptists to take part in it; and the Baptists said "We don't want a state church at all. We want an England where the church is made up of a visible, gathered, covenanted community of saints who have been baptized by immersion and the government doesn't sponsor or give favoritism to the church." This debate is the rock upon which the Puritan revolution foundered.

Even in the American colonies, two-thirds of the original thirteen states had tax-supported, official state churches. None of them were Baptist. In New England, churches were Congregational, in the South they were Episcopal, and in the middle colonies they tended to be Presbyterian. Indeed, in the ten years prior to the American Revolutionary War, we have documented over five hundred Baptist preachers who were thrown in jail by the Episcopal government authorities of Virginia for "disturbing the peace." Although that's not the worst definition of preaching I've ever heard, what the authorities meant was that they were preaching without a license from the government to do so; Baptist preachers like John Leland said, "We don't need a license from the government—we've got a license from Jesus and the church."

In spite of many of the hardships, the Baptist view triumphed in the American Constitution, at least at the federal level. You know well the story of John Leland and the Baptists and their role in the ratification of the Constitution.[4] The Baptists, in spite of persecution, had reached the

---

[4]Cited in H. H. Hobbs and E. Y. Mullins, *The Axioms of Religion* (Nashville: Broadman, 1981).

place where they were the balance of power in several states, particularly Virginia. Leland, a Baptist evangelist, cut a political deal whereby he would withdraw his opposition and do what he could to get Baptists to vote for ratification. In return, James Madison promised that the first congress of the new government would pass an amendment to the Constitution that would guarantee that "Congress shall make no law affecting an establishment of religion nor prohibiting the free exercise thereof." Thus, the First Amendment is really the codification and the triumph at the federal level of the Baptist view of the church and its relationship to the state. There will be no national establishment of religion. Government is not going to get into the religion business. And the government is not going to interfere with the free exercise of religion. Also, please note that all the restrictions in the First Amendment are on the government—not on Christians, and not on churches. It's the government that is restricted in the sphere of religion in the First Amendment—not the people, and not religion.

Note the first half of the First Amendment: "Congress shall make no law affecting an establishment of religion." At the time, nine of the states had tax-supported state churches. Some of them didn't get rid of their tax-supported state churches until 1832, when the last two established state churches were finally declared dead and disestablished in Massachusetts and Connecticut.

Sometimes when I recite this history, people say to me, "Well, if that's the case, and only the *federal* government is restricted from having an establishment of religion and interfering with the free exercise thereof, then how come we don't have a *state* Mormon church in Utah?" The reason for this is the Fourteenth Amendment to the Constitution, which has been determined by the Supreme Court for well more than a century to say, in effect, that what the federal government is forbidden from doing in the first ten amendments, *all* government is forbidden from doing. There are some who want to pretend the Fourteenth Amendment was never passed, or who would like to do away with the application of the Fourteenth Amendment to the states, but that is a very bad idea. The best defense that people of faith have today in the judicial system is the free exercise clause of the First Amendment. Weakened as it has been by the Supreme Court in the *Smith* decision,[5] it is still the best protection of religious liberty that we have. For example:

---

[5]See 1990 U.S. Supreme Court decision, "Employment Division v. Smith," in *A Companion to the United States Constitution and Its Amendments*, John Vile, ed., 4th ed. (Westport, CT: Greenwood Press, 2003).

- In Connecticut, a zoning commission told a couple they could not have a Bible study of more than ten people in their own home because it would cause parking problems and traffic congestion. The couple lost the case in state court; however, they won against the zoning commission in federal court, based on the First Amendment's guarantee of no governmental interference with the free exercise of religion.
- In the Northwest, we have had churches where zoning commissions have said "You can only build an auditorium of a certain size, no bigger, and you can only have a certain number of worship services at a certain number of specified times on Sundays because otherwise it would interfere with traffic flow." The churches have won—not in state court, but in federal court—based on the First Amendment.

At the time that the First Amendment was ratified, the religious, cultural, and political situations were completely different than they are today. The great depth and diversity of religious conviction and belief in the early days of the federal republic produced the First Amendment because, as constitutional scholar Michael McConnell has said, "Every religion was a minority religion in some part of the new United States of America."[6] There was no ability to have a majority religion because there were too many of them. McConnell has also said, "The First Amendment's clauses were not intended as an instrument of secularization or as a weapon that the non-religious or anti-religious could use to suppress the effusions of the religious. The religion clauses were intended to guarantee the rights of those whose religious practices seemed to the majority a little odd." "Enthusiastic" was the word often used to describe the Baptists of that day, with much the same meaning that we would use for the words "charismatic" or "fanatical" today.

First Amendment religion clauses were put in place to protect religious minorities (of which Baptists were one) in most parts of the country at the time of the ratification of the First Amendment. This ensured that the majority could not trample upon the minority's right to religious expression and freedom. It was never intended by our first founding fathers to be freedom *from* religion, but freedom *for* religion.

We have all heard about the infamous letter from Thomas Jefferson to the Baptist preachers of Danbury, Connecticut. Remember, those dear brothers were suffering under the discrimination of a state church—not a federal church, but a state Congregational church they all had to pay

---

[6]Michael McConnell, *Religious Freedom, Separation of Powers, and Reversal of Roles* (Salt Lake City, UT: Brigham Young University Press, 2001).

taxes to and that got a favored position vis-à-vis all other religions and all other denominations in Connecticut. Thomas Jefferson said, "Believing with you that religion is a matter which lies solely between a man and his God, that he owes account to none other for his faith or his worship, that the legislative powers of government reach actions only and not opinions, I contemplate with sovereign reverence that act of the whole American people which declare that their legislators should make no law respecting the establishment of religion or prohibiting the free exercise thereof, thus building a wall of separation between the church and state." The important thing to note is this: Jefferson was talking about a wall of separation dividing any institutional connection between the church and the state. He was not talking about a separation of religious belief, opinion, and expression from public life and public policy.

Let me give you the immediate context of that letter. John Leland, the great Baptist evangelist from New England, went to Virginia, spent more than two decades there, and then went back to his native Massachusetts in 1791. In his valedictory sermon, Leland made a statement that almost found its way into the *Baptist Faith and Message*. He said, "I believe that the preaching which is most blessed of God is the preaching of the sovereignty of God mixed with a little of what we would call Arminianism and the two can be tolerably well reconciled."[7] That sounds an awful lot like, "Election is the gracious purpose of God according to which He regenerates, justifies, sanctifies, and glorifies sinners."[8] It seems to me that the Southern Baptists were listening to John Leland.

Leland went back to Massachusetts and got far more involved in politics than I think a Baptist preacher should. He was very much involved in the election campaign of 1800—the nastiest, most caustic, most controversial election campaign in the history of the United States, which resulted in Thomas Jefferson, by the narrowest of margins, becoming the president. Leland was so much identified with his old friend Jefferson that when the Democrats of Western Massachusetts wanted to give a gift of gratitude to show their affection for their Jefferson, they asked Leland to be the head of the delegation. A multi-hundred-pound cheese was made. They hauled it by wagon down to Washington, D.C., and on Friday morning, New Year's Day, 1802, Leland called on President Jefferson at the White House and presented him with the gift of cheese. He reassured the president that no

---

[7]Cited in Timothy George, *Amazing Grace: God's Initiative—Our Response* (Nashville: Liteway, 2001).
[8]"Article V: God's Purpose and Grace," in "The Baptist Faith and Message" (2000), http://www.sbc.net/BFM/bfm2000.asp.

Federalist cows had contributed any milk to this cheese—only Democrat cows. Leland prayed for the president, praised the president, prayed for God's blessing on the president, and then the delegation left. Jefferson went back into the White House and had lunch. (It is not recorded whether he had any of the cheese.) That same Friday, Jefferson wrote the letter to the Baptist ministers of Danbury, Connecticut.

On Sunday morning Jefferson went to a worship service in the House of Representatives where Leland preached a sermon from the speaker's rostrum of the House of Representatives. One of the Federalist congressmen who was there—and was much irritated—said, "Jefferson, that great reprobate who never came, came to the worship service this Sunday to hear this untutored frontier preacher preach in his holy whine." Obviously, Jefferson saw no contradiction between his understanding of a wall of separation of church and state and voluntary religious services being held in the House of Representatives, from the speaker's rostrum, and a sermon being preached with the president of the United States sitting in the front pew.

Unfortunately, the society in which we have been called to live is much more hostile to religion than the society of the eighteenth century, and we have a judicial establishment that has done its best to turn the First Amendment on its head, saying that the First Amendment means "freedom from religion," or the right of Americans not to hear religious opinions they don't want to hear. As Yale law professor Stephen Carter said, "Our culture has a secular bias that holds not only that religious beliefs cannot serve as the basis of policy, they cannot even be debated in the form of public dialog. Religion is like building model airplanes—it's another hobby. Something quaint, something trivial, not really fit activity for intelligent, public-spirited adults."[9]

America's secularization of society seeks to say that it is all right to believe—we have freedom of conscience, and you can believe what you like—but we should keep those beliefs to ourselves, without bringing them into the public square. That is dangerous nonsense. Every great social evil in our history that has been corrected has been corrected because people of religious conviction brought their religious convictions to bear on public policy.

Here is the way it is supposed to work: We have the right to preach the gospel. When people get saved, and their lives, attitudes, and understandings are changed, they have the right to bring their religious convictions to bear on public policy as private citizens, and if we convince enough of them

---

[9]Stephen Carter, *The Culture of Disbelief* (New York: Knopf, 1994).

that we are right, we have the right to make those moral convictions law. That is not called a theocracy; it is called the democratic process.

America and the world will not get the proper balance of separation of church and state without our articulation of our heritage as Baptists. And I believe that if we are willing to be the salt and the light that we have been commanded to be by the Lord Jesus Christ, it is possible that we can turn this culture around. We need certainly to be salt and light and to leave the results up to the Lord. I am a pretribulation premillenialist (which, as you know, means that the world is going to be in really sorry shape as described in Revelation 4 onward until the Lord comes back). However, there's nothing in my Bible that tells me that we can't have another reformation before the second coming.

Southern Baptists can make a difference. Our task is to engage the culture with uncompromising biblical truth and leave the results to the providence of God.

CHAPTER FOURTEEN

PRIORITIES FOR A POST-RESURGENCE CONVENTION

Nathan A. Finn

THE YEAR 1979 MARKED THE beginning of a movement in the SBC that successfully wrested control of the denomination's bureaucracy from a moderate coalition that included theological progressives and those who tolerated their convictions. This "conservative resurgence," called a "fundamentalist takeover" by its moderate detractors, gradually subsided as the Convention's leadership was increasingly (re-)claimed by theological conservatives. Moderates began to distance themselves from the SBC in the late 1980s, forming new networks like the Southern Baptist Alliance (1988; now Alliance of Baptists) and Cooperative Baptist Fellowship (1991). They founded alternative entities, including periodicals like *SBC Today* (1983; now *Baptists Today*) and theological schools like Baptist Theological Seminary of Richmond (1991) and George W. Truett Theological Seminary (1991). For most moderates, the proper response to the new Convention leadership was to curtail cooperation in much the same way that separatist fundamentalists had done a generation earlier.[1]

Conservatives began to capitalize on their gains during the mid 1990s. In 1995, the SBC authorized a total denominational restructuring under the name "Covenant for a New Century," streamlining the Convention's

---

[1]For conservative assessments of the conservative resurgence, see Jerry Sutton, *The Baptist Reformation: The Conservative Resurgence in the Southern Baptist Convention* (Nashville: B&H, 2000), and Paige Patterson, *Anatomy of a Reformation: The Southern Baptist Convention, 1978-2004* (Fort Worth, TX: Southwestern Baptist Theological Seminary, 2004). For moderate interpretations, see Bill J. Leonard, *God's Last and Only Hope: The Fragmentation of the Southern Baptist Convention* (Grand Rapids, MI: Eerdmans, 1990), and David M. Morgan, *The New Crusade, The New Holy Land: Conflict in the Southern Baptist Convention, 1969-1991* (Tuscaloosa: University of Alabama Press, 1996).

bloated bureaucracy. In 1998, the Convention voted to amend the denomination's confession of faith, the *Baptist Faith and Message*. Two years later,
Southern Baptists adopted a substantial revision of the *Baptist Faith and
Message*, an event that signaled the completion of the conservative resurgence. By the turn of the twenty-first century, every Convention agency
and board was under conservative control and advocating conservative
theology and practice. The battle had shifted from the national Convention
to the various state bodies that cooperate with the SBC through the
Cooperative Program, the central funding mechanism for the denomination's various ministries.

Despite the success of the conservative resurgence, a number of contemporary challenges threaten the conservative coalition that ascended to
denominational leadership in the 1980s and 1990s. Conservatives continue
to debate theological issues like Calvinism, "miraculous" spiritual gifts,
and how Baptists should relate to other Christian groups. Social issues such
as alcohol consumption, global climate change, and the role Christians
should play in secular politics prove equally controversial. Like most
American denominations, Southern Baptists disagree among themselves
regarding worship music styles, the seeker-sensitive movement, and the
various emerging church movements. Because of these debates, perhaps
the most pressing issue facing the SBC in the early twenty-first century is
whether or not all the varieties of Convention conservatives can continue
to cooperate together in the same denomination.

This chapter attempts to address these challenges by offering a
constructive proposal for a post-resurgence SBC. Because this proposal
originates from a particular vantage point, a word of biography seems
appropriate before proceeding. I am a thirty-year-old Baptist historian
who teaches at a Southern Baptist seminary. I am a third generation
conservative denominational servant, having been mentored by men who
were mentored by the generation that captured the Convention's reigns
during the previous two decades. I was converted at a Southern Baptist
youth camp, married a Southern Baptist pastor's daughter, and was educated by a state Baptist college and Southern Baptist seminaries. I am
strongly committed to my denomination and gravely afraid that many of
my generation do not share that commitment, sometimes for understandable reasons. It is because of my background in and great love for the SBC
that I propose the following three priorities for post-resurgence Southern
Baptists' consideration.

THREE PRIORITIES FOR A POST-RESURGENCE CONVENTION
Priority 1: The Renewal of Baptist Identity

In a day of what Timothy George has called "spiritual amnesia" and "ecclesiastical myopia," post-resurgence Southern Baptists must be careful to maintain our commitment to historic Baptist convictions.[2] The renewal of Baptist identity is necessary if the SBC is to have a viable future. I believe this renewal must include both retrieval of the best of historic Baptist confessional identity and constructive thinking about how to live as Baptist Christians in the twenty-first century. This renewal must also balance a focus on essential Baptist distinctives while allowing for some diversity in the application of those distinctives. This post-resurgence renewal of Baptist identity should be characterized by at least three aspects.

First and most important, the renewal of Baptist identity must be an uncompromisingly *biblical* renewal. On at least some level, the conservative resurgence was a protracted battle about the nature of Baptist identity. Each side was convinced it was more "Baptist" than the opponent. For the moderate coalition, the heart of Baptist identity was freedom of conscious, sometimes called "soul freedom." Moderates argued that Baptists have always been dissenters who champion religious freedom for all people. Expanding upon the insights of early twentieth-century theologian E. Y. Mullins, Convention moderates argued for the primacy of personal religious experience and the value of private interpretation of Scripture. This emphasis led to considerable theological diversity within the moderate coalition.[3]

Conservatives agreed with moderates that freedom of conscious has indeed been a crucial emphasis in Baptist history, but responded that all freedom must be tethered to biblical authority. Conservatives argued that Baptists have always been primarily Biblicists, and all of the movement's theological distinctives, including a dedication to religious freedom, flow from a primary commitment to the supreme authority of Scripture.[4] Appropriately, conservatives chose to emphasize the inerrancy of Scripture

---

[2]Timothy George, "The Renewal of Baptist Theology," in *Baptist Theologians*, eds. Timothy George and David S. Dockery (Nashville: Broadman, 1990), 13.

[3]See Alan Neely, ed., *Being Baptist Means Freedom* (Charlotte, NC: Southern Baptist Alliance, 1988), and Walter B. Shurden, *The Baptist Identity: Four Fragile Freedoms* (Macon, GA: Smyth & Helwys, 1993). For the influence of Mullins on moderate understandings of Baptist identity, see the Spring 2008 issue of the journal *Baptist History and Heritage*, which includes several articles about Mullins written by moderate authors.

[4]See R. Stanton Norman, *More Than Just a Name: Preserving Our Baptist Identity* (Nashville: B&H, 2001).

as the main plank in their agenda. There were at least two reasons for this emphasis: (1) From a strategic standpoint, by focusing mostly on one issue instead of a range of issues, Convention conservatives were able to avoid infighting among themselves on those matters where there was no uniformity. (2) From a theological standpoint, by maintaining the centrality of biblical inerrancy, conservatives believed they were providing the epistemological framework necessary to eventually adjudicate all of the matters they debated among themselves.[5]

One of the most obvious results of the conservative resurgence is that a commitment to inerrancy is now the norm among all denominational servants, whether missionaries, professors, or trustees. In full agreement with the *Baptist Faith and Message*, all conservatives believe that Scripture has "God for its author, salvation for its end, and truth, without any mixture of error, for its matter."[6] Post-resurgence Southern Baptists are committed to the full inspiration and integrity of Scripture. But in order to move forward, we need to turn our focus to the related issues of biblical authority and sufficiency.

For post-resurgence Southern Baptists, the Bible must be our highest authority for faith and practice. If the Bible is God's written Word, and if it is trustworthy, then, agreeing with the *Baptist Faith and Message*, the Bible must also be our "supreme standard by which all human conduct, creeds, and religious opinions should be tried."[7] Furthermore, Southern Baptists must be committed to the Bible's sufficiency to guide us in all matters of doctrine and life. This means that every theological conviction, every denominational program, every historic practice, and every treasured tradition must be scrutinized according to the standard of God's Word. And if any of the above is found wanting, it must be appropriately altered or discarded with no regard for present popularity or historic precedent. Biblical inerrancy, though foundational, is not enough; we must become better Biblicists if we are to become better Baptists.

Second, the renewal of Baptist identity must also be a genuinely *catholic* renewal. This terminology will undoubtedly rub some readers the wrong way, but rest assured I am not suggesting that Southern Baptists embrace the Roman Catholic Church. Nor am I advocating a liturgical approach to worship, though there are certainly some Southern Baptist churches that

---

[5]Patterson, *Anatomy of a Reformation*, 7. See also Paul Pressler, *A Hill on Which to Die: One Southern Baptist's Journey* (Nashville: B&H, 1998), 149–60.
[6]"Article I: The Scriptures," in "The Baptist Faith and Message" (2000), http://www.sbc.net/BFM/bfm2000.asp.
[7]Ibid.

embrace elements of the liturgical traditions. Rather, I am arguing that one key to the renewal of Baptist identity includes Southern Baptists embracing the reality that we are part of the universal ("catholic") Christian tradition that includes all believers everywhere.

During the first four centuries of Christian history, the early church arrived at a remarkable theological consensus on the core of the Christian faith. While there was certainly theological diversity among professing believers, it was during this period that the church worked out the heart of orthodox theology, often in response to new heresies and other challenges. This catholic consensus was not simply the one "orthodoxy" among many competitors that happened to win out in the end.[8] Rather, what emerged as orthodox theology in the great ecumenical creeds was a faithful con-textualization of the biblical doctrines in the milieu of fourth- and fifth-century Eurasia. The tradition of the apostles was preserved in the books that came to be recognized as Scripture and was propagated orally and in print through various versions of the rule of faith, brief summaries of the grand story-line of Scripture. When heretics and sectarians challenged the traditional theological convictions, the church's leadership responded by fleshing out definitive articulations of the triune Godhead and the person of Christ in creedal statements.[9] And it should be noted that much of this happened in the century before pedobaptism became the dominant practice among Christians.[10]

Traditionally, most Baptists have downplayed the significance of the early church's creedal statements. The Baptist tradition began as a revolt against perversions of the catholic tradition by medieval theology and Constantinianism, the latter of which was present even among the Magisterial Reformers in the form of territorial churches and pedobap-tism. Because our ecclesiology is different from most professing Christians, including many other Protestants, some Baptists overemphasize the restora-tion of Baptist principles in the sixteenth and seventeenth centuries, virtu-ally ignoring the previous fifteen-hundred years of church history. Other Baptists, especially in America, contend that only Baptist churches are true churches, claiming that Baptist principles have endured in every genera-

---

[8]See Walter Bauer, *Orthodoxy and Heresy in Earliest Christianity* (Minneapolis, MN: Fortress, 1979), and Bart D. Ehrman, *Lost Christianities: The Battles for Scripture and the Faiths We Never Knew* (New York: Oxford University Press, 2005).

[9]See John Behr, *The Way to Nicea: Formation of Christian Theology*, vol. 1 (Crestwood, NY: St. Vladimir's Seminary Press, 2001), and Behr, *The Nicene Faith: Formation of Christian Theology*, vol. 2 (Crestwood, NY: St. Vladimir's Seminary Press, 2004).

[10]See Steven A. McKinion, "Baptism in the Patristic Writings," in *Believer's Baptism: Sign of the New Covenant in Christ*, NAC Studies in Bible and Theology, ed. Thomas R. Schreiner and Shawn D. Wright (Nashville: B&H Academic, 2007), 163–88.

tion from the New Testament era to the present. Both of these approaches represent sectarian rejections of the catholic tradition because they assume that Baptists alone are biblical. Hence, many Baptists bristle at the idea of catholicity, believing it sounds a little too much like Roman Catholic.

Despite our sectarian tendencies, some Baptists have engaged the catholic tradition to great profit. Steve Harmon has convincingly argued that Baptist confessional articulations of the Trinity and Christology borrow from the patristic creedal tradition.[11] Trinitarian General Baptists went so far as commending the Nicene, Apostle's, and Athanasian creeds in the preface of the Orthodox Creed in 1678.[12] The eighteenth-century Particular Baptist pastor-theologian John Gill quoted extensively from the church fathers and the creedal tradition in his defense of orthodox christology and his apology for a Reformed understanding of salvation.[13] Delegates to the first meeting of the Baptist World Alliance in 1905 recited the Apostle's Creed in unison as a confession of their fundamental unity with other Christians throughout history.[14] Numerous contemporary Baptist theologians have constructively interacted with the broader catholic tradition in an effort to better articulate contemporary Baptist theology.[15]

Post-resurgence Southern Baptists must make sure that the renewal of our Baptist identity does not come at the expense of our Christian identity. We must not downplay the Trinity as we contend for congregational polity or ignore the cosmic scope of salvation as we advocate believer's baptism by immersion. Southern Baptists should humbly confess that we are only one part of the visible body of Christ and that our own interpretations of numerous doctrines have been influenced by the catholic confessional consensus. We should acknowledge that we have much to learn from other Christian traditions, even as we earnestly and often times prophetically contend for our unique Baptist distinctives. Perhaps when the *Baptist Faith and Message* is revised in another generation, we might commend

[11]See Steven R. Harmon, "Baptist Confessions and the Patristic Tradition," in *Toward Baptist Catholicity: Essays on Tradition and the Baptist Vision*, Studies in Baptist History and Thought, ed. Steven R. Harmon (Bletchley, Milton Keynes, UK: Paternoster, 2006), 71–87.
[12]See the critical edition of the Orthodox Creed published by the Center for Theological Research at Southwestern Baptist Theological Seminary, http://www.baptisttheology.org/documents/OrthodoxCreed.pdf.
[13]See Timothy George, "John Gill," in *Baptist Theologians*, 82–83, 90.
[14]Harmon, "Appendix 2: Confessing the Faith," in *Toward Baptist Catholicity*, 225–29.
[15]See James Leo Garrett Jr., *Systematic Theology: Biblical, Historical, Evangelical*, 2 vols. (Grand Rapids, MI: Eerdmans, 1990–1995); Timothy George, "Is Jesus a Baptist?" in David S. Dockery and Timothy George, eds., *Building Bridges* (Nashville: Convention Press, 2007), 37–64; David S. Dockery, *Biblical Interpretation Then and Now: Contemporary Hermeneutics in Light of the Early Church* (Grand Rapids, MI: Baker Academic, 2000); Bruce A. Ware, *Father, Son, and Holy Spirit: Relationship, Roles, and Relevance* (Wheaton, IL: Crossway Books, 2005); Jason K. Lee, "The Regula Fidei as a Guide for Biblical Preaching" (paper presented at the annual meeting of Young Scholars in the Baptist Academy, Summer 2006), http://www.georgetowncollege.edu/ysba/past_participants.html.

the ancient creeds to our people as aids in catechesis and discipleship and encourage their use in corporate worship.

Finally, the renewal of Baptist identity must obviously be a distinctively *Baptist* renewal. I wholeheartedly believe that a more robust biblicism and a greater appreciation for catholicity will result in a renewed commitment to the essentials of Baptist identity. Historically, though we have been orthodox Christians, Baptists have emphasized a cluster of ecclesiological beliefs that have distinguished us from most other types of Christians. We humbly embrace these convictions because we believe that they are both more clearly biblical and better represent the fruit of the gospel than other forms of ecclesiology.

The most foundational Baptist conviction is a commitment to regenerate church membership, the idea that only believers are to covenant together as members of local churches. Most of the other Baptist distinctives are simply consistent applications of this primary doctrine. Regenerate church membership is currently being threatened by a number of trends and practices in the SBC. These include incomplete or spurious articulations of the gospel, shallow discipleship, and a lack of redemptive church discipline. Many pastors and theologians in recent years have called upon Southern Baptists to pursue regenerate church membership as both the foundation of our ecclesiological identity and a crucial means in the spiritual renewal of our local churches.[16] Reclaiming regenerate church membership is a necessity in a post-resurgence SBC.

Closely tied to regenerate church membership is the most visible Baptist distinctive, the full immersion of believers who can give a credible testimony to their salvation. Baptists have always baptized believers because of our conviction that this practice is both more biblical than pedobaptism and better safeguards the principle of regenerate church membership than the christening of infants. The integrity of believer's baptism is also being threatened in at least two ways. Some conservatives, especially those influenced by the revivalist tradition, have de-emphasized *believer's* baptism by immersing very young children (sometimes under five) and other individuals who have not really understood the gospel, particularly the necessity of repenting of one's sin. Other conservatives, especially those who are more Calvinistic in their theology, have denigrated believer's *baptism* by flirting

---

[16]See John H. Hammett, "Regenerate Church Membership," in *Restoring Integrity in Baptist Churches*, ed. Thomas White, Jason G. Duesing, and Malcolm B. Yarnell III (Grand Rapids, MI: Kregel, 2008), 21–43; R. Stanton Norman, *The Baptist Way: Distinctives of a Baptist Church* (Nashville: B&H, 2005), 47–63. Florida pastor Tom Ascol and Texas pastor Bart Barber have each been politically active on this front, proposing resolutions to the SBC to address the inconsistent application of regenerate church membership among the Convention's churches.

with an "open membership" approach that allows paedobaptists to join Baptist churches without submitting to New Testament baptism. Both of these tendencies must be repudiated by post-resurgence Southern Baptists.

Another threatened Baptist distinctive is congregational church polity, which argues that the final earthly authority in every local church is the membership. A healthy congregationalism hinges upon two prior commitments: submission to the lordship of Christ as understood through his written Word, and a church membership that, inasmuch as is humanly possible, does not include nonbelievers. Contemporary congregationalism is being challenged on at least three fronts. Some churches, especially large congregations influenced by corporate business models, bequeath virtually all authority to the senior pastor. Other churches, normally of the Calvinist persuasion, invest almost all authority in a plurality of pastors (elders). A perennial problem in many smaller churches is deacon "boards" or key committees that unofficially rule the church. While Scripture clearly teaches pastoral authority (1 Pet. 5:1–4), such authority is entrusted to the pastor or pastors by the congregation as a whole, which collectively submits to the lordship of Christ.[17] Deacon or committee authority is simply unbiblical. Post-resurgence Southern Baptists must not abandon congregationalism for more hierarchical and authoritarian approaches to local church polity.

Thankfully, many post-resurgence Southern Baptists are emphasizing the importance of historic and biblical Baptist distinctives. Authors such as Stan Norman, Mark Dever, and John Hammett have authored helpful books advocating Baptist identity.[18] Union University and Southwestern Baptist Theological Seminary have each hosted multiple conferences on the topic.[19] Dever, Greg Wills, and Jason Lee have written historical works with an eye toward application to contemporary Baptist practice.[20] Tom Nettles has authored a three-volume history of the Baptists that uses Baptist identity as its primary organizing principle.[21] Popular material is regularly disseminated through position papers, sermons, and blog posts. Though

---

[17]See Norman, *The Baptist Way*, 102–4.

[18]See John S. Hammett, *Biblical Foundations for Baptist Churches: A Contemporary Ecclesiology* (Grand Rapids, MI: Kregel, 2005); Mark Dever, *Nine Marks of a Healthy Church* (Wheaton, IL: Crossway Books, 2000); Norman, *The Baptist Way*.

[19]Southwestern Seminary has produced two different volumes of conference proceedings to date. See Thomas White, Jason G. Duesing, and Malcolm B. Yarnell III, eds., *First Freedom: The Baptist Perspective on Religious Liberty* (Nashville: B&H, 2007), and White, Duesing, and Yarnell, eds., *Restoring Integrity in Baptist Churches*.

[20]Mark Dever, ed., *Polity: Biblical Arguments on How to Conduct Church Life* (Washington, DC: Center for Church Reform, 2001); Gregory A. Wills, *Democratic Religion: Freedom and Authority in the Baptist South, 1785–1900* (New York: Oxford University Press, 1997); Jason K. Lee, *The Theology of John Smyth: Puritan, Separatist, Baptist, Mennonite* (Macon, GA: Mercer University Press, 2003), 127–65.

[21]Tom Nettles, *The Baptists: Key People Involved in Forming a Baptist Identity*, 3 vols. (Fearn, Ross-shire, UK: Christian Focus, 2005–2007).

there are minor differences in how the above individuals have articulated or applied traditional Baptist distinctives, there is a common commitment to the core essentials of our identity. A post-resurgence Convention must cling tightly to that core, even as we recognize that there are diverse expressions of that center among our multitudes of autonomous churches.

Priority 2: A Great Commission Resurgence

Since 1845, one consistency among Southern Baptists has been an unwavering commitment to gospel proclamation. According to the original constitution of the SBC, the Convention was formed for the purpose of "eliciting, combining and directing the energies of the whole denomination in one sacred effort, for the propagation of the Gospel . . . "[22] It seems, however, that we have become distracted from this sacred effort. Southern Baptists have less evangelistic impact on American culture than we did in 1979. While the number of missionaries serving with our two mission boards continues to climb, both boards have been rocked by scandal and controversy in recent years. Some argue that Southern Baptists have become so used to fighting among ourselves that we have taken our eyes off the prize of every tribe, tongue, and nation. Fortunately, there is a movement afoot to build upon the foundation of the conservative resurgence and redirect our energies toward missions and evangelism. There are three necessary elements to the Great Commission resurgence we must pursue over the next generation.

First, Southern Baptists must recover a robust understanding of the gospel. I use the word "recover" because, regrettably, some SBC churches have come perilously close to losing the gospel. I do not mean to imply that they have rejected the gospel, nor that they have embraced theological liberalism or doctrinal heresy. But it is possible to attend any number of Southern Baptist churches on a Sunday morning and not hear the gospel proclaimed from the pulpit. This is likely due to a combination of factors.

In too many of our churches, the gospel is being downplayed, confused, dumbed-down, or redefined. I believe almost none of this is deliberate, but it is still a reality in too many of our churches. Sometimes the gospel is ignored or downplayed, perhaps because the pastor assumes that his audience understands the gospel. I have seen the following scenario played out on a number of occasions. The pastor has not mentioned the gospel in his sermon, but as he reaches the conclusion he calls upon people to make a decision for Christ. He rightly asks sinners to trust Christ, but he has not

---

[22]"Preamble and Constitution of the Southern Baptist Convention, 1845," http://baptiststudiesonline. com/wp-content/uploads/2007/02/constitution-of-the-sbc.pdf.

explained what this means or why it is necessary for one's salvation. No doubt some who respond have heard the gospel previously and the Lord has convicted them at this moment, but what about those who have not previously heard the gospel but nevertheless make some sort of public decision? To what are these people looking for their salvation? Post-resurgence Southern Baptists must be diligent to make the gospel a central part of all our preaching and evangelism.

Sometimes the good news is confused when the facts of the gospel are collapsed into one or more ways to respond to those facts. When this occurs, the gospel becomes something different from the glorious truth of what God has done through Christ. Regrettably, the gospel itself is substituted with calls to "pray this prayer," "sign this card," "walk this aisle," "speak with this counselor," "raise that hand," or "enroll in this class." Some of this becomes so formulaic that we assume anyone who has jumped through the proper hoops has been reconciled to God. Post-resurgence Southern Baptists must passionately call upon all people to respond to the gospel without confusing those responses with the gospel itself.

Sometimes the gospel is cliché-ed or dumbed-down, transformed into little more than lingo. Such dumbing-down transpires every time a pastor throws out some trite description of the Christian life as a substitute for a gospel presentation: "God loves you and has a wonderful plan for your life"; "If you trust Jesus, he will help you get your life back in order"; or "Jesus will be the one who stands by your side when everyone else abandons you." I am not claiming that any of these things are necessarily untrue statements, but they are not in and of themselves the gospel. The fact that "God strengthens families" is not the gospel, but is one way the gospel works itself out in the lives of those who have believed the good news. Post-resurgence Southern Baptists must avoid dumbing-down the gospel by substituting clichés and popular terminology in its place, even if some of those substitutes are true and helpful statements.

Most tragic of all, sometimes the gospel is actually redefined, resulting in an articulation of something that is "sub-gospel"—in some cases "non-gospel." This scenario occurs when anyone describes the good news as something different from the biblical gospel. It also takes place when only one aspect of the gospel is equated with the entirety of the good news. So the gospel becomes "God loves you," or "God wants to save you," or "You should just trust God," or "God wants you to be the best person that you can be," or "God is in the business of second chances," or "God loves you just the way you are," or "Jesus wants to be your best friend."

On at least two occasions in recent years, I have personally heard two theologically conservative Southern Baptist megachurch pastors preach sermons where the gospel was defined in one or more of these terms. Post-resurgence Southern Baptists must make sure that what we are articulating is the biblical gospel in its entirety, lest we preach a sub-Christian, or even non-Christian, message.

So what is the biblical gospel that must be at the center of a post-resurgence SBC? Perhaps the most well-known biblical summary of the gospel is found in 1 Corinthians 15:3–4 (ESV):

> For I delivered to you as of first importance what I also received: that Christ died for our sins in accordance with the Scriptures, that he was buried, that he was raised on the third day in accordance with the Scriptures . . .

Though these truths about the death and resurrection of Christ stand at the heart of the gospel, they must be teased out. There is an implied "back story" in these verses: why did Christ die for our sins, why was he buried and raised, and how is this "in accordance with the Scriptures"? These details must be filled in if the gospel is to be adequately explained, defended, and commended to our lost neighbors and to the uttermost parts of the earth. To that end, David Dockery helpfully lists a number of theological truths that must be expounded if the gospel is to be proclaimed, including God's creation of humanity in his image and his sovereign rule over all things, humanity's rejection of God's rule and fall into sin, God's provision for humanity's sin in the perfect life, penal substitionary death, and victorious resurrection of Jesus Christ, God's actual salvation of men and women when they repent of their sins and trust in the person and work of Christ, and God's ultimate redemption of the entire created order.[23]

This gospel is preserved for us in the pages of Scripture, appearing as the central element that draws together and ultimately makes sense of all the individual stories within the Bible's grand narrative. In a helpful statement titled "Theological Vision for Ministry," the Gospel Coalition notes that the good news is found both "along" the Bible as a story of creation, fall, redemption, and restoration, and "across" the Bible as the true understanding of God, sin, Christ, and faith.[24] Post-resurgence Southern Baptists

---

[23]David S. Dockery, *Southern Baptist Consensus and Renewal: A Biblical, Historical, and Theological Proposal* (Nashville: B&H, 2008), 70.
[24]"Theological Vision of Ministry," adopted by the Gospel Coalition, http://www.thegospelcoalition.org/about/foundation-documents/vision.

must adequately explain these biblical facts in order for the gospel to be preached. It is only when these wonderful truths are proclaimed that we can call upon men and women to turn from their sins and trust in Christ (Rom. 10:9–13). And it is only after men and women have responded positively to the good news that we can teach them how to conduct themselves in a manner worthy of the gospel (Phil. 1:27). Our Great Commission resurgence must first and foremost be a gospel resurgence.

Second, post-resurgence Southern Baptists must believe that the Lord is a missional God and that his church is a missional people. That God himself is missional is made clear as the grand narrative of Scripture unfolds. John Piper argues that the Lord desires that his name be glorified among all people and that his purpose for cross-cultural missions is that the gospel be preached to all people groups so that a redeemed people can be called out from all the nations of the earth.[25] Christopher Wright argues that the Bible itself is a product of God's mission because "it witnesses to the self-giving movement of this God toward his creation and us, human beings in God's own image, but wayward and wanton."[26] God's missional purposes are made clear through his self-revelation in his covenantal dealings with Israel and his ultimate self-revelation in the incarnation and saving work of Jesus Christ.[27] Through all that he has done, culminating in the person and work of Christ, God is sovereignly bringing about his redemptive purposes for humanity and the entire created order.

We are privileged to play a role in the Lord's redemptive purposes. All of God's missional prerogatives are extended through the earthly means of his missional people, the church. Drawing upon the insights of noted missiologist-bishop Lesslie Newbigin, Darrell Guder claims, "God's mission is calling and sending us, the church of Jesus Christ, to be a missionary church in our own societies, in the cultures in which we find ourselves."[28] Speaking specifically of local churches, Charles Van Engen argues that Christians should not divorce ecclesiology from missiology, but should understand each church to be "God's missionary people in a local context."[29] Southern Baptist missiologist Ed Stetzer warns that most SBC

[25]John Piper, *Let the Nations Be Glad! The Supremacy of God in Missions*, 2nd ed. (Grand Rapids, MI: Baker, 2003), 17, 157.
[26]Christopher J. H. Wright, *The Mission of God: Unlocking the Bible's Grand Narrative* (Downers Grove, IL: IVP Academic, 2006), 48. See also David Bosch's discussion of the missional nature of the New Testament in David J. Bosch, *Transforming Mission: Paradigm Shifts in the Theology of Mission* (Maryknoll, NY: Orbis, 1991), 15–55.
[27]Wright, *The Mission of God*, 75–135.
[28]Darrell L. Guder, ed., *Missional Church: A Vision for the Sending of the Church in North America* (Grand Rapids, MI: Eerdmans, 1998), 5.
[29]Charles Van Engen, *God's Missionary People: Rethinking the Purpose of the Local Church* (Grand Rapids, MI: Baker, 1991), 27.

congregations will continue to fail to impact the lostness of North America unless Southern Baptist churches begin to "think of themselves as missionary churches in missionary settings."[30] Post-resurgence Southern Baptists must understand that we worship a missional God and that the church is his missional people.

Finally, post-resurgence Southern Baptists must (re)commit to being active participants in God's mission as we passionately engage in personal evangelism and church planting, both in North America and to the ends of the earth. Baptists have historically been pioneers in global missions. The seventeenth-century Baptist missionary William Carey famously argued that the Great Commission was a binding command on every individual Christian in every age. Though Carey strongly affirmed God's sovereignty in salvation, he challenged the popular hyper-Calvinism of his era by contending that individual Christians are the means God uses to bring non-Christians to faith in Jesus Christ.[31] Adoniram and Ann Judson agreed with Carey, and these Congregationalists-turned-Baptists were among the first foreign missionaries to be sent out from America.[32] Like Carey and the Judsons before us, if we will "own" the Great Commission as individuals and local churches, perhaps we will see more Southern Baptists serve as international missionaries and more local churches become globally minded by giving generously, praying fervently, and going obediently.

The Great Commission also has implications for reaching North America. For all of our talk about evangelism, post-resurgence Southern Baptists have an unremarkable track record in this matter. It is common knowledge that denominational baptism statistics have remained steady over the last five decades—around 350,000 per year—while the American population has grown exponentially. With these statistics in mind, particularly over the last thirty years, Thom Rainer has shown that the conservative resurgence has not yet yielded evangelistic fruit in most of our churches.[33] According to one recent study, the SBC actually experienced

[30]Ed Stetzer, "The Missional Nature of the Church and the Future of Southern Baptist Convention Churches," in *The Mission of Today's Church: Baptist Leaders Look at Modern Faith Issues*, ed. R. Stanton Norman (Nashville: B&H, 2007), 75. See also Ed Stetzer and David Putnam, *Breaking the Missional Code: Your Church Can Become a Missionary in Your Community* (Nashville: B&H, 2006).
[31]See William Carey, *An Enquiry into the Obligation of Christians to Use Means for the Conversion of the Heathens*, ed. John L. Prestlove (Leicester, UK: Anne Ireland, 1792; reprint, Dallas: Criswell Publications, 1988). For the context of Carey's missiological contributions, see Timothy George, *Faithful Witness: The Life and Mission of William Carey* (Birmingham, AL: New Hope, 1991), 47–66.
[32]For a fine biography of Adoniram Judson, see Courtney Anderson, *To the Golden Shore: The Life of Adoniram Judson* (Valley Forge, PA: Judson, 1987).
[33]Thom S. Rainer, "A Resurgence Not Yet Realized: Evangelistic Effectiveness in the Southern Baptist Convention since 1979," *Southern Baptist Journal of Theology* 9, no. 1 (Spring 2005): 54–69.

a numeric decline in 2006, the most recent year with available statistics.[34] Some will argue that these statistics only measure results, not efforts, noting that while we share the gospel, God is the one who does the converting. Fair enough, but remember that while it would be naïve to think that these statistics give a *complete* picture of Southern Baptist evangelistic engagement, it would be equally foolish to believe that these numbers are *unrelated* to our outreach efforts. The numbers are still troubling because they indicate that, as a general rule, Southern Baptist churches are simply not reaching North America with the good news of Jesus Christ.

Post-resurgence Southern Baptists must be diligent to share the good news with all types of people. The church may be a missional people by nature, but as Danny Akin has well said, "No church will be evangelistic by accident."[35] We must be *active* in our personal evangelism. Churches must work hard to cultivate an evangelistic atmosphere and effectively equip members to share the gospel with non-Christians. We should be burdened for the lost, because as Mark Dever notes, "If we are to follow a biblical model of evangelism, we must emphasize the urgency with which people ought to repent and believe if they will be saved."[36] We must also be *creative* in our personal evangelism, recognizing that North America is just as much a mission field as the two-thirds world. Southern Baptists must thoughtfully and biblically contextualize the gospel in order to reach different subcultures with the good news.[37] Most important, we must be *biblical* in our evangelism, ever careful to make sure that the good news we are sharing is actually the gospel.[38] There is no more exciting priority among post-resurgence Southern Baptists than the hope for a Great Commission resurgence.

Priority 3: Graciously Confessional Cooperation

The SBC exists because autonomous local churches believe that they can accomplish more when they work together than they can as individual congregations. As Cecil and Susan Ray observe, "Cooperation is not a Southern Baptist invention, but it is certainly one of our trademarks."[39]

---

[34]The statistics in question are available from LifeWay Research, a division of LifeWay Christian Resources, http://www.lifeway.com/lwc/mainpage/0,1701,M%253D200905,00.html.
[35]Daniel L. Akin, "Ten Mandates for Southern Baptists," in *The Mission of Today's Church*, 16.
[36]Mark Dever, *The Gospel and Personal Evangelism* (Wheaton, IL: Crossway Books, 2007), 55.
[37]See Will McRaney Jr., *The Art of Personal Evangelism: Sharing Jesus in a Changing Culture* (Nashville: B&H, 2003), 140–65, and the essays in D. A. Carson, ed., *Telling the Truth: Evangelizing Postmoderns* (Grand Rapids, MI: Zondervan, 2002).
[38]Dever, *The Gospel and Personal Evangelism*, 31–44.
[39]Cecil Ray and Susan Ray, *Cooperation: The Baptist Way to a Lost World* (Nashville: Stewardship Commission of the Southern Baptist Convention, 1985), 1.

This has always been the case among Baptists. Almost from our beginnings in the seventeenth century, Baptists have cooperated together in associations and conventions. According to the *Baptist Faith and Message*, these bodies are not connectional synods or hierarchical dioceses, but are "voluntary and advisory bodies designed to elicit, combine, and direct the energies of our people in the most effective manner."[40] Generally speaking, there have been two different approaches to interchurch cooperation taken by Southern Baptists during the course of our history.

The first historic approach was sectional and theological cooperation, a paradigm that more or less prevailed for the first century of the Convention's history. When the SBC was founded in 1845, almost all of the original delegates came from the Deep South. Sectional differences were among the many factors that contributed to the division between American Baptists. The Civil War and Reconstruction only exacerbated the sectional divide, effectively ending any hopes for the reunification of missionary Baptists in America. At the Fortress Monroe Conference of 1894, representatives of the Home Missionary Society (North) and the Home Mission Board (SBC) drafted comity agreements that carved America into distinct territories for the different Baptist groups to do their respective mission work. The result was that Southern Baptists mostly remained in the South and Southwest until the 1930s and 1940s, when for a variety of reasons Baptists outside of Convention territory sought to align with the SBC. By the mid-twentieth century, Southern Baptists had transformed into a national denomination, though one with a decidedly southern "flavor."[41]

Although there has never been uniformity in the theological convictions of Southern Baptists, there was a general doctrinal consensus into the first quarter of the twentieth century, despite the absence of a Convention-wide confession of faith. Most Southern Baptist leaders were generally Calvinistic, though not always holding to the doctrine of particular atonement. There was widespread acceptance of biblical inerrancy and a general hesitancy about the historical-critical method of biblical interpretation. Although divided into Landmark and non-Landmark camps, almost all Southern Baptists took ecclesiological matters seriously and were hesitant about ecumenical entanglements and practices that downplayed unique Baptist convictions. Arminianism, liberalism, and ecumenism were normally not tolerated, and dissenters in these matters were often silenced or

---

[40]"Article XIV: Cooperation," in "The Baptist Faith and Message" (2000), http://www.sbc.net/BFM/bfm2000.asp.
[41]This paragraph relies heavily on H. Leon McBeth, *The Baptist Heritage* (Nashville: Broadman, 1987), 381–91, 430–32, 623–32.

ostracized. The theological nature of SBC cooperation began to change with the wane of Calvinism and the de-emphasis on biblical inerrancy, both of which began in the 1920s. The shifting theological emphases only furthered the paradigm shift in Convention cooperation at mid-century.[42]

The second historic approach to cooperation was programmatic and pragmatic. This model of cooperation was the status quo from the post-World War II era until the 1990s. During the first half of the twentieth century, the bureaucratization of the SBC began in earnest. During the nineteenth century, one could argue that the SBC only existed during the few days that messengers from cooperating local churches gathered together for their annual meeting. That changed with the programmatic expansion marked by the formation of the Executive Committee in 1917, the Seventy-Five Million Campaign of 1919–1924, and the creation of the Cooperative Program in 1925. The Executive Committee grew in both size and influence for a generation while the Cooperative Program emerged as the center of Southern Baptist cooperation. The 1950s was the crucial decade: the Executive Committee wholly embraced modern business efficiency practices and "A Million More in '54," arguably the most successful program in SBC history, added over six-hundred thousand new members to SBC Sunday school roles. This programmatic emphasis continued into the early years of the conservative resurgence.[43]

The emphasis on programs, coupled with the evolution in our theological identity, resulted in a cooperation that was more pragmatic than principled. Although the *Baptist Faith and Message* had been adopted in 1925, Convention conservatives were disturbed by the increasingly non-theological character of denominational cooperation. Progressive theology was tolerated at SBC seminaries and state colleges while Cooperative Program support was emphasized. Public controversy would sometimes arise over the beliefs of a particular professor, as was the case with Frank Stagg's rejection of penal substitution, Ralph Elliott's rejection of the historicity of Genesis 1–11, the Broadman Bible Commentary Controversy, and Dale Moody's belief that true believers can fall from grace. Conservatives

---

[42]See Dockery, *Southern Baptist Consensus and Renewal*, 2–5, and Tom J. Nettles, *By His Grace and For His Glory: A Historical, Theological and Practical Study of the Doctrines of Grace in Baptist Life*, rev. and exp. 20th Anniversary Edition (Cape Coral, FL: Founders Press, 2006), esp. chs. 5–9. See also the essays in Paul A. Basden, ed., *Has Our Theology Changed? Southern Baptist Thought Since 1845* (Nashville: B&H, 1994).

[43]See Jesse C. Fletcher, *The Southern Baptist Convention: A Sesquicentennial History* (Nashville: B&H, 1994), 147–218, and Nancy Tatom Ammerman, *Baptist Battles: Social Change and Religious Conflict in the Southern Baptist Convention* (New Brunswick, NJ: Rutgers University Press, 1990), 44–71. For an introduction to the Cooperative Program, see Chad O. Brand and David E. Hankins, *One Sacred Effort: The Cooperative Program of the Southern Baptist Convention* (Nashville: B&H, 2005).

considered some entire schools theologically suspect, particularly Southern and Southeastern Seminaries and Wake Forest and Baylor Universities.[44]

Periodically, steps would be taken to address the issues, such as Elliott's termination from Midwestern Seminary in 1962 and the revision of the *Baptist Faith and Message* the following year. But many conservatives considered these events to be mostly symbolic gestures undertaken by pragmatic denominational leaders who were attempting to pacify outspoken conservative dissenters while avoiding substantive changes. Hundreds of fundamentalists left the SBC to align with the Independent Baptist movement between the 1940s and 1970s. Conservative dissenters who remained within the denomination networked together, with varying degrees of success, and finally devised a plan that successfully captured the bureaucracy and set the Convention's agencies and boards on a rightward trajectory.[45]

With the collapse of this second paradigm during the 1990s, the time is ripe for a post-resurgence approach to cooperation that avoids the twin errors of atheological pragmatism on the left and uncharitable separatism on the right.[46] We stand in need of a graciously confessional cooperation that flows from our renewed Baptist identity and aids us in our corporate pursuit of a Great Commission resurgence. This graciously confessional cooperation should appreciate genuine diversity within the context of broadly accepted doctrinal parameters and other expectations the Convention deems appropriate.

A new paradigm for cooperation is necessary because Southern Baptists remain quite diverse, albeit not as diverse as we were prior to 1979. David Dockery argues that SBC conservatives are a loose-knit coalition of at least seven broad groups: fundamentalists, revivalists, traditionalists, orthodox evangelicals, Calvinists, contemporary church practitioners, and culture warriors.[47] I would add Landmarkers, Cooperative Program apologists, and miraculous gifts advocates to Dockery's list. Tensions exist between some of these groups that can hinder our corporate ability to cooperate with each other. The question before post-resurgence Southern Baptists is how to determine acceptable diversity within the SBC.

According to the Convention's constitution and bylaws, any local

---

[44]See Gregory A. Wills, "Progressive Theology and Southern Baptist Controversies of the 1950s and 1960s," *The Southern Baptist Journal of Theology* 7, no. 1 (Spring 2003): 12–32.
[45]See Nathan A. Finn, "The Development of Baptist Fundamentalism in the South, 1940–1980" (PhD diss., Southeastern Baptist Theological Seminary, 2007), 140–57, 177–90; Sutton, *The Baptist Reformation*, 6–59.
[46]See Morris Chapman, "The Fundamentals of Cooperating Conservatives" (an address before the 2004 annual meeting of the Southern Baptist Convention, June 15, 2004), transcript available at http://www.morrischapman.com/article.asp?id=14.
[47]Dockery, *Southern Baptist Consensus and Renewal*, 11.

church is free to cooperate with the SBC, provided that it financially supports the denomination and does not endorse the homosexual lifestyle. Cooperation at this level is defined as the right to send up to ten messengers to the denomination's annual meeting, depending upon a church's contributions and/or membership.[48] This minimalist approach means that a church can believe virtually anything, including pedobaptism, and at least in theory cooperate with the SBC! At this time, there is no confessional basis for denominational cooperation, which is probably a bit too close to the pragmatic cooperation of the pre-resurgence era.

Post-resurgence Southern Baptists need to embrace a confessional basis for cooperation, but it would probably not be a good idea to mandate complete adherence to the *Baptist Faith and Message* by all cooperating churches. To do such would demand a degree of doctrinal uniformity that would exclude too many conservative Southern Baptists who are uncomfortable with aspects of the *Baptist Faith and Message*. David Dockery helpfully suggests that Southern Baptists should not seek such uniformity, but should commit to the best of the Baptist confessional tradition.[49] Perhaps Jim Richards offers a helpful proposal to this end:

> The future for the Southern Baptist Convention is to become a confessional fellowship. The *Baptist Faith and Message 2000* may be too restrictive. A minimal set of doctrinal statements is necessary for the expansion of the SBC. We cooperate not because of common geography, heritage, or goals. We cooperate because we believe the same essentials (Amos 3:3). At some point someone needs to move the SBC to adopt doctrinal affiliation requirements. Cooperation will be based on agreement regarding the nature of the Word of God and certain doctrines that define who we are. Preaching and teaching doctrine is the only way Baptists will retain their identity.[50]

This seems like a wise suggestion. I would propose that post-resurgence Southern Baptists adopt a brief abstract of the *Baptist Faith and Message* that affirms a high view of Scripture, an orthodox statement of the Trinity and christology, an evangelical understanding of salvation, and a basic Baptist understanding of ecclesiology. This would form an adequate confessional basis for churches cooperating with the SBC.

---

[48]The Convention's constitution and bylaws are available at http://www.sbc.net/PDF/SBC-CharterConstitutionByLaws.pdf.
[49]Dockery, *Southern Baptist Consensus and Renewal*, 215.
[50]James W. [Jim] Richards, "Cooperation among Southern Baptist Churches as Set Forth in Article 14 of the Baptist Faith and Message," in Norman, *The Mission of Today's Church*, 151.

In recent years, much of our debate about cooperation ignores local churches and centers around the question of who qualifies to serve in positions of denominational leadership and work for Convention entities. The requirements for trustees and institutional employees are considerably more stringent than those for local churches; all denominational leaders must affirm the current edition of the *Baptist Faith and Message* as a condition of service or employment.[51] In addition, most Convention entities have adopted a variety of policies, guidelines, and expectations that are not addressed in the denomination's confession of faith. This raises two questions. First, is it appropriate for trustees to establish parameters that are not spelled out in the *Baptist Faith and Message*? Second, is it appropriate for a denominational leader, either paid or elected, to conscientiously dissent from particular points in the *Baptist Faith and Message*?

Post-resurgence Southern Baptists should answer the first question in the affirmative. Trustees are elected by the Convention to provide leadership to particular institutions, each with its own unique history, needs, and purpose. The Abstract of Principles (1858) has historically been the confession of faith for Southern and Southeastern Seminaries, in some points clarifying (though not contradicting) the *Baptist Faith and Message*. The two mission boards have strict personal stewardship expectations for missionaries because they are personally responsible for managing funds in their mission work. Each of the Convention's entities requires any number of moral expectations that are not explicitly stated in the denomination's confession of faith. For these reasons, the *Baptist Faith and Message* is probably best understood as a minimalist document that provides the fundamental basis for governing Convention-funded agencies and boards.

Many post-resurgence Baptists are uncomfortable with this understanding of the *Baptist Faith and Message* because they object to specific additional parameters that have been established by some institutions and boards. For example, many object to the 2005 guidelines adopted by the International Mission Board (IMB) to more closely regulate baptism and forbid so-called private prayer languages. The latter issue is not addressed in the *Baptist Faith and Message* and the former issue is not as strictly defined in the confession as it is in the IMB guidelines. Others object to seminaries' using the Abstract of Principles because it affirms a more clearly Calvinistic understanding of the doctrine of election than the *Baptist Faith and Message*. Because of these controversial issues, a growing number of Southern Baptists argue that the *Baptist Faith and Message*

---

[51]Ibid., 152–53.

should be understood not as a minimalist statement but as a totally sufficient confession for all Convention entities and boards. A motion was even passed at the 2007 SBC annual meeting that seemed to advocate a total sufficiency view of the *Baptist Faith and Message*, though subsequent events at that meeting indicated that there was widespread confusion about the issue.[52]

It seems unwise for post-resurgence Southern Baptists to reject in principle the freedom of SBC boards and agencies to establish parameters in addition to the *Baptist Faith and Message*. At the same time, it is entirely possible that a trustee board could impose a specific extra-confessional requirement that would be rejected by a majority of Southern Baptists. Our governing documents should provide a way to rectify this situation if and when it arises. This would involve revising bylaw 26B, which states that motions made concerning the internal operations of an entity are to be referred to the trustee board, a procedure that is virtually impotent to address an issue arising from the trustee board itself.[53] Because trustees are ultimately accountable to the Convention that elected them, if a trustee board imposes any additional parameters that are controversial, it should be possible for the issues to be addressed during the annual business session of the SBC if necessary. If the Convention chooses to take up the matter, then both the trustees and those who disagree with them should be allowed to make their respective cases.

Admittedly, the above scenario runs the risk of both encouraging pandemonium at the annual meeting and ultimately undermining the ability of trustees to efficiently govern their entities. To preserve the integrity of the trustee system and to guard the Convention's time, a procedure would need to be adopted to manage those situations where an institution's trustees are being challenged. I would suggest a policy similar to the following:

- In order for messengers to be able to make an informed decision and to allow for sufficient time on the Convention's program, it would be necessary for those who wish to challenge the trustees to announce their intentions well in advance of the annual meeting. I would recommend sixty days.
- At the Convention itself, messengers would of course reserve the right to decide whether they would even hear the matter. Messengers may decide some challenges are not worth their time.

---

[52]See Keith Hinson, "BF&M Motion Grabs Attention at SBC," *Baptist Press*, June 13, 2007, http://www.bpnews.net/bpnews.asp?id=25853 , and Morris Chapman, "Postscript to the 2007 SBC Re the Baptist Faith and Message," June 21, 2007, http://www.morrischapman.com/article.asp?id=71.
[53]See bylaw 26B of the SBC Constitution and Bylaws, http://www.sbc.net/PDF/SBC-CharterConstitutionByLaws.pdf.

- A substantial majority would be necessary to actually reverse a policy established by an entity's trustee board. I would recommend a two-thirds supermajority.
- If the Convention should vote to reverse or revise a trustee decision, trustees would need enough time to implement the change. I would recommend implementation by the next annual meeting.
- Should the latter occur, the president of the institution would need to include details about the matter during his annual report to the following year's Convention.

I believe this type of approach would preserve both the right of individual trustee boards to govern their entities in a manner they believe to be most appropriate and the accountability of trustees to the Convention that elected them.

The second question is whether it is ever appropriate for an individual trustee or denominational employee to disagree with a portion of the *Baptist Faith and Message* or any additional parameters established by an entity's trustee board. These are actually two different but related issues. It seems inappropriate for a trustee or employee to openly oppose any entity-specific parameters established by an individual board or institution. When there is disagreement with a decision made by a trustee board, there are proper channels to express dissent. Trustees or administrators who disagree with specific extra-confessional requirements should have the right to express their opinions to the full trustee board and attempt to persuade it to reverse the decision. If there is no change, it is incumbent upon dissenting trustees and administrators to either accept the decision or, if one's conscience forbids acceptance, resign from their position and possibly attempt to take the matter before the Convention. It is not appropriate for a sitting trustee or paid administrator to voice *public* opposition to board decisions; to do so only exacerbates whatever controversy is already present. Non-administrative employees should be free to express their concerns to their administration, but must also ultimately either abide by institutional policies or resign if they cannot do so.

The question of dissenting to portions of the *Baptist Faith and Message* is a bit more complicated. In an effort to include as many conservatives as possible, the confession is deliberately ambiguous on a number of controversial issues, most notably the doctrines of grace, eschatology, so-called alien immersion, the validity of female deacons, and the number of elders (or pastors) a congregation should have. But in some matters the confession is quite specific. This is especially true of ecclesiological convictions, no doubt due to the central role that ecclesiology plays in Baptist identity.

Two examples will suffice. The *Baptist Faith and Message* explicitly states that, "Being a church ordinance, [baptism] is prerequisite to the privileges of church membership and to the Lord's Supper."[54] It is not at all clear that this position, historically called "strict" or "closed" Communion, is embraced by a majority of Southern Baptist churches. In fact, the relationship between baptism and Communion is one of the oldest and longest running debates among Baptists.[55] In a different section, the *Baptist Faith and Message* says regarding sin, "Through the temptation of Satan man transgressed the command of God, and fell from his original innocence whereby his posterity inherit a nature and an environment inclined toward sin."[56] The problem for many Southern Baptists is the word "inclined," which seems to suggest a softer view of human depravity than most Baptists have historically affirmed in their confessions. I personally know many Southern Baptists, from a variety of theological persuasions, who believe the statement on sin is too weak.

So should all "open Communion" Southern Baptists be excluded from denominational service or employment, particularly when that position might even be the majority view among post-resurgence Southern Baptists? Should those who believe the confession articulates an insufficient view of sin be excluded from service? Perhaps contra-confessional questions could be addressed in a similar manner to how trustees approach extra-confessional guidelines.

Every trustee board and administration should have the freedom to expect any level of adherence to the *Baptist Faith and Message* that it deems appropriate. If a particular trustee board is willing to allow a prospective trustee or employee to reject belief in strict Communion, then that is within their rights as that institution's trustees. By the same token, if a trustee board believes that the *Baptist Faith and Message* should be closely followed in its definition of human sin, this is also appropriate. The same principle would also apply with additional entity-specific confessions. For example, potential trustees, administrators, and professors might disagree with the Abstract of Principles' articulation of the doctrines of election and the Lord's Day. Trustees of the schools that employ that confession should

---

[54] "Article VI: The Church," in "The Baptist Faith and Message" (2000), http://www.sbc.net/BFM/bfm2000.asp.

[55] See Timothy George, "Controversy and Communion: The Limits of Baptist Fellowship from Bunyan to Spurgeon," in *The Gospel in the World: International Baptist Studies*, ed. D. W. Bebbington (Carlisle, Cumbia, UK: Paternoster, 2002), 38–58.

[56] "Article III: Man," in "The Baptist Faith and Message" (2000), http://www.sbc.net/BFM/bfm2000.asp.

determine how closely those under their authority should be expected to abide by its theology. I would suggest that one can embrace the *substance* of a confession of faith without agreeing on a particular, oft-disputed point.

I admit that entity-specific expectations regarding confessional affirmation pose a potential problem for post-resurgence Southern Baptists. During the conservative resurgence, a major point of contention among conservatives was that moderates at some seminaries were signing confessional statements with which they obviously had numerous disagreements. If trustee boards and administrators allow minor disagreements with the *Baptist Faith and Message* or other institutional confessions, does that make conservatives hypocrites who now do the very thing they opposed twenty years ago?

I think the answer should ultimately be no, for two reasons. First, the Convention itself should reserve the right to reject the practices of any trustee board that it judges to be too lax in its confessional expectations, per my above suggestions about amending bylaw 26B. Second, and more important, the climate of the SBC is different than it was a generation ago. One of the products of the conservative resurgence was a 1997 document titled "One Faith, One Task, One Sacred Trust." This statement was a covenant between the presidents of the six Southern Baptist seminaries and the Convention itself wherein the seminaries pledged to be more accountable to the Convention than was the case prior to the 1990s.[57] Other Convention agencies and boards have similarly regained the trust of the denomination. At the moment, there are closer ties and greater trust between the Convention and its entities than perhaps at any other time in SBC history. For this reason, if a trustee board allows an inappropriate degree of confessional dissent, then the Convention could and should intervene.

CONCLUSION

In 1993, Timothy George wryly suggested, "The mere replacement of one set of bureaucrats with another doth not a Reformation make."[58] Despite the title of a recent conservative history of the movement, the conservative resurgence was not a "Baptist Reformation."[59] Instead, the conservative resurgence was a combination of the *Ninety-Five Theses* and Luther's

---

[57]"One Faith, One Task, One Sacred Trust," Southeastern Baptist Theological Seminary, June 17, 1997, http://www.sebts.edu/prospective_students/what_we_believe/faith_task_trust.cfm.
[58]Timothy George, "Toward an Evangelical Future," in *Southern Baptists Observed: Multiple Perspectives on a Changing Denomination*, ed. Nancy Tatom Ammerman (Knoxville: University of Tennessee Press, 1993), 277.
[59]See Sutton, *The Baptist Reformation*.

famous "Here I Stand" speech before the Diet of Worms, establishing a theological foundation within the Convention's institutions to aid local churches in their pursuit of biblical reformation. The last thirty years have witnessed the successful takeover of the bureaucracy and a recommitment to a biblically conservative theological center among the Convention's seminaries, mission boards, and other ministries. The time is ripe to build upon that foundation and pursue true reformation.[60]

This chapter has suggested three priorities for a post-Resurgence SBC. Southern Baptists must pursue a biblically driven and historically conscious renewal of Baptist identity, lest we forget who we have been and lose sight of who we ought to be. We must embrace a Great Commission resurgence with an even greater vigor than the conservative resurgence, lest we gain the whole denomination only to lose the souls of multitudes who have not heard the good news. Both of these priorities must result in a graciously confessional cooperation, lest intramural squabbles and even future divisions cause us to fail to reach our full kingdom potential as a Convention of local churches. Now is the time for post-resurgence Southern Baptists to build upon the victories of the past as we look toward future victories, both for the glory of God and to the benefit of our churches.

---

[60]Others are calling upon Southern Baptists to do this very thing, though several different approaches are being advocated. For example, see White, Duesing, and Yarnell, eds., *Restoring Integrity in Baptist Churches*; Dockery, *Southern Baptist Consensus and Renewal*; and Tom Nettles, *Ready for Reformation? Bringing Authentic Reform to Southern Baptist Churches* (Nashville: B&H, 2005).

A FUTURE-DIRECTED PROPOSAL FOR THE SBC

Daniel L. Akin

SOUTHERN BAPTISTS HAVE A colorful and fascinating history by any standard of measure. From the Convention's humble beginnings in Augusta, Georgia, on May 8, 1845 (only 293 persons attended the Inaugural Convention and 273 came from three states: Georgia, South Carolina, and Virginia),[1] our denomination now is comprised of over sixteen million members in forty-three thousand churches. This is quite remarkable any way you look at it, and for all of this and more, Southern Baptists are grateful to God. We give thanks to our Lord for what he has done for us and through us.

However, what does the future hold? Our nation continues to grow more secular and our world more hostile to "the faith that was once for all delivered to the saints" (Jude 3, ESV).

Southern Baptists, in the midst of the swirling tides of modernity, have attempted to stake their claim and send a clear message on who we are. The conservative resurgence initiated in 1979 charted the course, and it can be argued that the *Baptist Faith and Message 2000* was something of a defining moment.[2] Still, it is not clear that we have a clear understanding and vision

---

[1] H. Leon McBeth, *The Baptist Heritage* (Nashville: Broadman, 1987), 388.

[2] The best treatment, and really the only treatment, of the Conservative Resurgence is Jerry Sutton, *The Baptist Reformation* (Nashville: Broadman & Holman, 2000). Paul Pressler provides an autobiographical look from one of the Resurgence's key leaders (*A Hill on Which to Die* [Nashville: Broadman & Holman, 1999]). From the moderate perspective there has been a flood of books. Two, however, stand out in scholarship and balance. See Nancy Ammerman, *Baptist Battles* (New Brunswick, NJ: Rutgers University Press, 1990) and Barry Hankins, *Uneasy in Babylon* (Tuscaloosa: University of Alabama Press, 2002). In addition to the adoption of "The Baptist Faith and Message" in 2000, other watershed moments would include the re-election of Charles Stanley in Dallas in 1985, the Glorieta Statement issued by the six seminary presidents in 1986, the adoption of the Peace Committee Report in 1987, Jerry Vine's sermon, "A Baptist and His Bible," preached in St. Louis in 1987, and the election of Morris Chapman as president

of who we are and what we should be. The conservative resurgence gave Southern Baptists a second chance, but it did not secure our future. Has there been a resurgence? Yes. Has there been a restoration? Doubtful. Have we experienced revival? Clearly the answer is no. These latter observations are not intended to cast a cloud of despair. On the contrary I am hopeful and optimistic, *if* (and the emphasis purposefully falls on the word "if") we will embrace with a radical, laser-beam devotion the "Ten Mandates" that historically have defined who Southern Baptists are and what Southern Baptists should be as we move ahead in the twenty-first century. Here is the face we need to display for the glory of God in the days before us.

TEN MANDATES FOR SOUTHERN BAPTISTS IN THE TWENTY-FIRST CENTURY

The Nonnegotiable of a Regenerate Church

A regenerate church has always characterized Baptist theology. This does not mean that unbelievers are not invited and welcomed as they attend. We should be "seeker sensitive" when we gather for worship. We should not be "seeker driven." The membership of the local church is made up of those who confess Christ as Savior and Lord, and whose life gives evidence of conversion. Baptist commitment to this principle set them apart from the magisterial reformers, but they did so because of their commitment to the teachings of the New Testament. There is no hint whatsoever of unregenerate church membership in the Bible. That the unregenerate are often present among the people of God is not denied. John the apostle acknowledges in 1 John 2:19, "They went out from us, but they did not really belong to us . . . their going showed that none of them belonged to us" (NIV).

The failure to uphold this principle with the most fervent commitment has always brought hurt to the church. This is certainly true in our own day. Stan Norman is correct when he notes, "Failing to emphasize regeneration as a prerequisite for church membership has historically resulted in the loss of emphasis upon the church as a holy community and has given rise to moral corruption and heretical teaching within the fellowship."[3] What issues might Southern Baptists need to address in maintaining our devotion to a regenerate church in the twenty-first century?

First, we need to make it clear that church membership is a privilege,

---

of the SBC in New Orleans in 1990. Chapman's election is important because it was "the last straw that broke the camel's back" leading the liberal/moderate faction of the SBC to form what has become the Cooperative Baptist Fellowship (CBF).

[3]Stan Norman, "Ecclesiological Guidelines to Inform Southern Baptist Church Planters" (position paper presented to North American Mission Board, September 28, 2004), 15–16.

not a right. There are requirements and expectations that are clearly defined and articulated when it comes to local church membership. This involves more than raising a hand, walking an aisle, or filling out a card. It requires an understanding of the gospel, public confession of one's faith evidenced by a clear verbal testimony, and a pledge to walk in the newness of life in Christ. The issue here is not and has never been perfection, but rather a change in direction and the pursuit of Christian maturity.

Second, we must guard against easy "believism" and a compromised gospel. The gracious invitation to believe on Christ must be complemented with the call to repent of sin. To leave out repentance is to preach only half the gospel. It is to ignore the first public preaching of John the Baptist (Matt. 3:1–2), Jesus (Matt. 4:17), and Peter (Acts 2:38). It is to neglect the missionary proclamation replete in the book of Acts where persons are called to "turn to God in repentance and have faith in our Lord Jesus" (Acts 20:21, NIV).

Third, we must be careful with respect to our own theological integrity concerning infant or early adolescent baptism that lacks a clear understanding and confession of the gospel. Now, I am not one who believes an individual cannot be saved until they reach their teenage years or later. There is no scriptural defense for such a position, and psychological arguments carry no weight in this discussion. Still, the large numbers of rebaptisms of those who underwent what they now perceive as a meaningless dunking in their adolescence must concern us, as well as the inflated membership roles filled with the names of persons who now give little or no evidence of faith. Maintaining the nonnegotiable of a regenerate church will demand both better evangelism and discipleship at every level of church life.

The Essential Nature of Believer's Baptism by Immersion

In the New Testament, public confession of Jesus Christ as Savior and Lord was not done by walking an aisle. Now, I do not wish to be misunderstood. I am a strong advocate of the public invitation because I find it clearly practiced in Scripture. The criticisms of extreme Calvinists at this point should be heard, but their solution not heeded. Public invitations have been abused, but this does not justify their dismissal any more than spousal abuse justifies the dismissal of marriage! Still, public confession of Jesus Christ as Savior and Lord was not by coming forward to the front of the church at the time of invitation. Public confession in Christ was by baptism. Indeed, an "unbaptized believer" is an oxymoron in light of the New Testament. Closely connected to but distinct from regeneration/ conversion,[4] baptism is the means whereby one publicly declares faith in Jesus Christ for salvation and is initiated into the believing community.[5]

That baptism involved a particular member (a believer), mode (immersion), and meaning (public identification with Christ and the believing community) is grounded in New Testament witness and has been a hallmark of Baptists throughout their history. To be a Baptist is to champion believer's baptism by immersion. The *Baptist Faith and Message 2000* says it well:

> Christian baptism is the immersion of a believer in water in the name of the Father, the Son, and the Holy Spirit. It is an act of obedience symbolizing the believer's faith in a crucified, buried, and risen Savior, the believer's death to sin, the burial of the old life, and the resurrection to walk in newness of life in Christ Jesus. It is a testimony to his faith in the final resurrection of the dead. Being a church ordinance, it is prerequisite to the privileges of church membership and to the Lord's Supper.[6]

What should concern us regarding this Baptist distinctive in the twenty-first century? Where do the dangers lie?

First, we must see evidence of regeneration for those we baptize. Second, baptism of young children must be administered with the greatest possible care. The example of W. A. Criswell—who fostered the concept of "a step toward God," provided a short catechetical booklet, met personally with every child before his or her baptism, and would not baptize any child until the age of ten—is worthy of our careful consideration. That we might do more than this is commendable. That we would do less is shameful and irresponsible. Third, baptism should be viewed and emphasized as a first and necessary step of discipleship and obedience to Christ. Fourth, we will reject as inconceivable the idea of admitting anyone into our membership without believer's baptism by immersion. Fifth, holding high the New Testament teaching on baptism will impact our understanding of the nature of the public invitation. I believe it will aid us in practicing it with greater care, wisdom, and integrity.

---

[4]See Robert Stein, "Baptist and Becoming a Christian in the New Testament," *The Southern Baptist Journal of Theology* 2, no. 1 (Spring 1998): 6–17.

[5]For an expanded treatment on the significance of baptism see Daniel L. Akin, "The Meaning of Baptism," in *Restoring Integrity in Baptist Churches*, ed. Thomas White, Jason Duesing, and Malcolm B. Yarnell III (Grand Rapids, MI: Kregel, 2008), 63–80.

[6]*The Baptist Faith and Message 2000* (Nashville: Lifeway, 2000), 14.

The Recovery of the Lost Jewels of Church Discipline and Genuine Disciple-Making as Essential Marks of the Church

Church discipline is clearly and repeatedly taught in the New Testament. Jesus addresses it in Matthew 18:15–20 and Paul does so in 1 Corinthians 5:1–13; 2 Corinthians 2:5–11; Galatians 6:1–4; and Titus 3:9–11. Unfortunately, it is rarely practiced in Christ's church today. Its absence is deafening, and this is theologically, historically, and practically untenable.

Theologically, to ignore the practice of church discipline is to disobey the plain teachings of Scripture and ignore the necessity of church discipline in maintaining the purity of the church. An undisciplined church will lose its distinctive character as a holy people. Historically, Baptists have viewed church discipline as an essential mark of the church along with the Word rightly preached and the ordinances properly administered. We find this evidenced in our earliest confessions, going back to the Anabaptists. Anabaptism was known for its emphasis on church discipline from the beginning with the Schleitheim Confession of 1527. Article 2 on the Ban states,

> Second. We are agreed as follows on the ban. The ban shall be employed with all those who have given themselves to the Lord, to walk in His commandments, and with all those who are baptized into the one body of Christ and who are called brethren or sisters and yet who slip sometimes and fall into error and sin, being inadvertently overtaken. The same shall be admonished twice in secret and the third time openly disciplined or banned according to the command of Christ (Matt. 18). But this shall be done according to the regulation of the Spirit (Matt. 5) before the breaking of bread, so that we may break and eat one bread, with one mind and in love and may drink of one cup.[7]

Sadly and surprisingly, there is no specific mention of church discipline in our most recent confessions: the *Baptist Faith and Message* 1925, 1963, or 2000.

Practically, the absence of church discipline has resulted in a spiritually and morally weakened witness to the lost. J. L. Dagg warned us almost 150 years ago, "When discipline leaves a church, Christ goes with it."[8] And one can hardly disagree with R. Albert Mohler Jr. who writes, "The decline of church discipline is perhaps the most visible failure of the contemporary

---

[7]Text and commentary can be found in Daniel L. Akin, "An Expositional Analysis of the Schleitheim Confession," *Criswell Theological Review* 2.2 (1988): 345–70.

[8]J. L. Dagg, *A Treatise on Church Order* (Charleston, SC: The Southern Baptist Publication Society, 1958), 274.

church. . . . The present generation of both ministers and church members is virtually without experience of biblical church discipline."[9]

Where do we go from here? First, we must teach our people what the Bible says about church discipline. They must see its biblical basis and its spiritual necessity. Second, we must begin to implement church discipline lovingly, wisely, gently, and probably slowly. A cram-course is a certain formula for disaster. Third, we must apply discipline to areas like absentee membership as well as the specific list provided by Paul in 1 Corinthians 5. I am sure this list is not exhaustive, but it is a proper place to begin and a proper guide to direct us. This is not optional; it is desperately essential. To again cite Mohler, "Without a recovery of functional church discipline—firmly established upon the principles revealed in the Bible—the church will continue its slide into moral dissolution and relativism."[10]

The Emphasis and Practice of a Genuinely Word-Based Ministry

In John 8:31–32 Jesus said, "If you hold to my teaching, you are really my disciples. Then you will know the truth, and the truth will set you free" (NIV). If what our Lord said is true, and it is, many Baptists along with their fellow Americans are still in slavery. Why? Because there is, to quote the prophet Amos, "a famine through the land—not a famine of food or a thirst for water, but a famine of hearing the words of the LORD" (Amos 8:11, NIV). Stephen Prothero writes that America is "A Nation of Faith and Religious Illiterates." Prothero, a teacher at Boston College, notes,

> The sociologist Peter Berger once remarked that if India is the most religious country in the world and Sweden the least, then the United States is a nation of Indians ruled by Swedes.
>
> Things are different in Europe, and not just in Sweden. The Dutch are four times less likely than Americans to believe in miracles, hell, and biblical inerrancy. The euro does not trust in God. But here is the paradox: Although Americans are far more religious than Europeans, they know far less about religion. . . .
>
> In Europe, religious education is the rule from the elementary grades on. So Austrians, Norwegians and the Irish can tell you about the Seven Deadly Sins or the Five Pillars of Islam. But, according to a 1997 poll, only one out of three U.S. citizens is able to name the most basic of Christian texts, the four Gospels, and 12% think Noah's wife was Joan of Arc. That

---

[9]R. Albert Mohler Jr., "Church Discipline: The Missing Mark" in *Polity: Biblical Arguments on How to Conduct Church Life*, ed. Mark E. Dever (Washington, DC: Center for Church Reform, 2001), 43.
[10]Ibid.

paints a picture of a nation that believes God speaks in Scripture but that can't be bothered to read what he has to say. . . .

When Americans debated slavery, almost exclusively on the basis of the Bible, people of all races and classes could follow the debate. They could make sense of its references to the runaway slave in the New Testament book of Philemon and to the year of jubilee, when slaves could be freed, in the Old Testament book of Leviticus. Today it is a rare American who can engage with any sophistication in biblically inflected arguments about gay marriage, abortion, or stem cell research. . . .

How did this happen? How did one of the most religious countries in the world become a nation of religious illiterates? Religious congregations are surely at fault. Churches and synagogues that once inculcated the "fourth R" are now telling the faithful stories "ripped from the headlines" rather than teaching them the Ten Commandments or parsing the Sermon on the Mount (which was delivered, as only one in three Americans can tell you, by Jesus). But most of the fault lies in our elementary and secondary schools.[11]

I take issue only with Prothero's last statement. The fault lies not with the schools but with the churches and, in particular, the pulpits. Seduced by the sirens of modernity we have jettisoned a word-based ministry that is expository in nature. We have, in our attempt to be popular and relevant, become foolish and irrelevant. Skiing across the surface needs of a fallen, sinful humanity, we have turned the pulpit into a pop-psychology sideshow and a feel-good pit stop. We have neglected preaching the whole counsel of God's Word and the theology of God's Word. Too many of our people know neither the content nor the doctrines of Scripture. Preaching the cross of Christ and the bloody atonement accomplished by his death is the exception rather than the norm. Some choose to focus on politics, others on the emotions, still others on relationships, and so on. If the Bible is used at all, it is usually as a proof-text out of context with no real connection to what the speaker is saying. For those of us who profess to believe both the inerrancy and sufficiency of Scripture, there must be in our pulpits what I call "engaging exposition." That is, there must be preaching that is biblical in content and dynamic in delivery, preaching that is expositional and theological on the one hand, and practical and applicable on the other. We must advocate an expositional *method* with a theological *mindset* under an evangelical *mandate*. It is preaching that models for our people how they should teach the Bible. Before it is too late, we need to heed the wise words of a liberal

---

[11]Stephen Prothero, "A Nation of Faith and Religious Illiterates," *Los Angeles Times*, January 12, 2005, http://articles.latimes.com/2005/jan/12/opinion/oe-prothero12.

Methodist who has been down this modernist road and found it to be a dead-end street. Listen to what William Willimon of Duke Divinity School says, and weep. In a fascinating article written in 1995 titled "Been There, Preached That," Willimon sounds a prophetic warning to Southern Baptists:

> I'm a mainline-liberal-Protestant-Methodist-type Christian. I know we're soft on Scripture. Norman Vincent Peale has exercised a more powerful effect on our preaching than St. Paul . . . I know we play fast and loose with Scripture. But I've always had this fantasy that somewhere, like in Texas there were preachers who preached it all, Genesis to Revelation, without blinking an eye. . . . I took great comfort in knowing that, even while I preached a pitifully compromised, "Pealed"-down gospel, that somewhere, good old Bible-believing preachers were offering their congregations the unadulterated Word, straight up.
>
> Do you know how disillusioning it has been for me to realize that many of these self-proclaimed biblical preachers now sound more like liberal mainliners than liberal mainliners? At the very time those of us in the mainline, old-line, sidelined were repenting of our pop psychological pap and rediscovering the joy of disciplined biblical preaching, these "biblical preachers" were becoming "user friendly" and "inclusive," taking their homiletical cues from the "felt needs" of us "boomers" and "busters" rather than the excruciating demands of the Bible.
>
> I know why they do this. . . . It all starts with American Christians wanting to be helpful to the present order, to be relevant (as the present order defines relevance). We so want to be invited to lunch at the White House or at least be interviewed on "Good Morning America." So we adjust our language to the demands of the market, beginning with the world and its current infatuations rather than the Word and its peculiar judgments on our infatuations.
>
> If you listen to too much of our preaching, you get the impression that Jesus was some sort of itinerant therapist who, for free, traveled about helping people feel better. Ever since Fosdick, we mainline liberals have been bad about this. Start with some human problem like depression; then rummage around in the Bible for a relevant answer.
>
> Last fall, as I was preparing in my office for the Sunday service, the telephone rang. "Who's preaching in Duke Chapel today?" asked a nasal, Yankee-sounding voice. I cleared my throat and answered. "The Reverend Doctor William Willimon." "Who's that?" asked the voice. "The Dean of the Chapel," I answered in a sonorous tone. "I hope he won't be preaching politics. I've had a rough week, and I need to hear about God. My Baptist church is so eaten up with politics, I've got to hear a sermon!" When you have to come to a Methodist for a biblical sermon, that's pitiful.[12]

---

[12]William Willimon, "Been There, Preached That," *Leadership Magazine* (Fall 1995).

The Vision for a Faithful and Authentic Biblical Ecclesiology

The doctrine of the church has become a point of significant debate, especially in terms of polity. Recent books are exploring again the nature of church government and the nature of church offices in terms of function and number, particularly that of the elder.[13]

In spite of the absence of any direct word concerning church discipline, article VI on "The Church" in the *Baptist Faith and Message 2000* is well stated. It reads as follows:

> A New Testament church of the Lord Jesus Christ is an autonomous local congregation of baptized believers, associated by covenant in the faith and fellowship of the gospel; observing the two ordinances of Christ, governed by His laws, exercising the gifts, rights, and privileges invested in them by His Word, and seeking to extend the gospel to the ends of the earth. Each congregation operates under the Lordship of Christ through democratic processes. In such a congregation each member is responsible and accountable to Christ as Lord. Its scriptural officers are pastors and deacons. While both men and women are gifted for service in the church, the office of pastor is limited to men as qualified by Scripture.
>
> The New Testament speaks also of the church as the Body of Christ which includes all of the redeemed of all the ages, believers from every tribe, and tongue, and people, and nation.[14]

Drawing from and building on this article, allow me to narrow the focus and address several crucial observations as to what constitutes a faithful and authentic ecclesiology in our day. First, there must be a regenerate church membership that is carefully guarded and held to the highest scriptural standards. Second, there must be the additional marks of (1) the Word, (2) ordinances, and (3) discipline. Third, the local church should be elder/pastor led and congregationally governed. Here, in my judgment, there is room for flexibility in terms of patterns, structure, and implementation. Scripture does not specify the number of elders, though they are almost always in the plural. It is interesting to note that throughout our Baptist history, until recently, our confessions favored the terms "bishops" and "elders." These terms also were almost always in the plural, though there has been debate concerning plurality vs. single elder.[15] However, there

---

[13]See Chad Brand and R. Stanton Norman, eds., *Perspectives on Church Government* (Nashville: Broadman & Holman, 2004).

[14]*Baptist Faith and Message 2000*, 13.

[15]One need only survey William L. Lumpkin, *Baptist Confession of Faith* (Valley Forge: Judson, 1959, rev. ed. 1969). See also Daniel Akin, "The Single-Elder-Led Church," Brand and Norman, eds., *Perspectives on Church Government*, 57–59.

is no debate that a properly constituted church will have both elders and deacons.

Scripture also does not set forth the specifics of congregationalism, though congregationalism in some form clearly is the most defensible form of church government based upon the New Testament.

As we move forward in this century, Southern Baptists will need to give particular attention to stewardship and discipleship, not that these two issues are unrelated. Every member a minister and every member a giver is biblical and essential. The members of our churches must move from being *shoppers*, to *buyers*, to *investors*.

The Continued Nurturing of a Fervent Missionary and Evangelistic Passion That Is Wedded to Healthy and Robust Theology

Southern Baptists are known for their missions and evangelism. In so many ways they define who we are. Former SBC President James Draper has well said of evangelism and missions, "Those things are in our DNA." However, Draper goes on to note, "Unfortunately we as a denomination and as churches have strayed somewhat from that [evangelism and missions] foundation, often focusing on a lot of things that have nothing to do with either of those."[16] In my thirty-plus years in ministry I have become absolutely convinced of an unquestionable truth. *No church will be evangelistic by accident.* There are some things churches will do well with some ease or naturalness because of their interest, context, and membership, but no church is inclined to do evangelism. It must be intentional, it must be a priority, and it must start at the top. Any pastor not committed to doing the work of an evangelist should not be in the ministry. He has disqualified himself based upon 2 Timothy 4:5.

To offer a practical perspective on this issue: we must understand that there are multiple ways churches can do missions and evangelism. That they do it is the key. In the American context a multipronged approach is certainly in order. We can train personal evangelists in *FAITH, EE, NET,* and a dozen other excellent witnessing programs. There is the ministry-based approach to evangelism of First Baptist Church of Leesburg, Florida, a model that more of our churches should adopt. There is the sports evangelism of Prestonwood Baptist Church that fits a large church in a context like Plano, Texas. Do what works best for you, but do something. We can dream and we can innovate.

---

[16]Chris Turner, "Draper Expounds on Young Ministers Involvement, Decline in Baptisms," *Facts & Trends* (January/February 2005), 26–29.

Marketplace evangelism—evangelism that reaches into the work-place—is an area in need of attention, strategizing, and training. Youth and student evangelism needs renewed emphasis. A generation of unregenerate teens is growing up in our churches. We can train and we can preach on evangelism, but we must act. Genuine, biblical evangelism must be a constant drumbeat throughout our denomination, in our seminaries and agencies, and in our state conventions and associations. On any level, if this is not happening, the entity has become irrelevant in fulfilling the Great Commission and should be radically overhauled or shut down and buried for the spiritual corpse it has become.

Seminaries in particular should take the lead in this area. We should train our students as personal evangelists and we should teach them models for church evangelism that will be easily transferable into the local church context. We should challenge them to evangelize without bias or prejudice, loving and going after the exploding ethnic and minority groups across America. The authenticity and integrity of the gospel is at stake. Bigotry and prejudice must be confronted for the ugly, putrid sin that it is. God has brought a mission field to our land. If we ignore or neglect it, he will certainly and rightly judge us with severity.

We should continue to emphasize missions training in partnership with the IMB, cultivating healthy dialogue every step of the way. Aggressive evangelism, especially on the mission field, must be rooted and grounded in healthy theology, a theology that will guard and protect our partnerships, our methods, our strategies, and our planting of New Testament churches.

The Pursuit of a First-Century Biblical Model for Church Planting

The twenty-first century is more like the first century than has ever been the case in our Western culture. The religious marketplace looks like the book of Acts, and so should our church planting strategies and methods. We are losing America and the West because we are losing the great metropolitan areas where there is a concentration of people. Mohler points out that most of the people who attend Southern Baptist churches now live in the cities and suburbs.[17] Paul's strategy for evangelizing the Roman Empire must become our strategy with a clear focus and intensity. Prayer, planning, money, and resources need to flood the great metroplexes that continue to bulge and explode across our nation and around the world. To this challenge I offer a couple of thoughts for consideration.

---

[17]See R. Albert Mohler Jr., "Southern Baptist Identity: Is There a Future?" chap. 1 in this volume.

First, explore creative methods, but make sure that they are faithfully filtered through the purifying waters of Holy Scripture. Our manual must be the Bible, not a marketing book. Can we learn from the ideas of the latter? Yes. Can we baptize their methods? No! (I believe no individual is doing better work and analysis in this area than Thom Rainer, president of LifeWay. We would be wise to read his books, weigh his insights, and hear his counsel.) Second, be wise fishers of men. Fish come in all sorts of varieties, so drag the net, throw in multiple hooks, and use various forms of bait. Be sensitive to your context, but stay grounded in the Word of God. Third, we (that includes the seminaries, NAMB, and megachurches) need to work together recruiting our best and brightest for strategic church planting. Some need to provide the resources and some the training. Those who exhibit godly, biblical character with passion, vision, and wisdom should find us willing to invest in them. We should find opportunities and provide avenues whereby young leaders can step up and soar for the glory of God, exercising the gifts and abilities given to them by God.

The Recovery of the Bible's View of Marriage as a Sacred Covenant Designed by God to Last for Life

In Matthew 19:4–11, Jesus gave us his view of marriage, divorce, and singleness. It was consistent with the teaching of the Old Testament, emphasizing in particular God's ordaining of marriage and the home in Genesis 2. Today our Lord must weep at what he observes in Southern Baptist churches. Few men are willing to stand in their pulpits and utter with a prophetic voice the sin of divorce. Indeed the debate on same-sex union and marriage is the inevitable result of the culture of divorce we have embraced.

In 1999 George Barna reported that "Baptists have the highest divorce rate of any Christian denomination, and are more likely to get a divorce than atheists and agnostics. . . . The survey . . . found that twenty-nine percent of all Baptists have been through a divorce."[18] In 2001 Barna reported that those who profess to be "born again" are less likely to cohabit but just as likely to divorce. He noted,

> Born again Christians are just as likely to get divorced as are non-born again adults. Overall, 33% of all born again individuals who have been married have gone through a divorce, which is statistically identical to the 34% incidence among non-born again adults. . . . The adults analyzed in the born again category were not those who claimed to be born again,

---

[18]Reported in *Associated Baptist Press* (December 30, 1999).

but were individuals who stated a personal commitment to Christ, having confessed their sins, embracing Christ as their savior, and believing that they have received eternal salvation because of their faith in Christ alone. *More than 90% of the born again adults who have been divorced experienced that divorce after they accepted Christ, not before.* It is unfortunate that so many people, regardless of their faith, experience a divorce, but especially unsettling to find that the faith commitment of so many born again individuals has not enabled them to strengthen and save their marriages.[19]

And yet again in 2004, Barna informed us that the trend continues virtually unchanged.[20] You would think we would be concerned, but apparently we are not. LifeWay discontinued the "Kingdom Family" emphasis that grew out of the Family Council appointed by Morris Chapman and chaired by Tom Elliff. It was my honor to serve on that council. In correspondence with Dr. Draper, I asked if he could share with me what happened and here is his heartbreaking response: "We just were not able to build any momentum for the Family Conferences, etc. . . . [it was] just that the whole emphasis didn't take off. I'm not sure why. We had some great personnel on conferences and tried it for quite some time . . . the response was low."[21]

Where do we go from here? Let me offer several ideas for us to implement. First, we must teach our people in a comprehensive manner the divine covenant nature of marriage: that it is, as the *Baptist Faith and Message 2000* says, "the uniting of one man and one woman in covenant commitment for a lifetime. It is God's unique gift to reveal the union between Christ and His Church. . . . "[22] We must also teach that God hates divorce (Mal. 2:16) and that divorce is sin. It is neither unpardonable nor unforgivable, but it is serious sin in the eyes of God and should be avoided at all cost.

Second, we must affirm the value and necessity of premarital counseling and mentoring. Any church that allows a single marriage to take place on its property without requiring intensive premarital instruction should be ashamed of itself. We must also begin to implement in an intentional and comprehensive approach the mentoring principles taught in Titus 2:1–8. Never has there been a greater need for older, godly men to mentor younger

---

[19]"Born Again Adults Less Likely to Co-Habit, Just as Likely to Divorce," *The Barna Update* (August 6, 2001). Italics added.
[20]"Born Again Christians Just As Likely to Divorce As Are Non-Christians," *The Barna Update* (September 8, 2004).
[21]Jimmy Draper, personal e-mail correspondence with author, January 29, 2005.
[22]*Baptist Faith and Message 2000*, Article XVIII, 21.

men, and for older godly women to mentor younger women. The potential such an emphasis has for marriage, family, evangelism, and discipleship is enormous.

Third, we must acknowledge the gift of singleness that God gives to some (Matthew 19; 1 Corinthians 7), tap into their tremendous potential for service, and stop harassing them because they are single. We should not forget the significant singles of Scripture: persons like Elijah and Elisha, Daniel, Simeon, Anna, Paul, John the Baptist, and, of course, Jesus.

Fourth, in a culture that seems to be going in the opposite direction, we must affirm in word and practice the gift of children as a "heritage from the LORD" (Ps. 127:3, NIV). Godly parents will be disciple-makers beginning in the home. They will understand that no greater investment can be made than that they would raise a brood of godly children who will live for Jesus just like they saw in Mom, and especially Dad.[23] Our churches must train parents to evangelize and disciple their children.

The Cultivation of Vibrant, Sound, and Productive Seminaries That are Really in Touch with the Churches They Serve

God did not ordain seminaries. I do believe he raised them up and has used them for his glory, but there is nothing that would require their existence for the ongoing work of the gospel and the church. The fact is that seminaries must justify their worth, value, and existence. If they fail to demonstrate their merit and importance, then they should cease to exist and go the way of all flesh. What then should seminaries be and do in order to serve the churches that support them and that send their men and women to be trained by them?

First, seminaries must never lose sight of the fact that they are servants of the churches and not the academy. We may speak and engage the world of scholarship, but our first and primary calling is to serve and equip the churches of the SBC. We should strive to serve all the churches on every level that we possibly can. This was the vision of our founding father of theological education, James Petigru Boyce (1827–1888). His inaugural address, delivered as professor of theology at Furman University on July 30, 1856, entitled "Three Changes in Theological Institutions," remains a monument and a map for training ministers by means of the seminary.[24]

---

[23]For a popular take on this see Henry G. Brinton, "Praying for More Men," *Washington Post*, December 19, 2004, http://www.washingtonpost.com/wp-dyn/articles/A9471-2004Dec17.html.
[24]The address is summarized and analyzed in John A. Broadus, *A Gentleman and a Scholar: A Memoir of James Petigru Boyce* (1893; repr. Birmingham, AL: Solid Ground Christian Books, 2004), 120–145.

He hoped to "see the means of theological education increased . . . open to all who would embrace them."[25]

Second, we must be doggedly confessional, taking with the utmost seriousness the confessions we affirm. Mohler rightly argues that the theological battle of the last quarter of the twentieth century was fought between a truth party (the Conservatives) and a liberty party (the Moderates). The truth party prevailed as Southern Baptists recovered their theological roots.[26] All six seminaries affirm the *Baptist Faith and Message 2000*. Two seminaries, Southern and Southeastern, also adhere to the *Abstract of Principles* (1858), which was primarily the work of Basil Manley Jr. The *Abstract* was the first theological confession formally adopted by Southern Baptists.[27] Concerning our commitment to our doctrinal confession, Boyce issued both a warning and a challenge:

> It is with a single man that error usually commences; and when such a man has influence or position, it is impossible to estimate the evil that will attend it. Ecclesiastical history is full of warning upon this subject. Scarcely a single heresy has ever blighted the Church which has not owed its existence or its development to that one man of power and ability whose name has always been associated with its doctrines.[28]

Therefore, given this ever present danger, our institutions should require a public declaration of all its teachers to teach in "accordance with and not contrary to" our doctrinal statements. To do so is right, honest, and unfair to no person. Boyce adds,

> You will infringe the rights of no man, and you will secure the rights of those who have established here an instrumentality for the production of a sound ministry. It is no hardship to those who teach here to be called upon to sign the declaration of their principles; for there are fields of usefulness open elsewhere to every man, and none need accept your call who cannot conscientiously sign your formulary. And while all this is true, you will receive by this an assurance that the trust committed to you by the founders is fulfilling in accordance with their wishes, that the ministry that go forth have here learned to distinguish truth from error, and to embrace the former, and that the same precious truths of the Bible which were so dear to the hearts of its founders, and which I trust are equally dear to yours,

---

[25]Ibid., 122. See also 132.

[26]See R. Albert Mohler Jr., "Southern Baptist Identity: Is There a Future?" chap. 1 in this volume, and Greg Wills, "Southern Baptist Identity: A Historical Perspective," chap. 3. in this volume.

[27]H. Leon McBeth, *A Sourcebook for Baptist Heritage* (Nashville: Broadman, 1990), 305.

[28]Broadus, *A Gentleman and a Scholar*, 139.

will be propagated in our churches, giving to them vigor and strength, and causing them to flourish by the godly sentiments and emotions they will awaken within them. May God impress you deeply with the responsibility under which you must act in reference to it![29]

Southern Baptists must produce and foster a positive theological agenda, not merely one that is defensive and reactionary. We must teach doctrine, love doctrine, and proclaim doctrine. Mohler challenges us to have a thick theology, not a thin theology.[30] I am with him 100 percent on this agenda.

Third, seminaries in the twenty-first century need to be more active in partnering with local churches in providing a wholesome and well-rounded educational experience. Seminaries are often criticized for what they do not teach (e.g., John Maxwell became a wealthy man by addressing our perceived and real shortcomings). I, however, have come to a conclusion on the matter that I am all but certain is correct, and if it is, it will require some changes in our thinking and in how we do theological education. While seminaries are guilty of numerous imperfections and shortcomings, it is time for us to stop criticizing them for what they cannot do both by design and culture. We cannot so easily teach our students leadership and interpersonal relationship skills, and give them pastoral/ministry experience. Those things are best learned and refined in the furnace and fire of the local church under the mentoring of a mature senior minister who can more adequately fulfill this aspect of 2 Timothy 2:1–2. Our curriculums are hardly set up to fulfill this need in theological education, and we are only fooling ourselves if we think what is popularly known as "SME" (Supervised Ministry Experience) is delivering what is needed. Further, the types of persons drawn to the teaching ministry of the seminary are not wired to teach leadership, relational skills, etc. This is not who they are and this is not what they know.

On the "intensive side," I would direct you to the partnership of Lakeview Baptist Church in Auburn, Alabama, and Southern Seminary. Al Jackson, as well as men like Mark Dever, John Piper, and Johnny Hunt, have chosen to pour their lives into others' in an intense, intentional mentoring method of theological/ministerial training. "Less intensive," but more conducive to seminary-based education, means partnering with healthy churches in your geographical area where students can go through a struc-

---

[29]Ibid., 140–41.
[30]Mohler, "Baptist Identity"; also see David S. Dockery, *Southern Baptist Consensus and Renewal: A Biblical, Historical, and Theological Proposal* (Nashville: B&H, 2008).

tured and well-planned mentorship, earning six to twelve hours toward their degree and learning the pastoral ropes from those who do it every single day. Here I have in mind the mentoring program of Highview Baptist Church in Louisville, Kentucky, under the leadership of Senior Pastor Kevin Ezell and Student Minister Jimmy Scroggins (who also serves as dean of Boyce College), and that of Providence Baptist Church in Raleigh, North Carolina, led by Pastor David Horner. Southeastern Seminary partners with this church and others in this model of ministry preparation. Such an approach to theological education allows the seminaries to focus on and do what they do well, and it allows local churches to play a vital role in educating ministers for the churches, something they should have been asked to do all along.

The Wisdom to Look Back and Remember So That as We Move Forward We Will Not Forget Who We Were

The SBC today is not the SBC of your parents, and certainly not your grandparents. Theirs was the SBC of Sunbeams/Mission Friends, RAs and GAs, Acteens, Brotherhood, and WMU. Ours is the SBC of Awanas, Upward Basketball, Promise Keepers, Precept Bible Study, and BSF (Bible Study Fellowship). The SBC monopoly over its thousands of churches is gone. We have moved from the country to the city, from the lower to the middle class, from isolation to significant participation, from loyal customer to mall shopper. Not everything involved in the old SBC was good, but neither was it all bad. There was present a structure and a plan that, if implemented and followed, could provide an education of our history and heritage. That mechanism is simply gone, and the results are far reaching. We now have several generations who know almost nothing of William Carey, Adoniram Judson, Bill Wallace, Lottie Moon, and Annie Armstrong, and absolutely nothing of Boyce, Broadus, Manly, Carroll, Robertson, Frost, Mullins, and Truett. Many who are now entering our seminaries were only small children or not yet born when the conservative resurgence began in 1979. They have never heard Criswell, Rogers, or Vines preach, and they are not really sure who they are. Pressler means next to nothing, and Patterson simply was the president of Southeastern who is now the president of Southwestern.

This is unacceptable. This must change. To lose sight of our heritage is to forget who we are. It is to be ignorant of the great theological issues that shaped and molded us into who and what we are today; it is to be unaware of the wonderful heroes on whose shoulders we now stand. In creative and dynamic avenues fitting a twenty-first-century context, we need to retell the Baptist History story in a way that will grab the attention and stir the heart of our people. As we look to the future we must not forget our past, a past rooted in the New Testament itself and amazingly played out on the screen of history for almost five-hundred years now.

CONCLUSION

I do not always agree with Ron Sider, but I do strongly concur with him on this: "If Christians do not live what they preach, the whole thing is a farce." Sider poignantly illustrates this in his book, *The Scandal of the Evangelical Conscience*. He writes,

> Graham Cyster, a Christian whom I know from South Africa, recently told me a painful story about a personal experience two decades ago when he was struggling against apartheid as a young South African evangelical. One night, he was smuggled into an underground Communist cell of young people fighting apartheid. "Tell us about the gospel of Jesus Christ," they asked, half hoping for an alternative to the violent communist strategy they were embracing.

Graham gave a clear, powerful presentation of the gospel, showing how personal faith in Christ wonderfully transforms persons and creates one new body of believers where there is neither Jew nor Greek, male nor female, rich nor poor, black nor white. The youth were fascinated. One seventeen-year-old exclaimed, "That is wonderful! Show me where I can see that happening." Graham's face fell as he sadly responded that he could not think of anywhere South-African Christians were truly living out the message of the gospel. "Then the whole thing is a piece of sh—," the youth angrily retorted. Within a month he left the country to join the armed struggle against apartheid—and eventually gave his life for his beliefs.[31]

North Carolina evangelist Vance Havner said, "What we live is what we really believe. Everything else is so much religious talk." By God's grace and for his glory may we know who we are and what we should be; may we know what we believe, and live as we should. If we do, we have a bright future. If we do, our Lord will be well pleased.

---

[31]Ronald J. Sider, "The Scandal of the Evangelical Conscience: Why Don't Christians Live What They Preach?" *Books & Culture: A Christian Review*, January 1, 2005, http://www.christianitytoday.com/bc/2005/janfeb/3.8.html.

GENERAL INDEX

abortion, 39, 249
Abstract of Principles, 295
Acteens, 108
adultery, 248–49
Advent Baptists, 71
Agee, Bill, 226
Ainsworth, Henry, 152
Akin, Danny, 270
Aldredge, E. P., 228–29
altar calls, 197, 210
American Constitution, 251–52
Anabaptists, 71, 124–37, 249–50, 285
annihilationists, 72
anti-intellectualism, 82
Apollinarianism, 140–41
Apollinarius of Laodicea, 140
Apostles' Creed, 141–42, 262
Arianism, 139
Arius, 139
Arminianism, 95–97, 113, 271
Arminians, 72
Armstrong, Annie, 13
Armstrong, J. C., 73
Asplund, John, 70
Athanasian Creed, 141, 262
atheism, 16
atonement, 54n49. *See also* universal atone-
    ment; Jesus, substitutionary atonement of
Augustine of Hippo, 99, 141–42

Bailey, J. W., 76–77
Bailey, Josiah, 84
Baker, Robert, 161–62
"the ban," 126–27, 131
baptism
    as a faith witness, 128–29
    believer's, 19, 26–27, 38, 48, 54, 126,
        154–55, 262, 283–84
    and children, 31, 48, 283
    by immersion, 48, 52, 71, 108–9, 146,
        250, 263, 283–84
    See also paedobaptism
Baptist church
    and church succession, 124, 142–43

history of, 139–55
identity of
    before the twentieth century, 70–74
    diversity in, 197–98
    as method and practice of church
        tradition, 196–97
    as missional focused, 183–202
    renewal of in Southern Baptist
        churches, 259–65
    in the twentieth century, 74–77
    unity in, 72–74
origins of, 108
    See also Southern Baptist Church; South-
        ern Baptist Convention
Baptist Faith and Message, 33, 234, 248,
    258, 260, 262–63, 272–81, 284, 289,
    295
Baptist Union, 29
Baptist, Why and Why Not, 11
Baptist World Alliance, 66, 142, 167–68,
    262
Baptist Young People's Union, 110, 118
Barrow, Henry, 152
Barth, Karl, 103
bishops, 289
Blaurock, George, 146
bloggers, 119–21, 208, 264
Bloom, Harold, 53n48
Bohemian Brethren, 143
Bosch, David, 180
Boyce, James P., 112, 294–95
Brethren, 71
Broadus, John, 112
Browne, Robert, 152
Bucer, Martin, 144, 155

Calvin, John, 144, 155
Calvinism, 95–97, 112–13, 258, 272, 283
Campbell, Alexander, 160
Carey, William, 100, 269
Carroll, Benajah Harvey, 45n6
Carson, D. A., 18
Carter, Stephen, 255
Carver, W. O., 77–78